LANDSCAPE WITH FIGURES

ALSO BY MALCOLM GOLDSTEIN

The Political Stage:
American Drama and Theater of the Great Depression

George S. Kaufman:
His Life, His Theater

The Art of Thornton Wilder

Pope and the Augustan Stage

Landscape

with Figures

A HISTORY OF ART DEALING IN THE UNITED STATES

Malcolm Goldstein

OXFORD
UNIVERSITY PRESS
2000

OXFORD
UNIVERSITY PRESS

Oxford New York
Athens Auckland Bangkok Bogotá
Buenos Aires Calcutta
Cape Town Chennai Dar es Salaam Delhi
Florence Hong Kong Istanbul
Karachi Kuala Lumpur Madrid Melbourne
Mexico City Mumbai
Nairobi Paris São Paulo Shanghai Singapore
Taipei Tokyo Toronto Warsaw

and associated companies in
Berlin Ibadan

Published by Oxford University Press, Inc.
198 Madison Avenue, New York, New York 10016

Library of Congress Cataloging-in-Publication Data
Goldstein, Malcolm, 1925-
Landscape with figures: a history of art dealing in the United States/Malcolm Goldstein.
p. cm. Includes bibliographical references and index.
ISBN 0-19-513673-X
1. Art dealers—United States—Biography.
2. Art—United States—Marketing—History.
I. Title.
N8659.G65 2000 380.1'457'0973—dc21
99-044087

9 8 7 6 5 4 3 2 1
Printed in the United States of America
on acid-free paper

ILLUSTRATION CREDITS

Page
7 Archives of the Pennsylvania Academy of the Fine Arts.
22 The Metropolitan Museum of Art, Edward W. C. Arnold Collection of New York Prints, Maps, and Pictures, Bequest of Edward W. C. Arnold, 1954 (54.90.1056).
32 Prints and Drawings Collection, The Octagon Museum, Washington D.C.
35 Courtesy of Knoedler & Company.
48 The Metropolitan Museum of Art, Gift of Amy and Emma Welcher and Alice Welcher Erickson, 1967 (67.844.2).
55 Courtesy of Patricia Olivier.
60 Courtesy of Vose Galleries of Boston.
68 Courtesy of Kraushaar Galleries.
70 Courtesy of Kraushaar Galleries.
79 Archives of American Art.
96 The Metropolitan Museum of Art, Alfred Stieglitz Collection.
100 Alfred Stieglitz Archive, Beinecke Rare Book and Manuscript Library, Yale University.
138 New York Times Pictures.
198 The Joseph and Robert Cornell Memorial Foundation/ Licensed by VAGA, New York, NY.
217 Solomon R. Guggenheim Museum.
228 Photograph by Berenice Abbott. Courtesy of Lillian Kiesler.
242 The Museum of Modern Art, The Sidney and Harriet Janis Collection.
248 Photograph by William Raynor.
256 Photograph by Nina Leen/LIFE Magazine.
267 Photograph by Ralston Crawford.
278 Courtesy of Artes Magnus.
285 Courtesy of O. K. Harris Gallery.
295 Photograph by Lisa Romerein.
304 Photograph by David Armstrong.
306 Photograph by Barbara Alper/ New York Times Pictures.
309 Photograph by Elaine Mayers Salkaln, 1985.

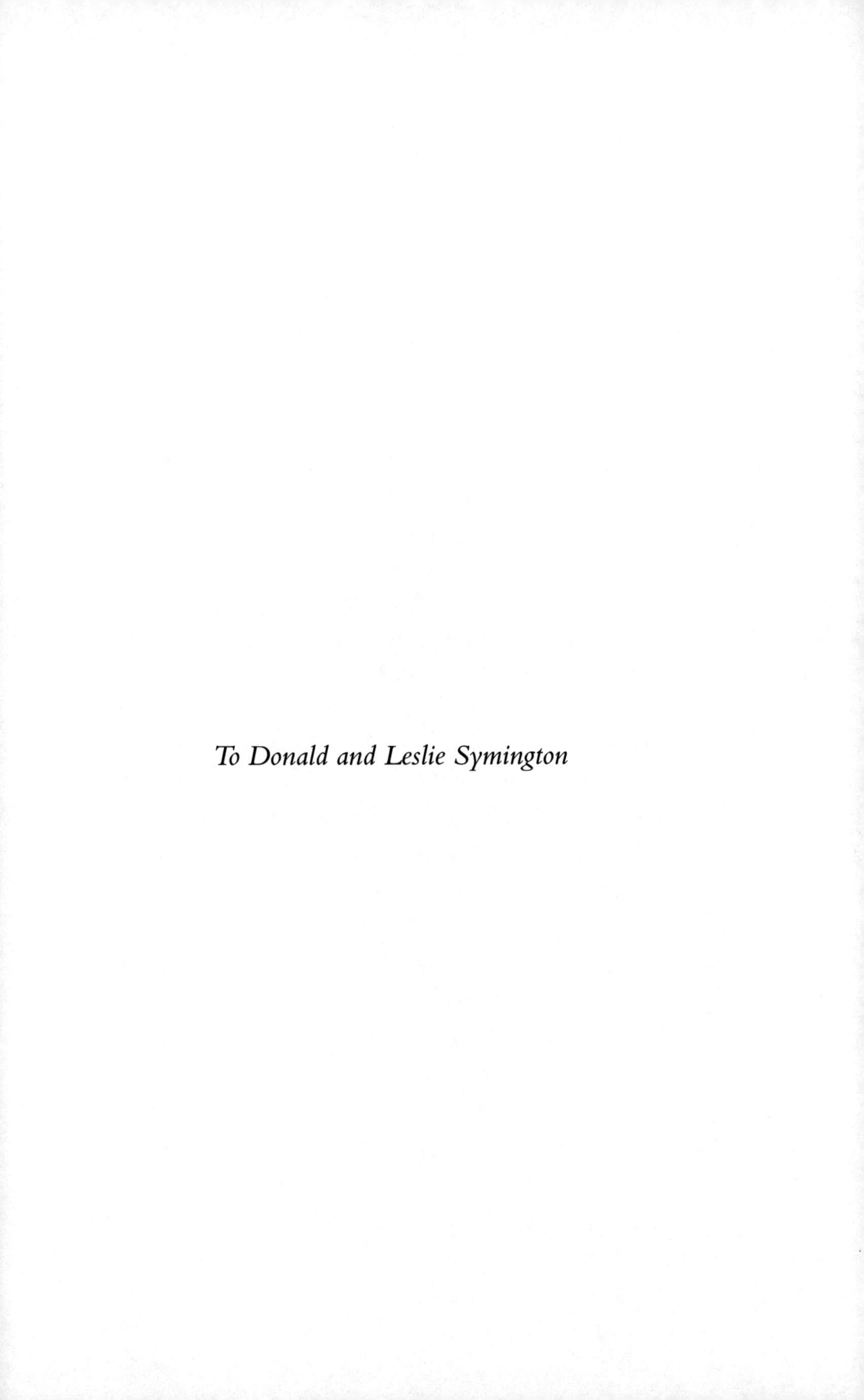

To Donald and Leslie Symington

CONTENTS

INTRODUCTION AND ACKNOWLEDGMENTS

Roy Lichtenstein (1923-1997), the most popular living American artist of the late twentieth century, declared in the 1960s that the public for art was about as large as the public for chemistry. Perhaps with that ironic observation in mind, he twitted the art market in 1970 by creating a large bronze relief titled *Peace Through Chemistry* and four equally large lithographs on the same subject. These camp extravaganzas, whose images were based on themes borrowed from social-realist art of the 1930s and decorative details of the buildings of the 1939 New York World's Fair, found ready buyers among art enthusiasts. It may even have been—who knows?—that some of the buyers were members of the public for chemistry.

The public for art was in fact much greater than Lichtenstein's offhand remark would suggest. The remark would not have been worth repeating here were it not for the fact that one of the individuals most responsible for the public enthusiasm for art even as Lichtenstein spoke was Leo Castelli, his own dealer. Although art as the ultimate luxury item is within the financial reach of only a relatively few fortunate individuals, the increased attendance at museums since the Second World War by all but the least sophisticated members of American society provides unquestionable evidence of the hold that art has gained on the consciousness of the nation.

In the interim between the end of the war and the opening of Castelli's gallery in 1957 came the displacement of Paris by New York as the capital of the international art market and the rise of members of New York's very own school, Abstract Expressionism, to status as world figures in their profession. The principal dealers who promoted this astonishingly strong art of broadly gestural strokes or, as with the work of Jackson Pollock, drips of paint onto canvas were Peggy Guggenheim, Samuel Kootz, Betty Parsons, Charles Egan, and Sidney Janis. To them first of all may be credited the newly charged, widespread interest in art and its creators. Castelli's embrace of Pop Art, the very likable, easy-to-take art of familiar objects as created by Lichtenstein and Andy Warhol, served even more strongly to alert the public to the pleasures to be derived from gazing with an open mind at the product of an artist's creative power.

The chapters that follow will offer a close examination of the careers of these six and many other dealers of the nineteenth and twentieth centuries. Not as much information as we would like is available about the lives of the earliest entrants into the art trade in America. But to understand the rise of that trade to its position of eminence today, it is essential to examine the meager facts at hand about the pioneers as well as the abundance of information about modern-day dealers. It took a long succession of sellers of art to create the environment into which such a supersalesman as Leo Castelli stepped when he opened his gallery, and every piece of the available information has its value.

It is essential for readers to understand at the outset, however, that not every person receives mention in this book who at some time in his or her life set up a shop in America for the sale of art. Had I introduced the names of all the dealers I came across while looking into the past and present of the profession, the result would have been not a book but a data bank. Such a publication might be useful, but hardly readable. As for the many dealers I do take up, most were or are based in New York, which since the early nineteenth century has been the center of the art trade in the United States. There are many dealers active today in cities across the country whom I respect but whom I have found no opportunity to include. I hope that they and all other dealers currently on the scene who do not find their names in the index will not feel hurt for being left out.

I also feel obliged to make clear at the outset that this book is not about every sector of the trade. Although the intense interest in art so much in evidence today has been fueled partly by the high prices major works of art have fetched at auction, this book is not about the auction houses. They are, to be sure, mentioned here and there in the chapters that follow, but only briefly. They deserve their own historians and of late have been attracting them. I should also make it clear that I have not included dealers in all categories of art. For present purposes, my concern is with dealers in American and European art as it has evolved over the many centuries of its creation. Surely that is enough for one book. Folk art and video art come in for very brief mention, and Asian art, despite its seductive beauty, is not mentioned at all. Nor do I deal with performance art, which, because it is impermanent and involves live participation, cannot be bought or sold in commercial galleries.

My interest in galleries and their owners dates from my graduate-student days at Columbia University in the 1950s and the rare occasions when I pulled away from my books and took a bus down to Fifty-seventh Street to look at art. I was always amazed at the politeness and patience of most of the dealers whose galleries I visited, when it must have been clear to them that I could hardly afford even a $50 etching, let alone a painting by Pollock or Franz Kline. I particularly remember with gratitude three eminent dealers, Grace Borgenicht, the late Edith Gregor Halpert, and the late Antoinette Kraushaar, all of whom let me pay for relatively inexpensive works over a period of months and gave honest answers to my perhaps tiresome questions about the history and workings of their galleries.

Their attitude has had much to do with the regard that I have for the trade. In the long period during which I was engaged in the writing of this book, friends and acquaintances queried me repeatedly about the honesty of dealers. I startled most of them, just as I may startle my readers, by saying that I have found dealers *in general* to be aboveboard in their treatment of collectors, myself as well as others. The fact that most dealers will back down from the announced price of a work if the prospective buyer asks for a discount is not, it seems to me, a mark of dishonesty; bargaining has always been an accepted part of the process of buying a work of art or, for that matter, an antique piece of furniture.

Nor do I find it immoral that many dealers offer preferential treatment to long-standing clients, to whom alone they may show certain major works; it is the dealers' right to sell to whom they please if this means placing works to the advantage of their artists. To be sure, the art business has its rogues, just as has any other business. Having been the victim of what I now believe to be the ingrained, habitual dishonesty of four dealers, I am all too sadly aware of this. I have, incidentally, ruled out any mention of the four, but of course they know who they are. Fortunately for the integrity of this book, none is of any consequence to the trade. Certain more eminent dealers have been guilty of wrongdoings that are now a part of the public record, and I have not failed to comment on them.

It is a pleasure to acknowledge the help provided me by many dealers, critics, historians, artists, and collectors. Profound thanks go again to the three dealers mentioned above, who provided me with much valuable information at the same time that they made it possible for me to begin a collection of art. The many others who answered my questions, some in brief conversations on the telephone or at social gatherings, others in extensive interviews, are, in alphabetical order, Joe Amrhein (Pierogi 2000), William Appleton, Hildegard Bachert (Galerie St. Etienne), Charles C. Bergman (Pollock-Krasner Foundation), Avis Berman, the late Michael Blankfort, Irving Blum, Mary Boone, Elizabeth Broun (National Museum of American Art), the late Leo Castelli, the late Toiny Castelli, Sylvan Cole, Melissa De Medeiros (Knoedler and Company), John Driscoll (Babcock Gallery); André Emmerich, James Thomas Flexner, Gray Foy, Allan Frumkin, Larry Gagosian, Arnold Glimcher (PaceWildenstein), Gracie Mansion, the late E. D. H. Johnson, Paul Kantor, Ivan Karp, Klaus Kertess (Bykert Gallery), Margo Leavin, Jason McCoy, Carole M. Pesner (Kraushaar Galleries), Joan Peterson, Robert Pincus-Witten, Paul Resika, Bernice Rose, Irving Sandler, Charles Seliger, the late Dorothy Schneiderman (Harbor Gallery), Michael Sundell, Nina Castelli Sundell, Eugene V. Thaw, Esteban Vicente, the late Désirée Goudstikker von Saher, the late Eleanor Ward (Stable Gallery), and Gerold Wunderlich.

I owe a special debt to my late friend Lily Harmon, who allowed me to read and make full use of her unpublished biography of the dealer J. B. Neumann; I wholeheartedly wish that she were here to receive a copy of this book. Before his untimely death, Paul Cummings read the first ten chapters of my typescript and made helpful comments on them; I regret that he too is not here to receive a copy. I wish to express my thanks also to Patricia Olivier and David H. Whittier, sister and brother whose stepfather was the grandson of the dealer William Schaus. Mme. Olivier supplied me with a photograph of a portrait of Schaus, and Mr. Whittier provided me with much information about Schaus and his family. Thanks, too, and many of them, to Tom Wallace, my ebullient agent.

I am more indebted than I can say to the Frick Art Reference Library; the Avery Library of Columbia University; the New York Public Library, especially its Rare Books and Manuscripts Division; the oral history collections of Columbia University and the University of California, Los Angeles; the Beinecke Library of Yale University; W. Gregory Gallagher and Jonathan Harding, respectively the librarian and archivist of the Century Association; the library and archive of the Museum of Modern Art; the library of the New-York Historical Society; the New York Society Library and Mark Piel, its director; and, most of all, the New York branch of the Archives of American Art and Nancy Malloy and Valerie Komor, its ever helpful staff. I was also most pleasantly treated on my two visits to the archives' headquarters in Washington, but on neither visit did I find anything helpful to me that was not also available on microfilm in the New York branch. I am grateful to the library of the Metropolitan Museum for permission to read the museum's correspondence with William Schaus.

It has been a major disappointment to me that I was unable to consult the Duveen Brothers archive. When I inquired about it in the early 1990s at the Metropolitan Museum, where it was then housed, I was told that although other researchers had had access to it, it had since been declared off-limits because of its fragility. Inquiring again at the Metropolitan much later, I was told by Katherine Baetjer, who had been in charge of it, that the archive had been transferred to the Getty Research Institute in California. Mark Henderson at the Getty informed me that the archive was being photocopied at the University of California, Los Angeles, but might not be available to scholars until as late as 2002. When at last it becomes available, it is sure to yield a trove of valuable information.

In order to avoid an excessive swelling in the notes, I have not given my sources of information on the dates of exhibitions. I beg my readers to trust me on this important matter. Although the notes include references to all my other archival and secondary sources, as well as to interviews, I feel obliged to make special mention here of certain men and women whose books and essays have been of such great help to me that without them I would have required another lifetime to finish this project. The writers and their publications are as follows: Edward Fowles, *Memories of Duveen Brothers;* Lee Hall, *Betty Parsons: Artist Dealer Collector;* Julien Levy, *Memoir of an Art Gallery;* Sue Davidson Lowe, *Stieglitz: A Memoir/Biography;* Lynn H. Nicholas, *The Rape of Europa;* Ernest Samuels, *Bernard Berenson: The Making of a Connoisseur* and *Bernard Berenson: The Making of a Legend;* Calvin Tomkins, "A Keeper of the Treasure" and "A Good Eye and a Good Ear" (*New Yorker* profiles), and *Off the Wall: Robert Rauschenberg and the Art World of Our Time;* and Robert C. Williams, *Russian Art and American Money*. I can only hope that my book will be as useful to other writers.

For invitations to speak on the general subject of this book, I wish to express my thanks to the Century Association, the Drawing Society, the art department of Stanford University, the Whitney Museum of American Art, and the members of the biography seminar of New York University. I also wish to thank the American Council of Learned Societies for a most helpful research grant.

Nowadays a peruser of the art press may come upon references to a gallery owner as not a dealer but a "gallerist." This term strikes me as spurious and self-aggrandizing, on the order of "beautician," and I have refrained from using it. (It gives me a certain measure of amusement to report that the spelling checker on my word-processing program does not recognize the word.) I have also declined to convert to current values the sums mentioned as having been paid by collectors and dealers for various works of art; with inflation an ongoing fact of life, the resulting figures, were I to give them, would mean little to anyone who picks this book up ten or even five years from now.

Malcolm Goldstein

I

PIONEERING THE MARKET

One piece missing from the mosaic of modern history and not likely to be found is the name of the first person ever to sell a work of art in the colonies that were to become the United States. It may have been a self-taught New Englander who completed a likeness of a neighbor and turned it over to him for a few shillings, or perhaps a settler in Nieuw Amsterdam who, on finding that he had brought over one more landscape from the old country than his walls had room for, inquired among his friends for a buyer. Or it may have been . . . but what voices from the past can tell us?

And it is just as unlikely that anyone will ever discover the name of the first American to establish himself as a dealer in art, let alone art by itself, unaccompanied by an assortment of more practical goods. Probably, to pile conjecture on conjecture, he (whoever he was) dealt in prints, for although newspapers of the colonial and early federal years seldom published notices of the sale of paintings, they carried the advertisements of print-shop proprietors with some frequency. When advertisements of paintings did appear, they usually included lists of other available items, such as artists' supplies, maps, and toys. The few newspaper mentions of paintings alone do not give the impression that the sellers were conducting an ongoing trade; instead, the notices appear to be for collections of pictures to be sold by venture capitalists—men who risked their money on a quick turnover, as when in 1720 a Mr. Shore of Queen Street in Boston offered a sale "at the Crown Coffee House in Long Wharf of a collection of pictures fit for any gentleman's dining room or staircase."[1] So far as is known, it was not until the second decade of the nineteenth century that an establishment for the sale of paintings alone, without household or other goods, came into being.

If earlier it made sense to shopkeepers to offer such mundane objects as toys alongside paintings and teapots alongside prints, the reason is clear enough: They could not make a living on art alone. Few if any colonists or, after independence, citizens of the young United States thought of art as something to "collect." Most considered pictures to have no value above their utility as decorations, unless it was the value inherent in portraits as dynastic emblems. Although landscapes and history paintings could be found in some colonial and federal homes, it was portraits that had the greatest appeal, especially in New England, along with engravings of old and modern masterpieces. Engravings were expensive, however, and therefore not to be found in many homes, for publishers passed along to buyers the cost of the heavy presses required for printing them. Sculpture, apart from tombstone carvings, ships' figureheads, and architectural decorations, was not to become an American art until the early nineteenth century, and even then it made its way slowly.

No middlemen entered the scene to scout out sitters for the portraitists. They acted as their own dealers. To announce their availability and their whereabouts, they hung out a shingle or placed advertisements in local papers. As dealers, they operated in a narrowly confined market, and although the number of early portraits that have survived is not small, the commissions that the artists received were not so numerous as to guarantee a comfortable living. A measure of their economic frustration is evident in their willingness to back away from their easels long enough to teach their art to aspiring youngsters and to perform a variety of other services apart from painting. There was no other way to avoid a lifetime of short rations and cramped quarters. Gerardus Duyckinck of

New York let it be known that he would undertake the painting of pictures of almost any sort, as well as "varnishing, japanning, gilding, glazing, [and] silvering of looking glasses." Gustavus Hesselius and John Winter of Philadelphia would provide not only conventional works of art but also "signs, show-boards, ship and house painting, writing in gold and color, [and] the cleaning and restoring of pictures."[2] The ads suggest that the portraitists would have been grateful for the occasional commission of a landscape or a still life, and this is even more strongly suggested by the landscape vistas to be glimpsed behind the heads and shoulders of the sitters in their portraits.

In the opening years of the nineteenth century, the ranks of furniture and toy dealers, gilders, mirror makers, and framers who sold art as a sideline was on the increase. But to take the bold step of establishing a gallery for the sale of art alone in any form other than prints required more courage than most shopkeepers could muster. City directories give us names but no insight into character, addresses but no word on what sort of art was for sale.

Like their counterparts in other walks of life, the few early dealers who found a place in history were shrewd, resourceful, or personable (seldom *and* personable). One such was John Doggett, a skilled craftsman who, after devoting ten years to cabinetry, mirror making, and wood carving, opened a shop in Boston in 1810 for the sale of pictures and frames. A shrewd Yankee trader, Doggett scoured the countryside for works of art to buy outright for resale, commissioned pictures from artists, including Gilbert Stuart, and took still others on consignment at a commission of only 5 percent, a tenth of what in the course of time many dealers would demand of artists. From a series of portraits painted for him by Stuart, he commissioned a group of highly regarded lithographs. In 1845, rich and still hardy, he retired, having turned the business over to his brother and Samuel S. Williams of Boston. When the brother, Samuel Doggett, retired in 1854 and Williams took on a new partner, the firm was renamed Williams and Everett. As such, it became one of the most prestigious art galleries of the nineteenth and early twentieth centuries.[3] William Dunlap, the painter-historian whose *History of the Rise and Progress of the Arts of Design in the United States* (1834) is essential to the study of artist life in the early years, writes of having exhibited one of his paintings in Doggett's gallery, which he describes as "[a] great room, a noble place." Offering a hint of the keenness of the dealer's eye, he tells us that Doggett, on a visit to the Philadelphia studio of Thomas Sully, spotted and admired a painting that had long languished there for want of a buyer. Doggett made an offer, bought the painting, and then resold it to a Boston museum for $500, at that time no small figure.[4]

In 1811, soon after Doggett began to deal in art, a man of puzzling character named Pierre Flandin set up a gallery in New York, where he continued to pursue the trade for more than forty years, dealing mainly in old masters and achieving such eminence as to secure a place on the board of the American Academy of the Fine Arts, the august association of artists, businessmen, and civic leaders founded in 1820. Flandin's chief claim to fame was that one of his customers was Robert Gilmor Jr., a Baltimore financier and the enthusiastic collector of not only old-master paintings but also works by modern English and American artists. However, not all the pictures Flandin sold Gilmor had the pedigree that the dealer claimed for them. A "Holbein," for instance, eventually proved to be the work of Cornelius de Lyon, and a "Raphael," which Gilmor questioned even as he paid for it, the work of Jan Grossart.[5] Yet no matter how far downward the attributions were to drift, no one could say that Flandin dealt in rubbish. His flaw, one not unique to him among dealers, was a disconcerting high-handedness, as when he told Gilmor, who liked to trade canvases with him, that some of the works offered by the collector were not quite good enough, even though both men knew that Gilmor had bought them from Flandin himself.[6]

Successful as both Flandin and Doggett were at their calling, it would seem that neither had the color or the magnetism on which personal legends are founded, for not much is known about their days and ways.[7] Not so, however, with Michael Paff, a dealer whose personality was composed of such odd streaks that visitors to his gallery not only remembered his looks but claimed to remember his very words.

A German émigré who never lost his accent, "Old Paff," as eventually he was called by everyone who knew him, arrived in New York in the winter of 1784, aboard the same ship that brought John Jacob Astor to the New World.[8] The fur trade provided the foundation of the Astor fortune, but early in his career Astor also ran a profitable business in musical instruments. According to the *New-York Register and City Directory* for 1797, Paff in partnership with his brother, John, also owned a music shop.[9] In the shop the two Paffs stocked pianos, music boxes, handwritten sheet music, and music published under their own imprint. From time to time, according to contemporary advertisements, they also sold paintings and engravings on consignment.[10] They were successful, and to such an extent that in 1802 they were able to buy out Astor, their rival.[11]

By 1811 Michael Paff was on his own; for the first time, he was listed

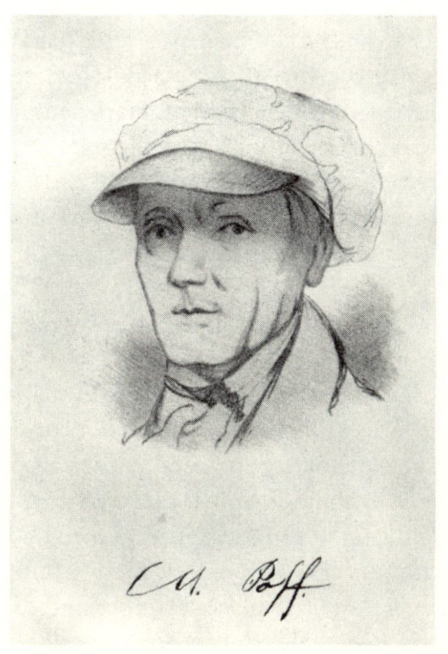

Michael Paff

in the directory without John and with the words "picture gallery" after his name. Art, not music, was now his only game. He had relocated frequently in the past and was then at still another new address, 228 Broadway. Astor lived across the street at 223, and in 1812, when Paff moved yet again, to 221, the two men became next-door neighbors.[12] That year and that move marked the beginning of Paff's rise in the art community.

Long before 1812 Paff had been forming a vast collection of pictures, and he had now made up his mind to earn some money with it. In a prospectus dated March 30, 1812, six weeks before the opening of his new premises, Paff noted that although the United States could boast among her sons such distinguished painters as John Trumbull and Benjamin West, "it was beyond the Atlantic that their genius unfolded itself," not at home, as it might have done had fine pictures been at hand for them to study. Paff proposed to enlighten the public—"professors, students, and amateurs"—by means of just such works, which he was proud to say he had collected "at vast expense." He gave no hint in the prospectus that the pictures were for sale; for the time being he apparently meant to keep the collection together and make his living by exhibiting it. To view it, art lovers had to pay 50 cents per visit or take out an annual subscription, for which the rate varied. If, for example, a gentleman wished to subscribe for his entire family, he paid $10, but a subscription for himself and two ladies cost him only $8. As a museum, if that was what Paff wanted his new gallery to be, this was not the first in America. Charles Willson Peale, portraitist and sire of artist children named Raphaelle, Rembrandt, Titian, and Rubens, had preceded him. In Philadelphia in 1785, Peale opened what he believed to be the first American museum; it was not limited to art, however, but also included scientific displays. Paff showed nothing but art. In time for the opening he issued a catalogue of his extensive holdings.

If Paff owned what he thought he owned—that is, if his pictures were authentic—then a visit to his gallery promised a treat. Listed in the catalogue were works by three Americans, West, Stuart Gilbert, and Thomas Sully, along with William Winstanley, an Englishman who somewhat earlier had lived and painted in America. But primarily the catalogue was a roll call of European names, including Rembrandt and Rubens, Titian and Tintoretto, Correggio and Carracci, along with many other works by masters, minor figures, and artists unknown. There were 230 pictures in all, some of which Paff described in detail. "An Italian landscape painted by *Claude Lorraine,* with figures dancing, playing music and amusing themselves,—a Shepherd, Horses, and a flock of Sheep. A scene a quarter of an hour after sun-set, the light striking against the sky, mountains and hills, in a most beautiful manner. This is supposed to be the only Painting by this great and illustrious Master in this country"—so ran the description of item 86. No prices were given.

But if on making his debut as a gallery owner Paff was unwilling to sell his paintings, only a few years passed before he could be tempted to part with all of them, except for a few personal treasures. By 1818, if not before, he was in the picture trade. Early in that year he made an offer of $10,000 to the Academy of the Fine Arts for a selection of works—an offer that was rejected, although with a note of thanks.[13] In July of the same year he placed an advertisement in a newspaper, the *National Advocate,* beckoning art lovers to the gallery, then located on Wall Street, where they would find pictures "worthy of their attention . . . at the smallest expense, with the most extensive gratification." To this he added, "N.B.: Old Paintings restored to their original lustre, or purchased at their utmost value."

Paff, like Flandin and Doggett, had made his commitment to art at an auspicious time, the beginning of an era when art was coming to mean something more than decoration, a time when the idea of forming a collection would begin to take hold. In the hearts of some wealthy men, of whom Gilmor was a leading example, had been born a passion for the works of old masters. Paff was standing by, ready to supply them.

He had been on to something important when he asserted in his prospectus that familiarity with masterworks was fundamental to the cultivation of taste in art. But the principles of connoisseurship, the ability to discern the true, magisterial hand and to examine a work systematically for evidence of overpainting, lay beyond his intellectual grasp—and no wonder, for this was a field not yet seriously explored in America or, for that matter, far advanced abroad. As with others who followed close on his heels in the old-master trade, in his search for art to show and sell he cast his net broadly through pawn shops and auction rooms, the attics of private houses, and the warehouses of importers who brought in paintings by the shipload, often having first cut them from their frames for easy transport.[14] But he looked and bought with knowledge limited to only what he could pick up from books, and they, of course, were books published before the invention of photography, an indispensable tool to later students of art. No doubt he was sometimes correct in his attributions. The Claude catalogued in 1812 may have been a Claude; at this late date, who is to argue? But given the state of scholarship in that year, it is unimaginable that all five, if even one, of the alleged Rubenses were Rubenses.

With both buyer and seller indulging in wishful thinking, it is just as unimaginable that many of the collectors who bought from Paff got what they paid for. But there is a difference between deliberate fraud and unrestrained optimism such as Paff's, even when abetted by ignorance. The available facts of the dealer's life do not suggest that he knowingly sold false goods. When he bought a picture, he cleaned it (using methods that would drive a present-day conservator to tears) and would then decide for himself who had painted it. Often after a purchasing foray he found, or believed he found, cause for jubilation. Reminiscing about him some sixty years after Paff's death, C. L. Beaumont, the son of the obscure dealer John P. Beaumont,[15] wrote, "He would wash, scrape, study, and ponder over an old picture; would sit up nights with it consulting books, and when he had made a discovery, his enthusiasm carried him off the earth."[16]

An iconophile and fantasist who fooled himself as well as his customers, Paff enjoyed his occupation to the fullest. Michelangelo seems to have figured in his fantasies above all other artists. Having read that no works had been recorded for a certain period in Michelangelo's life, Paff became convinced that one of his holdings was from the great master's hand. "Vot vas he doing all dot time, my poy?" he asked young Beaumont. "He vos paint dot picter."[17] John Durand, in his biography of his father, the artis Asher B. Durand, wrote that Paff once declared a *Last Supper* in the gallery to be Michelangelo's because the stones painted across the floor of the scene amounted to ten, the very number of letters in the artist's surname, Buonarotti.[18]

Of the collectors who visited Paff's emporium, two, Robert Gilmor and Luman Reed, were art patrons of discriminating taste and money enough to buy whatever took their fancy. Gilmor was not tempted by Paff's bogus wares, however.[19] Not so Reed, who made a few purchases—the number is uncertain—before he saw them for the poor things they were.[20]A retired wholesale merchant and a New Yorker, Reed maintained a private gallery in his home on Greenwich Street, spent liberally to stock it with pictures, and opened it to the public one day a week. After his disappointment with Paff's goods, he turned to a new field of collecting where authenticity was no problem: the landscapes and allegories of the Hudson River artists, whose talents and vision he and Gilmor were among the first to appreciate. Henry T. Tuckerman, in his *Book of the Artists,* tells of one of Paff's dealings with Reed. "Ah, Mr. Reed," Paff said to him one day, "der is a gem for you, but I don't think I sell it to you. I was cleaning a landscape I bought at auction, and I cleaned one corner a leetle hard and I thought I saw something underneath, and sure enough, someone has stolen an old master in Italy, and painted a landscape over it to avoid detection, and now I have him. I don't know, but I think it is a Correggio. I sell him for one t'ousan' dollar. But come tomorrow." Reed returned the next day to find the painting cleaned, varnished, and framed, and a print of the same image near by. "Ah, Mr. Reed," Paff said, "I can't sell him for one t'ousan': it is a fine Vandyke, here is the original engraving of it; no doubt about it. I must have five t'ousan' dollars for it."[21]

It may have been just this incident that caused Reed to look more closely at Paff's pictures. But if Reed left the gallery in disgust, knowing perfectly well that the work on view was more likely a copy of a Van Dyck than an original, a steady stream of less sophisticated buyers made up for the loss of his custom. Despite such bizarre sales pitches, Paff prospered. His own belief in the worth of his acquisitions and the warmth with which he expressed it were irresistible to most collectors. For a quarter of a century he did good business. Asher B. Durand, in a letter to Thomas Cole, recalled hearing "poor old Paff" exclaim about certain exciting works that they "make boys of us all."[22] There was something charming about both the phrase and its sentiment that alongside such works most other human accomplishments count for little. Another of Paff's assets was his quaint appearance: a face and shape that gave him a little of the look of a German statuary garden dwarf. "He was," wrote Beaumont, "a little, old, white-faced Schwartzwalder, in a broad-brimmed, low-crowned hat and a short-waisted, long, full-skirted coat, a merry, happy, good-natured man."[23]

Surrounded by art, sought after by collectors, and courted by both the American Academy and its young rival, the National Academy of Design, he had every reason to be merry.[24] Friends came to the gallery to pay social calls and sometimes to lead him to an understanding of the iconography of a new acquisition. A group whose members included a physician, Dr. Wainwright, was summoned one day to inspect a baffling recent purchase: a rendering of a supine man with an apple at his mouth and a frog resting on his private parts. After looking it over, the friends concluded that it represented life's very last moments. The apple, as they saw it, signified the extreme weakness that comes with death, because the man appeared unable to bite into it, and the frog signified that other phenomenon that signals the end, extreme cold. Some time afterward, Paff fell ill and Dr. Wainwright paid a house call. "Doctor," said Paff, looking up from his sickbed, "Doctor. I have got the frog."[25]

Luman Reed, himself a good-natured man, appears to have remained well disposed toward the dealer even after his break with the gallery. After Durand painted Reed's portrait under a commission from Jonathan Sturges, Reed's partner, Reed wrote Durand with no hint of rancor that Paff had seen it and declared it first-rate, "& you know," said Reed, "he spares nobody but the oldmasters."[26]

The artist Daniel Huntington described Paff's gallery as "a dimly lighted and musty den," and it may have been just that with, as was the custom, pictures hanging from floor to ceiling, frames touching, and scarcely a patch of blank wall to provide rest for the eye.[27] But late in his career Paff graced its exterior with a plaster Cupid holding a palette and brushes.[28] With this decoration, the god of love equipped with a painter's gear in place of the usual bow and arrows, Paff gave three-dimensional form to his feeling for art and artists. Toward young painters he made gestures of kindness, lending them works to copy and assisting in the sale of their pictures. The painter Robert W. Weir wrote of one such thoughtful move on Paff's part back when Weir was eighteen years old: "At that time [1821] I became acquainted with Mr. Paff, who kindly lent me several pictures, which I took great pains, as well as pleasure in copying, and succeeded so well as to attract the attention of many connoisseurs of high standing."[29] One connoisseur whom Weir met was the artist John Trumbull, who bought Weir's small canvas *Distress* from Paff for only $6.00, rendering Weir himself distressed. Why Trumbull, who took a dim view of Weir's talent, wanted the painting is something of a mystery. His advice to the artist was, "Give up painting and take to making shoes."[30]

For a time, visitors to Paff's shop could find a very personal testimony to his iconophilia: a painting from his own hand. This, according to *Blunt's Stranger's Guide to the City of New-York* for 1817, was the only modern work in the gallery. Because it was the first and only work Paff had ever attempted, the guide described it as a "virgin" painting. For a virgin painting, it had an appropriate title: *Love Without Success*.

The most eloquent tribute to Paff that has come down to us was composed by the politician and art lover Philip Hone, who after the dealer died on June 10, 1838, took a few minutes to immortalize him in his diary. "Our old friend Michael Paff," he wrote, "died yesterday of apoplexy, aged 65 years. His house was a perfect museum. He bought, sold, exchanged, and jobbed pictures, and when required repaired, varnished, and reframed them, translating many a dark mass of undefinable objects into the sunlit landscapes of Ruysdael or Poussin, and recovering from the thick veil of antiquated varnish the graceful form of Correggio and the rich tints of Guido."[31]

Five months after Hone wrote this eulogy, Paff's holdings were sold under the hammer of Aaron Levy, a front-running auctioneer. The catalogue, whose cover was decorated with a portrait of the dealer (the only one now known), ran to forty-two pages. It listed more than 1,100 lots: 1,031 paintings and 84 engravings, in a thunderous cascade of impressive names. Raphael, Michelangelo, Velásquez, Dürer, Rembrandt, Carlo Dolci—all those and more, many more, were there. But Levy and his cataloguers held back a little from endorsing every work. "The Compilers of the Catalogue," they wrote, "having been on intimate terms with the late proprietor for many years, had thereby an opportunity of becoming acquainted with his leading pictures, and with the names of the artists to whom he ascribed them; they have chosen, therefore, to adhere to the Authorship of the pictures in *all* cases where they have been named by him, which they have denoted with an asterisk thus*." *Caveat emptor* was the real message written in those stars.

But astute readers of the catalogue may have had some doubts about the unstarred items as well, for the cataloguers neglected to say how they arrived at their identifications. Many items both starred and unstarred were annotated. An alleged Van Dyck (starred), *Queen Esther Supplicating King Ahasuerus,* drew more than fifty lines of comment, including the information that Paff had refused an offer of over $9,000 for it. When the cataloguers came to Michelangelo's *Last Supper* with its ten stones across the floor, they proceeded cautiously. "If," they suggested, "the picture is by the illustrious master to whom it is assigned, it must be of value far beyond what would be prudent to name, for fear of [our] being named visionary and extravagant. The merits and authorship of this picture are respectively submitted to the discrimination of an enlightened and liberal public."

Knowledge of Paff's holdings comes to an end with their dispersal at auction. If a record was kept of the buyers, as it must have been, it was neither published nor preserved. The name of only one buyer is known: the New Haven architect Ithiel Town, who may have bought as many as 170 works.[32] Nothing, however, is known of their whereabouts. This absence of information is unfortunate in the extreme, because the pictures, if they could be traced and found, would provide insight into the American response to artistic values at an early stage of art collecting and, just as important, of art dealing.

2

THE AMERICAN ARTIST AND HIS FRIENDS

Paff's collectors, like Paff himself, preferred the art of Europe to the home product; the bulk of his inventory as listed in the prospectus of 1812 and the auction catalogue of 1838 consisted of imported works. It was art such as he enjoyed, and he assumed that his customers would be eager to buy it. But Paff was no enemy to American artists, nor was he alone in his time in offering them moral support and sometimes buying their canvases. As the nineteenth century sped along, framers and gilders, civic leaders, and collectors themselves began to recognize that American artists were no less capable of creating art of high quality than their European contemporaries and could even produce works that an art enthusiast might hang alongside his "old masters" without embarrassment. But acceptance of the native product, when it came, was gradual; citizens of the New World would for many years regard the Old World's artistic accomplishments with an awe that their own accomplishments did not inspire.

Opportunities, if sometimes meager ones, were provided for the display of contemporary works by the academies of fine arts that sprang up around the turn of the century. The success of England's Royal Academy, which had advanced the careers of its members through annual exhibitions since its founding in 1768, was the model for these new institutions. The first move in this direction on American shores was made in Philadelphia by Charles Willson Peale in 1795. But his organization, the Columbianum, was open scarcely a year before internal disputes caused its members to abandon it. Next, and longer-lived, although ultimately collapsing for the same reason, was the American Academy of the Fine Arts in New York. After it came the durable Pennsylvania Academy of the Fine Arts, which with its school and busy exhibition program continues to exist in Philadelphia. Other academies were organized in other cities, and all with only one end in view: the promotion of art. This was expected to come about through the development of collections of painting and sculpture, the scheduling of classes of instruction (for which the collections were of obvious importance), and the hanging of temporary exhibitions of old and new work. Beginning in 1827, the Boston Athenaeum, then twenty years old, was especially helpful to artists in the last of these activities. Although conceived as a library, which it remains, the Athenaeum held frequent exhibitions of art and purchased works by American artists with funds from its admission fees.[1]

Joining with the artists to develop and maintain the academies were the pillars of society: politicians, members of the learned professions, and merchant princes. The success of these gentlemen in opening channels of communication between the artists and the public, as well as in providing classes, did not always match the artists' hopes. This was glaringly true of the American Academy, whose well-to-do patrons never allowed the social gulf between themselves and the artists to narrow. The artists were permitted to draw from plaster casts in the academy's collection, but only between the hours of six and nine in the morning, chronically a sore point with them. In both New York and Philadelphia it seemed to the artists that the leaders of their cities' academies paid more attention to the idea of developing a museum than to the artists' needs for instruction and for the exhibition of their work.

In New York matters came to a head in 1826. Although the presidency of the American Academy was held by a renowned painter, John Trumbull, years of adulation at home and in England had dulled his sense of identification with his fellow artists. Arrogant, officious, aloof, Trumbull so alienated a group of men who planned to meet in the academy's quarters in the evening for drawing sessions and mutual criticism that they broke away to found a new organization, the National Academy of Design. With Samuel F. B. Morse as its first president, the National Academy soon became the stronger of the two societies. Only artists and architects were elected to membership. In 1841 the American Academy, its membership having sharply declined, was dissolved, to the regret of few. The National Academy meanwhile had moved from strength to strength. Firmly established in the art community long before the older society had given up the ghost, it drew the attention of the press with annual exhibitions of its members' work, and should any of the civic, intellectual, and business leaders barred from membership care to make a purchase, their money was cordially accepted.[2]

Remaining as outlets for artists at least through the 1820s were shops whose owners sold art but specialized in goods of other kinds. Just as Paff in his earliest years of shopkeeping had done, and as others had done before him, framers and gilders were willing to take pictures on consignment and give them window or wall space. These were tradesmen who owed the artists a favor, inasmuch as they derived their income, or a substantial part of it, from them.

It was owing to one such man that the romantic landscapes of Thomas Cole first met the public eye. In 1825 George Dixey, a carver and gilder, was kind enough to hang three of Cole's latest pictures in his shop, where they were seen by a Mr. G. W. Bruen. Bruen, according to William Dunlap, bought one of them for $10. So pleased was he with his purchase that he persuaded a framer named Coleman to hang three others. Ten dollars was no longer considered an adequate price; Coleman offered these canvases at $25 apiece. John Trumbull happened upon them, bought one, and later in the day told Dunlap about them. While the two men were chatting in Dunlap's house, Asher B. Durand dropped by, and all three then went to Coleman's to have a look at the young artist's work. There they found Cole himself, and, moved by his modest manner as well as by his pictures, Dunlap and Durand each chose one of the remaining two. For works of their dimensions, approximately two by three feet each, at $25 they were a steal, and Dunlap knew it.[3] Nevertheless, he could not afford to keep his purchase permanently; when Philip Hone offered him $50 for it, Dunlap turned it over to him. Remembering this transaction a few years later, Dunlap wrote, "[A]nd my necessities prevented me from giving the profit to the painter."[4] But Cole managed well enough without Dunlap's gain from the resale; after these early sales in Dixey's and Coleman's shops, he went on to receive a steady flow of commissions that increased in volume in the thirteen years remaining to him.

The frame shop of Parker and Clover (later owned by Lewis P. Clover alone) became another prominent New York outlet for American artists, including, at times, Morse, Cole, John Quidor, and William Sidney Mount. Eventually Clover became an active dealer and a publisher of prints, and his son, Lewis Junior, perhaps inspired by the art surrounding him in his boyhood, apprenticed himself to Asher B. Durand and became an engraver and painter. Dunlap took his own pictures to Parker and Clover for framing and in his rounds of the city dropped in to other shops and galleries as well, including Paff's. [5]

To reach a larger public than frame-shop visitors and the cognoscenti who attended exhibitions at the academies, enterprising artists staged exhibitions on their own. They wooed the public, not just with easel paintings such as were on view in their "painting rooms," but with large-scale biblical or historical pictures or landscapes: "Great Pictures," as they came to be called. This method of showing work to the public had been pioneered in England in the late eighteenth century by the American expatriates John Singleton Copley and Benjamin West.[6] It was not sales that the artists had in mind. They were looking for a generous reward from exhibition fees, usually set at 25 cents, although it was true enough that any commissions coming in as a result of the exhibitions would be most welcome. Such shows were not confined to the cities where the artists lived. Works calculated to be of general interest were trouped from city to city and installed in whatever accommodations could be found. If no permanent structure was available, a tent would do just as well, provided it kept out the rain.

These exhibitions were the period's equivalent of the twentieth century's film extravaganzas and touring versions of Broadway hits. They offered an experience of spectacle, and to residents of the smaller cities they brought something more: a taste of the artistic life of the metropolis. Beginning in 1818, each of the four large canvases painted by John Trumbull for the Rotunda of the Capitol in Washington went on the road. Congress commissioned the pictures for the immense sum of $32,000, and the exhibitions brought Trumbull thousands more. In a mere three weeks during 1818 *The Declaration of Independence* earned the artist $1,701.56. In 1822 *The Court of Death*, by Rembrandt Peale, began a tour that lasted over a year and brought in $8,886. William Dunlap sent out his *Christ Rejected* in the same year and also offered it to the American Academy for exhibition, with the stipulation that half the proceeds come to him. This painting and three others by Dunlap, *The Bearing of the Cross, Death on a Pale Horse* (after a painting by Benjamin West), and *Calvary*, were sent across the country from Maine to Ohio. In New York in 1817 John Vanderlyn erected the Rotunda near City Hall at his own expense for the exhibition of panoramas of European sights painted by himself and other artists. They remained on view until 1830.[7]

Unfortunately, not all the exhibitions met the artists' expectations of financial rewards. Samuel F. B. Morse suffered three severe disappointments in this way, first with his *Dying Hercules* and *Congress Hall* in the 1820s and then in 1833 with *The Exhibition Gallery of the Louvre*, a work of some six by nine feet in which Morse painstakingly rendered in miniature fifty of the Louvre's holdings. At Morse's home in New York the *Louvre* drew an average weekly gate of only $15, and it did poor business in New Haven and Boston also. When Morse, despairing of making any money on the painting in this way, sold it in 1834, he got only $1,200 for it, less than half the amount he had counted on. Ironically, it was this work that, when sold at auction in 1982 by its then owner, Syracuse University, to a private collector, Daniel J. Terra, fetched what was at the time a record price for an American painting: $3.25 million, easily surpassing the $2.5 million fetched by Frederic Edwin Church's *Icebergs* in 1979, then the highest price ever reached at an auction in America.[8]

For two weeks in the spring of 1859, Church, having taken up residence in the new and fashionable Tenth Street Studio Building, used his quarters there as exhibition space for a sweeping landscape, *The Heart of the Andes*, a work five and a half feet high and almost ten feet wide, and made to seem even bigger by the immensity of the elaborately carved black walnut frame surrounding it.[9] He elected to show the picture at night, illuminated by gaslight and surrounded by foliage, so as to create the illusion that paint and canvas were nature herself. Viewers had the sensation of peering at a mountain through a forest.

And the viewers arrived in droves; over twelve thousand men and women came to the studio to see this exotic vista, each paying the usual 25 cents. On the last day of the show, May 23, when more than two thousand people trooped through the Studio Building, the line of eager viewers stretched from Sixth Avenue to Broadway.[10] Even before this event, Church had sold the painting for $10,000, then a record price.[11] Under the guidance of John McClure, a sometime employee of the firm of Williams, Stevens and Williams (originally Williams and Stevens), an art gallery that previously had exhibited Church's panoramic *Niagara, The Heart of the Andes* then went on tour to London, returned to the Studio

Building for a stay of three months, and then moved on to Boston, Philadelphia, Baltimore, Cincinnati, Chicago, St. Louis, and Brooklyn.[12] From the tour and from the black-and-white engraving made after the painting (issued in 1862) Church also lined his pockets.[13]

The frame-shop hangings, academy exhibitions, and special one-object shows, as beneficial to many artists as they undoubtedly were, could hardly compensate for the lack of galleries of modern art where new work could be seen on a day-to-day basis. As late as the 1830s such businesses did not exist, and in 1838, with the death of Paff, even the most famous "old master" gallery was gone. But in that same year the moderns found a champion, and a series of events was set in train that would do wonders for the cause of their art. One of their own, an artist named James Herring, opened the Apollo Gallery, where contemporary American art could be seen and purchased. Herring, born in England in 1794, was a portraitist who in 1833 with James B. Longacre, an engraver, embarked on the serial publication of *The National Portrait Gallery of Distinguished Americans*, a four-volume set of engravings after painted portraits. The series was completed in 1839. Herring was also the owner of a circulating library and a dealer in books and prints. As secretary of the American Academy, he had come to know the art community, and his new enterprise, the Apollo, was intended to introduce it to new patrons.[14]

The Apollo Gallery was located in rooms at 410 Broadway, where Herring also housed his library. He had no trouble gathering examples of the work of leading artists; clearly they saw his invitation as the answer to a long-felt need. Missing at first were pictures by Cole, Durand, and Morse, but Herring secured works by J. W. Casilear, Thomas Doughty, Rembrandt and Raphaelle Peale, Hiram Powers, Thomas Sully, and many others, for a total of 260 items by ninety-six artists. Bravely counting on admission fees to support the gallery, Herring charged the artists no commissions. Half of what remained after accounting for the expenses of each exhibition he thriftily set aside, hoping that these monies would eventually provide sufficient funding for a national museum of American art.

Herring's scheme was too generous to succeed in 1838. He overestimated the general interest in the art of native sons. Despite press notices favorable to his conception and to the opening exhibition, not much was sold. But generous even in disappointment, Herring attributed the lack of sales to the depression then affecting the economy, not to the apathy of the public. He could not afford to run the gallery at a loss, but word luckily reached him from Edinburgh at just this time of another scheme for promoting art, one that had been tried successfully in several cities abroad. In January 1839, calling together a group of New Yorkers prominent in business and the professions, he proposed that they form an organization such as the one that eminent citizens of Edinburgh had run for the past two years. The plan involved the purchase of works of art through public subscriptions and the distribution of them to the subscribers in an annual lottery.

Herring had no difficulty persuading his band of patrons of the merit of the scheme. It was calculated to please everyone involved: the artists would have a new market for their works, and the public would have a chance of acquiring them at modest cost. An appeal was issued for subscriptions at $5 each under the name of the Apollo Art-Union. The name was changed in 1844 to the American Art-Union, but the principles behind the organization remained essentially the same for its entire thirteen years of life.

Aiding in the Art-Union's growth was the dawning awareness that much (probably most) of the old-master art on sale was not really that. Luman Reed was not the only disenchanted purchaser. Popular journals of the 1830s and '40s offered cautionary memoranda, warning prospective purchasers off the available "Rembrandts" and "Titians" and stressing the absurdity of the notion held by speculators and pretenders to wealth that great art of the past was to be had cheaply. The *New-York Mirror,* for example, reported in 1836 a conversation with "an acquaintance" who at a sale had snapped up works by some of the greatest names for about $15 apiece, which he expected to sell at a markup of 500 percent. Troubled by this, the *Mirror* observed, "The fact is, that the sweepings of Europe—the daubs which would be considered as encumbering the servants' hall of a gentleman's house in England, are bought and shipped for America; and it is in order to open the eyes of the unenlightened, that we have taken the trouble to pen these remarks."[15]

The Art-Union's exhibitions were held at its premises, which at first were Herring's rooms at 410 Broadway. But as the membership expanded, so did the space requirements, until in 1847 the society's managers chose to construct a building of their own, at 497 Broadway, with a gallery that their president described as "stately." Although at first the exhibitions required copies of old masters to fill up the space, the primary purpose of the shows was to promote and sell new American art. For the first three years the public paid to see the exhibitions, as they had done at the Apollo Gallery, but after that came an art-community innovation: every visitor was admitted free of charge. In the usual style of nineteenth-century exhibitions, the pictures were hung one above

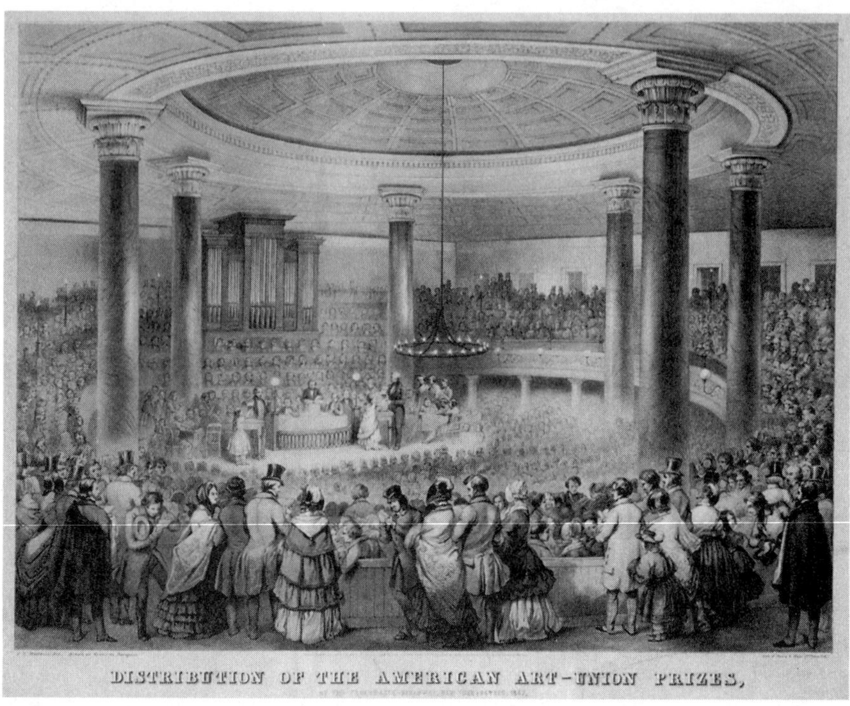

Distribution of the American Art-Union Prizes, December 24, 1847

another and side by side, frame touching frame far up the walls, placing a severe demand on the patience of viewers. When the Art-Union devoted its gallery space exclusively to the paintings of Daniel Huntington in 1850, this was believed to be the first one-artist show of work by a contemporary to be held in New York.[16]

One of the benefits of membership was the distribution each year of an engraving after a painting in the Art-Union's collection. Pictures by Durand, Cole, William Sidney Mount, and George Caleb Bingham were among the works chosen for this treatment. But far and away the greatest attraction for subscribers was the lottery. Each subscription entitled the holder to one ticket to it, but any individual was free to purchase as many subscriptions as he could afford. Off to a promising start, the Art-Union attracted 814 subscribers in its first year and distributed thirty-six paintings, chosen from among those not sold at the exhibitions. In its peak year, 1849, the numbers climbed to 18,960 subscribers and 460 paintings along with 550 statuettes, models, and prints. Growing increasingly crowded and fashionable as the years went along, the lotteries attracted the attention of the press, whose reports mentioned not only the prizes and the winners but also the dignitaries in attendance. These events were held on the Friday evening before Christmas and took on the festive air of the season—as well they might have, in view of the quality of the prizes. Listening closely as the winning numbers were called out, the well-dressed subscribers hoped to come away with a John F. Kensett, a Church, a Durand, or a Cole, Christmas presents of a high order. In 1848 Cole's *The Voyage of Life,* a series of four canvases, was offered as a single prize.[17]

No money from the subscribers ever found its way into the pockets of the Art-Union's managers. They expected no compensation. From the outset, when Herring first presented the idea to his band of civic leaders, the Art-Union was governed by prominent figures who participated out of a genuine love of art and the hope of promoting American culture. The first president, John W. Francis, was a physician who often looked after sick artists free of charge; the third was William Cullen Bryant, poet and newspaper editor. Although at the annual elections the officers and board were inclined to reelect themselves, the continuity of management engineered in this way probably contributed to the Art-Union's stability. In any event, no harm came from it. Nor were difficulties created by the decision, made at the outset and maintained to the end, not to ask a panel of artists to choose the pictures to be distributed, lest professional jealousy get in the way of sound judgment.

In some years the managers faced charges in the press that not every work shown was of the highest quality. But they replied with dignified paternalism that although this was true, there was a good reason for it: the pictures of lesser quality were painted by artists of promise and therefore deserved to be shown. Above all, it was American art that the Art-Union wished to popularize. Works could be submitted by Americans living abroad and Europeans living in the United States, but what the managers looked for in art was American subjects: American landscapes, American life. "It is the object of art not to reproduce itself," the selection committee told the artists in 1842, "but to look to Nature for its models, and these exist within the limits of our own territory, in as grand and imposing forms as in France and Italy, but even although they did not, it is not only nature that we want in our works of art, but it is our own nature, something that will awaken our sympathies and strengthen the bonds that bind us to our homes."[18] It was all right, in the managers' eyes, for American artists to study abroad, and they went so far as to offer funds in support of those who were doing so, but they hoped for American content in the painters' output after they returned.

The Art-Union's board knew that to make their organization grow they would have to prime the pump. They hired travelers to go about the country and drum up subscriptions, with the happy result that the membership roll extended from Maine to Wisconsin and down into Florida. Eventually it leapt across the border into Mexico and overseas to Munich and Rio de Janeiro. In 1848 the board inaugurated a monthly magazine, the *American Art-Union Bulletin.* This was not their first publication, but it was much superior to the routine catalogues and accounts of the lottery distribution that preceded it. It was the first American magazine devoted exclusively to art and the art world. Its contents informed readers of exhibitions held at home and abroad and offered criticism of art old and new. And, realizing that nothing would more effectively generate curiosity and a sense of belonging among the members than gossip of the art world, the editors also printed such news of American artists as who was sailing for Europe, who had just returned, and who was spending the summer in the mountains or at the seashore. There was also room for artists' advertisements or "cards," among them the frequently appearing address of "Frederic E. Church, landscape painter."

The Art-Union stirred up so much excitement that it created not only friends—the subscribers and artists—but rivals and enemies. Although not an art union, a Free Gallery opened its doors in Philadelphia in 1844 and in its ten years of existence sold only American art.[19] Eventually that city as well as Cincinnati, Newark, San Francisco, and still others had art unions of their own. But the American Art-Union's managers, blessed as they were with an ever-increasing roll of subscribers, did not see these upstarts as a threat to their organization's health. The *Bulletin* reported on the birth of each of them and commented occasionally on their procedures. A threat, when it eventually came, arose in another quarter.

For most of its thirteen years as a buyer and distributor of art, the American Art-Union was engaged in a quarrel with the National Academy of Design. It was a running battle intermittently marked by periods of truce. Since both institutions mounted exhibitions of American art, neither wished to surrender the right of first call on the artists' output. Nor did either institution care to show works that had previously been exhibited by the other. Worrying and wrangling over the issue, the opponents battered away at each other in their publications and sought the aid of the commercial press on their respective sides. At one time the National Academy demanded that the Art-Union show no work by living Americans, a demand that the Art-Union necessarily rejected out of hand. At another time the National Academy's officers elected to bar from their annual exhibitions any works previously shown by the Art-Union. The Art-Union did not adopt the same procedure, but insisted that all works offered to it for purchase be made available for exhibitions as well.

Another severe, unresolvable point of conflict stemmed from the Art-Union's early decision to open its exhibitions free of charge. The National Academy, which counted on the receipts of admission fees to underwrite its programs, felt a severe threat on that score. "Our deadly enemies" was the phrase used by Charles C. Ingham, one of the academy's founders, in a letter to its president, Asher B. Durand, in September 1849, when tempers were highest.[20]

That fall the academy contemplated setting up an art union of its own, the Painters' and Sculptors' Art-Union. In its *Bulletin* the American Art-Union applied the needle of criticism to the academy's procedures, the color of its exhibition rooms, and the quality of the works on view. But with a sudden about-face the American Art-Union enabled the academy to pay off a floating debt by buying a bloc of its members' works, thus lowering the heat. By that time, however, the days of the American Art-Union had slowly and sadly begun to fade to a close.

It was neither the competition from provincial rivals nor the wrath of the National Academy that brought about the collapse. What destroyed the Art-Union was the very thing that had made it a success: the annual lottery. Disapproval of the lottery had been voiced in the press from the beginning, but criticism on that score had never troubled the managers, who always insisted that the lottery was not the most important event in their program but merely one of many measures for promoting American art. They claimed that in the first place the lottery was not what it appeared to be, a kind of gamble, but the only possible means of distributing to individual subscribers the works that were the common property of them all. Still, it *was* the lottery that drew in the subscribers, as was evident in their tardiness in paying the annual $5 fee until shortly before the date of the drawing. In 1852 the attacks in the papers grew more clamorous, and the district attorney decided to look into the matter. A suit was brought against the Art-Union for violation of the constitution of the state of New York, and both the state Supreme Court and the Court of Appeals (New York's highest) found against the association. The managers hoped to carry on by substituting an auction for the lottery, but that dream died when the first sale, held in December 1853, failed to spark public enthusiasm. The funds remaining in the managers' hands were given to the New York Gallery of the Fine Arts, the museum created to display Luman Reed's collection. By stages through 1885 that collection and the papers of the Art-Union became the property of the New-York Historical Society.

The court rulings that closed down the American Art-Union dealt American artists a blow from which they only gradually recovered. Its operations had benefited them financially and had increased their prestige. Now in a sense they had to make a new beginning, under new auspices. But that was difficult to accomplish, because in the meanwhile the old, snobbish preference for European art over the native product had begun to reassert itself. John Durand and William J. Stillman, the editors of the *Crayon,* the leading art journal of the 1850s, suggested that needy artists offer their works at auction, since that would surely bring in some money. On the other hand, when one destitute painter wrote to say that he was contemplating a raffle of his works, they were scandalized. A raffle, they maintained, would cheapen the art market; if his pictures were worthy of purchase, they would sell by more acceptable means, since every thoroughly accomplished picture in New York, they also maintained, found a buyer. A more reasonable comment from the same source was prompted by the successful auction held by Jasper Cropsey in 1857 to finance a trip abroad:

> We have always insisted that the reason our painters seemed neglected was because they did not direct their labors towards public taste, preferring generally to display themselves on huge canvasses and labored compositions, which very few have a love for, or house-room enough to spare to accommodate them, rather than works which concentrate all their thought in small space, with comparatively little manual labor.[21]

At midcentury it was new art from abroad, not old-master paintings, that attracted collectors and dealers. Even as the enrollment of the American Art-Union was reaching its highest figure, dealers in French and German art were finding a market in the United States.

In 1846 the Parisian firm of Goupil (then Goupil, Vibert) chose to start up a branch in New York and sent over a young man, Michael Knoedler, to head it. The firm had been founded in 1827; the opening of this outpost was one of the measures of its success. Although in its Paris gallery Goupil dealt mainly in high-quality prints, its inventory also included paintings and sculptures, and the stock that Knoedler brought to New York was just such a mixture.[22] To sell this stock, Knoedler set up the International Art-Union. This new rival, unlike the provincial societies, was a constant irritant to the managers of the American Art-Union, who saw it for what it was: strictly a commercial enterprise.

Also imported from France and making inroads on the American market were pictures by the Barbizon school, which included such major painters as Corot, Millet, and Daubigny. In the main, the works of this school were sunny landscapes and scenes of rural life; thousands of American schoolchildren of the decades to come would look up from their desks at sepia reproductions hanging on their classroom walls of such manifestations of the Barbizon esthetic as Millet's *The Gleaners* and *The Angelus*. The young artist William Morris Hunt became attracted to the art of the Barbizon painters when he became friends with Millet in France in 1844. On his return to the States, he advised New England collectors to buy Barbizon pictures. In 1850 the small Westminster Gallery of Providence, Rhode Island, was taken over by Joseph Vose of the same city. Acting on Hunt's advice, Vose began to deal in the Barbizon artists in both Providence and Boston.[23]

Of equal interest to Americans in the same years were the works of Germany's Düsseldorf school.[24] For the most part these resembled Barbizon pictures in content, but they also included historical paintings, such as Emanuel Leutze's celebrated *Washington Crossing the Delaware*, and rugged, romantic mountain landscapes. The meticulous detail of these works lent them immense appeal. In 1849 the German-born John G. Boker, a wine merchant of New York who had interrupted his business career to serve as American consul in Remscheid, the city of his birth, and later in Basel, turned to a new trade and opened the Düsseldorf Gallery with a collection of some 150 works of the school. The Broadway building that housed the gallery was a church in the Gothic style that had formerly served a Unitarian congregation. To permit nighttime viewing of his collection, Boker installed gas jets, an innovation that no other dealer in the city had yet tried.[25]

For his pictures, which he gathered over a period of twenty years, Boker was later said to have paid a total of $230,000.[26] For the 1830s and '40s, this was an immense sum to invest in art, and although Boker did not fail as a dealer, neither did he greatly prosper. He at first kept the original collection intact but each year brought in new paintings which then went on sale. But business was not brisk, and in 1857 he thought it prudent to sell the entire contents of the gallery to the Cosmopolitan Art

Association for $180,000. This organization was an art union, one of the most successful and best-publicized organizations of its kind to come along since the American Art-Union had pioneered the route. The Cosmopolitan's headquarters were located in Sandusky, Ohio, well beyond the reach of New York's constitution and the jurisdiction of its district attorney.[27]

Among the most satisfied visitors of Boker's premises (sometimes referred to by patrons as "Mr. Düsseldorf's Gallery") were young lovers, who were quick to discover that the screens set up for the hanging of paintings provided sheltered corners for furtive kisses.[28] Their name for the gallery was the "Lovers' Tryst." One of their number was Elihu Vedder, who would achieve fame with symbolist pictures of sea serpents and female faces mysteriously materializing out of clouds, but whose memoirs, *The Digressions of V.,* have a robust earthiness that contrasts nicely with the romanticism of his art. Reminiscing about his young adult life, he wrote that during his early years in New York he had frequented the Düsseldorf Gallery in the company of young women with whom he was on terms of affection. "This trysting," he confided, "serves to explain why I was not more influenced by the Düsseldorf School."[29]

Although in the years from 1840 to 1860 at least forty Americans studied at Düsseldorf, American artists on the whole were not pleased by the presence of so many of the school's works in New York. Looking back in 1894 on Boker's gallery, John Durand recalled it as "the first appearance among us of foreign art on a large scale" and also said that it had caused an "eclipse" of American art.[30] This was somewhat misleading, for although never before had so much *contemporary* European art been exhibited in the United States, older art from abroad, whether genuine or spurious, had been shown in plenty since the days of Paff and Flandin. Yet Durand was essentially right in asserting that the opening of the Düsseldorf Gallery marked the beginning of an eclipse. The eclipse was only partial, however, inasmuch as American art continued to have its champions, some of whom possessed as much of the spirit of enterprise as Herring and his associates in the American Art-Union.

3

MIDCENTURY MOMENTUM

Although the work of European artists challenged American paintings for space on well-to-do collectors' walls through the 1850s and the Civil War years, it could not crowd them out altogether. Commissions and on-the-spot purchases made by callers at the studio (the word came into familiar American usage in the '50s, gradually replacing "painting room") still accounted for most of the sales of the typical American artist. But among his purchasers were dealers also. In New York, galleries opened one after another in the three- and four-story buildings on Broadway below Tenth Street. Other cities, with Boston in the forefront, also witnessed the establishment of new galleries and a consequent enrichment of artistic life. None of these just-opened midcentury galleries specialized in American art; they offered a small stock of domestic works amid a preponderance of foreign art. But at least they gave American artists a chance to show what they could do.

At the same time, and despite the inability of Luman Reed's relations and friends to generate public enthusiasm for a permanent exhibition of his collection, the museum idea caught on as new collectors began to dream of the final placement of their holdings in handsome buildings that could provide for the education of the public and stand as memorials to themselves. In 1857 American financial institutions experienced a sharp, severe panic, but the decade could be counted a prosperous age nevertheless, and those who prospered the most found a gratifying release from the tensions of business in collecting art. As the 1850s moved along, the art season in New York, which previously had run from winter to spring, culminating in the annual exhibition of the National Academy of Design each May, was gradually lengthened to include the fall as dealers perceived that patrons might long for the refreshment of art after the miseries of a humid summer. But earlier in the decade, as one reporter noted, only a "stray work of art" might have been on view in the fall, perhaps at the galleries of Schaus, Goupil, or Williams and Stevens where "the inevitable rustling ladies" could be counted on to rush in for a quick look and a chat, although hardly for the serious contemplation of art.[1]

In the same decade, what was to become an "inundation" (to use John Durand's word) of European art commenced as European dealers elected to tap the American market.[2] The Civil War years, from 1861 to 1865, which saw the birth and growth of many American fortunes and the founding of powerful dynastic families, created not only great wealth but also the wish to spend it on the building of mansions and on pictures and marble statuary to decorate them. In less than a year after the Confederacy's collapse, the *New York Times* editorialized at length, and not altogether approvingly, on the "picture mania," but conceded, "If we must have a fanciful epidemic among us always, how much better that it should take this form than develop itself again in a mania for the mulberry plant or the Dutch tulip bulb!"[3]

But despite the proliferating activity in the buying and selling of art, at midcentury even the most popular American artists were still obliged to promote themselves. They were not lacking in allies. One real-estate development of 1857 was especially beneficial to the artists of New York and so widely praised that it was soon duplicated in Boston. This was the construction of the first building in the city designed to be tenanted exclusively by painters and sculptors: the Tenth Street Studio Building. Although Richard Morris Hunt's design for the building may have resulted in "a somber pile," as one magazine article described it, the artists themselves were more than satisfied with it.[4] Until it was demolished in 1955 to make way for an apartment house, the Studio Building provided comfortable working space and, if required, lodging for many distinguished artists, among them Albert Bierstadt, William Merritt Chase, Frederic Edwin Church, John F. Kensett, and Worthington Whittredge, to name only five. Studios—well lighted, if quite plain—were provided for some twenty-three artists along with bedrooms for a few of them and a large exhibition hall. A typical room, decorated and occupied by Launt Thompson, the lone sculptor in the building, drew this description from Thomas Bailey Aldrich:

> Imagine a large square room lighted by a double window, to which are fitted two movable cloth screens, so arranged that the light can be increased or subdued at pleasure. With the exception of this window, and a heavy oiled-pine mantel-piece . . . there is nothing very striking about the room itself. The walls and ceiling are plainly finished, and the neatly swept floor uncarpeted. The furniture is as simple, consisting of five or six camp-chairs, an uncomfortable lounge, and a mahogany table with rather uncertain legs, but very quaintly carved—a relic of our great-grandmothers.[5]

Conceived and built by the financier James Boorman Johnston, brother of the railroad magnate and art collector John Taylor Johnston, the Studio Building was popular and prestigious from the start.[6] Rents ranged between $200 and $300 per year, a trifle high, but not so high as to prevent full occupancy.[7] Although studio space was available elsewhere—for example, in the New York University building on Washington Square (described by Aldrich as "dingy and despondent") and Appleton's and Dodsworth's buildings on Broadway—this was the only structure whose entire area, all three floors of it, was designed for occupancy by artists alone, and they rushed to move in.[8] Not surprisingly, the *Crayon* observed that the city could well support another such structure, should "some capitalist" come forward to back it.[9] Of the first tenants, only one out of twenty-one was a woman, Anna Mary Freeman. She remained for two years, a brief tenancy compared to that of Frederic Church, who kept his studio until 1889, or John La Farge, who kept his until 1910. Perhaps she was made to feel self-conscious by so very masculine an environment. The men in the building soon became a band of brothers who jubilantly and sometimes raucously celebrated one another's successes. Later, however, married couples took up residence.

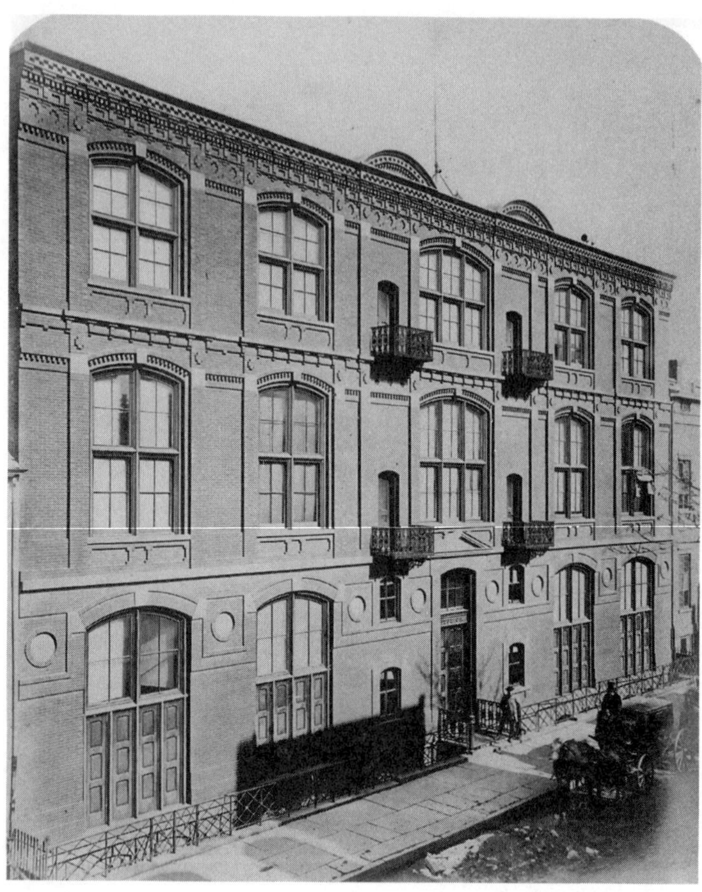

Tenth Street Studio Building

The Studio Building served the artists not only as a place for practicing their profession, but also as a place for showing and selling their latest works—and, with those artists of scant success, their older works as well. Visitors were always welcome, whether they came to buy, to take works on consignment, as dealers sometimes did, or merely to ogle. The tenants' "cards" in the *Crayon* and elsewhere notified the public of their at-home days. In addition to keeping those hours open for the public, the artists of the Studio Building, like those at Dodsworth's, held receptions a few times each season, when most of the individual studios were open and their occupants on hand to welcome callers.

The large, central exhibition room, well supplied with gaslight fixtures, also was available on such occasions. Of the first reception, held in March 1858, the *Crayon* reported, "There was a large and highly gratified assembly of ladies and gentlemen present; the company visited the several studios in the building, and took much interest in the arrangements of this unique structure. . . . We have never seen better night-light for pictures, nor a better constructed exhibition-room—thanks to Mr. R. M. Hunt, the architect."[10]

A lengthier description was offered by the *New York Times* on the occasion of a reception held in January 1859:

> No pictures or works of art of any kind were admitted, except the productions of the artists of the Studio, and a most brilliant and attractive display they made. The only drawback to the pleasure of the exhibition was the trifling one of not being able to see any of the works exhibited. The great charm, however, of these receptions is not the pictures, nor the sculpture, nor the drawings, but the company. You find yourself, on entering the rooms, if you succeed in entering them, in the midst of a brilliant assemblage of youth, beauty, and fashion; of men worth knowing and women worth seeing; and being hemmed in on all sides by orbicular spreads of brocade and velvet, you stand still, with your hat above your head, or suffer yourself to be swayed hither and thither by the pressure of the crowd. You catch glimpses of gilt frames in the distance, and now and then find yourself thrust against a white but unresisting object, which you discover, on turning your head, to be a hideous group of Italian peasants in marble. You know there are charming pictures on the walls . . . [b]ut, what's the use? You cannot see them. Nobody sees them. But everybody sees everybody, and there's the delight of it.[11]

Less crowded but also less decorous events took place from time to time, when the building spontaneously developed a party atmosphere. The artists, most of them young in the building's early years, were disposed to relax noisily when their long day at the easel had ended. On one much reported occasion, they dressed up in whatever costumes each man's rooms provided, paraded through the corridors, and ended their revel with a war dance.[12] All this jollity faded, however, during the summer, when the artists took them selves away from the sweltering city to retreats in the country. In 1860 the *Crayon* quoted a reporter from another journal who paid the Studio Building a midsummer visit:

> We entered its portals a day or two ago, hoping to meet a familiar face and shake a friendly hand; but the lonely air of the place made

> us sick at heart, if not melancholy. The chair of the polite janitor stood vacant, a few dusty newspapers only hanging over its back. The letter boxes were empty, and the eye traced in vain for something to indicate life in the establishment.[13]

But with the return of cool weather, the artists themselves also returned, and the combined activities of socializing and making art commenced again.

Not until two decades after the Civil War did dealers begin to play a crucial role in the life of most American artists. The principle of exclusivity, under which an artist entrusted his entire output on consignment to a single dealer, came even later. At midcentury, artists set their own prices and sold where they could. The notion of remaining loyal to a dealer did not enter their minds. For their part, the dealers took the same line. At this early stage in the rise of the gallery system, they had not yet formed the practice of developing a stable of artists, unlike the leading dealers of Europe, who were beginning to buy up "not pictures but artists," as the *Times* put it, and to control the market in those artists' work.[14] One of the first galleries to take that step was the eminent Boston firm of Williams and Everett, which gave subsidies to George Inness, as, later, did Doll and Richards of the same city.[15] Visiting studios and exhibitions of the National Academy of Design and other artists' associations, the dealers took on consignment from the artists as many works as they admired and believed they could sell. Some of their stock was acquired for resale from collectors. If, as sometimes happened, the dealers had work on hand that did not move, they gave up the struggle to sell it themselves and called in the auctioneers.

But to the men growing rich from railroads, shipping, and mines in the 1850s and destined to grow richer during the Civil War, American art was somewhat less alluring than the latest thing from Europe. A few men of means, such as Charles M. Leupp, Robert M. Olyphant, and Marshall O. Roberts of New York, preferred the Americans, but most well-to-do collectors bought only the occasional native work and indulged themselves with purchases of meticulously painted salon pictures from Paris and Düsseldorf on religious and historical themes, as well as landscapes and scenes of rural life from the Barbizon painters. The sumptuously illustrated three-volume *Art Treasures of America*, published between 1879 and 1882 by the artist Earl Shinn under the pseudonym Edward Strahan, showed American works to have no more than a 10 percent representation in leading private collections. Had Shinn published in 1865, the list-

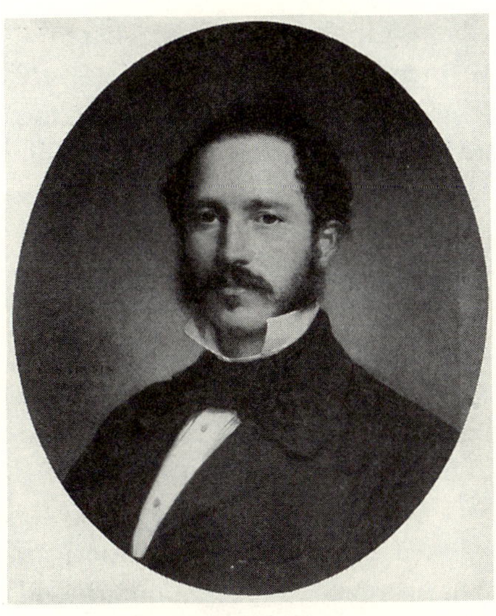

Michael Knoedler

ings would have been somewhat more favorable to American art, although foreign—chiefly French—art would still have dominated.

The bellwether for the many young dealerships of the 1850s was Goupil, whose director, Michael Knoedler, had a keen sense of the market.[16] With four busy years of the merchandising of art in New York behind him when the decade began, Knoedler not only understood the prevailing taste of the times but played a role in the shaping of it. German by birth, he had moved when young to Paris and there secured a position as clerk in the Goupil firm.[17] In Paris the pronunciation of his first name became gallicized, so that more often than not among friends and family he was addressed as Michel. The adventurous spirit that led him from his home near Stuttgart to the French capital served him well in 1846, when Goupil asked him to represent the firm in New York. The firm chose wisely, for Knoedler had the qualities that make for leadership in the field: "a frank heartiness and a genial diligence that are irresistible," as one writer put it.[18]

But in 1846, with collecting not yet a pulse-quickening enthusiasm among even those Americans who could easily afford the still modest prices asked for art, making a go of a new gallery required perseverance as well as charm. Knoedler's International Art-Union may have rendered the older American Art-Union anxious and wrathful, but to set it up was nevertheless a shrewd business maneuver, inasmuch as it introduced the public to the firm's wares and, of course, contributed to its income. At Goupil's first New York premises, at 289 Broadway, Knoedler established a free gallery, following the American Art-Union's innovation, where the curious could enter and examine the merchandise without the costly nuisance of having to part with 25 cents for the privilege, and that too was an aid to business. Knoedler's cordiality was matched by his intelligence. A portrait of him painted thirteen years after his arrival in New York shows not merely a handsome face but observant eyes that look out beneath a high and generous brow.

Although, as noted, Goupil's New York branch at the outset was primarily a shop for engravings, paintings were always available. Typical among Knoedler's goods were the elegantly finished, spiritually uplifting creations of such fashionable continental artists as Paul Delaroche and Ary Scheffer. Visitors to the gallery could see, for example, a *Dead Christ* from Delaroche's hand, a *Head of the Savior* from Scheffer's. In its first catalogue, published in 1848, the firm offered greetings to the American public that were cordial to the point of effusiveness: "The salutary and elevating effect of cultivating amongst the people a taste for the Fine Arts is indisputable. . . . It is, therefore, the true mark of a great people to accord a liberal support to the Arts in general; and the flattering encouragement they have met with in this country, clearly indicates that there exists among the people a high appreciation of Art, which is destined to make rapid progress in the future." Proudly, but with an odd inability to understand the dynamic that he himself was creating in the trade, he wrote back to Paris in 1856 that he had sold a work for $300, "the highest price that will ever be paid for a painting in America."[19]

But Knoedler was imaginative enough to see that one way of impressing the American public, no matter how taken it may have been with a passion for European art, was by encouraging native art as well. In that way his gallery could place itself firmly in the American scene. Goupil's International Art-Union, according to a prospectus of 1849, made a practice of sending a fledgling American artist abroad every year for two years of study. One of the first to be offered such an opportunity was William Sidney Mount, the Long Island genre painter; he turned down the invitation, however, because it would have obliged him to paint four pictures for the firm during his time abroad.[20]

Not only did the Goupil firm support American artists in this generous fashion, but, to return to the catalogue of 1848, "we desire to identify ourselves, as far as we may be encouraged, with the productions of American artists, seriously contemplating to engrave in Paris the most remarkable works of the American School of Art." In the same year the firm published its first such print, a skillfully lithographed rendering of

Mount's *The Power of Music*. It sold for $5. Never before had an American painting been sent to Paris for "engraving."[21]

By 1854 Goupil's had outgrown its original premises at 289 Broadway. After a trip to France from which he returned a married man, Knoedler moved the gallery slightly north, to 366 Broadway. Although he could not afford to deal in American art exclusively or, for that matter, to let it dominate the gallery, he remained true to his promise by continuing to keep his eye on it. When Knoedler presented a group of paintings by George Henry Hall, an American genre painter, in 1856, the concept of the one-artist show was still so rare as to invite comment in the press. Observed one reporter, "Mr. G. H. Hall was given a public exhibition of his works at Messrs. Goupil & Co.'s store, which mode of exhibiting an artist's productions is entitled to some consideration. We think it has many advantages. The artist can choose his own place and light, and his works can be seen much more satisfactorily, than when placed in the midst of others."[22]

In 1857 Knoedler bought out the Goupil interest and became the sole owner of the gallery, but retained the original name. In 1859, after only two years, he found he had done so well as his own man that he required still more space and bought the house at 722 Broadway, near Ninth Street, belonging to A. T. Stewart, the department store owner and collector.[23] Stewart, who came to own Rosa Bonheur's much prized *Horse Fair,* now in the Metropolitan Museum of Art, collected art in what could be called a Knoedleresque mixture of American and European works—one, that is, in which European works outnumbered the American products.[24] By 1864 Knoedler occupied a position of such eminence in the New York art community that three artists, William S. Haseltine, Louis Lang, and William J. Hays, proposed him for membership in the Century Association, a club for artists, writers, and "amateurs of the arts." He was the first dealer to become a member.

At Goupil's, Knoedler bought paintings directly from the artists for exhibition, engraving, or resale. The gallery sought works not only by Mount but by other talented Americans, including George Caleb Bingham, whose *Canvassing for Votes* Knoedler bought in 1852.[25] By the late winter of 1859 he had gathered up so many American pictures that he employed what was then the leading auction house, Henry H. Leeds & Company, to sell them at a gala two-evening event at the National Academy of Design. Some of the artists and the prices their works fetched were Jasper Cropsey ($24, $25, $80), Mount ($185), and Church (*Homage to Cole,* $510).[26] The idea was to clear the decks, not to signal an abandonment of American art; the firm continued to stock the work of American artists. Sculpture by the mid-1800s having become an American form of artistic expression, Knoedler showed three works in 1860 by Emma Stebbins, who, after devoting herself to brush and palette for some two decades, had lately turned sculptor. Her exhibition was a critical success; the *Crayon*'s reviewer, in keeping with the attitude of his time, praised Stebbins for her "masculine energy."[27] But Knoedler, his patronage of American creativity notwithstanding, was never one to turn his back on European art, as he demonstrated in the same year by exhibiting a collection of 206 French and English paintings brought over by Ernest Gambart, the Belgian-born London dealer.[28]

Ever quick to get in on a good thing, in this instance the striking success of Church's *Heart of the Andes,* Knoedler held an exhibition of the artist's *Twilight in the Wilderness* in 1860. In the following year, when the gallery opened what a journalist described as "an elegant exhibition room" on its second floor, Knoedler inaugurated the new space with a showing of Church's monumental *Icebergs*. Also in 1861 he showed Church's *Our Banner in the Sky;* in 1862, *Under Niagara;* and in 1863, *Cotopaxi,* one of several paintings by Church of that craggy mountain. For a mere $200 Knoedler acquired the copyright of *Our Banner,* a rendering of the American flag as composed of the stars and striated clouds of an early evening sky, a painting calculated to stir patriotic hearts at the outset of the Civil War.[29] The firm's chromolithographic reproduction afforded art lovers of modest means a colorful symbol of Yankee determination.

Among still other Americans whose work appeared from time to time at Goupil's was Daniel Huntington. In 1863 Knoedler exhibited Huntington's *Mercy's Dream,* along with an engraving after it. At that time the artist was serving the first of two lengthy terms as president of the National Academy of Design.[30] In 1865 Knoedler bought William Trost Richards's *June Woods* directly from the artist and sold it to Robert L. Stuart, a sugar refiner and, incidentally, one of Knoedler's clubmates at the Century. Works by Mary Cassatt, a rising young painter, caught Knoedler's eye in 1872 and then went on view in the gallery.[31]

In 1847 Goupil's sent another young man, Wilhelm (later William) Schaus, over from Paris to work in the New York branch. Like Michael Knoedler, he was of German descent, and, also like Knoedler, he was enterprising.[32] It was Schaus, an admirer of Mount, who persuaded the artist to permit the firm to issue the lithograph of *The Power of Music* and who prodded, cajoled, and importuned him to let the firm show whatever works he might have on hand. "You say that you are pleased to know that I would like your 'Just in Time' for the new gallery," he wrote to Mount in 1849, "but can I obtain it? *To have it,* that is the question. It would afford me the *utmost* pleasure to have this picture, because it is a real gem in every respect. . . . Of course this would be *in addition* to the large picture you promised me for next year. *Pray, do let me be the happy possessor!*"[33] Over the years, Schaus succeeded without noticeable strain in persuading Mount to let him send nine paintings to the Paris lithographers, five for publication by Goupil and four to appear under Schaus's own imprint.[34]

Once their business dealings had begun, the artist and dealer formed a warm friendship. Schaus was frequently a guest, and a most welcome one, at Mount's Long Island home, and Mount customarily dropped into Goupil's to chat with Schaus when he came into town. Schaus was too talented an operator in the art world to stay permanently in a secondary position at Goupil's. The first sign of his restlessness was his request for a share of the profits from the prints he commissioned of American paintings. When this was refused, he told himself that it was time, after fifteen years with the firm in Paris and New York, to leave and start up a gallery of his own. At what seems to have been the last minute, however, either he or his superiors relented, and he stayed on for a while longer. "I thought it very strange," Mount wrote to him, "that Goupil & Co. should let you run away from their establishment. To tell you the truth, they might rake Germany, France, England, and the United States, with a fine tooth comb before they could find a man that understands so well as you do their interest with the Americans—even at double *your sallery* [*sic*], the house would be the looser [*sic*] in parting with you." Nevertheless, Schaus was determined to set up on his own, and in August 1852 he notified Mount that he had broken with Goupil.[35] In the following year he found suitable rooms on Broadway and opened the doors of William Schaus and Company.

At the outset, Schaus's enthusiasm for American art remained hearty. He showed, for example, the landscapes of Jasper Cropsey, the domestic scenes of Lilly Martin Spencer, of whose works he also commissioned lithographs, and the marble *White Captive* of Erastus Dow Palmer.[36] "Objectionable" was the verdict pronounced by the *New York Times* on Palmer's elegant nude, which, like the more famous *Greek Slave* of Hiram Powers, depicted a woman caught and bound, although, unlike the slave, not employing a free hand to preserve her modesty. "That the art displayed is of a high order, and the workmanship above criticism," declared the scandalized writer, is not to be disputed, and it is for that very reason all the more objectionable. That it almost needs a touch of the marble to persuade one that it is not really a lovely young woman suddenly unveiled to the vulgar gaze, makes all the stronger our protest against this attack on the decorum of American manners. . . . And in this connection we take occasion to speak of the unblushing effrontery with which the exhibition room of the "White Captive" is sometimes made a convenient lounging and flirtation place.

The newspaper, always friendly toward the dealer, allowed Schaus space for a rebuttal of the suggestion that any offense against propriety might occur in his premises. Angered by the indictment of his taste, he described the charges as "libels on every lady and gentleman who has [*sic*] visited the 'White Captive.' " And with this rejoinder the flare-up was extinguished.[37]

Yet for all his genuine admiration of American art, Schaus, like Knoedler, was soon exhibiting expensive European art as well. In 1858 the *Times* reported that "Mr. Schaus, to whom Art in this City is under divers obligations, lent his rooms awhile to the owner of a noble picture claiming to come from the easel of Peter Paul Rubens." It was for sale at $18,000. Schaus also had on hand at the time a stock of recent French paintings lent to him by Gambart. "We ought to take care," said the *Times,* "that Mr. Schaus is not allowed to send them back to Mr. Gambart."[38] Gradually the firm, which was to remain in business for sixty years, transformed itself into a venue for the sale of European painting and sculpture almost exclusively, and Schaus became a rich man in the process.

Although Schaus and Knoedler very clearly led the pack of New York dealers at midcentury, Williams, Stevens & Williams and the firm of John Snedecor were not far behind them. Williams, Stevens, and Williams received almost as much press coverage as the galleries of the two émigré dealers, while Snedecor was so successful that the firm he founded, renamed Babcock in 1916, remains in business.

Williams, Stevens, & Williams rose to eminence from commonplace origins as a shop where mirrors were made and sold. As Williams and Stevens, it was first listed in a business directory for the year 1843. Gradually the firm expanded. It frequently exhibited new work by American artists, but, like Goupil's, it conducted a busy trade in prints. In 1854 the partners exhibited the most sensational large-scale picture of the year:

Rosa Bonheur's *Horse Fair*. One of their shrewdest ventures was the purchase for $6,000 in 1857 of Church's *Niagara* along with the copyright, with which they were empowered to reproduce the painting as a lithograph.[39] Gallery visitors were stunned by Church's ability to depict the iridescent cascade with a virtually photographic literalism. From the gallery, *Niagara* went on the road in America and was subsequently shipped to England, where it drew crowds and an enviable sheaf of enthusiastic notices. The firm had overspent its resources, however, and had begun to feel a severe financial pinch, one upshot of which was that Church was unwilling to let the partners have more of his pictures. Maneuvering on the edge, they were in so perilous a plight that in England *Niagara* was threatened with seizure by their creditors. It may have been this experience that led Church to select an agent, a Scot named John McClure, to arrange his future large-scale single-picture exhibitions.[40] When the painting returned to New York, it was purchased by John Taylor Johnston for $5,000.[41]

Williams, Stevens & Williams continued in business, if shakily, until 1865, when the firm's name made its last appearance in New York City directories. Among other Americans whose work the partners showed before calling it a day was John Rogers, the creator of plaster sculptures of a size to fit comfortably on a tabletop or sconce and usually composed of two, three, or four figures and cast in large numbers according to demand. These "Rogers groups," as they came to be known, were a three-dimensional equivalent of the more sentimental hand-colored lithographs of the leading American print publishers of the nineteenth century, Currier and Ives. "All day and every day, week in and week out," wrote a reporter for the *New York Times* during the Civil War,

> there is an ever-changing crowd of men, women and children amid the ever-surging tides of Broadway, before the windows of Williams, Stevens & Williams, gazing, with eager interest, upon the statuettes and groups of the sculptor, John Rogers. These works appeal to a deep popular sentiment. They are not pretentious displays of gods, goddesses, ideal characters or world-compelling heroes. They are illustrations of American domestic, and especially of American military life—not of our great Generals or our bold Admirals, or the men whose praises fill all the newspapers; but of the common soldier of the Union . . . in the ordinary moments and usual occupations of everyday camp life.[42]

The firm did not have an exclusive right to the Rogers groups, however—in fact, far from it. Blessed with a good head for business, Rogers managed to have the groups shown from coast to coast, from Williams and Everett in Boston to, by 1866, a gallery in San Francisco. In that year he published his first catalogue and established his own, highly successful mail-order business for marketing the groups, with prices ranging from $10 to $25.[43]

John Snedecor, who would seem to have been less clever in public relations than many of his contemporaries, got little attention from the press in the years immediately following his opening, on Broadway at White Street, in 1852. Yet there can be no doubt of his prominence. For the most part he sold American art, but like any other dealer he had to make a living, and when the demand for European art surged in the 1870s, he stocked and sold it, along with Americn pictures.

Not much is known about Snedecor apart from the fact that he was a successful dealer. No documents have come to light to give a glimpse into his personality or knowledge of his origins or insight into his private life at any stage of his career. In the city directory for the years before he opened his gallery appears a J. Snedecor whose occupation was goldbeater—that is, someone who beats gold to such airy thinness that it can be used for the gilding of furniture and frames. Given the close relationship of that trade to the art market, this Snedecor was probably the dealer-to-be. Much later Snedecor makes an impressive appearance in F. Hopkinson Smith's novel *The Fortunes of Oliver Horn,* set on the brink of the Civil War but published in 1902, when Snedecor was still alive and still in charge of the gallery. The novel's young southern hero, a painter just starting out in his profession, paints a sketch of a bewitching countess of indeterminate origin and presents it to her, only to find it later in Snedecor's window, where it attracts a crowd. Delivered to the dealer by the countess herself, whose conscience is quite unconcerned about the ethics of disposing of a gift in this fashion, the portrait has already been sold, and for a good price. Thanks to the countess's ingratitude, Horn, as the creator of this beautiful work, is set on the road to fame, and Snedecor is happy to have received a substantial commission on the sale. For what it is worth (not much, to be sure), this may have been the first appearance in American fiction of a dealer, living or dead, under his own name.

If it tells nothing more about the dealer, Smith's novel at least presents a man who has made a commitment to sponsor American art. So do the surviving catalogues of his exhibitions. In the 1860s he had, along with European works, pictures by George Inness, Eastman Johnson, Jasper F.

Cropsey, Lilly Martin Spencer, Jervis McEntee, James D. Smillie, and many other prominent Americans.[44] As Michael Knoedler had done before him, in January 1860 and again in December he engaged Henry Leeds to sell at auction works from his inventory by several of those artists as well as others. Also like Knoedler, and possibly taking his cue from him, Snedecor was an early sponsor of one-artist shows. In 1859 he offered a solo show of works by J. A. Oertel, and this was followed by many other such exhibitions: in 1861, of 208 pictures by George Loring Brown, a mammoth display; in 1862, of 47 pictures by Louis Mignot; in 1866, of 40 works by George Inness, including the now well-known *Peace and Plenty,* a treasure of the Metropolitan Museum, which then somehow failed to find a buyer; in 1869, of works by Elihu Vedder; and there were still more. In 1864 he revealed a laudable public spirit (as well as good business sense) by lending pictures to the New York Sanitary Fair, one of many such fairs organized under the sponsorship of the United States Sanitary Commission for the purpose of raising money to provide clothing, food, and medical supplies for the Union forces through donations of cash and salable items.[45]

One artist whose works were stocked by Snedecor and who has left a brief record of their association was Jervis McEntee, a Hudson River painter whose landscapes more often than not were tinged with brown where one might expect to find green. Muddy though they were, the pictures sold well, but never rapidly enough to relieve McEntee's perpetual anxiety, an anxiety that persisted despite his ability to have a comfortable domestic life, pay the rent on his room at the Tenth Street Studio Building, where he lived with his wife, and also pay his bills at the Century Association. He noted in a diary entry of 1874 that when he went to collect a small sum owed him by Snedecor, all he received was the news that the dealer did not have the money to pay him.[46] Needless to say, he was distressed. But that stony response does not necessarily reflect poorly on the dealer, who very likely was telling the truth when he said that he did not have the cash on hand. One year earlier a depression had hit the country, and in 1874, when McEntee presented his bill, the economy had not yet recovered.

In the best galleries, such as Snedecor's, Knoedler's, and Schaus's, the proprietors made an effort to show their wares to good advantage by decorating their premises with care, although by twentieth-century standards their decorative schemes of dark walls and rich draperies might seem claustrophobic. And, in spite of the good examples provided by the American Art-Union, Knoedler, and the Free Gallery of Philadelphia in doing away with an entrance charge, most galleries continued to demand it.[47] It was news when Snedecor had a show in 1864 and let the public in free.[48] Writing in 1860 from Boston to Frederic, Lord Leighton, the English actress Fanny Kemble touched on both matters:

> Here people exhibit their pictures at a shilling a head, i.e., put them in a room hung around with black calico, light up a flare of gas above them, and take a quarter of a dollar from every sinner who sees them. Pictures of very high pretensions are exhibited, like scenes in a theater, by gaslight, advertised in colored posters all over the streets, like theatrical exhibitions.[49]

At least one artist, Elihu Vedder, resented the fee, because in no way did it benefit him. Writing, as usual, in a light vein about one exhibition of his work, coincidentally also in Boston, he recalled,

> Admittance was charged and went to swell the already high percentage of the dealer. The young lady who received the admission money—a sweet pretty girl—under the effect doubtless of the glamour [of the exhibition's success], whispered to me that she wished to say something to me in private, but could not do so in the Gallery. I became interested and told her that as it was near closing hour I would wait for her down the street. We met, and I did gallantly escort her to a retired Ice-Cream Saloon. Nothing can be more proper than ice-cream. Then she said she could stand it no longer to see how they were taking in the admission money, and I not getting a cent of it, and that she thought it her duty to let me know the state of affairs and begged me not to think hardly of her for the step she had taken to inform me. "Think hardly of you, my dear girl!"—this was not said hardly—"I shall always hold you a true friend."—Also adding other things.[50]

This exhibition took place at Williams and Everett in 1880, twenty years after Fanny Kemble's visit to Boston, and the gallery kept 15 percent of the sales.[51]

Yet one more dealer to join the midcentury set of preeminent merchants of art, and ultimately surpassing Snedecor in eminence, was Samuel Putnam Avery, originally an engraver and publisher of engravings as well as an ardent collector. In this early phase of his career, before the outbreak of the Civil War, Avery was chosen by William T. Walters, a Baltimorean, to aid him in the development of a collection of American art. In 1861 Walters, who sympathized with the South, like many other Marylanders, fled to Paris with his family to avoid arrest. From France he dispatched works of art to Avery for sale in New York. Thus began Avery's career as a dealer. In 1864 Walters provided him with the financial backing to open a gallery.[52]

Avery found suitable space for this new venture at Broadway and Fourth Street.[53] At this turn of his career, he planned to cater principally to collectors of American art. In an announcement dated December 19, 1864, in which, as the formal fashion of the day required, he referred to himself in the third person, the fledgling dealer told the public,

> He has made arrangements to receive occasional consignments of superior Paintings and Drawings directly from distinguished foreign artists, but he especially solicits orders to purchase on commission works of art from American Artists. Many years of association with, and earnest love and study of their works, will enable him, he is assured, to present peculiar advantages to those who desire to procure choice selections. In this connection he has the cordial cooperation and the privilege of referring to the following gentlemen.

There followed a list of forty-eight American artists, including Bierstadt, Church, Durand, Kensett, and Vedder. But however prominently the work of those eminences figured in his original plans, the time was not far off when they and the others on his list would account for only a fraction of the sales of his firm.

At the start of his career as a gallery owner, Avery's respect for American art served to place him on the committee to choose the works intended to represent the United States at the Paris Universal Exposition of 1867. It also secured him the position of commissioner. In that capacity he oversaw the crating of the works and their installation at the fair. From that year on, he traveled annually to Europe in search of art for his gallery, although he, like his peers, did not wholly neglect American art. Quick to acquire wealth and power in the heady postwar economy, he stood out as a leading figure among New York dealers by 1870, when a writer for *Appleton's Journal,* commenting on the uses of money, observed, "Not the least of what it commands is to be seen in the fine art emporiums of New York, in Goupil's gallery, in Schaus's and in S. P. Avery's art rooms."[54] He was to stay a close rival to Knoedler and Schaus until his retirement from the trade in 1887, at the age of sixty-four. The dealings of all three were equally responsible for and responsive to the shifting preferences of American collectors.

4

NEW MONEY, OLD CONFLICTS

The lavish and much publicized world's fair that opened in Paris in April 1867, a scant two years after Lee's surrender at Appomattox, provided an opportunity for the reunited nation to demonstrate its recovery and the unimaginable extent of its inventiveness and resources. The exhibition of works of art from American collections, which Samuel P. Avery was named to supervise, provided the lenders with an opportunity of another, yet not so very different, sort: to show themselves to the world, through the paintings and sculptures that their money could buy, as men of cultivated taste. The consequences were far-reaching and strangely at odds with such expectations.[1]

Along with Avery on the committee organized to select works to be exhibited in Paris were fourteen other men. Among them were the collectors Marshall O. Roberts, Robert M. Olyphant, Robert L. Stuart, and John Taylor Johnston and one other dealer, the well-liked Michael

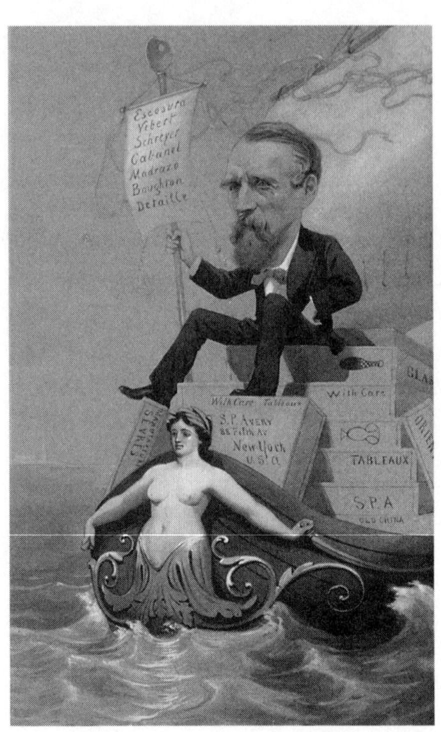

Samuel P. Avery returns from Europe with a boatload of merchandise.

Knoedler. The committee members lent works from their own collections and sought others from such prominent collectors as Jonathan Sturges and A. T. Stewart. Included in their choices were works by Church, Bierstadt, Cropsey, Durand, Inness, Kensett, Homer, and forty-one other painters and sculptors, along with twenty-four etchings by James Abbott McNeill Whistler and some miscellaneous engravings. Pictures by the Hudson River school predominated, but the collection also included portraits and European scenes. It went without saying that to their owners these works represented the very apex of American artistic expression.

But to their grave disappointment, French and English critics, and some American critics as well, offered only a little in the way of praise. For the most part, what the critics liked about this New World painting was the authenticity—the realness—of depiction. One American observer, although finding the exhibition good on the whole, complained nevertheless that too few aspects of the American social and physical climate were on view.[2] Only Church's panoramic *Niagara,* lent by Johnston, was honored with a medal—a silver medal, however, hence second-class. Disappointment was general, and in consequence well-to-do American cognoscenti, who had already been treated to displays of European art in Knoedler's and Schaus's galleries and in the exhibitions staged in New York by Ernest Gambart, began to look with heightened appreciation at what those and other dealers offered in the latest fashions from the Continental art centers and from England. If American art was not worthy of even one gold medal, they reasoned, there must be something not quite right about it. They had, to be sure, bought European art before the Paris fair, with Delaroche, Scheffer, Bonheur, and Horace Vernet their favorites. With their interest in the output of their own country dampened by the weak response to it in Paris, they began to invest more heavily in French artists and members of other European schools. American artists also began to be impressed by the accomplishments of their European counterparts and sailed in increasing numbers to France for instruction in the ateliers of Paris, with as one result a lessening in American painting of the meticulous detail that had been a hallmark of the Hudson River school and, as another, a depiction of scenes not of their native land but of France and other European countries.[3]

Months before the Paris exhibition opened, American artists had already begun to put pressure on Congress to place a stiff tariff on imported art. It was no mystical foreknowledge that the fair would increase the ardor of collectors for European art that moved them to act, but the fact that a great number of works had already been imported and placed on view. Duty had been collected on imported art since the early years of the republic, but not at a sufficient rate to satisfy native artists. What they petitioned for was steep: a duty of $100 per work and an additional 10 percent of the value over $1,000. Public opinion was against them, however, and for the time being Congress decided not to act on the issue. Writing to the *New York Times,* one distressed member of the public, signing himself "An Anti-tariff Art Lover," after noting that among "civilized nations," only in America was art taxed "in any manner," went on to say, "I can hardly believe that this movement has been set on foot by our leading artists, as they must be aware, as well as the art public, that in no country in the world are artists as well paid, as well cared for, and as comfortably situated, as in this."[4] The artists, even the leading ones, would not have agreed, but the *Times* and other organs of opinion concurred. "No class of producers," the newspaper insisted, "is so well patronized by the whole people of this country as artists."[5] The *Tribune* argued that while a high tariff would keep out inferior works and forgeries, it would also prevent the importation of pictures by such artists as Delaroche, Gérôme, Leys, and Vernet.[6]

And so, unhindered for the moment by a heightened tariff, the great flood of foreign art continued to sweep in, and collectors lined their walls all the way to the ceiling with the creations of Bonheur, Delaroche, Meissonier, Frère, Jacque, Diem, and Zamaçois. This was *new* art, of course, not the work of old masters; the dealings of Paff and other sellers of questionable Raphaels and Michelangelos had put a damper on the American enthusiasm for the art of the distant past. Sophisticated collectors had taken heed of the warnings issued intermittently over the decades by journalists that the unwary were always in danger of being duped. In 1860, in an article praising the collection mustered by James Jackson Jarves, America's most advanced connoisseur, the *Times* took the occasion to recall a recent auction in which obvious forgeries had been passed off as masterworks. Such sales, the newspaper noted, were injurious not only to the public but also to the auctioneer, who apparently was unable to bear up under the pressure of collectors to conduct them.[7]

Jarves himself, having amassed a large collection, was quite aware of the dangers faced by collectors of old-master art. In his *Art Studies,* published in 1861, he cautioned: "As the taste for collecting objects of art is rapidly developing in America, it may not be without profit to print some of the pitfalls which attend the amateur in their pursuit, especially in Italy, that exhaustless quarry of 'originals' and 'old masters.'" Forgeries, he pointed out, were ever urged upon the unwary collector: "Great is the commotion among dealers, and their 'sensali,' or jackals." As a result of incautious buying in the past, Jarves noted, "[o]ld masters are almost a byword of doubt or contempt in America, owing to the influx of cheap copies and pseudo-originals, of no artistic value whatever."[8]

Having read the pulse of the art-buying public, Avery began to deal energetically in modern Continental art. His first salesroom, at the corner of Broadway and Fourth Street, would no longer serve. In 1868 he took rooms at 86-88 Fifth Avenue, where the gallery remained until 1902, long after Avery himself had retired, when it was moved farther north to 360 Fifth. During his first year in the new premises he held two auctions; the first was made up of works he had purchased in Europe, the second of watercolors. In the following year he sold at auction his entire inventory, which included both European and American works.[9] From 1871 until 1882, when he handed control of the gallery over to his son, Sam Jr., Avery made an extended trip abroad every year in search of pictures to sell. He bought contemporary art exclusively. Why take the risk of putting his or his clients' money into Raphaels and Correggios that might prove to be the latest products of some criminally mischievous dauber's atelier? "They come," he wrote from France to John Taylor Johnston in 1872, his irritation blinding him to the niceties of spelling and punctuation, "They come, do these self-sacrificing foreigners of all languages before I am out of a morning, all got up finely with red ribbons in their button holes, sometimes with a Raphael or so under their arm. Telling them that I don't talk french that I don't buy old masters ... they keep right on in french, spanish, or (and) Italian."[10]

Early in his quests abroad, before he became familiar with the European art community, Avery was aided by George Lucas, an American art agent from Baltimore who had been living in Paris since 1857. As a young man, Lucas worked as a civil engineer in New Haven and other cities near New York, having been trained in that profession at West Point. The cultural advantages of New York were a constant lure to him, and in the early 1850s he began buying minor, inexpensive works of art for himself and, at their request, for his friends and his brother. In this random fashion he set out on what was to be his true career, the trade for which he was suited by temperament. As with Whistler, who became his friend, his first crossing of the Atlantic was also his last. So far as is known, he traveled abroad in 1857 (at age thirty) purely for the pleasure of travel. But on reaching Paris and falling in love with both the city and a woman who resided there, he claimed ever after to have suffered such horrors of *mal de mer* on the voyage that he could never risk another transatlantic crossing. Commissions from Baltimore collectors began to reach him in 1858, and when in the following year he received his first commission from William T. Walters, he was firmly set in a vocation far more attractive to him than engineering.[11]

The diaries that Avery faithfully kept during his sojourns in Europe (and which mention his frequent meetings with Lucas) reveal a comfortable mixture of pleasure and business. From time to time his American clients turned up in Paris while he was there, and he dined with them or saw them in other social circumstances, when, inevitably, their collections and the state of the art market came under discussion. His colleagues Schaus and Knoedler also traveled to Europe on the prowl for salable items, and on occasion his path crossed theirs. In the golden decades of the post-Civil War expansion, and in spite of the financial panic of 1873, there was room in the marketplace for all three of these busy dealers, as well as for many others less frequently in the news. Not until 1883, when Congress at last passed a stiff tariff bill—one that increased the price of imported art by 30 percent—was there even a brief weakening of the art-buying mania in this opulent world.

Among Avery's purchases abroad were works by such salon painters as Mario Fortuny, William-Adolphe Bouguereau, Alexandre Cabanel, Zamaçois, and Hugues Merle, among others. An insight into the prevailing taste of the time is provided by a description in the *Art Journal* for 1875 of Merle's *The Knight's Betrothed* at Avery's gallery:

> The lady has been seated in a richly carved old Gothic chair, and has risen to her feet to look at a procession of knights, led by trumpeters, and men-at-arms carrying banners which is passing the window. . . . The fair lady evidently recognizes her lover's colours in the procession, and the warm blood, as it courses through her veins, suffuses her girlish yet thoughtful face with a crimson tinge and lends to it an additional charm.[12]

Here was a picture that told a story! The anonymous reviewer obviously enjoyed it.

As his diary notifies us, Avery's clients included such prominent businessmen as August Belmont, John Taylor Johnston, A. T. Stewart, and William H. Vanderbilt as well as other dealers, among whom were John Snedecor and Boston's Williams and Everett. Avery saw his rich collectors socially in New York as well as abroad and shared in their very full life. An outgoing, engaging man, he was invited to join New York's leading clubs devoted to the arts—the Century Association, The Players, the Grolier Club, and the Lotos Club—as well as other social clubs, including the Union League, whose roster of members included such prominent artists as John Kensett, Worthington Whittredge, and the sculptor John Quincy Adams Ward.

Avery was generous, not only with money but with time. When a group of Union League men, inspired by the lawyer John Jay, determined to establish a museum of art in New York, Avery, a member of the club's art committee, was one of the men who developed the idea of what such a museum might be.[13] In consequence of their collective effort, the Metropolitan Museum of Art was incorporated in 1870, and from 1872 until his death, in 1904, Avery served it as a trustee. That such a position of power in a public institution might create a conflict of interest for a dealer does not seem to have entered the minds of Avery's fellow trustees or the Metropolitan's officers, as it undoubtedly would have a hundred years later. At any rate, there could have been no reason for concern, for Avery served honorably and effectively. He not only offered good counsel but was instrumental in securing major gifts for the Metropolitan.

However, there was one proffered gift that the Metropolitan declined late in the dealer's life: his own vast holding of prints, some fifteen thousand of them. At that time prints were excluded from the Metropolitan's collections.[14] The trustees were too shortsighted to see that Avery's prints could form the basis of a major department of the museum, such as it was later to develop. Avery next approached the New York Public Library, where the prints were gratefully accepted.

Like Avery, William Schaus found his interest in American art waning after he learned the lesson offered by the Paris fair, and not until late in his career did he take it up again. Of what one might call the "big three" of American antebellum dealers, only Knoedler, while never failing to provide his mogul clients with the best of the new art of Europe, continued to show the native product regularly. He demonstrated his gratitude toward the American public not only in this way but by becoming an American citizen, in 1866.[15]

Works by such American painters as J. G. Brown, John W. Casilear, Jasper Cropsey, Daniel Huntington, and Worthington Whittredge graced the walls of his gallery, but expensive imports by Gustave Brion, Gérôme, Jules Breton, Eugène Isabey, Jacque, and Meyer von Bremen, among many others, streamed into the premises—and soon went out to the homes of the Vanderbilts, H. O. Havemeyer, Henry M. Flagler, Leland Stanford, and Jay Gould (who bought twenty-two pictures from Knoedler in two days).[16]

The three most prominent dealers, along with Charles Kraushaar, Daniel Cottier, and still others in New York and other cities, sought art from almost every outpost abroad where it could be found. Kraushaar, after years on Schaus's staff, set up on his own in 1885. His inventory, a mixture of European and American art, resembled Schaus's. After his death, in 1917, the gallery was managed by his brother, John, who continued the same sort of program. Cottier, a Scotsman by birth, had had a gallery in London for some six years before opening his New York branch in 1873. He designed and created furniture and stained glass, and sold these items as well as fine art. In his gallery, which he maintained until his death, in 1891, visitors might see not only American art but also the work of the seventeenth-century Dutch masters, Corot, Millet, Delacroix, Adolphe Monticelli, Matthijs Maris, and many other Europeans.[17] In Boston, Doll and Richards showed in 1872 what Henry James described as "a small but remarkable" group of French paintings from local collections. It included works by Delacroix, Decamps, Troyon, Théodore Rousseau, Daubigny, Duprez, and Diaz. Said James, "They form a group interesting in more ways than one—as to the reciprocal light they shed upon each other as members of a school, and as to their opportune and almost pathetic testimony just now to the admirable aesthetic gifts of the French mind."[18] In the same year Williams and Everett exhibited a painting of a cockfight by Gérôme that James described as "a capital example of the master," although the subject and the presence of a nude young man and young woman in the same picture disturbed him.[19]

As for the "big three" in New York, in one month of 1878 Avery had a "school-room interior by Piltz, of Weimar," Knoedler had a "moonlit snow-scene in Poland, by the Polish artist Chelmusky," and Schaus had a " 'Herzogovinian Captive,' by Cermak, the Herzogovinian painter."[20] Yet the same magazine that reported glowingly on these pictures evidenced distress when later in the year at a new Paris exhibition the American painters revealed themselves to be slavishly imitative of the Europeans:

> The fair faces of American girlhood (a race unparalleled for beauty on either side of the seas), the scenes of American daily life, events of our war, illustrations of our history or our literature—such, judging from the Art departments of the other nations, were the subjects that our painters should have chosen to show what American art could reproduce: instead of which we find Italian peasants, French reapers, Breton interiors, a Bavarian sheep-shearing on one side; a scene from the war in La Vendée on another; even a drunken Parisian quean [*sic*], leering vulgarly at her jeering parrot, this last the coarsest picture that is to be found within the limits of all the art galleries of the Exhibition.[21]

Having studied abroad, and understanding the current taste of American collectors, these artists were doing their best to compete in a market dominated by European scenes.

In 1869 Michael Knoedler moved his gallery, still known as Goupil & Company, to 170 Fifth Avenue, at the corner of Twenty-second Street, and in the following year he took his brother John into the firm. He renovated the gallery's rooms in 1876. In 1877 he gave his eldest son, Roland, a partnership and renamed the firm M. Knoedler & Company.[22] Michael had long been ill with respiratory troubles and early in the decade had taken up residence in France. There, in 1878, his death occurred, a death much lamented by the art world. Roland in his early years with the firm showed works by William Merritt Chase and Winslow Homer. Other contemporary Americans were to follow as

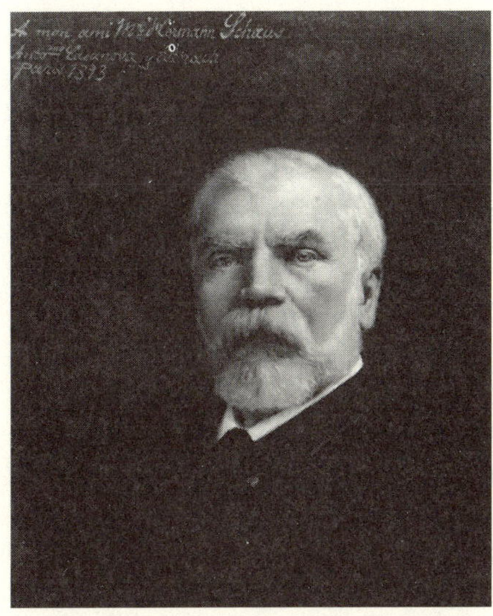

William Schaus

Roland continued his father's policy of nonspecialization. That policy meant that the gallery must make room, as it always had, for contemporary Europeans as well. In 1880, for example, Roland sold Gérôme's typically exotic *Almeh Performing His Sword Dance* to Charles Crocker, one of California's great railroad and mining magnates.[23]

Under Roland's stewardship, M. Knoedler & Company soon entered its greatest period. Like his father, he retained the tie to Goupil's in his ads and gave up this reference only when sued, in 1889, by Boussod and Valadon, the Paris firm that was the true successor to Goupil's.

William Schaus pursued a path different from Roland Knoedler's. His youthful enthusiasm for Mount, Lilly Martin Spencer, and other Americans notwithstanding, in the 1870s he embraced wholeheartedly the new cult of European salon pictures and their three-dimensional counterparts, sleek marble sculptures on edifying themes and classical lines. He also dealt extensively in those older favorites, the Barbizon artists. And, looking farther back into the history of art, Schaus bought and sold old-master paintings on occasion, continuing a practice that, it will be recalled, he had instituted as early as 1858 with his purchase and resale of a Rubens. A Rembrandt and a Van Dyck are known to have been for sale in his gallery in later years. His prestige and reputation for probity grew rapidly as time passed. So respected was he by 1886 that the *New York Times* complained roundly in his behalf over the severe duty imposed on the Rembrandt by U.S. Customs.[24]

Like Avery and Knoedler, Schaus was an international figure, a frequent voyager to Europe in search of irresistible temptations for his clients. It would seem that in a purely personal (as opposed to commercial) sense, Schaus's greatest attachment abroad was to Germany, not France, in view of the fact that two of Schaus's daughters married officers in the Prussian army. Nevertheless, he was made a member of the Legion of Honor. Family legend had it that he received his rosette for locating and returning to the Louvre a piece of a painting cut out by a thief.[25] He was also honored by the king of Spain for recovering a stolen Murillo, which he identified by examining the brush strokes.[26]

After some forty years in the trade, in 1886 Schaus sold the business to his nephew Hermann Schaus and Augustus W. Conover, his brother-in-law. In the following year he grandly saluted the Metropolitan Museum with a letter to Louis Palma di Cesnola, its director: "It is my wish that my children should forward something to the Metropolitan Museum of Art in New York." He proposed a gift of five works, a "statue in marble" by Raffaele Monti and paintings by Blaise Degoffe, Charles Hermann-Léon, Emile Renouf, and Léon-Germain Pelouse.[27]

So passé have these artists become that a search through the pages of such a standard reference work as Robert Rosenblum and H.W. Janson's compendious *19th-Century Art* turns up a reference to only one of the five: Monti.[28] Nevertheless, the five works were not the sweepings of the gallery's storerooms or items from Schaus's personal chamber of horrors, if in fact he had one. The Metropolitan was pleased to get them. Cesnola, in his note of thanks, replied, "You are always good, kind, and generous toward our dear Museum, and if our rich fellow citizens would follow your example, this institution would soon become the richest in the world." After a diplomatic interval of two and a half months, Schaus asked for a quid pro quo. He requested that his two elder daughters be designated patrons of the museum and that his son and youngest daughter be made members.[29] A grateful museum granted his wish.

Schaus could well afford such seignorial gestures, for his years in business had secured him a fortune. At his death, in 1892, he left an estate of over $1.2 million in railroad bonds.[30] The estate also included some valuable works of art, many of which went to Roland Knoedler at auction in 1896.[31] The gallery remained open for business until Hermann's death in 1910.

Remarks on the interrelations of the major dealers by DeCourcy E. McIntosh in an account of Pittsburgh collectors and collecting at the turn of the century gives insight into the workings of the market. A sale conducted by the Knoedler gallery in 1893 included Delacroix's *Arab*

Horseman Giving a Signal, which the firm bought in 1889 from the Paris gallery of E. LeRoy. At the sale it went to a Detroit dealer, William O'Leary, for $3,500. O'Leary apparently could find no buyer for it and sold it back to Knoedler's for the same $3,500. Cottier then paid Knoedler's $4,500 for it and sold it to Anthony McBurney Byers of Pittsburgh. Byers also owned Jules Breton's *Sunrise at Dournenez,* which had a similarly circuitous provenance. Knoedler's had bought the painting from Petit *aîné* in Paris and then sold it to the Schaus gallery for $8,200. But, as with the Delacroix, it came back to the Knoedler firm, which then sold it to Byers.[32] In the eighteen years of his management, Hermann Schaus proved a worthy successor to his uncle. Like William, he was a man of daring when the occasion demanded it, as when at an auction in 1908 he paid the highest price then recorded in America for a painting: $65,000 for a work by Troyon, beating out Senator William A. Clark of Montana. The painting, a typical Troyon, showed two cows headed for a pasture. It had belonged to William Schaus himself and in 1896 was sold from his estate for $24,500.[33] It was risky business for Hermann Schaus to reclaim his uncle's picture for the gallery at such a price. Long before the auction took place, fashions in art, unstable as always, had begun to shift away from the Barbizon painters.

Summing up Hermann Schaus's career in a brief obituary, William Macbeth, then the leading specialist in American art, took occasion to praise him, but not without offering a few chiding words as well:

> Mr. Schaus had so little sympathy with new movements in art that it is doubtful whether he could, in a longer career, have adapted himself to changed conditions. What he aimed to do in the world of art he did well, but younger men have joined a procession in which he could never have taken a part.[34]

It was an accurate assessment, and it might have applied to Hermann's uncle William as well. With his early enthusiasm for American art, William Schaus had been in a procession of younger men at the outset of his career, but at its close he too had lost sight of the art developing all around him.

5

COMPETING FOR DOLLARS

As it had been from the beginning, New York in the 1880s was the center of the American art world. The wealth and prestige of the Knoedler, Schaus, and Avery galleries—to say nothing of the wealth of their clients—could not be matched by galleries in other American cities. Yet elsewhere across the land ever more galleries began to spring up, their owners undaunted by the supreme eminence of the New York dealers and the dwindling of enthusiasm for art that came about in 1883 when Congress gave in to the American artists' plea for a high tariff on imported art. In fact, the new tariff did not distract collectors for long; like the twentieth century's ever rising taxes on income and sales, it was a matter to which art addicts eventually adjusted.

Among the new galleries in cities distant from New York, the M. O'Brien and Roullier galleries of Chicago provided art for midwestern collections, and on the Pacific coast the Vickery Gallery of San Francisco

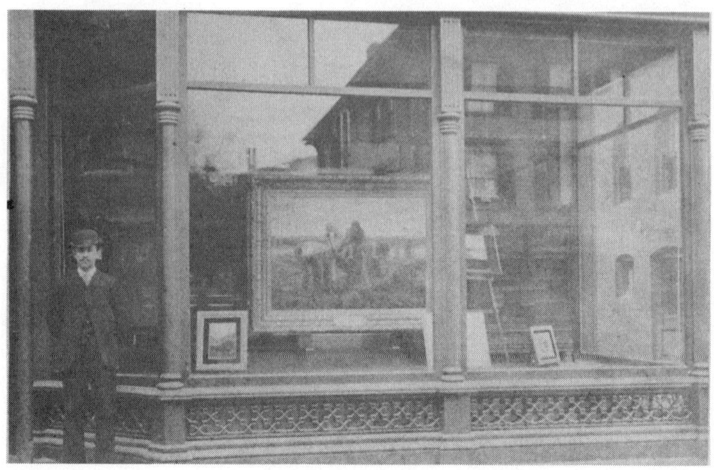

The early location of the Vose Galleries, in Providence, Rhode Island

did sustaining business in California art as well as European art and the work of American artists from the eastern seaboard. Boston, then the trade's second city, having been well served in art since 1810 by Williams and Everett and their predecessor, John Doggett, and since the 1840s by Doll and Richards and their predecessors, Sowle and Shaw, was supplied in the 1880s with works from a new source when Seth Vose of Providence brought paintings up from his gallery in that city.[1]

The arrival in the national art community of the Vose family, who were destined to maintain one of the most successful galleries specializing in American art, occurred in 1850, when Joseph Vose of Rhode Island bought the Westminster Gallery in Providence.[2] Seth Vose, his son, joined the gallery within a year of its opening. Industrious and apparently tireless, Seth enlarged its business and began a trade in the Barbizon artists. In 1852 he held the first Corot show in the United States; unhappily, not a single work sold.[3] In the 1880s he commenced a schedule of daily travel southwest from his home in Attleboro, Massachusetts, by horse to Pawtucket, Rhode Island, from there by train to Providence, where he opened up his gallery for the day and then went northeast again by train to Boston, where he showed his stock in rooms in that city's Studio Building.[4]

In 1897 his son, Robert C. Vose, a recent college graduate, opened a small branch of the Westminster Gallery in Fall River, Massachusetts, where he sold the work of such prominent Americans as, among others, A. T. Bricher and George Inness. In the same year he established a gallery in Boston as well.[5] Although the Voses still sold French and also British paintings through the 1920s and into the 1930s, with the opening of the

Boston gallery the family made a strong commitment to American art and consequently an identification with it in the minds of collectors.

Robert C. Vose, as energetic as his father, toured the nation with a supply of art to sell. His first cross-country foray took place in 1905, when he traveled to Portland, Oregon, at the time of that city's Lewis and Clark Exposition. From then on, he took canvases from the Vose Galleries from city to city every winter. So successful a salesman was he that in 1914 dealers in St. Louis invoked a law against itinerant vendors to have him evicted from his hotel suite, which he had fitted out to simulate a gallery, as was his custom on the road. But the story had a happy ending: with loyal and locally prominent clients hastening to the rescue, he was allowed to stay.[6]

The firm was well regarded even before achieving national prominence with its stock of American art, and so when it found itself on the brink of bankruptcy in 1861 it was saved by a consortium of colleagues in the trade led by Roland Knoedler. As Robert C. Vose Jr. was to acknowledge in print in 1981, similar kindnesses from bankers and others secured the continuity of the firm during the most challenging period of its history, the Great Depression of the 1930s.[7] In good times, the Voses sold—and continue to sell—works to virtually every major American museum for whose collections their wares might be appropriate. Among their notable private clients in the past were Ima Hogg, sometimes known as the "first lady of Texas," for her estate Bayou Bend, in Houston, and Henry Francis du Pont for Winterthur, in Delaware, which houses a great collection of antiques along with pictures to set them off.[8]

As prominent in the marketing of American art as the Vose firm was to become, it was not the first to specialize in the field. That distinction was held by William Macbeth, who established his gallery in New York in 1892.[9] The Scotch-Irish Macbeth was born in Madden, in the north of Ireland, in 1851. After a brief stint in Dublin as a clerk in the clearinghouse of the banks of Ireland, he sailed for New York in 1873, where his brother James was established as a businessman and inventor. Within a month of his arrival in the city he found a job at $5 a week with the gallery of Frederick Keppel, a dealer in fine prints. This was his introduction to the art trade. "Think I will like it," he noted in his diary.[10] His prediction was correct. So well did he like it that he stayed with Keppel for nearly twenty years, until he felt it was time, at last, to strike out on his own.

Young Macbeth had good reason to be happy in his position with Keppel, a man who thoroughly enjoyed his trade, as the Macbeth diary strongly suggests, and was therefore easy to work with. More than that, he possessed an engaging personality. The sketch of his life offered in the *Dictionary of American Biography* lists among his attributes "a genius for friendship." Macbeth, also a man of great good nature, was well matched with him.

Keppel, born in 1845, was senior to Macbeth by only six years. He too was a native of Ireland. He arrived in Manhattan in 1864, after migrations to England, Canada, and upstate New York. As a youth in Canada, he worked on a farm and would have remained contentedly at it if he had not been severely injured when a cart piled with hay and pitchforks overturned and the prongs of a fork pierced his lungs. In New York City he first established himself as a book dealer but turned to prints when an elderly Londoner, a print dealer eager to return home, came to him with a portfolio of prints for sale. Keppel reluctantly offered $100 for the portfolio and was dismayed to hear the old man promptly accept. With help from print collectors in Philadelphia and a bookseller of the same city, Keppel disposed of six of his new acquisitions for the price he had paid for the entire lot and immediately set about to train himself to become an authority in the field of fine prints. In this he was altogether successful. He went to Europe to collect prints and on his return in 1868, at age twenty-three, he opened his first shop.

Keppel's connoisseurship of prints became so advanced, as he boasted in his memoirs, that he could spot an excellent counterfeit of Rembrandt's *Ecce Homo* for what it was by a minuscule difference from the original in the drawing of the hand of one of the many figures in the picture.[11] By the time Macbeth joined his firm, he was, although not yet out of his twenties, a leader in the city's print trade, with a stock that included old-master prints from the age of Dürer to works by such moderns as Whistler, Robert Swain Gifford, and Thomas Moran. As his business expanded, he set up subsidiary operations in Chicago and Paris. The announcements and catalogues of his exhibitions were nicely designed, as befitted a firm specializing in graphic art; many were provided with introductions by Keppel himself. For a man as industrious and affable as William Macbeth, Keppel's busy, highly regarded shop provided the best possible berth.

From almost the start of his employment, Macbeth became a valued member of the firm. As the diary makes clear, Keppel and his wife looked after him with the care they might have lavished on a younger brother. Macbeth was grateful for the relationship. A model young man, in his diary he never failed to refer to his employer respectfully as Mr. Keppel.

In January 1874, a mere two months after he was hired, Macbeth was given the responsibility of managing the gallery entirely by himself while Keppel was in Europe on business. Along with this test of his ability he was given a raise of $2 a week and a 10 percent commission on the gallery's profits during Keppel's absence. Keppel was "satisfied" with his management, Macbeth noted on his employer's return. This must have been an understatement, since additional increases in his salary followed in short order, as did invitations to the country house the Keppels then maintained on Staten Island. The Keppels moved about from place to place within commuting distance of Manhattan, and wherever they went Macbeth remained their frequent visitor. Usually he spent Monday nights with them.

Macbeth's other diversions from his duties at the gallery included faithful attendance at Episcopal services in Brooklyn, where he lived; teaching a Sunday school class at the church; and, a portent of things to come, visiting exhibitions held by such organizations as the National Academy of Design and the Society of American Artists.[12] Brooklyn remained his principal place of residence throughout his life.

In 1876 he fell in love with Jessie Walker of that city (not yet a borough of New York) and repeatedly over the next six years reported to his diary his disappointments over broken dates and the young woman's seeming reluctance to be married. At last, however, on Christmas Day 1882, she consented, and four months later the wedding took place. Had Jessie been allowed her way, however, it would have been delayed by yet another twelve months; Macbeth had a brother who was enrolled in an Episcopal seminary, and it was Jessie's exasperating notion that they should postpone the wedding until he was ordained and could perform the ceremony.

Although his position at Frederick Keppel and Company was financially rewarding, Macbeth eventually acquired enough knowledge of art and the art world—and enough cash—to believe that he could strike out on his own without danger of failing. Such funds as he had amassed were bolstered, moreover, by loans from Henry T. Chapman, an ardent collector, and other collectors who helped him financially in the early years.[13] He also had an abundance of goodwill from Keppel. On March 31, 1892, he broke away to found his own business, on Fifth Avenue, the fashionable venue for art. Although there is no evidence that Keppel was one of his backers, the parting was altogether amicable; in no way did it create an estrangement between the two men. Macbeth had no intention of competing with Keppel. American art, not international prints, was to be his field. The two men remained close until Keppel's death, in 1912. Keppel's letters to him over the years, invariably warm, bore the complimentary close "Ever and always." It was typical of him and emblematic of their friendship that when in 1906 a rumor reached Keppel's ears that the steel magnate Charles M. Schwab intended to furnish his new mansion on Riverside Drive with American art exclusively, he immediately passed it on to Macbeth so that he could beat out his rivals in the field.[14]

Macbeth not only had visited exhibitions of American art during his Keppel years, but after becoming a partner had organized exhibitions of American watercolors in the gallery.[15] His decision to go into business for himself would seem to have been arrived at gradually as he became increasingly aware of the need for a distinctly American gallery. While with Keppel he had been a good salesman of prints, as his elevation to partner demonstrated, but his diary contains very little comment on Keppel's stock. Prints, provided they were by American artists, were not excluded from Macbeth's gallery when it opened, but the emphasis nevertheless was distinctly on painting. Macbeth was proud that his was the first gallery specializing in American art, and he frequently referred to it as such in *Art Notes,* an occasional publication that he inaugurated in October 1896 "in the interest of the Macbeth Gallery."

To explain his intentions to the public, Macbeth offered the following printed announcement of his opening:

> The work of American artists has never received the full share of appreciation that it deserves, and the time has come when an effort should be made to gain for it the favor of those who have hitherto purchased foreign pictures exclusively. As I shall exhibit only that which is thoroughly good and interesting, I hope to make this establishment known as the place where may be procured the very best our artists can produce.

He very soon attracted the attention and the eye of enthusiasts of American art. Thomas B. Clarke, a leading collector of the native product whose income derived from the manufacture of linen collars, recognized the potential of the gallery in its first year. He formed an alliance with Macbeth for the sale of works from his collection or that he had on consignment from the artists. From October 1892 to May 1894 he brought Macbeth an impressive array of paintings by Charles H. Davis, Winslow Homer, George Inness, Louis Moeller, and Dwight W. Tryon, valuable additions to the fledgling dealer's inventory.[16]

But despite his determination to deal in American art alone, for the first six years Macbeth offered annual exhibitions of European paintings, mainly Dutch, and employed agents, the artists Arthur B. Davies and Henry Ward Ranger, to scout the European market for him.[17] The proceeds from the sale of European works, particularly those of the Dutch artist Anton Mauve, helped to keep the gallery afloat in the early years, when the depressed national economy frightened many clients away from art lacking the glamorous cachet of a European origin. Once the business climate improved, as it did at the turn of the century, Macbeth dropped his Europeans and never brought them back.

The first premises of the Macbeth Gallery were at 237 Fifth Avenue, near Twenty-seventh Street. For a time it was the northernmost gallery in the city, but not so far out of the way as to discourage collectors.[18] Protected by ample capital, Macbeth built an inventory that appealed to those few who in the 1890s not only professed to an enthusiasm for American art but were willing and able to put up good money for it. Among the many artists he showed with success in the early years were Arthur B. Davies, Charles H. Davis, Homer Dodge Martin, Alexander H. Wyant, and, when he could get their pictures, George Inness, Winslow Homer, and the older painters of the Hudson River school. Eventually he added works by colonial portraitists and miniaturists to his stock. In the early years of the twentieth century American Impressionist painting became one of the gallery's staples and remained so until the gallery closed in 1954, as did the work of artists influenced by the Barbizon school.

One of the qualities that established Macbeth's credibility with collectors and helped to make him a leader in the trade was his willingness to speak frankly about speculation in art. This troublesome issue—art as a commodity rather than as an enhancement of the spirit—would seem to have pressed as heavily on the minds of collectors and dealers in his time as it would in the boom market of the late twentieth century. In his issue of *Art Notes* for April 1897 he wrote:

> I must confess I have never had much sympathy for the collector who buys pictures in the hope of seeing their value increase in the course of time; and yet why should a man not buy pictures as an investment?
>
> Many a businessman has been saved from financial disaster by the collection of pictures wisely purchased in prosperous days. The

cautious buyer who really appreciates the pictures he invests his spare money in, must not be classed with the picture speculator, who can never be a lovable person.

In 1902, on the tenth anniversary of the opening of his gallery, he took this theme up once more, but this time in phrases suggesting a degree of self-interest:

> The greatest change in the attitude of the public towards American pictures has occurred in the past four or five years. . . . [and] it has been shown in the auction room that well selected American pictures have been very profitable investments, while on the other hand the average foreign picture, as a dividend earner, has proved to be a snare and a delusion. . . . So it seems reasonably certain that the buyers who think more of the money value of a picture than of its artistic quality will in future be found competing with the few who have always recognized the good in native art.[19]

From time to time Macbeth wrote enthusiastically of works to be seen in other galleries, particularly Keppel's, but he also liked to show that he was aware—as what dealer is not?—of disingenuous doings in the trade, as in this brief imaginary exchange:

> *Scene*. New York Auction Room.
> *Art Patron*. How much do you think I ought to pay for this fine Corot?
> *Picture Dealer*. What! You think of buying a picture like that? Don't you know it is false? Corot never saw it.
> *Art Patron*. That was not your opinion when you urged me to buy it from you eight years ago.
> Exit picture dealer from presence of lost customer.[20]

But on at least one occasion Macbeth, the most honest and morally upright of men, found his own morality questioned. Like all other gallery owners as well as publishers, theatrical producers, actors, and dancers, Macbeth was constantly in danger of offending Anthony Comstock, the imperious secretary and militant chief operative of the Society for the Suppression of Vice, an organization founded in 1873. Incessantly patrolling in what he assumed to be the public interest, in 1887 Comstock had staged a raid on the Knoedler Gallery, whose walls were then hung with nudes somewhat too nude for his approval. In February 1905 it was Macbeth's turn. When he placed in his window a painting by Bryson Burroughs called *The Explorers*, which showed five very young unclad children, two boys and three girls, wading in a brook on a summer's day, he unknowingly asked for trouble. An idyllic depiction of early childhood, the painting nevertheless put Comstock in a rage. Accompanied by one of his agents, he entered the gallery and, in the absence of Macbeth himself, ordered an office boy to take the picture out of the window. It would be all right, he said, to hang it indoors, but he would not allow it in a window, where presumably every innocent passerby who saw it would suffer an immediate debasement of his morals. Bewildered but also amused, Macbeth later spoke to a reporter about Comstock's demand: "I can corrupt the public as much as I like in one part of the gallery, but must not do so in another. . . . I have another picture here of some boys at a swimming pool, and that one there showing a baby's foot. Who knows? Maybe they will have to be turned toward the wall."[21] Nevertheless, he took the picture out of the window.

Quaintly pretty as well as innocent, *The Explorers* was typical of the gallery's inventory in its Impressionist style. Although endowed with enough of the pioneer spirit to specialize in American art, Macbeth could never manage a wholehearted embrace of the avant-garde. He took his boldest step as a dealer in 1908, when he offered a show of sixty-three works by Arthur B. Davies, William Glackens, Robert Henri, George Luks, Ernest Lawson, Maurice Prendergast, Everett Shinn, and John Sloan, eight artists who soon came to be known as "*the* Eight" when a reporter for the *Evening Sun* gave them that collective title.[22]

Before this exhibition, Macbeth had already shown works by Henri, Luks, Prendergast, and Davies, and had puffed Davies extravagantly in the first number of *Art Notes:* "Mr. Arthur B. Davies has spent a very busy summer as usual, taking little rest except in the variety of his work. The favored few who have been allowed to see his pictures grow from month to month speak with great enthusiasm of his new work." Yet Macbeth was not so enthusiastic about the artists as to let them have the run of the gallery for their group show without some hedging. He asked, reasonably enough, for 25 percent of the take, but also for a $400 guarantee.[23]

Despite the fame (tinged with notoriety) that the exhibition gave these eight artists as a group, they were not an ironbound society when Macbeth agreed to show them. The notion of staging a group show came up quite casually on March 13, 1907, when Henri and Luks went to dinner at the apartment of Sloan and his wife. "Some talk after dinner of an exhibition of certain men's work" is how Sloan recorded it in his diary.[24] Prendergast was a late addition, having been invited by Davies to show along with the others after Macbeth's commitment was in hand. Moreover, the artists were a mixed lot with respect to what they liked to paint and how they painted it; in their choice of subjects and their technique at least four of the Eight, Davies, Lawson, Prendergast, and Shinn, were closely akin to such American Impressionists among their older contemporaries as Frank W. Benson, Childe Hassam, and John Twachtman, men who late in 1897 along with seven other artists had formed a group that came to be known as the Ten American Painters.[25] The others among the Eight were less romantic in their subjects; their depictions of city life eventually caused the entire Eight and other American realists to be known as the "Ashcan school." The term was invented by Art Young, a cartoonist for the *Masses,* the satirical (eventually socialist) magazine to which Davies, Sloan, and Luks were contributors. The designation was not wholly accurate, but it stuck.

As measured by the crowds of visitors, the extent of press coverage, and the sale of seven pictures for a total of just under $4,000, a quite decent figure for the time, the show was a distinct success—so much so that in the fall it went on tour to the museums of Chicago, Toledo, Detroit, Cincinnati, Bridgeport, Pittsburgh, and Newark.[26] Macbeth believed that had the market not been weakened by another panic, this one arising in 1907 but still holding on in 1908, more pictures would have sold.[27] Yet when Henri spoke to him late in 1908 about a follow-up exhibition, Macbeth told him that the gallery was booked through May 1909, adding that he would be sorry to see the group showing anywhere else.[28] In 1962 Robert McIntyre, Macbeth's nephew and a member of his staff, recalled that Macbeth received "threatening letters, phone calls, and visits" while the show was on.[29] As a group, the Eight are not known to have approached him again, and he did not again approach the Eight, although he still occasionally had paintings on hand by five of them, the exceptions being Glackens, Shinn, and Sloan.

By way of parenthesis, mention should be made of the *Exhibition of Independent Artists,* a show that stemmed from the show at Macbeth's, at least insofar as several of the Eight were involved in it, although Macbeth himself was not. This very large display of American art was held in April 1910 on three floors of a building at 29–31 West Thirty-fifth Street. Such an undertaking had been first suggested by John Sloan in December 1909. It was taken up in March 1909 by Henri, Sloan, Davies, and Walt Kuhn, each of whom advanced $200 toward the project. Contributions

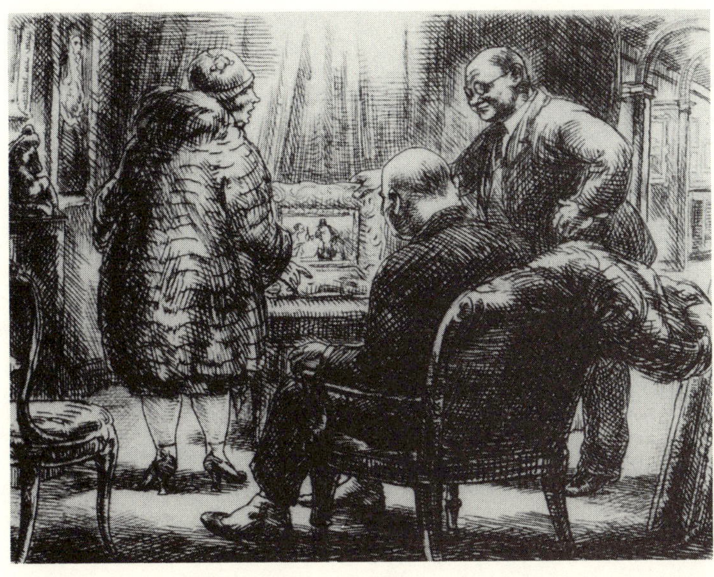

John Sloan, Kraus-haar's. *John Kraushaar shows a painting to two doubtful prospects.*

to make up the rental came from other artists. In degree of fame, the exhibitors ranged from the Eight and their friends down to artists quite unknown. Any artist who could get up the entry fee was free to submit work. Unfortunately, the show, while well attended, produced next to nothing in the way of sales. Of the 260 paintings, 20 sculptures, 219 drawings and prints on view, only five works were sold, for a total of $75.[30] Three years later Kuhn and Davies devoted their organizational skills to a more momentous event: the *International Exhibition of Modern Art,* which was to slip into history as "the Armory Show."

When in 1938 the Macbeth Gallery at last showed all the Eight at once for a second time, in a thirtieth-anniversary celebration of the first exhibition, it was directed by Robert Macbeth, the founder's son, in association with Robert McIntyre. Of the Eight, only Glackens, Shinn, and Sloan were left to enjoy it. By that date every member of the group was recognized as a major American artist. They had all passed into such respectability that it was possible to fit them into the schedule of the gallery without disturbing its image as a showroom for what the two Roberts took to be the best in American representational art. The Eight were no longer on the cutting edge, and the gallery had long since lodged itself in a time warp where only the stylistically tried and true was welcome on its walls. Between their two group exhibitions, most of the Eight had shown at the Kraushaar Galleries. John Kraushaar, the brother of Charles Kraushaar and Charles's successor as the director of the

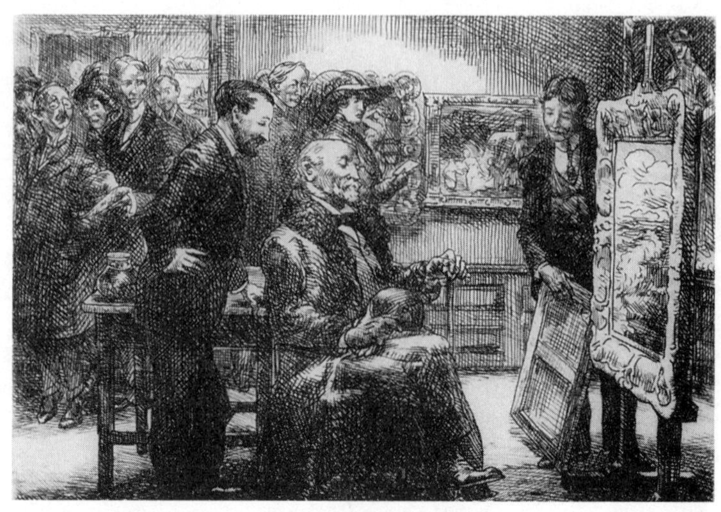

John Sloan, Picture Buyer. *William Macbeth, at left, hoping to make a sale. His nephew, Robert McIntyre, stands at the easel.*

gallery, liked the men and they liked him. Luks played baseball with him.[31] Sloan, whose paintings were never easy to sell, but whose career Kraushaar did his best to foster, called him "the most honest art dealer in the country."[32]

William Macbeth, like all but the most daring of dealers, was reluctant to show art of doubtful appeal to his clients but at the same time quite willing to offer work that he did not much care for, provided it would sell, as, for example, the paintings of Paul Dougherty, which he described to Sloan as potboilers.[33] Sloan, always a shrewd observer of character, caught the salesman side of Macbeth's personality in *Picture Buyer,* an etching of interest as both a document and a work of art. It has a sparkle that no formal portrait could provide. Dropping into the gallery on a day shortly before the Eight opening, Sloan spotted Macbeth in the act of attempting to sell a picture. The picture was placed on an easel, and the elderly client, grasping a cane in his left hand, sat before it. Macbeth stood behind him, purring into his ear, as Sloan later said, and Robert McIntyre stood awkwardly at the easel with another painting to show once the client had looked his fill at the first.[34] The etching portrays the entire scene: the very eager salesman-dealer, the earnest young assistant, the skeptical client (in actuality, H. H. Benedict, president of the Remington Typewriter company), and a throng of onlookers deriving some enjoyment from it all.[35] The picture on the easel suggests in a few vague lines one of Dougherty's bland landscapes.

Although Macbeth would not allow the Eight a second group show, he did give the public much else to enjoy, and not only the public for art residing in New York. Art lovers all over America had opportunities to see works from his inventory. Compulsively likable man that he seems to have been, he quickly became the leading figure in an informal nationwide network of dealers in American art. Searching out whatever would please their customers, the firms traded frequently with one another, and thus pictures found by Macbeth were shown in major cities from Massachusetts to California. Judging by the letters in Macbeth's files, now in the collection of the Archives of American Art, all the firms worked with one another in an amicably competitive spirit.

Macbeth's reliability as a specialist in American art was constantly in evidence throughout his years as a dealer. He was, for instance, the dealer to whom the press turned for information in 1908 when another dealer, William Clausen, was sued for selling allegedly bogus paintings by Homer Dodge Martin and George Inness to William T. Evans and Alexander C. Humphreys. At the time, Evans and Humphreys were the foremost collectors of late-nineteenth- and early-twentieth-century American art.[36] Both had bought from Macbeth. Lawyers for Humphreys had already received some funds in restitution from Clausen when the news broke. It was Evans who was the more vocal and persistent of the two. He had recently given fifty works to the federal government with the understanding that they would be installed in a national gallery, should such a building be erected. In the meanwhile, since the Smithsonian could not accommodate them, the paintings were put on view in Washington's Corcoran Gallery.[37]

When Evans, who said that he had bought the paintings from Clausen in "about 1903," was told by art-world friends that they were forgeries, he withdrew them from his gift and substituted two unquestioned Martins and one unquestioned Inness. He was determined to have Clausen imprisoned and equally determined to recover the $5,380 that the bogus pictures had cost him, and he succeeded to the extent of having Clausen jailed overnight. At the trial, which the papers considered important enough for the front page, a former employee of Clausen's said in a deposition that canvases were frequently prepared for painting at the gallery and then sent out to artists. He believed that they came back as pictures purported by Clausen to be by Martin, Inness, or Alexander Wyant. An artist, Frederick W. Kost, testified that Clausen once said to him, "Fred, don't you know that the whole picture business is a bunk game?" When still another collector, Lyman C. Bloomingdale, returned an alleged Martin, Kost asked Clausen whether an artist named [Arthur]

Dawson had "painted on it," only to be told, "No, Dawson don't paint no more `Homer Martins' for me." At the trial, Clausen's lawyer claimed that the dealer had purchased the pictures from men named Chittendon and Hamilton. Queried about the credentials of the two men, Macbeth could only say that he had never heard of either of them and had no idea who they could be.[38] *American Art News,* not afraid to take sides, championed Clausen throughout his travail. Both suits, that of Humphreys as well as that of Evans, resulted in hung juries in 1910, with the great majority of the jurors maintaining Clausen's innocence, and there the matter ended. In the meanwhile, however, Clausen, who had been dealing in art since 1889, had gone bust and shut the doors of his gallery for good.[39]

Macbeth maintained his all-powerful position in the American field until his death. The most prominent of the firms outside New York with which he did business was the Vose Galleries of Boston, but, as his correspondence reveals, it figured in his trade no more than, for example, the O'Brien and Vickery firms, or Pittsburgh's venerable J. J. Gillespie Gallery, founded in 1833. From the Vickery Gallery of San Francisco, with which he seems to have had an especially close relationship, Macbeth drew works by such California artists as William Keith, painter of redwood glades, and Helen Hyde, a talented orientalist printmaker. The first one-artist show that Macbeth held was of Keith's paintings.[40] William Vickery, in turn, took a variety of works from Macbeth. As early as 1893, only a year after Macbeth opened his gallery, the two dealers were in correspondence. Soon they were close enough to discuss problems common to both, such as the contrariness of buyers. Vickery, in a letter of May 4, 1896, for example, observed that although he was not doing too badly, he was having trouble making ends meet because of the tardiness of his "patrons" in paying their bills.[41]

In those times, so much more formal than our own, it took a while for the two Williams to arrive at a first-name basis—perhaps as long as ten years, from the evidence of Vickery's letters—but eventually they achieved it. After Vickery made his two "lieutenants," Henry Atkins (his nephew) and Frederic C. Torrey, partners in the gallery, they too became close to Macbeth. The firmness of the tie between the two galleries and, for that matter, the closeness among the many leading dealers in American art are strikingly reflected in a letter from the Vickery Gallery to Macbeth dated May 24, 1906. The letter, not from Vickery himself but from Torrey, was written seven weeks after the disastrous earthquake and fire that destroyed the firm's building on Post Street and much else in the business district of San Francisco, along with vast tracts of domestic property. It is a poignant reflection on the resulting havoc, which was made even worse by the treachery of insurers:

> It is two weeks since my return and I haven't sent you a line—which is proof of friendship for I've written almost everybody else! At the moment I must only scribble items for you. Everyone is well. Mr. Vickery seems cheerfulness itself and I've never seen him looking in better shape, and he assures me he feels it, sleeps well, eats well, is not worrying. I somehow suspect his welcome to me was genuine! He keeps office, and isn't overworked at this time. Mrs. V. too is very well. Henry [Atkins] has been under great stress and it shows more, being obviously very tired. We sent him off for some days last week. He was greatly improved by his walks in the mountains and seems in at least workable shape.
>
> Our main problems are temporary location of [our] framing shop so that we may get to work, and insurance settlements. We hope to get light on the first [of June], but affairs are very mixed—oh, you can well conceive it. Insurance matters are at a standstill. The English companies are not moving, awaiting legal advice as to liability; a few stronger American companies are paying small claims to householders, with $1000, but no commercial losses involving more than one company are being adjusted. Committees of adjustment have been appointed for over a month, and our name was #55 on the list, and our hopes of speedy adjustment raised. But as our schedules are ready I have been camping on the trail—as this insurance business will be mine and yesterday I discovered the truth in its lair, which is for all practical purposes that the local agents have been quoting sops [to] the public without any authority whatsoever. . . .
>
> The banks however have all opened and no stress is being laid on anyone so far as I know. In fact I believe a fine broad spirit is prevailing in these matters. We are under no immediate stress therefore and the check I borrowed from F.S.N. [?] I have returned to them unused. The community spirit is unshaken and the best of good feeling prevails everywhere. But no one really realizes the situation. Fine expressions of friendship reached us from all directions. One of them was so unexpected and considerate that I must tell you of it. When I was in Boston I saw Vose—father and son—and took on sale two paintings from them—net $825.00. As soon as the mails

> could reach us came a fine letter of condolence, and saying that they could not of course know whether we saved their pictures but enclosed a receipted bill in full! And this was my first business connection with that house. But we did save both of the paintings, which were small.

Ironically, even as Torrey described his firm's hardships Macbeth himself was settling into new, more spacious quarters at 450 Fifth Avenue. Three and a half years later, after a visit to California (not his first), Macbeth wrote with typical enthusiasm of the western gallery's rise from the ashes:

> I cannot refrain from paying tribute to the new home of real art in various forms, presided over by Messrs. Vickery, Atkins and Torrey, at 550 Sutter Street. Near the old location from which they were driven by the 1906 fire, these good friends have erected a fine building, unique in arrangement, where are displayed pictures, original designs in jewelry and furniture, choicest porcelains, and many other objects of unusual artistic value. The firm has richly earned its high reputation and increasing prosperity.[42]

The Vickery, Atkins, and Torrey Gallery remained in business until 1933. Of the three partners, only Torrey was then still living.[43]

Macbeth's comments in *Art Notes,* which sometimes are the rather rambling jottings of an enthusiast and sometimes reminders to the public of what was to be seen and bought in his gallery, confirm the profile of a friendly, well-disposed human being that is delineated in the diaries he so assiduously kept when young, along with justifiable pride in what he had accomplished. On the major anniversaries of the founding of the gallery, he liked to reminisce about the early years. In 1912 he wrote, "Twenty years ago there was not a single picture dealer in the country giving the least serious attention to native artists. The years of special exhibitions in my gallery have been acknowledged as a strong factor in leading to a very different condition."[44] Five years later, on the twenty-fifth anniversary of the opening, he recalled the early days in some detail:

> The opening of my gallery in 1892 . . . was a rash venture under the existing conditions, and disaster was freely predicted. There was, indeed, reason for gloomy views and I often wonder how I had courage to continue the hard fight. I had good friends among the

> artists who gladly lent their pictures for exhibiting, and though sales were not frequent, bare expenses were met until the tide turned and the small circle of buyers gradually became wider. I gratefully acknowledge that my first clients are still clients and friends.[45]

He thought it improper to name "friends who in the early years of my business were most helpful in many ways," but made two exceptions: Benjamin Altman, the collector and merchant, and Joseph Jefferson, the celebrated actor. Soon after the gallery opened, Altman bought one painting from him, a canvas by Davies, and never bought another, but in 1894, his taste having changed in favor of the old masters, he consigned his American collection to Macbeth for resale, a substantial boon to the young dealer.[46] Macbeth declined at this time to mention George A. Hearn, another of his major patrons, but on occasion in the past had cited him as a benefactor of the American art community. Hearn championed American art not only by collecting it but by establishing, in 1905, a fund for its purchase at the Metropolitan Museum, of which he was a trustee. Given the eminence of both men, it is not surprising that many of the American works bought by the museum were from Macbeth's gallery.[47]

In the miscellaneous comments that take up generous space in *Art Notes,* Macbeth often had kind words for his colleagues in the field, as in a brief elegy on the death of Leon Katz, owner of the Katz Gallery on West Seventy-fourth Street, also a venue for American art, and a note of sympathy for Newman E. Montross on the death of a son, an event that "has excited universal regret."[48] His wish to express sorrow may have been prompted by the memory of his own feelings when in the autumn of 1892 his firstborn son, William, and his daughter, Jessie, died in quick succession. The gallery had been open only six months at the time.

The April 1917 number of *Art Notes* was the last that he wrote. He died unexpectedly on August 10, leaving behind a thriving business. He had made his mark on the trade and on the taste of the art-conscious public. Few dealers have an effect on taste; most simply go with the tide, as we have seen was true of Knoedler, Schaus, and Avery once the public expressed a preference for European art. Macbeth did not, of course, change all that completely, but because of his strengths as a dealer he made American art desirable again. The business, far too important a component of the art scene to be abandoned with his death, remained in operation under Robert Macbeth until the spring of 1954. Although comparatively little can be said for most of the new artists shown at the Macbeth Gallery in its last decades, noteworthy is the fact that in 1937 the gallery gave Andrew Wyeth, then twenty years old, his first one-artist exhibition. It was an extraordinary success: everything on view sold, and so did almost all the works held in reserve.[49] The young artist was an instant star.

6

INVASION

In the decades following the Civil War and the rapid expansion of industry and interstate rail lines it necessitated, the United States found itself to be a stronger economic power than ever before in its brief history. Nevertheless, there were panics in the financial markets in the postwar decades: The panic of 1873 caused a downturn that continued through the decade and was followed by a five-year period of uneasiness, and when prosperity at last returned, it was crushed by another panic in 1893.[1]

Yet in these years many newly rich businessmen, their wives, and, in time, their widows and their children sought out costly art of the highest reputation and quality to adorn their walls. They became steady customers not only of such trusted New York dealers as Knoedler, Schaus, and Avery, but also of dealers whose principal base was either London or Paris. They wanted the best of the new art that was available from

Europe, of course, but many also set their sights higher: on the work of old masters.

Mark Twain brilliantly and lastingly named the period "the Gilded Age," as opposed to an age of solid gold, when he invented the phrase for the title of his novel of 1873, written with Charles Dudley Warner. The postwar decades were, undeniably, an age of ostentation. Great mansions sprang up on New York's Fifth Avenue and San Francisco's Nob Hill and in fashionable resort communities such as Newport, Rhode Island. When the Metropolitan Opera House opened in 1883, it possessed a "golden horseshoe" of two tiers of boxes: trophies of the very rich, who sat in sartorial splendor, quite aware of the envious glances cast at them by less fortunate persons seated above and below.

We would be unfair, however, to assume that the box holders did not enjoy the music they had lavishly paid to hear. Nor should we make a similar assumption about the purchasers of old-master art. No doubt for some wealthy men and women this art, possessing, as it did, unquestionable cachet, was valued because it provided the means of establishing to themselves and others that they had arrived. But there is in fact no reason to believe that *any* of these well-heeled collectors did not truly and profoundly love what they bought, regardless of what may have been the thoughts of some of them on gaining through art an entrée into the highest reaches of social life. No one has to be poor to admire a Raphael. European dealers were on hand to cater to their tastes. Duveen Brothers and Durand-Ruel, firms that set up branches in New York in the 1870s and 1880s respectively, were the bellwethers; other dealers were to follow after the turn of the century. All knew the market and could satisfy the reasonable demands of any American collector—and sometimes, in the case of Duveen Brothers at least, the unreasonable demands.

Knoedler and Schaus, as employees of Goupil, had constituted the first wave of Europeans to enter the American market, along with the naturalized John G. Boker, proprietor of the Düsseldorf Gallery. These men, it will be remembered, began their courtship of American collectors in the 1840s. Later, in the '60s, Ernest Gambart had come from London to stage three exhibitions of his holdings. In the immediate postwar years, only Schaus showed a strong interest in older European art. Although the Duveens confined themselves to decorative wares when they opened their New York branch in the '70s, later, in the early years of the twentieth century, the firm developed as a giant in the old-master trade. In the 1880s the enterprising Paul Durand-Ruel came over to exhibit and, he hoped, to sell a collection of paintings from his gallery in Paris. With the

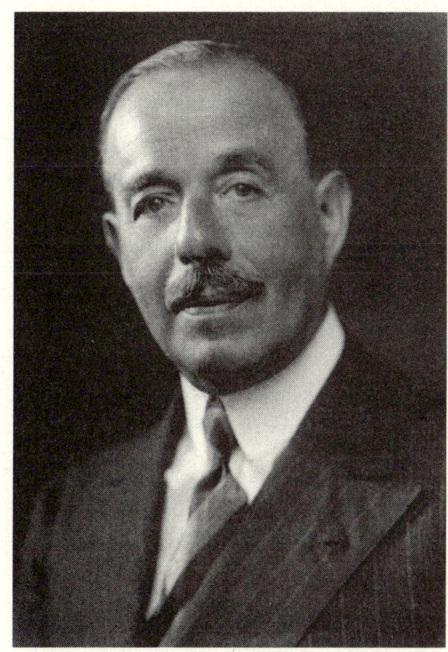

Joseph Duveen

establishment of beachheads by these two firms, New York was put on the way to becoming one of the great art centers of the world.

The Duveens, a Jewish family, peregrinated from France to Holland before finally putting down roots in England.[2] In 1810, during the Napoleonic wars, one Henoch Joseph fled from France to Holland, taking the name Du Vesne, the spelling of which he later saw fit to alter to Duveen, rendering it less French and more Dutch. He prospered, originally as a blacksmith and then, in a move that improved his fortune, as a manufacturer of weights and measures. After his death his son, Joseph, found himself incapable of managing the business and closed it down.[3] From Holland in 1863, Joseph Duveen's elder son, Joel, then twenty-three, went to seek his fortune in England as a salesman in a produce firm.[4] It was he who, when still a very young man, laid the foundation for the firm by turning from produce to porcelain as a commodity from which to derive a living.

Joel's maternal grandfather, Joseph Hangjas, of Haarlem, was a wholesale dealer in blue-and-white delft and other pottery. When Joel, on a visit to his grandfather's house, eyed some of these wares, he was struck with the thought that there might be a market for them in England. With his grandfather's blessing, he set out to sell them there. He had guessed right about the market. The English proved to be ready buyers.[5]

Joel Duveen's first partner was Barney Barnett, his future brother-in-law. Barnett had been traveling in Holland with him when he visited the Hangjas home. From their base in Hull the two young men took their goods, which included valuable Asian porcelains, to antique dealers in Liverpool, Manchester, and other cities in the north of England. Their finances flourished, but the partnership was doomed to end eventually because of Joel's growing desire to establish himself in London. The break occurred, amicably, in 1876, when Barnett's father decided to retire from his jewelry business and asked his son to take over the management of it. In 1877 Joel and his brother-in-law Henri Hangjas Duveen elected to establish a partnership.[6]

Their plan was that Henri would scour the continent for goods that Joel would sell in London, where he set up premises in Oxford Street. At the same time it was decided that Henry Duveen, Joel's young brother, would go to Boston to develop relations for the firm with American dealers, to whom they would sell goods at wholesale. Meanwhile, Joel and Henri had concluded that it would be wise to tap some markets beyond that for pottery and porcelain. They expanded to include tapestries, furniture, and paintings and formed connections with continental dealers to that end. The decorative items were to be supplied by Jan Theunissen of The Hague and the Paris firm of Lowengard, the paintings by the Paris firm of E. Gimpel and Wildenstein.[7]

In 1877, the very year that the arrangement between Joel and Henri was created, but before the partnership agreement could be signed, Henri died of typhoid fever, leaving Joel and his brother to carry out their plans alone, without the security of a formal, signed document. When Henry arrived in Boston in the summer of 1877, it appeared to him that that city was a good spot for a business such as theirs, as he reported to Joel in an enthusiastic letter. "I like America very well," he wrote. "It is a fine rich country. It beats England in everything, and you will be astonished at what it is like, it is A.1."[8]

Within a year of his arrival Henry relocated to New York, the North American center of the trade in which the firm was engaged.[9] His premises were a small shop downtown on Jones Street.[10] There Joel sent him goods to sell: porcelains, silver, furniture, tapestries, and some seventeenth- and eighteenth-century Dutch portraits. In those early years of its development, the firm was still not prepared to make a full-scale entry into the market for fine art. Both brothers doubted the practicality of such a move at the time. As late as the turn of the century Henry remained opposed, on the grounds that "pictures were the last thing a man buys. First of all he needs a house, then furniture for it, and probably he would change the house before he got around to worrying about anything except run-of-the-mill or 'furnishing' pictures."[11]

Relations between the brothers Joel and Henry were not always smooth. Not until 1889 did they get around to formalizing their working arrangements as a partnership, under the name Duveen Brothers.[12] Up to that time Henry was the minor figure in their dealings; Joel wished to retain control. At his base in New York Henry grew tired of taking orders from his brother overseas, and quarrels broke out whenever the two were together despite the existence (according to their nephew James) of a deep fraternal bond between them. Their sister, Betsy, managed to restore cordiality between them for a while, but a final break was certain to come, the formal partnership notwithstanding. It was a question of time.[13]

The major cause of disruption and disagreement was the scarcely concealed desire of young Joseph Duveen, the eldest of Joel's eight sons, to take the lead in the firm. Joe, as he was called by everyone in the family and everyone else who knew or had only as much as heard of him, had gone to work for his father and his uncle in Oxford Street in 1887, at the age of seventeen.[14] On arriving at twenty-one, in 1890, he was given a 10 percent share of Duveen Brothers stock at the insistence of his father. It was he, not his father or his uncle, who was eager for the firm to tap into the picture business. Very soon after the bestowal of stock on his son, Joel fell critically ill with pneumonia. Although he recovered, he was never again strong enough to keep the firm on the path he wished it to follow—that is, with decorative items the primary stock in trade. Annually for the rest of his life he followed the sun to warm climates, returning to England for only four months of the year. With Joel now reduced to a minimal presence in London and Henry occupied in New York, Joe found it possible to enlarge his role.[15]

In 1894 he saw an opportunity to move into fine art when on Joel's decision Duveen Brothers bought rooms in Old Bond Street, the center of the London dealers' world. Joseph wheedled permission from his father and uncle to show some paintings in the new rooms, and asked for a consignment from Gimpel and Wildenstein. This tactic proved disappointing, for not much was sold, but it brought him to the attention of the owners of the prestigious New Gallery, who invited him to secure loans of old-master paintings from private English collections for an exhibition in their rooms. He took to the assignment with gusto. For the most part the pictures had been sold to their owners by London galleries. The exhibition was popular but after its opening was decried in print by the young American connoisseur Bernhard (later Bernard) Berenson as a mass of incorrect attributions. Ironically and paradoxically, this fact in itself was ultimately of use to Joe Duveen once he had become an all-powerful force in the old-master trade.[16]

The firm's first important venture in fine art occurred at last in 1901, when Henry decided to buy at auction John Hoppner's portrait of Lady Louisa Manners with the expectation of selling it to Benjamin Altman, the New York merchant prince whose realm was a spacious department store on Fifth Avenue. The amount paid by Duveen Brothers for the Hoppner was £14,050, the highest price ever fetched at an auction in Britain to that date. Altman had authorized the purchase but shipped the painting back to London after examining it in New York; the lady was too plump and too old for his taste in portraiture. Eventually the firm placed the picture elsewhere and, although no doubt disappointed that Altman, potentially a major client, had reneged, committed themselves thenceforth to dealing in fine art. Without consulting Joel, Joe and his uncle Henry began to look around for a large collection they could purchase as a sign of their commitment.[17] Two came to their attention, both of epic value and size.

The first, which became available in 1906, was the collection of Oscar Hainauer, a Berlin banker of great wealth who had died in 1894. Hainauer's holdings, bought with the advice of Wilhelm von Bode, the director of the Kaiser Friedrich Museum in Berlin, included not only paintings and sculptures but rugs, tapestries, and *objets de vertu* of the highest quality such as the Duveens had traded in for years. A distinguished connoisseur, von Bode had also catalogued the collection for Hainauer, making attributions of various works of uncertain authorship in the collection. It had been the intention of Kaiser Wilhelm to buy the collection for von Bode's museum from Hainauer's widow with the absurdly low offer of (translated from marks) $375,000 and a fiat intended to bar all dealers, German or otherwise, from bidding. Although Frau Hainauer was in danger of angering the kaiser if she spurned the offer, she showed interest when Godfrey von Kopp, a dealer of questionable scruples and modest means, made a counteroffer of $750,000 and accompanied it with a promise to get the collection out of Germany in a hurry, before von Bode, who was away on vacation, returned to Berlin.[18]

To complete the deal, von Kopp then turned to the Duveen Brothers, who went to Frau Hainauer with an offer of $1 million, made possible by a loan in that amount from J. P. Morgan. (Henry told Morgan that he intended to pay $5 million.) Without this method of financing, Henry would have had to disclose his intention of buying the collection to Joel, who might have tried to prevent it on the grounds that there was something shady about the scheme. Henry and Joe gave von Kopp a commission of $80,000, exported the collection speedily, and deposited Frau Hainauer's $1 million in a Swiss bank, in accordance with her wishes. On learning at last of these covert arrangements, Joel was indeed unhappy that the firm had maneuvered behind the backs of the kaiser and von Bode and, of course, himself. He was pleased enough, however, with the profit of some $4 million that the firm made very quickly on the sale of the sculptures in the collection, leaving vastly more still to be offered to collectors. Nevertheless, the Hainauer transaction led the way to a break in Duveen family relationships.[19]

Not satisfied with von Bode's catalogue, the Duveens hired Bernhard Berenson, now an art historian and connoisseur of vast reputation, to provide a new one. He was the firm's second choice, after the English connoisseur Robert Langton Douglas had demurred. The assignment to Berenson was primarily Henry's idea; initially, both Joe and Joel were opposed, having heard that Berenson was not well regarded in all circles. Henry's view prevailed, however, and soon Berenson was to be become the firm's specialist in attributions, a man whose say-so on the authorship of a painting could move its price skyward if he pronounced it the work of a major artist. His connection with the Duveens made him rich—and, to be sure, also added to the wealth of Henry and Joe. His recataloguing of the Hainauer collection, meanwhile, gave him an opportunity to cast doubt on the knowledge and insight of his rival, von Bode, by reattributing many of the paintings downward. In time, however, von Bode's judgment was reaffirmed; in the 1930s Berenson himself allowed that the original attributions were correct.[20]

Although Joel had been in agreement with his father on the matter of hiring Berenson to make the new catalogue, they agreed on little else. Joe, along with his uncle Henry, was determined to push Joel out of the firm. He was willing to work with Henry and with his younger brothers, but with no other Duveens, not even his father. As the uncle and nephew knew, the sad truth was that Joel was too ill, and also too preoccupied with his real-estate interests, another source of wealth for him, to give proper attention to the firm's affairs. In 1906 Henry and Joe, although minor partners in the firm, demanded a new division of the shares.[21] With that matter settled in their favor, a restructuring of the firm, pushing Joel out and establishing Henry and Joe in complete control, became inevitable.

The second major collection, for which the firm negotiated in 1907, was composed of the combined estates of the brothers Rodolphe and Maurice Kann. The Kanns, who were acclaimed for their connoisseurship, had lived in houses side by side in Paris. They had broken through the walls to provide a single large gallery for their collections, but soon fell out over who should claim possession of certain works and as a result had ceased to speak to one another. After the death of Rodolphe in 1905, the Paris dealer Nathan Wildenstein obtained an option from Edouard Kann, Rodolphe's son, to buy the collection and promised to underwrite the cost of a catalogue by Wilhelm von Bode of both brothers' collections.[22]

At that point Nathan Wildenstein drew the Duveens into his plans; they would pay for the catalogue and in turn would participate in his option to buy. Maurice, in poor health at the time, could not be expected to live long, and Wildenstein hoped eventually to purchase both collections. On the death of Maurice in 1907, the two collections were inherited by Edouard Kann. At that point, Wildenstein persuaded Edouard to sell the collections for 23 million francs. For a second time without consulting Joel, Henry and Joe agreed to put up most of the money, half of which came, as before, in the form of a loan from J. P. Morgan, who was to have first choice of the Kanns' treasures. Wildenstein was to have a commission of 8 percent on everything sold from the collections.[23]

The Kanns had gathered a spectacular and very large mass of works: ceramics, tapestries, and antique furniture as well as paintings and sculpture. Among the pictures were works of the Flemish, Italian, and Dutch masters, including an amazing clutch of eleven late Rembrandts. James Henry Duveen, who was astounded on hearing that the Kann collections could be bought, later recalled that it "was equivalent to telling me that the National Gallery was for sale."[24]

Joel was crushed when he discovered that once again Henry and Joe had plotted a major maneuver without consulting him. At the same time, he was angry enough to wish to leave the firm, thus playing into the hands of Henry and Joe. It took the soothing personality of his nephew James, to whom he was a surrogate father, to quiet him down. Joel went with James to examine the Kanns' vast assortment of marvels, without being asked by Henry and Joe, and concurred that the firm should make the purchase. He was mollified, presumably, when the pictures began to fly out of the firm's warehouse to buyers; Benjamin Altman, for example, bought three Rembrandts and a Ruysdael from the collection. Still, the break was soon to come.[25]

With Henry and Joe now more active in the firm than Joel, their insistence on a new division of the firm's shares was not altogether unreasonable, painful to Joel though it may have been. One move that Joel could and did make to put a rein on Joe was to change his own name from Joel Joseph to Joseph Joel and insist that Joe do business under the name of the firm and that he refer to himself as Joe, not Joseph. Joel would be *the* Joseph Duveen for the brief remainder of his life. It was under that name that he was knighted by Edward VII in 1908. He died in November of that same year.[26]

Knowing that Joel was critically ill and not likely to live much longer, Henry and Joe were willing to let him remain the titular head of the firm. It would continue to be called Duveen Brothers, but its destiny was now in their hands, with Louis Duveen, another of Joel's sons, also a member. Two more of Joel's many sons, Ernest and Benjamin, were also employed by the firm.[27]

Four other sons, Edward, Henry, John, and Charles, did not care to be a part of the organization. Edward and Henry assisted Joel in managing his extensive real properties. John made it clear that he had no wish to take part in *any* Duveen affairs, a position understandable enough after the internecine fighting, but probably brought on by severe rebukes from his uncle Henry that his habit of going to tea parties with clients was the wrong way to conduct business. Charles opted to strike out as a dealer on his own. Joe, who was incensed on hearing that his brother intended to do business as Charles Duveen, offered him $7,500 (£1,500 in the exchange rate of the time) a year and his choice of $120,000 (£24,000) of the firm's holdings if he would take another name. Charles accepted the offer and set himself up as Charles of Bond Street. Joe permitted only his brothers Louis, Ernest, and Benjamin to as much as enter Duveen Brothers' premises in the years to come.[28]

Along with the Hainauer and Kann purchases, another event occurred to help the firm on the path toward leadership in the old-master trade. With many wealthy Americans establishing residences for themselves in Paris, the city that unquestionably was the art capital of the world in the early decades of the century, Joe conceived the notion of opening a branch of Duveen Brothers there. As early as 1903 he began a search for a suitable location in the Place Vendôme. In 1907 he found what he was looking for and chose a Paris architect, René Sargent, to create plans for the new gallery. Sumptuous and meticulous in all details, the Paris quarters of Duveen Brothers opened for business in 1908.[29]

With the Paris gallery running to his satisfaction, Joe contemplated an expansion of the firm's New York operation. Ever the optimist, he was unfazed by a scandal in which the firm was embroiled with U.S. Customs in 1910. The year before, Congress passed a law freeing of duty all imported work over one hundred years old. When it was discovered that the firm had imported works *before* 1909 on which it had not paid the import duty based on market value, Henry and his nephew Ben, Joe's brother, who was working in the New York branch at the time, were arrested. By a great stroke of irony, the arrest took place on Yom Kippur, the Jewish Day of Atonement. Customs demanded a payment of duties amounting to $10 million and also a fine of $10,000. But thanks to the acuity of a young lawyer, Louis S. Levy, hired by Joe, the duty was reduced to $1.4 million. All the Duveens connected with the New York branch—Joe, Henry, Ben, and Louis—pleaded guilty, and their fines came to a total of $50,000.[30] Somehow, this contretemps with the law did not lessen the firm's prestige and its ability to satisfy its clients. As for atoning, no, that would not have been Duveen style.

Even as the firm was struggling over its problems with customs, expansion was on Joe's mind. He had arrived at the opinion that if the firm was to continue to grow in its New York operation, a new building was required. He looked around for a suitable property in the most fashionable art neighborhood and found it at the northwest corner of Fifth Avenue and Fifty-sixth Street. Again he commissioned a design from René Sargent, requesting a building that would resemble France's Ministry of Marine on the Place de la Concorde, an Ecole des Beaux Arts edifice that he had long admired. With the opening of this building in 1912, the Duveens found themselves at the pinnacle of the international art community. In 1919, after more than fifty years in the trade, Henry Duveen died, leaving Joe in complete control of the firm for the twenty years of life remaining to him. But that pushes us ahead a bit too rapidly.

For Paul Durand-Ruel, unlike the Duveens, it was not the work of the old masters that held the chief interest. Although he sold great works of the past when he could get them and also did a good business in the Barbizon painters, he became known best as a champion of the newest of the new French art, the work of young painters who enjoyed painting out-of-doors and whose colors glowed with a brightness to which few of their elders were accustomed in art and of which few of them approved. These were the upstarts who came to be known as Impressionists. The designation was given them by the critic Louis Leroy in 1874 after he viewed Claude Monet's *Impression: Sunrise,* now in the Musée

Marmottan, Paris. Not only did the label stick; it became one of the most familiar terms in the lexicon of the arts.

The origin of the Durand-Ruel gallery in Paris was a stationery shop established by Paul Durand-Ruel's parents in 1803. After extending their inventory to include artists' supplies, the family began to accept the paintings of their customers in payment for them. By 1833 the shop was doing more business in art than in stationery, and in the following year, when its only competitor died, no other shop in Paris dealt in modern art. It was in 1846 that Paul Durand-Ruel entered the business. In 1865 he took over its management.[31] A few years later, in 1869, he expressed the principles that had guided and would continue to guide him in his work: "A good dealer must be an enlightened *amateur,* ready—if need be—to sacrifice his own interest to his artistic convictions, as well as someone fighting against speculators rather than involving himself in their schemes."[32]

Durand-Ruel's father had admired and supported the Barbizon artists; their success was in part due to his enthusiasm for their work. Paul Durand-Ruel also admired them and dealt in their pictures. But after meeting Claude Monet and Camille Pissarro in 1870, he was captivated by their fresh and vivid art. It was in London through the Barbizon painter Charles-François Daubigny that he made the acquaintance of these younger artists.[33] Having met them, he remained forever their admirer and protector. It was not easy for the Impressionists to reach a public even with Durand-Ruel's devoted attention, but they would have had a still more difficult time without it. The diary of the Paris dealer René Gimpel offers testimony to his kindness. Auguste Renoir once told Gimpel, "Durand-Ruel . . . alone helped me to eat when I was hungry." On another occasion Gimpel overheard Monet, old and in very comfortable circumstances, say to a rival dealer, Georges Bernheim, "There's only one person to whom I owe something, and that's Durand-Ruel, who was looked upon as mad and nearly attacked by bailiffs on our account." Later, reminiscing about the distant past with Gimpel, Monet described Durand-Ruel as "our guardian angel."[34]

The fateful introduction of Durand-Ruel to Monet and Pissarro came about during, and because of, the Franco-Prussian War. In 1870, when it appeared likely that Bismarck's armies would take Paris, the dealer fled to London with the inventory of his Paris gallery; in no other way could he protect his holdings. He calculated cleverly; had he waited much longer before taking flight, he would have been held in Paris by the Prussian blockade and siege. Also during the war years, taking advantage of the accessibility of Belgium, to which numbers of his compatriots had fled, he established a branch in Brussels.

Durand-Ruel's first attempt to introduce his artists to America occurred in 1883, when he sent a few pictures to an exhibition of European painting in Boston. Unfortunately, this proved to be an ineffectual effort. It was premature, for in the early 1880s few American collectors were ready to accept Impressionism.[35] Perhaps it was because he failed to make headway on this occasion that he offered no mention of it in his memoirs.[36] His subsequent efforts, carried out in New York, eventually succeeded.

It was through the agency of James F. Sutton, an art-world entrepreneur of solid organizational talent and substantial means, that Durand-Ruel was tempted to display Impressionist art in New York. The war had made life difficult for artists and their dealers; in 1874 Durand-Ruel found it necessary to close his London gallery. But, persevering (and never abandoning the Barbizon artists), he built a name for himself as a connoisseur of Impressionism. Sutton had previously worked with A. A. Vantine and Son, dealers specializing in Asian antiques and porcelains. In 1880 he joined Rufus Ellis Moore in the Kurtz Gallery, so named because it was housed in the Kurtz Building on East Twenty-fifth Street. With Sutton in control, the Kurtz Gallery was renamed the American Art Gallery. Although some paintings of the Impressionists had entered American collections, Sutton was the first American to recognize the merit of their work and to attempt to promote it.[37]

The American Art Gallery did not live up to Sutton's expectations. He broke away from Moore in 1882, and their joint holdings were sold at auction under the hammer of Thomas E. Kirby. Sutton's next move was to back Kirby in a new, opulently decorated gallery. This proved a sensible decision, for Kirby knew how to attract a clientele both wealthy and fashionable. The firm was renamed the American Art Association. It was the intention of Kirby and Sutton that the association be recognized as a noncommercial venture. Depite their seeming intention of concentrating on American art, in 1885 Sutton went to see Durand-Ruel in Paris and suggested that he stage an exhibition and auction of Impressionist art in New York in the association's galleries. In the following year, Durand-Ruel arrived with 289 paintings by his artists. It was a brave and chancy, perhaps foolhardy, move, because at that point, about a third of the way through his long history as a dealer, he was in debt for 5 million francs and threatened with bankruptcy.[38]

Monet's share in the exhibition was the largest: forty works. With only three, Seurat had the smallest representation numerically, but one of the three was his masterpiece, the glorious *Sunday Afternoon on the Island of La Grande Jatte,* now one of the greatest treasures of Chicago's Art Institute. The collection also included works by the American expatriate Mary Cassatt.[39]

Sutton skillfully arranged a deal with custom officials in the Port of New York to avoid a tariff on the pictures. For this occasion the association was declared a cultural institution and as such was required to pay a duty only on the works that sold. The newspapers, which had given the pictures a lukewarm reception, were not impressed by the association's newly elevated status and, egged on by dealers, staged a campaign to cut it down to size. Their position was that the association was just another commercial venture. This made sense because, despite the lofty ambitions avowed by Sutton and Kirby in their early press releases, soon after opening its doors the association began to stage auctions of minor collections. It was noted, moreover, that Sutton was the son-in-law of R. H. Macy, the dry-goods mogul. With this ruckus occurring in the press, the Customs officials reconsidered the matter and concluded that full duties should be paid. To avoid that heavy cost, the pictures were carted to the National Academy of Design, whose credentials as a promoter of culture placed it above suspicion. As it happened, visitors to the association and the National Academy of Design were not much inclined to invest money in this new style of painting even though, unlike the first Parisians ever exposed to it, they did not did not howl with indignation at the sight of it. It was still a bit too new, too radical, for most American collectors. Only 15 paintings out of the 289 found buyers, for a total of $17,500 in receipts. Not surprisingly, Monet, in whose work hardly a soul could fail to find beauty, was the biggest seller.[40]

Undaunted by the failure of the show to command the full approval of the public and the critics, Durand-Ruel tried again in 1887. Two of his three sons accompanied the shipment of pictures, which included works by the Barbizon painters and other, more conservative artists as well as by the Impressionists. This time, however, the problems over duties were even more troublesome. Other dealers were annoyed that the pictures had been allowed to enter duty-free, with the upshot that Durand-Ruel was not allowed to sell them in New York. If a collector wished to buy one of them, it had to be sent back to Paris and then shipped again to New York! Nor could Durand-Ruel exhibit the pictures in the association's galleries, because of prior bookings made by Sutton. Again he went, perforce, to the National Academy of Design.[41] But even after all this trouble, the story did not have a happy ending. The results of the auction demonstrated, once more, that most American collectors were not ready for Impressionism.[42]

None of this discouraged the dealer for long. Convinced that Americans would soon become enthusiastic admirers of his artists, he decided to open a gallery of his own in New York. He found suitable quarters for it on Fifth Avenue and sent his three sons over to run it. Predictably (although clearly Durand-Ruel himself did not predict it), he did not do well at the outset; in 1889, in the face of a still indifferent public, he had to auction off his New York holdings. But at that time the Paris firm of Boussod and Valadon formed an alliance with his New York branch, and gradually it began to prosper.[43] In 1890 he treated New Yorkers to a show of Dutch master paintings that included examples by Rembrandt, Rubens, de Hooch, Hals, Cuyp, ter Borch, and others. Over the next six decades, the gallery offered works by Impressionists, old masters, contemporary French masters, and many contemporary Americans. It closed its doors finally in January 1950 with a show of nineteenth- and twentieth-century French art, at which time its location was on East Fifty-seventh Street, then New York's most fashionable venue for fine art.

Next among the European dealers to try New York were Ernest Gimpel and Nathan Wildenstein, who through their dealings with the Duveens had known for years that the New World hungered for the arts of Europe. Their firm originated in a gallery that Nathan Wildenstein opened in Paris in 1877. After a little more than a decade of successful dealing on his own, he formed a partnership with Gimpel—hence the new firm and its name, E. Gimpel and Wildenstein.[44] By the turn of the century they could well afford the expense of operating a foreign branch, for which they found quarters at Fifth Avenue and Twenty-eighth Street. They opened for business in 1903. Since Wildenstein did not care to travel and not once in his life dared to make the long voyage to New York, Ernest Gimpel of necessity shouldered the burden of managing the branch.[45] After Gimpel's death in 1907, his son, René, took it over.

"The galleries," according to one report, were "richly appointed and a delight to the eye of art lover[s]."[46] The firm's net swept widely; in 1903 the partners showed paintings not only by Canaletto and Nattier but also by Gilbert Stuart. In the following year they offered Sir Thomas Lawrence, Lancret, and Van Dyck, and in 1905 they introduced an American, Everett Shinn, who offered oils, watercolors, and drawings. Also in 1905 it was reported that Ernest Gimpel sold "the most important example of Rembrandt ever imported, to a prominent New York collector, for the highest figure ever paid for an imported canvas here," but to whom and for how much it was sold the report neglected to say.[47] The partnership lasted until 1919, when René Gimpel, preferring to deal on his own, ended it. As Wildenstein and Company, the New York firm not only stayed on but grew, becoming the chief rival to Duveen Brothers and Knoedler's in the old-master trade. In that special branch of the art market, it would outlast both.

And it would outlast the next, but still not the last, European firm to test the enthusiasm of American collectors, the Parisian firm of Jacques Seligmann et Compagnie, founded by the three Seligmann brothers, Jacques, Arnold, and Simon. "About 1880" is the date given for its origin by Jacques's eldest son, Germain, in his memoirs; the destruction of the firm's papers during the Second World War make a more precise dating impossible. If that date is correct, Jacques Seligmann was only twenty-two when he met his first customers. What he exhibited and sold at the outset he scraped together with a tiny capital. But an eye for quality is also capital of a kind, and that he possessed even as a very young man. German by birth, he was already conversant in French when he left his native city, Frankfurt am Main, for Paris at the age of sixteen, having observed more of Prussian militarism than he could bear. Among the first major dealers with whom he became associated were the Wertheimer brothers, Ascher and Charles, of London's Bond Street. So favorable an impression did he make on them when he was young and strapped for cash that they gave him works on consignment whose value was far beyond his means. This proved a successful venture on the Wertheimers' part; in no time he sold the pieces they had let him have, and at a substantial profit. (After the death of Charles Wertheimer in 1912, Seligmann paid £27,000 for choice works from his firm.)[48] By 1900 he could afford to move out of his first location, on the grubby rue des Mathurins, to rooms in the posh and fashionable Place Vendôme.[49]

Painting interested Seligmann very little at any time in his career. Drawings, sculptures, tapestries, and *objets d'art* were his principal stock in trade; only infrequently might a painting be seen in his gallery. It was an *objet*—a German porcelain with two figures, a reclining nymph and an ogling shepherd—that served to draw him to America. In 1905 J. P. Morgan, who previously had made purchases from him, visited the Place Vendôme gallery, spotted the piece, called *Sylvie,* and decided to buy it. But when Seligmann delivered the porcelain to Morgan's hotel, he was firmly told that the sale was off. Apparently someone—Seligmann never learned who—had told Morgan that the piece was not authentic. Seligmann declared he would prove that the piece was indeed what he claimed it to be. He then took it to be inspected by German connoisseurs of porcelain and acquired written reports from them attesting to its authenticity. His next move, in 1905, was to take it to New York, where he offered it, not to Morgan for purchase, but to the Metropolitan Museum as a gift. The museum accepted it happily, and Morgan, properly impressed and just at that time appointed to the presidency of the Metropolitan, became his chief American client.

Seligmann had not traveled to New York before this visit. He had had representation there since 1901, however, through an associate, Emile Rey, who kept a small office on Fifth Avenue for him. Before the storm broke over *Sylvie,* Rey had already sold some items to Morgan, as well as to Henry Walters, the Baltimore collector. With the knowledge of Morgan's faith in him and the gratitude of the Metropolitan to gladden him, Seligmann was at last confident enough to make a real showing in New York. He took a building off Fifth Avenue on Thirty-sixth Street—as Germain points out in his memoirs, "about as far uptown as business dared go"—and turned it into a branch of the Paris gallery.[50] From then on, except for the early years of the First World War, he made an annual visit to New York, where his clients included not only Morgan but other men of great wealth to whom the buying of art had become an addiction. Among them were Benjamin Altman, Henry Clay Frick, William Randolph Hearst, Henry E. Huntington, the banker George Blumenthal, the merchants Jesse, Percy, and Herbert Straus, and Joseph Widener of Philadelphia, whose father, Peter, also a notable collector, had made a fortune in public utilities and streetcar lines.

In 1913 Seligmann moved still farther uptown, to Fifth Avenue and Fifty-fifth Street, taking part in the northern migration that was to halt for years at Fifty-seventh Street. The year before, after a bitter quarrel, he had broken with his brother Arnold, who started a firm of his own.[51] All this occurred while Seligmann still remained ill at ease with the commerce of paintings. Early in 1917, before America entered the First World War, a time when European dealers were of necessity curtailing their activities abroad, he sailed to America at the request of the French government on a Spanish, hence neutral, ship with a cargo of works of art to sell to American collectors. The underlying purpose of the mission was to offset the war-induced flow of dollars and gold from France to the United States. Sculptures and *objets* were included in the inventory Seligmann brought with him, but the collection also included paintings and works on paper. In sales over a period of two months he managed to net more than a million dollars.[52]

Yet with even this success he remained unconvinced that he should become a picture dealer. When he had sold pictures in the past, he had done so because they were included in a large collection of miscellaneous works that he had bought. After buying the large Wallace-Bagatelle collection in 1913, he sold most of the paintings to Roland Knoedler rather than, in his son's words, "bother about them."[53] At the war's end, observing that new collectors were less interested in the decorative arts than their elders had been and very much interested in paintings, Germain continued to press his father to take a major role in the expanding picture market.

But his efforts never quite succeeded. In 1918, in an atypical move, Jacques Seligmann bought seventy-one works by Degas from the sales at the artist's studio and sent them to New York to be sold at auction by the American Art Association. Unimpressed by what the auction house took in at the sale, he was no more inclined than ever to change the course of his gallery. But the beauty of the pictures so moved his son that after the death of Jacques in 1923, Germain not only made the sale of paintings a major function of the gallery but went on to deal in Impressionist and Post-Impressionist art.[54]

Of these dealers, the Duveens and Durand-Ruel affected the taste of the American public for art as no one had before them. To be sure, old-master art had long impressed the public, but with the Duveens' salesmanship, and that of Joe especially, the passion to own it grew as never before among those lucky enough to afford it. With the courageous effort of the steadfast Durand-Ruel to promote it, the art of the Impressionists became equally covetable and exerted an influence on American artists that, although no longer strong, has never quite lost its hold.

7

THE BIRTH OF MODERNISM

In the late decades of the twentieth century the term *modernism* came into use to describe the new, breakaway movements in the arts from the turn of the century through the 1920s. This use of the term has caused a shift in the language of esthetics: the art of the present and the very recent past, art that used to be called "modern," is now often described as "postmodern" or "contemporary." It is true that most of the art that William Macbeth preferred to sell was contemporary, in fact just off the easels of the artists who painted it, but it was "modern" only in that sense, not in the sense of representing the latest currents of creativity. Dealers bolder than Macbeth or the wave that had recently flooded in from Europe were needed on the scene if the attention of the American public was to be turned to the very latest European painters, those who had pushed art to a new form of expression, the painters for whom in 1910 the English critic Roger Fry invented the term *Post-Impressionist*

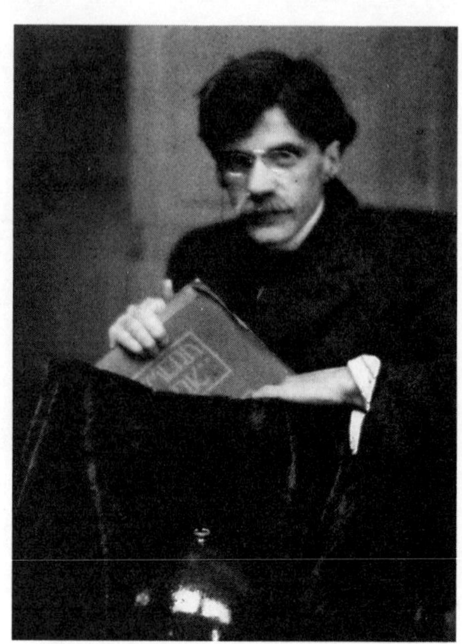

Alfred Stieglitz. Photographed by Edward Steichen.

and who today are regarded as the fathers of modernism in art. Among them, to list only five, were Cézanne, Matisse, Picasso, Braque, and Henri Rousseau. Foremost among American dealers to exhibit Post-Impressionism was Alfred Stieglitz, who, soon after introducing these artists in the early years of his gallery added many of their American followers to his roster.

Stieglitz rose to eminence as a dealer in the fine arts through the one form of art in which early on he himself was acclaimed a master: photography. Born in Hoboken, New Jersey, in 1864 to German-Jewish parents, Edward (originally Ephraim) and Hedwig Stieglitz, Alfred, the eldest of six children, became fascinated by photography as a child. Edward Stieglitz, a successful dry-goods merchant, was a man of more than moderate means, and provided a good life for his family. Having observed Alfred's enjoyment of a board game involving miniature lead horses, he took him and some of his friends to be photographed at their game. When the picture taking was over, young Alfred asked to look on in the darkroom as the photographer developed his plates and produced his prints. These were the years before George Eastman's Kodak became a household item enabling a family to immortalize itself easily with a series of snapshots.[1]

The photographs were an indication that Edward Stieglitz was proud of his family. He was also proud of his past. He spoke German at home and was eager to have his children see something of their parents' fatherland. When Alfred was only two and his sister, Flora, was not yet a toddler, Edward and Hedwig carried them off to Germany, and on a German ship, the *Germania,* for a six-month sojourn. After Edward retired from business in 1881, the family went again to Europe for a prolonged stay. This temporary displacement of the family had something to do with Alfred's education. Edward wanted his eldest son and favorite child to be educated in mechanical engineering in Berlin. Alfred had completed two years of undergraduate study at the College of the City of New York, which he entered in 1879 at age fifteen. Now his education was to be completed abroad.[2]

After a year of improving his German and his knowledge of science in the Realgymnasium in Karlsruhe, he entered Berlin's Technische Hochschule. He also attended lectures at the University of Berlin.[3] The engineering curriculum bored Alfred to distraction, and the distraction that he found, photography, proved to be something that would engage his mind as engineering never could. Spotting some inexpensive photographic equipment in a Berlin shop window in 1883, he bought it and began to experiment with making pictures. "The camera was waiting for me by predestination," he later remarked, "and I took to it as a musician takes to the piano or a painter takes to canvas."[4] But it took something more than just the purchase of the physical object to lead him to a life in photography. In conversation with another student, he discovered that Hermann Wilhelm Vogel, a professor of photochemistry at the Polytechnikum, offered a course on the esthetics of photography. To Vogel's instruction he attributed the real foundation of his career.[5] In 1885 he gave up his engineering studies altogether and spent his time in travel and in taking pictures, some of which won prizes and made his name known in photographic circles. He made a visit back to New York in 1887 but soon returned to Berlin. He traveled much in Europe, chiefly in German-speaking countries, absorbing culture wherever he went. Berlin remained his home base while he was abroad, and with a generous allowance to supply his creature comforts and underwrite his experiments, he might have stayed on in Europe indefinitely had his parents not asked him to come home for good in 1890 after the death of his sister Flora.[6]

It took Stieglitz a while to move along the path toward complete involvement in the twin professions of photography and art dealing that were to occupy the long remainder of his life. On his return to the United States, he went to work at the Heliochrome Company, a firm in which his father was a shareholder. Two close friends, Joe Obermeyer and Lou Schubart, joined him. The company, which was developing a process for color printing, soon failed, and the three young men, with money supplied by Edward Stieglitz, founded a new business of the same sort, the Photochrome Engraving Company.[7] But the independence that this arrangement gave him notwithstanding, commerce itself held little interest for him, as became apparent, even painfully apparent, to his associates in his years as an art dealer. At this early stage, photography alone interested him, and he was in the habit of jumping up from his chair in the office, grabbing his camera and his hat, and going out into the streets to take pictures, leaving the office to his two partners, who could manage perfectly well without him.

In 1891 Stieglitz joined the Society of Amateur Photographers on the urging of some of its members and within a year became a critic for and editor of the *American Amateur Photographer*. In these posts he was notoriously hardheaded. Amateurs who submitted prints in the hope of having them published in the magazine might open their mail to find a rejection slip reading "Technically excellent; pictorially rotten."[8]

As the nineties pushed along, Stieglitz stepped up his activities in photography. He also embarked on an unfortunate, loveless marriage with Emmeline ("Emmy") Obermeyer, the sister of one of his partners, in 1893. The couple had one child, a daughter, but the marriage was doomed from the start, for Stieglitz found his wife to be self-centered, unintellectual, and unrelievedly dull. Another consequential event of the decade was his giving up his shares in the photoengraving company, in 1895. Said his indulgent father, "Alfred, you'd better retire. I can't afford to keep you in business."[9] The pictures that he sent to exhibitions and to magazines for reproduction met with approval in camera circles, and with his reputation ever on the ascendant, in 1894 he was elected to the Linked Ring Brotherhood, a prestigious English photographic society.[10]

On Stieglitz's urging, in 1896 the Society of Amateur Photographers merged with the New York Camera Club. The name chosen for the new society was the Camera Club of New York. Stieglitz became the vice president. He then resigned his editorship of the *American Amateur Photographer* and next took control of the Camera Club's quarterly journal, *Camera Notes,* which until that time had been only a vehicle for reporting on the club's activities. Under Stieglitz, it turned into a quarterly for the reproduction of photographs, many of which were printed by the Photochrome Company. For new directions and new opportunities in photography, Stieglitz would sometimes go out into the streets at night, once even in a raging blizzard, to take pictures, using a long exposure. These, like all his earliest work, were simply records of impressions caught by his eye. Charles H. Coffin, an eminent critic of photography, linked him to the Impressionist painters.[11] He employed his medium, the camera, with the same intention—creating a fresh recording of a familiar scene—that had been the Impressionists' goal when applying their brushes to canvas.

Not content merely to enter his pictures in exhibitions, Stieglitz also began to publish them. His first portfolio appeared in 1897, his second in 1901, another in 1904. These professional successes were somewhat offset by problems arising within the Camera Club, whose members in general were more conservative than he. Moreover, they were put off, understandably, by the harsh treatment they and their pictures received from him in his capacity as editor of *Camera Notes*. Nor were all the members pictorialists who, like Stieglitz, hoped to elevate the status of photography to the level of fine art by creating images that emulated paintings. He resigned the editorship in 1902 and began to plan another quarterly, *Camera Work,* the first number of which appeared in January 1903. In 1908 he was expelled from the Camera Club without explanation; the apparent reason was that members held him responsible for the club's severe financial problems. He initiated a suit against the club, was reinstated, and then resigned.[12] *Camera Work* was completely independent of the club. Through June 1917, when the last number appeared, the journal published not only commentary on photography and other forms of art, but meticulous reproductions, usually in gravure, of original photographs, along with other plates of paintings, drawings, and sculptures.

Late in 1905 Stieglitz took the step that was to transform him into a leading figure in American cultural life. On the urging of the painter-photographer Edward (originally Eduard) Steichen, whom he had met in 1900, he opened the Little Galleries of the Photo-Secession at 291 Fifth Avenue. The number of the street address became the familiar name, and later the official name, of the gallery. Steichen was the cofounder; he too would one day have fame thrust upon him. Stieglitz's small studio at the top of the building and two small rooms adjacent to it made up the gallery's space. In the almost one hundred years since Michael Paff had begun to display his collection, New York still had few galleries. As the artist Guy Pène du Bois was later to note of the city's gallery scene at about this time, "In 1906 the exhibitions could be fairly covered by one critic in one day."[13] With his program of displaying photography and advanced art, Stieglitz had the field virtually to himself.

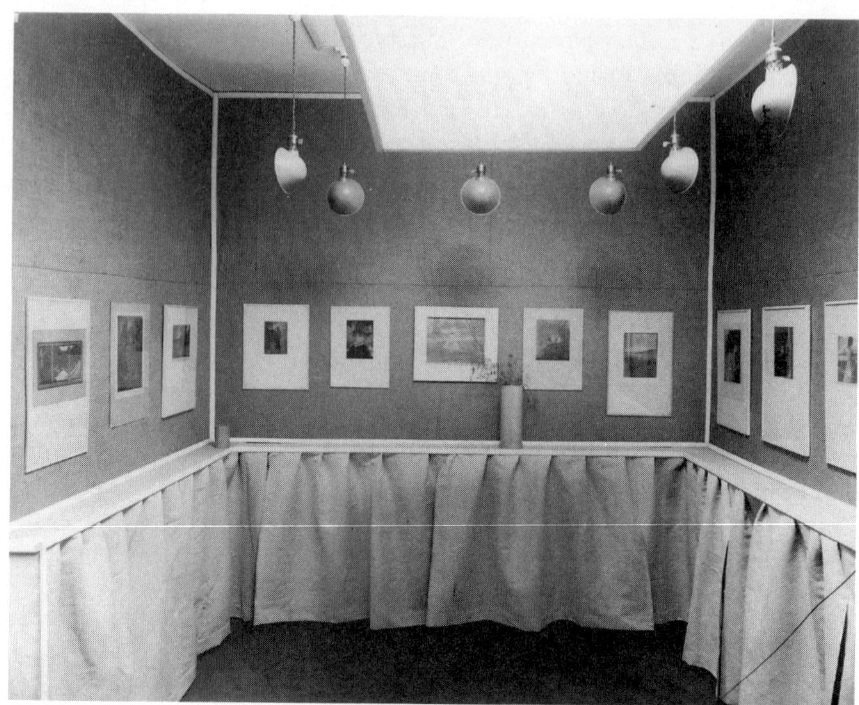

Alfred Stieglitz, The Little Galleries of the Photo-Secession

The gallery provided a venue for exhibitions of the Photo-Secession, a loosely knit organization of pictorialist photographers that he founded in 1902.[14] No suitable hall was available for the Photo-Secessionists, and had one been, the Little Galleries might not have come into being. Although the inaugural exhibition, which opened on November 24, 1905, was limited to the Photo-Secessionists and was highly successful, the founders' plan was to make room on the gallery's schedule for other photographers as well.

The name Photo-Secession, Stieglitz's invention, was in part a borrowing from the *Sezession* societies of modernist artists in Vienna, Berlin, and Munich, who used the term to signify their rebellion against conservative art. Since the members of Stieglitz's group were also in a state of rebellion against their elders and those photographers who, although not their betters as technicians, were better known than they, the name was appropriate, if obscure. That its meaning may not have been clear to gallery-goers does not seem to have mattered to Stieglitz. The members, who paid dues to their organization, decided that these funds and as much in addition as each felt able to contribute from the sale of prints should go to the maintenance of the gallery.

As designed by Steichen, the Little Galleries had a distinctly modern look. Wanting nothing to do with the conventional decor of brown or red plush favored by other dealers of the age, Steichen, with the approval of Stieglitz, chose earth tones and other correspondingly muted colors to produce a look reminiscent of the exhibition space in the building of the Wiener Sezession, constructed in 1898 to the design of Josef Olbrich. New York had nothing else like it. *Camera Work* provided the following description:

> One of the larger rooms is kept in dull olive tones, the burlap wall-covering being a warm gray; the woodwork and moldings similar in general color, but considerably darker. The hangings are of an olive-sepia sateen, and the ceiling and canopy are of a deep creamy gray. The small room is designed especially to show prints on very light mounts or in white frames. The walls of this room are covered with a bleached natural burlap; the woodwork and moldings are pure white; the hangings, a dull ecru. The third room is decorated in gray-blue, dull salmon, and olive-gray. In all the rooms the lamp-shades match the wall-coverings.[15]

This setting, handsome in its austerity, served a purpose beyond providing space for the display and sale of pictures. It was also a place where photographers, artists in other mediums, collectors, and friends could gather to exchange ideas and gossip. Having a well-to-do father to help him out with an allowance of $3,000 a year for the time being and a wife who also had money, Stieglitz took something of a horseback attitude toward mere trade. His gallery, as he viewed it, was a not-for-profit venue for the showing of works of quality that might not find another setting. He took no commission on sales and claimed, with truth, never to be interested in the commerce of art. In his memoirs, Man Ray, an artist whom Stieglitz befriended and instructed in the art of the camera, tells of an occasion when Stieglitz was asked by a woman of means to make a photographic portrait of her.[16] He agreed to do it, but for the unheard-of fee of $1,000. "I was surprised," Man Ray wrote, "and my opinion of him came down a peg"—until he learned that when the woman's husband agreed to the price, Stieglitz increased it to $1,500.[17]

In keeping with his lack of the commercial instinct, Stieglitz frequently displayed a curious reluctance to sell, often expressed in forbidding tones, a quirk that eventually became a major factor in the making of his legend. In his self-imposed role as an interrogator of would-be buyers, he was at his stubborn worst in a transaction during his second show of drawings and sculptures by Henri Matisse in 1911. The would-be purchaser was Mrs. George Blumenthal, whose husband, a partner in the investment banking firm Lazard Frères, sat on the board of the Metropolitan Museum and later became its president. Mrs. Blumenthal was tempted by three drawings; the price was $20 each. Knowing that she and her husband lived in palatial surroundings amid great art of the past that would provide an uncomplimentary setting for the drawings, Stieglitz was reluctant to let her have them. When Mrs. Blumenthal told him that she intended the drawings not for herself but for the Metropolitan Museum, he expressed doubt that the museum would accept them. Mrs. Blumenthal coolly replied, "The Museum will take what I offer it." The Metropolitan not only accepted the drawings but put them on view.[18]

Stieglitz had convinced himself that anyone truly determined to own something by one of his artists would eventually get it, and in truth the works he exhibited usually were for sale. But his mulishness made life hard for the artists, for whom the proceeds from their work put food on the table. Nevertheless, Stieglitz did what he could to protect them. In 1914, for one example of his efforts in their behalf, Stieglitz repeatedly implored one buyer, the dealer Charles Daniel, to pay up the $1,700 he owed, $1,100 for seventeen paintings by John Marin and $600 for five by Marsden Hartley. First he tried to make a joke of it: "How about a check for the fellows," he wrote seven months after Daniel had been taken possession; "they are waiting, and they 'knead' (need) the dough." In another six months, when Daniel still had not come through, he adopted a more serious tone: *The money must be raised.* . . . It is a question of *actual living* for both Marin and Hartley," as indeed it may have been.[19]

Stieglitz's inquisitorial manner necessarily elicited a defensive response from would-be customers, and that in turn provided him with an opening for further interrogation, a procedure that he seems to have enjoyed. He made the most of any opportunity to talk, and although his garrulity was accepted without evident distress by seasoned admirers, it was maddening to any stranger to the gallery who asked a simple question about a work of art on the wall and then was treated to a Niagara of explication and interpretation. In the early years, before his divorce and subsequent second marriage, to Georgia O'Keeffe, it may have been that he talked so much to visitors because the dullness of his wife Emmy made conversation impossible at home. Whatever the reason for it, this character trait only deepened with the passing years until it too became a component of his legend. Robert McBride, the critic for the New York *Sun*, noted, "It is sometimes a question in our minds whether it is Mr. Stieglitz or the pictures on the wall at the Photo-Secession that constitute the exhibition."[20] In his memoirs, Man Ray mildly observed, "He talked at length about modern art to anyone willing to listen to him. I listened fascinated, but at times it seemed a bit long-winded."[21] A more typical reaction was John Sloan's: "I went to 291 once, and he talked off one ear. It has grown back pretty well, but I never returned to 291. . . . I tried to keep away from him, out of his hair."[22]

In his first season Stieglitz showed only photographs. Thereafter, however, he began to exhibit works in other media, beginning, in the second season, with a show of drawings by Pamela Colman Smith, a young American who lived in England and whose work had an attractive symbolist quality. He had become impatient with the rivalries springing up among the photographers. To Steichen, who was then living in Paris, he wrote that he "preferred to [show the Colman Smith drawings] rather than to go on representing a lot of conceited photographers."[23] He had been expecting to receive some Rodin drawings from Steichen in Paris. They arrived in time for the third season, and Steichen was urged to send along anything else of interest that was to be found in Paris. Consequently, Steichen sent a shipment of works by Matisse: watercolors, drawings, etchings, lithographs, and one oil. These comprised the first American exhibition of Matisse's work and his first one-artist show outside France.

In the season of 1910–11 Cézanne also had his first American exposure, at the Little Galleries; his lithographs were shown in a group exhibition for which Steichen mustered other prints by Manet, Renoir, and Toulouse-Lautrec and drawings and paintings by both Rodin and Henri Rousseau. In March 1911 Stieglitz gave Cézanne his first one-artist exhibition in America with a display of twenty watercolors and, by way of a rather wicked prank, one imitation Cézanne by Stieglitz himself. This ersatz creation was the most admired work in the show.[24] Stieglitz made frequent trips abroad during the summers of these early years of the gallery and, with Steichen to guide him, saw what was going on in the ateliers of the advanced artists and viewed the expanding collections of the four Steins: Gertrude, Leo, Michael, and Sarah (Michael's wife). In these collections, works by Picasso, Cézanne, and Matisse were plenteously on view, scaling the walls in a fashion more typical of the nineteenth century than the early twentieth. The Steins and their friends Etta and Dr. Claribel Cone, of Baltimore, whom they frequently saw in Paris, were decidedly of the avant-garde in their tastes in art. These painters they admired were, above all, startlingly *new*, and the Steins and Cones helped to make them news.

When Matisse was given a second show at 291 in 1910, two drawings went to John Quinn, who in his brief life (1870–1924) assembled the greatest collection of the art of his time to be found in America.[25] A successful lawyer who ran his own firm, he made good money, and he spent it on art with the self-confidence of a connoisseur, as demonstrated by the fact that among the two thousand works in his collection at the time of his death were more than fifty by Picasso and almost as many by Matisse.[26] He was deeply attracted to women and they to him, but, in the words of one commentator on his life, "he adroitly avoided the altar," perhaps because, as one senses in reading about him, art was his truest passion.[27] Although he was a confirmed anti-Semite, he did not let the fact that Stieglitz was a Jew prevent him from crossing the threshold of 291. He was slow to take to the kind of art favored by Stieglitz, but once he learned to enjoy it he bought massively from the dealer: twenty-seven works in all, including examples of African tribal art. He thought well of Stieglitz because the dealer was so uninterested in making money on the works he sold and also because of his willingness to subsidize artists in need.[28] Quinn became a frequent caller at the gallery, and, given the depth of his regard for artistic talent, as well as his occasional flashes of temper, it is unlikely that Stieglitz ever subjected him to the barrage of questions that other, less distinguished collectors were made to endure.

Little by little, photography lost its position of eminence in the gallery as Stieglitz, his eye growing ever sharper, came to look on the modernist painters with constantly increasing enthusiasm. He held his last show of the Photo-Secessionists in December 1908. After it closed, he changed the name of the gallery formally to 291. Yet in fact this was no longer the street address; having heard from his landlord that the rent was going up, Stieglitz had left the old digs and had taken rooms across the hall. The new rooms were actually at 293 Fifth Avenue. One elevator served both addresses, making it possible for anyone entering 291 Fifth to reach the gallery, and 291 somehow sounded more pleasing to Stieglitz's ear than 293. The modern look remained; the decor of the old rooms was reconstituted in the new ones. Although easy to carry out, this move was expensive. Complicating matters, the Photo-Secessionists were lax in paying their dues, and Stieglitz's father, who had always come through with funds, was just then short of cash.[29] Stieglitz himself put up as much money as he could and gathered a group of friends to help out with the rest.

Among these patrons was a young Frenchman, Paul Haviland, a Harvard graduate (class of 1901) who lived in New York as the American representative of the Haviland china company of Limoges, which his father headed. He took Stieglitz's enterprise at 291 with the utmost seriousness, believing him to be a true revolutionary in the arts. Another major figure in the development of 291 was Agnes Ernst Meyer, the wife of the banker Eugene Meyer Jr. She came to know Stieglitz in 1908, before her marriage, when as a reporter for the *Morning Sun* she was sent to interview him. On that occasion she was so overwhelmed by what she saw and heard that she stayed six hours. To Stieglitz and Steichen she was "the Sun Girl."[30] After her marriage, she and her husband generously helped to support artists on the gallery's roster.

Not a patron but a friend and aide who served brilliantly in the development of 291 in the 1910s was the Mexican-born caricaturist Marius de Zayas, a lively, engaging, wealthy young man with a passion for the new art. Stieglitz visited his studio in 1907 and liked what he saw. In 1909 he gave de Zayas his first one-artist show. Although this exposure of de Zayas's art did not go down well with the public, the loyal Stieglitz, never in a hurry to abandon an artist, offered two more shows of his work, in 1910 and 1913. The second show, consisting of cardboard cutout figures of prominent New Yorkers, brought wall-to-wall crowds to 291, vindicating his judgment.[31] But de Zayas, as William Innes Homer has pointed out, "was more important to Stieglitz as a co-worker, critic, aesthetician, and link between 291 and the Parisian avant-garde" than as an artist.[32] Traveling to Paris in 1910 for a long visit, de Zayas discovered the vitality of the movement there in modern art. His enthusiasm for what he saw led to exhibitions at 291 of African sculptures and works by Picasso and Cézanne.

On February 17, 1913, the opening of the fateful Armory Show took place, towing in its wake many dealers who were as eager as Stieglitz to promote the best of the new art and more attuned to its commercial possibilities than he could ever be. The exhibition was destined to become the most lengthily described and carefully documented art event in American history. Its own history goes back to 1911 and discussions held by four artists, Walt Kuhn, Elmer L. MacRae, Jerome Meyers, and Henry Fitch Taylor, at the Madison Gallery, which was managed by

Taylor and owned by Clara Davidge. The four men pondered what steps might be taken to ease the task of securing exhibitions of contemporary art and determined to take action. The upshot was the formation of a new organization, the Association of American Painters and Sculptors.[33] Among its members were seven of the Eight, the exception being Shinn.[34] Under the presidency of Arthur B. Davies and with the legal assistance and general counsel of John Quinn (along with his help in securing the Sixty-ninth Regiment Armory as housing for the exhibition) and the energetic participation of Walt Kuhn as secretary and Elmer MacRae as treasurer, the members of the association intended the Armory Show to shake up the esthetic consciousness of the nation. And although seven of the twenty-five members were also members of the National Academy of Design, the association intended its exhibition to rebuke the academy for the staleness and stodginess of its annual exhibitions.

On top of this, every artist in the association hoped to sell some art, of course—his own as well as that of the many other artists represented. It was the plan of the association to stage a series of exhibitions, not just this one, for theirs was an organization that was meant to last. But in fact the Armory Show was the only one it staged, and in 1916 the association disbanded.[35]

Not all of the approximately thirteen hundred exhibits could be described as avant-garde; included among them were works by such past masters as Goya, Corot, Delacroix, and Ingres. Of the roughly three hundred contemporary artists represented, nearly half were eventually to drift into obscurity.[36] What chiefly brought the public and the press up short was the innovative art of those Europeans (mostly French) who were little known or, as with many of them, quite unknown to Americans. The artist and critic Walter Pach, a resident of Paris at the time, had done most of the scouting in European art centers for the new works to be shown. Quinn declared in his opening address, "This exhibition will be epoch-making in the history of American art." And so it was, insofar as it introduced visitors to works of art the likes of which they had never seen before.

Some liked it, some did not. Not everyone attending the show was as pleased as Theodore Roosevelt. Even though he found some of the works impossible to take, his happy cry of "Bully!" was heard repeatedly in the hall.[37] Nine years after the show, Carl Van Vechten, a novelist close to the New York avant-garde all his life, offered an impression of the public's response that catches the electricity of the event:

> Everybody went and everybody talked about it. Street-car conductors asked for your opinion of the Nude Descending a Staircase, as they asked you for your nickel. Elevator boys grinned about Matisse's La Madras Rouge, Picabia's La Danse à la Source, and Brancusi's Mademoiselle Pogany, as they lifted you to the twenty-third floor. Ladies you met at dinner found Archipenko's sculpture very amusing, but was it art? Alfred Stieglitz, whose 291 Gallery had nourished similar ideas for years, spouted like a geyser for three weeks and then, after a proper interval, like Old Faithful, began again.[38]

Many of the works on view were so radical—the examples of Cubism in particular, set apart in a room all their own—as to be met with hoots of laughter, disbelieving shakes of the head, and even alarm, as though vandals were rushing the gate. The most startling of all was the first painting mentioned in Van Vechten's account, Marcel Duchamp's Cubist *Nude Descending a Staircase #2*, which was described memorably in the magazine *Everybody's* as "an explosion in a shingle factory." Roosevelt found it faintly absurd. "There is in my bath-room," he wrote, "a really good Navaho rug which, on any proper interpretation of the Cubist theory, is a far more satisfying and decorative picture."[39] New York, the city that for at least half a century had imagined itself endowed with a degree of sophistication not to be found elsewhere in the United States, proved to be no more advanced in its response to Cubism than were Chicago and Boston, the cities where the show was later installed. If the general public had looked on artists as odd creatures before the opening, it took them to be even odder after strolling among the exhibits.

The Association of American Painters and Sculptors had made Stieglitz an honorary vice president in the hope of securing whatever promotional effort he might be willing to make. As Davies and his cohorts expected, he was indeed enthusiastic. Not only did he lend works generously to the show, but in a January 26 article in the New York *American* he exhorted the public to attend the show and to set aside its prejudices against the new and previously unknown. Charitably, he did not point out that many of the artists represented had already been introduced to the American public in his own gallery. Before the show ended its run in New York, he bought eight works: five drawings by Alexander Archipenko, a Davies drawing, a sculpture by Manuel Manolo, and a painting by Wassily Kandinsky, for a total of $767.50. The Kandinsky, *Improvisation #27*, now in the Metropolitan Museum, at $500 was much the priciest.[40]

Henry Clay Frick, then building the great collection that would be housed in his mansion on Fifth Avenue, was tempted by Cézanne's *Woman with a Rosary* (now *An Old Woman with a Rosary*, in the National Gallery, London), but, according to Walter Pach, was dissuaded from buying it by a dealer who accompanied him to the show. Pach does not identify the dealer, but very likely it was Joseph Duveen, fearful lest Frick's interest in his stock of old masters be supplanted by enthusiasm for the moderns.[41] The purchases of Walter Arensberg, an eager young collector, were four lithographs, one each by Cézanne, Gauguin, Jacques Villon (Duchamp's brother), and Vuillard. The crusty and rich Dr. Albert C. Barnes, who was outspoken in his disapproval of Cubism, also came for a look; after declaring, characteristically, that he owned "better stuff" (as perhaps he did), he bought an oil by Maurice de Vlaminck.[42]

Despite the laughter it provoked, Duchamp's *Nude* found a buyer, although not right away. Frederic C. Torrey traveled from San Francisco to New York for the show, saw the painting and admired it, but hesitated before writing a check. (The price was $324.) The fact that his gallery, Vickery, Atkins, and Torrey, had never sold anything remotely so daring as Duchamp's picture may have stayed his hand at first. But on his journey home the *Nude* began, apparently, to work itself deeply into his consciousness; at Albuquerque he wired back to New York his intention to buy. Luckily for him, the painting was still available. His thought was to keep it for himself, and after exhibiting it in Portland, Oregon, and at the gallery, he placed it in his Oakland home at, fittingly, the foot of a staircase. In 1919, however, feeling an economic pinch, he decided to sell. After Quinn, to whom it was first offered, turned it down, it went to Walter Arensberg. But Torrey never forgot the painting. He commissioned a full-size photographic reproduction and hung it where he had hung the original.[43] He may have been consoled for the loss of the painting by an early sketch by Duchamp from which the painting developed, a gift to him from the artist.[44]

Among those who gave moral support to the association, somewhat surprisingly in view of his conservatism, was Torrey's friend William Macbeth. All of three months prior to the opening he offered some advance publicity in *Art Notes:* "It will be an international showing with no limit named as to medium of expression. . . . The exhibition plans give promise of real importance to the art world." One month before the opening, he again praised the efforts of the planners: "I most heartily welcome the whole project, and am convinced that when the big show is all over, American art will have been justified and established on a firmer basis than ever before."[45] Once he had taken in the show and all its astonishments, Macbeth got back to it in *Art Notes,* this time a little less glowingly, but with no intention of condemning the enterprise: "On examining the pictures through several visits, my pleasure was in no measure marred because I found a few score of them to be utterly absurd, and, from my point of view, to bear no relation to art, except, possibly, in some cases, as decorations of a certain disagreeable sort." He concluded with "Hats off, say I, to the Association of American Painters and Sculptors."[46] Macbeth made one purchase from the show: *Picture Buyer,* John Sloan's amusingly satiric etching of the dealer himself. The price was right: $10.[47]

One important event of 1913 that can perhaps be described as a by-product of the Armory Show was the new tariff law, passed by Congress late in the year, regarding works of art. At last the tariff on virtually all new work was lifted. In theory at least, original paintings, drawings, etchings, engravings, and sculptures could come in free of duty, the undutiable sculptures being limited to the original and two replicas. (Unaccountably, woodcuts and lithographs were not mentioned in the bill, but in fact could enter without being taxed.) The act also provided that all reproductions and proven forgeries would be hit by duty. Although there would be trouble in later years when customs officials untrained to appreciate nonobjective works declared that this or that sculpture or painting was not art and therefore was dutiable at the value of the materials of which it was made, the new act established a turning point in the commerce of art in the United States.

Behind the passage of the act was the indefatigable John Quinn, not only a shrewd lawyer but a superb lobbyist as well, who claimed to be the author of the act's "every word and line." His campaign cost him some $2,500. He had long been offended by the fact that America was, as he put it, "the only civilized country in the world" that levied a duty on art. As an avid collector of French and English painting and sculpture, he served his own interest as well as that of other collectors in securing the passage of the act, and had he been able to achieve it a year or so earlier, he would have benefited the Association of American Painters and Sculptors, which was much vexed by the old tariff regulations in planning its exhibition.[48]

Even before the eye-opening revelations of the Armory Show, Stieglitz had held the first American showings of works not only by Matisse but by Toulouse-Lautrec, Henri Rousseau, Cézanne, Picasso, and Picabia, as well as John Marin and Arthur Dove, who would be among his stalwarts when in later life he focused on American art alone. A charcoal drawing by Picasso that he showed in 1910 he believed to be the first Cubist work to be exhibited in the United States.[49]

In these same years he also showed Marsden Hartley, Max Weber, and Arthur B. Charles, artists who had made their debuts elsewhere. And whereas he gave himself only a single one-artist exhibition at the gallery, in 1913, he gave Steichen four, in 1906, 1908, 1909, and 1910. But the familiar sort of figurative art, whether Impressionist or of the "Ashcan school" variety of realism, was not to his taste. In all his searches for art to present to the public, he took no interest whatever in the Eight. He told the photographer Dorothy Norman, his friend, "When it came to a showdown, I could not see anything truly revolutionary or searching in their paintings."[50]

After the Armory Show, but before 291 closed on July 1, 1917, Stieglitz offered the first American exhibitions of the work of Constantin Brancusi, Braque, Oscar Bluemner, Elie Nadelman, Abraham Walkowitz, Gino Severini, and Georgia O'Keeffe, and gave Stanton Macdonald-Wright his first one-artist exhibition.[51] His exhibition in November 1914 titled *African Savage Art,* consisting of sculptures from the Congo, the Ivory Coast, and Nigeria, was the first of its kind in the United States.[52] When charcoal drawings by Braque were shown at 291 (December 1914–January 1915), constituting the artist's first exposure in the United States, he was so little known to Americans that the weekly *American Art News* consistently misspelled his name as Brague.

Stieglitz was introduced to O'Keeffe's work by Anita Pollitzer, her close friend, who brought several of her charcoal drawings to 291 in 1915 without notifying the artist. On seeing them, Stieglitz exclaimed, "Finally a woman on paper," a remark that for some inexplicable reason has been so frequently repeated as to take on a mystic meaning.[53] He had, of course, already shown the work on paper of a woman, Pamela Colman Smith. But these early abstract works by O'Keeffe were so vital and so distinctive in their economy of line that they may have wiped Colman Smith's drawings from his memory.

Stieglitz exhibited the O'Keeffe drawings along with works by two now forgotten artists, Charles Duncan and René Lafferty, in May 1916, without her knowledge. Although she had been pleased to hear earlier that he might show the drawings, she was not pleased when she went to see them in the gallery. His failure to ask her permission annoyed her. Her appearance there at that time was her first meeting with Stieglitz. She demanded that he take the drawings down, but finally allowed herself to be convinced that it would be altogether wrong to withhold such impressive works from the public. And who, as she later said, could win in an argument with Stieglitz?[54] A romantic might like to fantasize that with this first meeting their love affair began, but that important turn in their lives did not occur until 1918.

Gradually the relationship of Stieglitz and Steichen, fraternally warm at first, began to disintegrate. The rupture came about as Stieglitz gave increasingly more space in *Camera Work* to the reproduction of paintings and drawings and revealed himself to be less interested in what Steichen had to say about the direction of 291 than in the advice of de Zayas, Haviland, and Agnes Meyer. Before the break, Stieglitz had devoted a special supplement to the April 1906 number of *Camera Work* to sixteen photographs by Steichen, and he published fourteen more in the April-July 1913 number. But by 1915 the break was complete, precipitated by Steichen's essay for an issue of the journal devoted to answers by friends of the gallery to Stieglitz's request for comments on what it meant to them. Of the sixty-eight respondents, only Steichen took a purely negative view, writing in part:

> During the past year, possibly two years, "291" has seemed to me to be merely marking time. It had obviously reached a result in one of its particular efforts and had accomplished a definite result within itself and for itself—and for the public at large it had laid the way for others to successfully organize the big International Exhibition of Modern Art held at the Armory in 1913.
>
> Whether it was the discouragement that follows achievement, or a desire to cling to success and permanently establish its value, or merely a consequent inertia caused by the absence of new or vital creative forces I am not prepared to discuss here—but "291" was not actively a living issue.[55]

Not until late in their lives did the two men resume cordial relations, so intense was the ill feeling between them.

In 1915 de Zayas, Haviland, and Meyer proposed that the gallery issue a monthly periodical devoted to advanced art and that it be called *291*. Stieglitz agreed, and he became one of its backers along with Haviland and Meyer. Twelve numbers of the magazine appeared, covering the twelve months from March 1915 through February 1916. Offering drawings by the French artist Francis Picabia, who with his wife, Gabrielle Buffet, was then living in New York, and by Steichen, de Zayas himself, and others, along with essays, reviews, poems, and reproductions of contemporary French art, *291* has been described as "unparalleled anywhere in the world as a total work of art."[56]

Each number consisted of only a few pages. More than a little space was given to satiric comment. The first number offered the report that "the masses" laughed at the works by Matisse in the exhibitions offered by Stieglitz and Newman E. Montross and that to Stieglitz "masses" meant "m asses," or a thousand asses. The second number got at the National Academy, although with some confusion as to its name:

> John W[hite] Alexander states as his reason for resigning the presidency of the New York [*sic*] Academy of Design that he is tired of his fruitless campaign to obtain larger quarters in which to display the productions of New York artists.
>
> The spring exhibition of the Academy does not convince us that we miss much by not seeing more canvases of the standard of those shown.[57]

In the mid-teens Stieglitz fell on difficult times. De Zayas, Meyer, Haviland, and Picabia, unhappy with his lack of a commercial sense, staged a mutiny and opened their own shop, the Modern Gallery, in 1915. But that was not the worst of his problems and did not trouble him at all in the beginning. The great and seemingly insoluble difficulty was that he was hard-pressed for money: money for the magazine *291,* money for *Camera Work,* money for the monthly stipends that he paid to Dove and Hartley. One sad but necessary move in the face of all this was the abandonment of *291* after the February 1916 issue, although that economizing step did not put an end to his worries. He soldiered on for another year. In 1917, having strained his financial resources almost to the breaking point by foolishly signing a new lease, he realized that he was in over his head and decided to close the gallery.[58] An exhibition of drawings, watercolors, and oils by O'Keeffe, which opened on April 3 and closed on May 14, was the last at 291. It was also O'Keeffe's first one-artist show. On May 18 Stieglitz wrote to Quinn in response to a letter received from him the previous day: "But I must smile what [that?] you talk of me as a business man like De Zayas and others. I am not in business and never have been. I have done all the work at 291, and all Camera Work, as what you term a 'thank you' job. Why I should have been such a fool I don't know. I have given my life to the country before it ever asked for volunteers or passed the conscription law."[59]

On the plus side was the deepening of his relationship with O'Keeffe in 1918 when she moved to New York from Texas, where she had been teaching. Emmy, out for a morning's shopping, returned home one day to find Stieglitz photographing O'Keeffe and, outraged, ordered him either to give up O'Keeffe or move out of their apartment. He moved out in only two hours' time, but was not free to marry O'Keeffe until 1924, when Emmy divorced him.[60]

The Armory show was followed by other large-scale roundups of new art that benefited from Stieglitz's participation: the *Exhibition of Contemporary Art,* held at the National Arts Club in 1914; the *Forum Exhibition of Modern American Painters,* held at the Anderson Galleries in 1916; and the first exhibition of the Society of Independent Artists, held in Grand Central Palace in 1917.

The first two of these exhibitions were limited to works by American artists. Stieglitz was one of the organizers of the *Forum Exhibition,* along with the critic Willard Huntington Wright and John Weichsel, the founder of the People's Art Guild, which from 1915 to 1918 staged exhibitions of contemporary art in schools and settlement houses.[61] The Society of Independent Artists continued to hold annual exhibitions through 1943. The first president of the society was William Glackens; serving with him as treasurer was Walter Pach. Both men had been instrumental in organizing the Armory show. The first, very large show of the society was not limited to modernist art. The hanging committee tacitly stretched the meaning of the term *art* so far as to make possible the inclusion of artificial flower arrangements and even a birdbath.[62]

Among the alleged works of art set before the committee was an object submitted by one Richard Mutt and titled *Fountain.* The object was a urinal, and its actual contributor was Marcel Duchamp, a fact known by some but not all of the society's officers and directors. Duchamp, who arrived in New York in 1915, had become the city's foremost exponent of Dada, the iconoclastic movement—*attitude* is perhaps a more appropriate word—founded in Zurich in 1916 as a protest against bourgeois values, including support for the traditional in art. Weary of painting, which he would give up entirely in 1923, Duchamp had conceived of a new sort of art, the found object that could stand as a sculpture if its "finder" wished to declare it a sculpture. The first of these was a bottle dryer, which he bought in Paris in 1914 and signed. In 1915 he invented the term *readymade* for such objects. The readymades grew in number over the years, but *Fountain* was the most notorious of the lot. Among others for which Duchamp became famous were a snow shovel, a bicycle wheel mounted on a stool, and a typewriter cover.

A heated argument arose over the suitability of *Fountain* as a possible exhibit, with artists who painted in a somewhat conventional mode—Glackens, the brothers Charles and Maurice Prendergast, John Sloan, and Rockwell Kent—against it. They and others of similar bent won the day. *Fountain* was rejected. Duchamp and Walter Arensberg resigned from the society's board and the society itself over the rejection. It was left to Stieglitz, who may not have known the identity of Richard Mutt, to come to the rescue of the object. Not only did he photograph it for inclusion in the short-lived (two issues) Dada magazine *The Blind Man,* giving it an unexpected touch of glamour, but he exhibited it briefly at 291, where it seems not to have to have provoked cries of outrage.[63] Eventually it was either lost or destroyed.

Fortunately for the modernist movement, when Stieglitz gave up 291 he did not give up dealing in art. One change in his taste and concerns as a dealer became evident, however: after the closing of 291 he sponsored only the work of American artists, with two exceptions—large paintings by Picabia in 1928 and the work of the refugee artist George Grosz in 1933. From 1917 to 1924, he arranged exhibitions of "his artists"—that is, those Americans he had shown at 291—in the galleries of Stephane Bourgeois, Charles Daniel, and Newman E. Montross, and the small, long-lived Weyhe Gallery (founded in 1919). He also busied himself to obtain shows for Marin and Hartley in major museums.[64] Arthur Dove, to whom he had first given a one-artist show in 1912, and Hartley were perpetually in need. Hartley, who wrote him often and voluminously, laid bare his anxieties with special pathos in a letter of 1924: "I wish now that things might go in N.Y. each year so that I could begin to store up a little for future needs. After all, Stieglitz, it isn't expecting too much. I'm tired of living in one room all my life. . . . [I] want to live my own private life in a way that brings peace to me."[65] Late in 1925 Stieglitz became a regular exhibitor at the Anderson with his own room, which he called the Intimate Gallery.

At this gallery, too, he favored the work of the artists who were at the center of his circle: Marin, Dove, O'Keeffe, Demuth, Hartley, Bluemner, Picabia, Macdonald-Wright, and the photographer Paul Strand. He also held one exhibition of the work of Gaston Lachaise and one of the work of Peggy Bacon. In 1929, backed by money from friends and $16,000 gathered by Paul Strand, Stieglitz established his last gallery, an American Place, high up in a building on Madison Avenue at Fifty-third Street.[66]

Although its opening coincided with the Wall Street debacle, he made a go of it. The gallery remained open through the Depression and did not close until June 1946, one month before Stieglitz's death, on July 13. Photographs by Ansel Adams, Eliot Porter, and Stieglitz himself sometimes occupied its walls, but An American Place was limited largely to the work of the painters who had long been his regulars. These artists had proved themselves worthy of attention in the first decades of the century, and, their talent never faltering, they were still among the best American painters of its fifth decade.

Stieglitz himself did not change, except to grow more crotchety with age. The challenging of prospective buyers went on as before. On one typical occasion during his last years a young collector came to his door hoping to buy a watercolor by Marin, only to be asked the searching question, "What makes you think you deserve to own a Marin?"[67] Worse than this, to be sure, was his inability to shake the conviction during the Hitler years that the rise of the Nazis should be blamed not on the German people, whom he profoundly admired, but on Americans, who had corrupted them by somehow exporting materialism and greed to their country.[68]

8

FOLLOWERS

Stieglitz was not only the father figure of modernism in America but also the modernist dealer whose time in the trade covered the longest span of years. But other, younger dealers who came along in his wake also steadfastly promoted the avant-garde. Still more dealers, influenced as much by the success (and publicity) of the epochal Armory Show as by the pioneering of Stieglitz, also took up the cause of modernism in the teens. The most notable of them were Martin Birnbaum; Newman E. Montross; Charles Daniel; Stephane Bourgeois; Harriett C. Bryant, director of the Carroll Galleries; Marius de Zayas, Francis Picabia, and Agnes Meyer, proprietors of the Modern Gallery; Robert J. Coady, proprietor of the Washington Square Gallery; and Joseph Brummer. These dealers were as patient as they were courageous. Presumably they sensed that time was on their side.[1]

The leading figure among their patrons, and, as we will see, something of a link among them, was John Quinn, a lawyer who, though touchy, irascible, and prejudiced, was welcomed by almost of all of them when he stepped inside their rooms.[2] But he was not the only eminent buyer. Among the other collectors who helped to drive the modernist movement forward were Agnes and Eugene Meyer; Walter Arensberg, a wealthy Harvard graduate powerfully swayed to modernism by the Armory Show; and Dr. Albert C. Barnes, the possessor of a discriminating eye for art along with a temperament even more volatile than Quinn's. Yet another major player in the modernist circle was Walter Pach, an artist who had studied with Robert Henri but who is chiefly memorable for his organizing effort on behalf of the Armory Show and his service as agent for both Quinn and Arensberg, as well as for Montross, Bourgeois, and Bryant. These men are also a part of the story.

Less involved with the latest currents of creativity than Stieglitz, but nevertheless a forward-looking figure in the art world of his time, was Martin Birnbaum. Like Stieglitz, he arrived at the trade by way of another profession, in his case the law. Born in Hungary in 1878, he came to America with his family when still a young boy. Like Stieglitz again, he entered the College of the City of New York, but, unlike Stieglitz, he was not tempted to leave in the middle of his undergraduate career. After graduating in 1897, he entered the school of law at Columbia, received his law degree, took his bar exams, began the practice of law, and found that he had no liking for the legal profession whatsoever. He might have known well before that late date that the arts held the dominant place in his repertory of interests. A very competent, well-trained amateur violinist, he played for his personal enjoyment and that of his friends all his life. But he also liked the theater, literature, painting, and sculpture, particularly the last two, and when the opportunity arose to abandon the law for a life in art, he seized it. A gregarious creature (and eventually a globe-trotting bon vivant with an international circle of friends), he was introduced early in his legal career to Annie Bertram Webb, an older, wealthy, socially prominent woman who needed a lawyer to conduct a suit in Capri for her against a hotel proprietor. Although lacking the credentials to practice law in Italy, Birnbaum went to Capri in her behalf and immediately cleared up the problem.[3] He became a member of Mrs. Webb's entourage and, so far as one can make out from his discursive memoirs, traveled with her off and on for about ten years, although still engaged, when he could not avoid it, in real-estate law. He was finally released from that drudgery in 1910, when through another older woman, Mrs. Leonard Weber, he met Emil Werckmeister, the owner of the Berlin Photographic Company.[4]

Although the primary business of Werckmeister's firm was the publication of reproductions of great paintings, the firm also held exhibitions of contemporary art. A new manager of its New York branch was needed, and Birnbaum got the job. He stayed at the gallery for six years, offering the work of European and American artists of the day and of the recent past. His first show, paintings by the Belgian artist Alfred Stevens, was well received, as was his introductory essay for the catalogue. After this good start, he went on to show paintings and drawings by Aubrey Beardsley, Robert Blum, Albert Sterner, Pamela Colman Smith, and Jules Pascin, and sculptures by Paul Manship and Mahonri Young, along with much more. His tastes were so eclectic that he exhibited not only the graphic art of the German Expressionists but Persian and Indian miniatures and paintings on silk panels by the English artist Charles Conder, which, Birnbaum notes in his memoirs, were intended for a lady's boudoir.[5]

Curiously enough, John Quinn, the lifelong bachelor, bought four of the Conder panels; according to Birnbaum, he was thinking of marrying at the time. Two of the panels, *Casino de Paris* and *Fantasia,* for which he paid $1,500 and $628, respectively, were still in his collection when he died, but the others he returned to Birnbaum for resale.[6] In view of the fact that Quinn disliked Germans as much as he disliked Jews, it is something of a wonder that he ever passed through the doors of the Berlin Photographic Company in the first place. But his correspondence and the records of his purchases reveal that he bought much more from the gallery, including Goya miniatures, Pascin drawings, and prints by John Singer Sargent and Maurice Denis.[7]

The Berlin Photographic Company lost its American public with the onset of the First World War and the intense anti-German sentiment that quickly developed. When the firm closed in 1916, Birnbaum moved on to Scott and Fowles, a firm whose chief interest lay in old-master paintings.[8] At Scott and Fowles, where he became a partner, Birnbaum sold masterworks by such artists as Velásquez, Rembrandt, and Goya, but he also managed to stage exhibitions of the modernist artists whom he admired. He showed, for example, the paintings of Maurice Sterne and Augustus John and the sculptures of Paul Manship and Elie Nadelman. Although he does not write in his memoirs of visiting 291, he was as much aware of its existence as everyone else in the art trade. His only reference to Stieglitz (with the name misspelled) is in connection with Stieglitz's exhibition of sculptures and drawings by Nadelman from December 8, 1915, to January 18, 1916, Nadelman's first in the United

States. Birnbaum himself had expected to introduce the artist to the American public and felt betrayed by his willingness to show with Stieglitz.[9] After ten years with Scott and Fowles, Birnbaum resigned his partnership to set up on his own as a consultant and arranger of private sales to collectors and museums.

The long career of Newman E. Montross had its start more than thirty years before the beginning of the modernist movement. In his teens Montross moved to Manhattan from Ellenville, New York, where he was born in 1849. Like William Macbeth, he "discovered" art through his first job—in his case, a position as clerk in a shop selling artists' supplies. As he began to meet the artists who patronized the shop, he became interested in their world. In 1870, at the age of twenty-one, he opened a shop of his own on Fortieth Street for the sale of the same products. With a move to Broadway and larger premises in 1885, he established himself as an art dealer. Such serious collectors of American art as Charles Lang Freer and Thomas B. Clark visited his gallery and added to their collections from his stock. The first American painting that Montross sold is believed to be a work of Thomas W. Dewing, which went to Freer.[10]

In 1885 Montross moved to Fifth Avenue and Twenty-fifth Street; his rooms at that location were the first top-lighted gallery in New York. Although he did not deal exclusively in American art, by 1889 he was already so well-known as one of its ranking champions that he was invited to direct an exhibition of American paintings in Washington, D.C., offered under the auspices of the Lady Managers of the Garfield Hospital. In her introduction to the catalogue, Mariana Griswold Van Rensselaer, a prominent critic of art and architecture, cited the exhibition as "the first important collection of works by living American artists that has been shown in the Capitol of their country."

Joining the march of dealers uptown, in 1900 Montross took new rooms at 372 Fifth Avenue. In 1909 he moved farther north, to 550 Fifth. Artists respected him and were happy to be represented by him, although an ambiguous note was struck in John Sloan's observation of 1907: "He is just as agreeable and soft and suave as George Luks' imitation of him."[11] But Luks, heavy drinker and general bad boy of the art world, may have meant no harm in spoofing Montross's rather lordly manner. The Ten American Painters moved to Montross's gallery from the Durand-Ruel Galleries, where, beginning in 1898, they had enjoyed seven annual exhibitions. After an interruption of two years, 1915–1916, when they showed at Knoedler's, they came back to Montross for their last commercial gallery show as a group.[12] Most of the Ten were successful enough to go where they pleased without fear of losing their admirers and collectors. That they all chose Montross's gallery as their New York venue provides strong evidence of his popularity and probity.[13]

Early on, Montross admired the American Impressionists in general, not just the several Impressionists among the Ten. In the first decade of the century he showed, in addition to the Ten, John La Farge and Gari Melchers. But he also showed paintings by Albert Pinkham Ryder, among works of many other artists not in the Impressionist camp. His introduction to modernism came through the art that he saw at 291. On first glance, the works on view there did not appeal to him, and he is reported to have dismissed them with the dry comment, "Surely, some time, Mr. Stieglitz, you are going into the art business."[14]

But, always open to new currents in art and the business opportunities they might provide, Montross soon began looking for modernist art to exhibit. According to the critic Henry McBride, it was the Armory show that turned him toward modernism as a product he could sell: "[H]e went to the armory exhibition—frankly as a scoffer, and he scoffed some, at the beginning, but the constant clicking of the turnstiles . . . sobered him and put him in proper mood for reflection."[15] He lent the show three works by Ryder, one of which, *Resurrection,* now in the Phillips Collection, Washington, D.C., was from his own collection.[16]

However, Montross's interest in modernism may have begun to develop several years earlier. Dropping in on Marsden Hartley's first one-artist show at 291 in May 1909, he was much impressed by Hartley's paintings and impressed, too, by the artist himself, whom he met at the gallery. Responding to an invitation from him, Hartley visited Montross's gallery. He found there a style of interior design quite unlike that at Stieglitz's place, but standard for the age: red plush and more red plush. He also found a patron. When Montross learned that Hartley needed only $4 a week to live and work in Maine, he offered him a stipend in that amount for the next two years, with no strings attached.[17] The following year Montross showed oils and photographs by Steichen, works snubbed by *American Art News* as evincing the "baneful influence of Matisse."[18]

In 1914, on the urging of Arthur B. Davies, Montross offered an exhibition of young members of the American avant-garde. Many of the artists were destined to fade from sight, but those whose reputations have remained secure include Davies himself, Glackens, Kuhn, the Prendergast brothers, Man Ray, Morton L. Schamberg, and Charles Sheeler. So much excitement built up among collectors when the show was announced as forthcoming that Montross felt obliged to issue a press release. In part it read,

> For one thing, I consider that the exhibition will prove to be a natural sequel to the international exhibition of modern art which created so much interest throughout the whole country last year. It will not be a chance collection of paintings. Every artist whose recent work is to be represented is familiar with the qualities of the work of those with whom he is to be associated on this occasion.... It must be clear to everybody that there can be no suggestion of a desire to startle the public for the sake of making a sensation....
>
> For those whose memories do not go back as far as my own, I should like to point out that many of the artists whose work I have been showing for the past twenty years, and who are now classed among the conservatives, were regarded as innovators at first.[19]

Matisse was given a comprehensive exhibition at Montross's gallery in 1915, with the pictures chosen by Walter Pach. This was the largest one-artist exhibition Matisse had yet had in America. Reporting on it to Gertrude Stein, Carl Van Vechten cynically observed, "Matisse has reached the Montross Galleries—in other words become old-fashioned."[20] Montross immediately followed up the show with a second exhibition of contemporary Americans. Possibly it was the shock of these exhibitions at a gallery they had thought of as "safe" that persuaded the Ten to take themselves to Knoedler's for two seasons.

With the help of Pach, other shows of contemporary French art followed at the gallery: Cézanne watercolors in 1916, works by Duchamp, Albert Gleizes, Jean Crotti, and Jean Metzinger in a group exhibition—"Four Musketeers"—also in 1916, and a memorable Van Gogh exhibition in 1920. But Montross turned down a request from John Quinn, one of his major clients, to hold an exhibition of the works of the Vorticist group of Britain, whose members included Wyndham Lewis and the sculptor Henri Gaudier-Brzeska, an act for which Quinn labeled him "yellow."[21]

Montross continued to promote the modernists of France and America, especially the Americans, until his death, which occurred in December 1932, when the nation was held in the seemingly relentless grip of the Great Depression. As he wished, the gallery did not close at his death. It remained in operation for another ten and a half years, through the summer of 1943, but with increasingly less distinction than it had maintained under the guidance of Montross himself. Noteworthy, however, were the exhibitions held there in 1935 and 1936 by a new crew of nine artists confusingly calling themselves the Ten. Behind this choice of a misleading group designation was their thought that they could always invite a tenth artist to join them once they had a space in which to exhibit.[22] The new Ten were promising modernist artists in whose work one might see hints of the bold style of the German Expressionists, artists whose paintings were usually on view in the gallery of J. B. Neumann. Among the group were Mark Rothko, who had not yet shortened his name from Marcus Rothkowitz, and Adolph Gottlieb, men to whom overtures from dealers, the praise of critics, and the attention of collectors would come in the '40s and '50s, when they moved from figurative painting to pure abstraction.[23]

Unlike Montross, Charles Daniel, born in 1878, fell in love with art in his infancy. As he wrote late in life, long after hard times had forced him to close his gallery, "I cannot remember when a picture was not a magnet to my eye. I cannot account for it. It must have been inherent in my birth. The interest was there and that interest grew." He bought his first painting at the age of sixteen, for $1.50. "It was a daub," he said, "but I was immensely proud of it, and hung it over my bed."[24]

Daniel's father owned a German restaurant at Twenty-eighth Street and Tenth Avenue. Nearby was a printing shop owned by the father of Glenn O. Coleman, later an artist of note, but in 1906, when Daniel met him, still a student, the two young men became friends and began to attend exhibitions together.[25] Enamored of art though he was, not until he came to know Coleman did Daniel have a proper introduction to the world of art and artists. Not everything about that world pleased him. For one thing, there was the oppressive "atmosphere of deep carpets and red plush" in the galleries. Nor did he admire the gentility of much of the art that he saw: "A lady in silks in the parlor, never a girl in the kitchen peeling potatoes." His mind and his very pores were open to the influence of modernism.

Before becoming an art dealer, Daniel, in partnership with his brother George, owned and ran a café—sometimes described unflatteringly but more accurately as a saloon—on Forty-second Street. Although Daniel, "a large, round-faced man," as described by Man Ray, had looks that may have seemed more suited to bartending than the genteel occupation of dealing in pictures, art was unquestionably his passion.[26] In 1908, he began buying paintings he could be proud of when a canvas by Ernest Lawson caught his eye. He paid $22 for it and $20 for a painting by Man Ray, and kept on buying.[27] One of his early enthusiasms was for the watercolors of John Marin, which he first saw at Stieglitz's in 1910. For two Paris scenes he paid $90.[28] He continued to buy from Stieglitz, adding paintings by Dove, Hartley, and Abraham Walkowitz to his collection.[29] Later, in 1914, he was to write, " 'Two Ninety-One was the original impulse of my going into the modern world of art. I had been seeing the conventional pictures of the day, and in a superficial way [had] been very enthusiastic about them. Then I happened at '291' and saw an exhibition of Water-Colors by John Marin which quite startled me at first, but held me and left me eager for a second view."[30]

George Daniel grew impatient with his brother's mania for pictures and his enjoyment of the companionship of Coleman, Max Kuehne, and other artists. "Charlie," he said, "you should not associate with artists. It gives you a bad name in business." But even had George's warning been worth taking seriously, it would not have swayed Daniel from the path on which he was set. Not yet a dealer, but a champion of modernism, and to such an extent that he offered stipends to needy artists, in 1912 he rented space on West Fifty-fifth Street and established the Daniel Studio, where he showed their works.[31]

In the following year, responding, like many others, to the impact of the Armory Show, Daniel began to envision a gallery of his own, a step beyond the Daniel Studio. In December, some nine months after the Armory Show closed in New York, the Daniel Gallery opened its doors. The first show, as Daniel later described it, was a "hodgepodge of what we could get together." It included Glackens, Samuel Halpert, Hartley, Man Ray, Claggett Wilson, and Max Weber. The address was 2 West Forty-seventh Street, in what was then the heart of gallery country, with the Knoedler, Macbeth, and Keppel premises close by. Daniel's rooms, which an artist friend, Rockwell Kent, helped to make ready for business, were on the top floor. The look of the place was pleasingly austere, a little like 291, with monk's cloth, not plush, covering the walls. Kent designed the gallery's logo, and Man Ray designed its first catalogues. To make all this possible, Daniel sold his share in the café to his brother. His friend Alanson Hartpence, a poet, became his second in command and stayed on until illness overtook him in the late 1920s.[32]

Acquiring a roster of artists, hodgepodge or not, was no problem for Daniel. The relationships he had developed with Coleman, Preston Dickinson, Halpert, Hartley, Kent, Lawson, Luks, Man Ray, and many others paid off in the availability of their work to him. The temporary withdrawal of Stieglitz from dealing in 1917 provided still others; noteworthy among them were Marin and Charles Sheeler, although even before the close of 291 Daniel had Marins for sale. Like Stieglitz, Daniel was strongly drawn to works on paper and promoted them, although he did not fail to show oils on canvas, which his collectors preferred. "We used to have magnificent exhibitions in the twenties," he wrote after his retirement. "Marin watercolors, India ink drawings by [Yasuo] Kuniyoshi, Dickinson pastels, and either black-and-white or colored drawings by Sheeler. I'd stand there and look at them—they were the finest things being done in America, but because they weren't big oils they weren't considered important."

Daniel's genuine interest in artists as human beings was the key to the workings of the gallery. He worried about Charles Demuth's diabetes, Lawson's lack of thrift, Hartley's poverty. Perhaps because he had run a popular drinking place, he was particularly sensitive to the drinking problems of some members of his stable, especially Dickinson. "One morning," Daniel wrote, "one of the artists came in and told me that he'd passed a little café on Christopher Street at two A.M. 'The door flew open,' he said. 'A hat, a coat were thrown out, and after them they threw Dickinson out.' "What help Daniel could provide, usually in the form of counseling, he did provide.

Just as he was careful to look after his artists, he seems to have been adroit at handling his clients. Unlike Stieglitz, Daniel was definitely in business to sell art, and, unlike Stieglitz in this respect as well, he had a salesman's sense of when to stop talking. "I was shocked by the unforeseen difficulties of running a gallery," he wrote. "Collectors were so ignorant, buying pictures for the social prestige of having a collection so conventional that you could never sell them a picture by an unknown artist. I shall never forget the time a collector said to me, 'But what will my friends say?' I couldn't insult him, but I wanted to ask if he was so chicken-hearted that he had no opinions of his own."

Daniel's steadiest collector was Ferdinand Howald, a mining engineer whose fortune was founded on a coal mine he operated in West Virginia. A bachelor and something of a loner, he eventually made his residence in New York, but built a home for his relations in Columbus, Ohio, the city in which he was raised. To Daniel he was "someone sent from heaven." After his initial purchase from Daniel of an oil by Edward Middleton Manigault in 1914, he made regular visits to the gallery. According to Daniel, Stieglitz made many efforts to add Howald to his list of clients, but without success. Even Howald's many Marins came from Daniel. On one evening when Daniel visited him in his New York apartment, he saw an O'Keeffe. Said Howald (as quoted by Daniel), "Mr. Stieglitz sent me this today. He wants me to get interested, but I am afraid I shall return it."

Although Howald bought oils on canvas, he was like Daniel in his appreciation of works on paper. On his death, in 1934, Howald left most of his collection to the Columbus Gallery of Fine Arts. The bequest included twenty-eight Marin watercolors, ten pastels and watercolors by Dickinson, six watercolors and drawings by Sheeler, and twenty-four watercolors and gouaches and one tempera by Charles Demuth, along with much more, on canvas or paper, by these and other artists.[33]

Albert C. Barnes was another of Daniel's clients, although, unlike Howald, not heaven-sent. Barnes's vast fortune, made from his invention and manufacture of Argyrol, an antiseptic, allowed him to buy modernist masterpieces by Cézanne and Matisse that not even Quinn could afford. He was introduced to the work of these artists by his friend William Glackens, whom he sent to Paris in 1912 on a $20,000 buying trip. But Barnes, a fast learner, was competent to choose for himself within six months of receiving Glackens's selections, and he chose brilliantly.[34] He was a shrewd and ruthless bargainer who knew how to use the power of the wealth he had amassed. He never failed to squeeze Daniel for a rock-bottom price. "[Barnes] always wanted to chop me," Daniel wrote. "He came in one summer during the First World War and bought a number of pictures, chopping me on the price of each of them. What could I do? In summer you gasp for money as you gasp for water. There was a man worth millions, I was struggling along and he wouldn't willingly pay the modest prices I was asking."

The 1920s were Daniel's great years. In 1924 he moved to 200 Madison Avenue, near Thirty-fourth Street. The artists in his stable were in demand, the prices of their work climbing steadily. Howald, for example, paid $130 and $140 in 1916 for his first two Marin watercolors, but by 1924 the price had risen to $1,200, and he paid it.[35] Daniel himself did not grow rich, however. Nor, according to one observer of his career, the critic Murdock Pemberton, did wealth much matter to him; he dealt in art for the love of the game.[36] Before the game ended for him, he had exhibited two hundred artists, to twenty-nine of whom he gave their first one-artist shows.[37] Nor did he limit his scope exclusively to American art. In 1921 he offered works by Alexander Archipenko, and in 1925 works by the group known as the Blue Four: Paul Klee, Wassily Kandinsky, Alexei Jawlensky, and Lyonel Feininger.

The end came in 1932, the third year of the Great Depression. The Wall Street debacle of 1929 and the loss of Howald's patronage caused by declining health were a double blow that forced the closing of the gallery. This was no ordinary retirement from business. Like countless other Americans in that painful year, Daniel was too hard up even to pay his rent. The building's owner brought marshals to the scene, and they locked Daniel's doors and seized his inventory—a melancholy conclusion to what had been an exemplary career. His personal collection was spared, but he could not afford to keep it. Ralph Chait, a dealer in Asian art who occupied space in the same building, bought it and sold it eventually to Knoedler's, where it was exhibited in 1942 in, sad irony, the plush-lined milieu (at Knoedler's it was chocolate, not red) he had so long deplored.[38] In 1943 Daniel's artists of old, who by that year were recognized as American masters, held a dinner in his honor.[39] He was never quite able to believe that these men whose careers he had guided and forwarded were now a part of the art establishment. "I still cannot get used to seeing my group at home in all the top galleries," he wrote to a friend in 1955.[40]

Nor, despite the fact that in his day he had been a champion of modernism, was he able as the years passed to alter his vision of what was art and what was not. Abstract Expressionism, the most striking development of the postwar years, was lost on him. In the same letter of 1955, he wrote, "Last week I was introduced to a young collector, a nice boy who belongs to the Modern Museum. It was disheartening to hear his attitude toward art. Healthy art is an anathema to his kind. I am sure the day will come when the Modern Museum will be excoriated for fostering so much decadent and degenerate art." Daniel spent his last years in poverty. At his death, in 1972, he was virtually a forgotten man.

Before coming to the United States, Stephane (variously spelled Stephan or Stephen) Bourgeois, a Frenchman, was the proprietor of a gallery in Paris. There he had formed an acquaintance with Walter Pach. Bourgeois's father, grandfather, and great-grandfather had been dealers before him. He made his first art purchase in 1905, a small Maillol sculpture that he spotted in the window of the Paris dealer Ambroise Vollard. He arrived in New York in 1911, bringing over with him a clutch of paintings.[41]

Impressed by the idea of the Armory show, he solicited loans for it and generously lent six works, all but one from his personal collection. The exception, which he held on consignment, was Toulouse-Lautrec's

Woman in a Garden; it was purchased from the show by Quinn. Bourgeois was disappointed that the show did not produce a tidal swell of sales, but he was not so shaken as to give up hope of improvement in the American market. Engaging the assistance of Pach to arrange exhibitions for him, in 1914 he set up a gallery at 668 Fifth Avenue.[42] His first exhibition included Cézanne, Manet, Monet, and Van Gogh, but he was soon to exhibit the American artists Maurice Sterne and Gaston Lachaise.

Thanking Quinn for his support in 1916, Bourgeois wrote that he planned to show Americans and Europeans "who have real talent and who are striving for personal expression."[43] In that year and at the same time that Montross was showing Duchamp, Crotti, Gleizes, and Metzinger, Bourgeois held an "Exhibition of Modern Art" that included among the works on view two of Duchamp's eyebrow-raising "readymades," the snow shovel and a typewriter cover.

After the Armory show, Quinn of course remained a client of the gallery. Among the artists whose works he took from Bourgeois were Raoul Dufy, André Derain, Matisse, Georges Rouault, and Joseph Stella. But as was usual in the negotiations of Quinn and his dealers, nasty flare-ups occurred from time to time. In 1917, not having been paid for works Quinn purchased in the previous summer and which he had promised to pay for in the fall, Bourgeois informed him that he had advanced the money owed to the artists from the sales and therefore "I practically financed your purchases." Brushing aside as an inconvenience Bourgeois's reminder that Quinn had not kept his promise, Quinn replied heatedly, but hardly convincingly,

> [I]f in the summer time you had told me that owing to the artists' needs you were advancing the money to them and suggested that I change the arrangement, I would have been very glad to do so. That is how far I am from asking you to do any "financing" for me, either for an "indefinite period" or any time. You never told me before the period had expired you had advanced the money. It takes two to make an exception. You mustn't complain now after having done something of which you never told me and in which you gave me no opportunity to share or to act.[44]

On another occasion, in 1922, Bourgeois, meaning merely to be helpful, sent Quinn into an epistolary rage by informing him of a Cézanne owned by the Paris dealer Paul Rosenberg that could be had for 160,000 francs (then about $17,500). Quinn, bristling at the price, replied,

I wonder whether you mentioned my name to him in the matter? I should be curious to know, for some dealers in Paris seem to think that the way to do business with me is to mark up their prices beyond what I know prices reasonably are. I never buy a picture "for investment." A man who buys art "as an investment" is an ass. If I were looking for an "investment," I would not buy art, but I would buy oil stock or tobacco stock or steel stock or lead stock, for stocks pay dividends and are readily saleable and can be used as collateral. Neither did I ever sell a picture or any other work of art. Neither have I ever played safe by buying merely old and established names. I think I have been a good sport in the buying of art, for I bought from living artists and to encourage living artists and have backed my judgment of artists and artists' work.[45]

Bourgeois remained at his uptown address for ten years, after which he moved to lower Fifth Avenue and ultimately to Fifty-seventh Street. Although he never abandoned contemporary art, he eventually developed expertise in another field, old-master painting. This, sad to say, was found wanting in 1946, when he lost a suit against the portraitist Johann W. de R. Quistgaard, who had sold him an alleged fifteenth-century painting. After listening to the arguments and noting that Quistgaard had not guaranteed the painting's authenticity, the jury concluded that, as an expert, Bourgeois should have known better.[46] It was the last time he made the news.

Robert J. Coady, born in 1876, was yet another of the young people whose lives in art were sparked by the modernist movement as it developed in France at the turn of the century.[47] He visited Paris between 1905 and 1912 (the dates are uncertain) and there met another young American, Michael Brenner. While in Paris they had the good fortune to gain the friendship of Gertrude Stein and her brothers, who furthered their education by introducing them to the latest developments in Continental culture.

Both Coady and Brenner had originally aspired to a career in art, Coady as a painter and Brenner as a sculptor. But on their return to New York in 1914, as war threatened in Europe, their lives took another spin. Although they had not seen the Armory Show, they joined the swelling band of men intending to take a advantage of the excitement it engendered. Forming a partnership, they opened the Washington Square Gallery at 47 Washington Square South.

Early in the year, with Brenner acting as agent, they secured a contract from Picasso's dealer, Daniel-Henry Kahnweiler, for consignments of works by Picasso and Juan Gris. The contract also gave them exclusive American representation for one year of the two artists and Braque and Fernand Léger as well. Very soon after the signing the terms were extended to May 1, 1916, and they were given representation of all of Kahnweiler's artists. Under the final terms of their agreement with the dealer, they were committed to the purchase of art valued at a total of 6,000 francs.[48] The gallery opened with a Picasso exhibition in the summer of 1914. In addition to the latest artistic products of France, the partners also showed African sculpture and art created by black children.

As attendance grew, the partners' original gallery space proved too small. They moved first to larger rooms next door, then in 1917 to 489 Fifth Avenue, where they adopted a new name, the Coady Gallery. A theorist as well as a dealer in art, Coady launched a magazine, *The Soil,* in 1916 in which he set forth the remarkably advanced argument that American art consisted in the vitality of American energy and enterprise. Manufacturing and the machinery that it developed and made use of he viewed as sculpture: "Today is the day of moving pictures, it is also the day of moving sculpture."[49] Unfortunately, *The Soil* failed to find a public. Coady shut it down after five issues.

Missing nothing of consequence in the art world, John Quinn quite naturally visited Coady's galleries and added to his collection from them. The men established a good rapport. But in 1919 Quinn bridled when Coady, always hopeful of aiding the cultural development of black Americans, suggested that Quinn give some of his holdings to Howard University, the leading black institution of higher learning. Quinn, declaring in effect that he took little interest in "art education 'for the masses,' " suggested that Coady apply to members of the Ashcan school instead.[50]

After 1917, when the war slowed their business, Brenner bowed out of the partnership. Coady maintained the gallery another two years. He died of pneumonia in 1921. The more robust Brenner, born in 1885, lived to the great age of eighty-four.

The Carroll Galleries, at 9 East Forty-fourth Street, had an even shorter life than Coady's galleries. The gallery opened in 1914 and came to an abrupt end in 1917—in sum, an unpleasant experience for everyone involved. This gallery was run by the "lean, long-legged, handsome" Harriett C. Bryant, a young woman who operated it as an extension of the decorating business she had opened some years earlier.[51] Quinn was not only her backer but her principal client. Walter Pach, Walt Kuhn, and Arthur B. Davies had urged him to support a gallery trading in the new art, and, agreeing, he chose to support the Carroll Galleries.[52] The ubiquitous Pach was briefed to select European art for the gallery, with Bryant and Montross sharing the cost of his expenses abroad.

All this sounded quite good when the gallery was in the planning stage. Yet as early as the first season Quinn grew impatient with Bryant. She staged important exhibitions of modern French painting on a level of excellence with those held by Stieglitz, Bourgeois, and Montross, but as a businesswoman, she was less savvy than he had expected her to be, although what prior evidence of her intelligence he had noticed the records do not show. Nor, he believed, was she altogether ethical. He accused her, rightly, of using her takings from gallery exhibitions to extend her decorating business instead of giving what she owed to the artists whose works she had received on consignment. Quinn's letters to her make clear his growing exasperation as artists and widows of artists complained of not being paid for consigned work they knew to have been sold.[53] Among her unhappy creditors were Roger de la Fresnaye, André Dunoyer de Segonzac, Georges Rouault, Raymond Duchamp-Villon, Raoul Dufy, and the eminent Paris dealer Ambroise Vollard.

Quinn, predictably, bought in quantity from Bryant. Complain though he might about her incompetence, he was happy to take advantage of it; often he was able to take the art home at steeply reduced prices, when, because of her poor management and salesmanship, the works had found no buyers by the season's end.[54] Among his purchases were the first Picassos to enter his collection, rose- and blue-period pieces consigned to Bryant by Vollard.[55] In an effort to make Bryant's gallery profitable, he tried to persuade Charles Daniel to merge his gallery with it and take over the management. Quinn had visited Daniel's gallery before, but had never been tempted to buy. Daniel, quite content with the way things were going for him, turned Quinn down, much to the collector's irritation. He never entered Daniel's premises again.[56]

Bryant's gallery was also the arena of a confrontation between Quinn and Albert C. Barnes. Barnes, whenever thwarted or annoyed—and it took very little to annoy him—behaved like a spoiled child, but a spoiled child with an adult's vocabulary of obscenities. When Bryant was unwilling to lower the price on some paintings by Maurice Prendergast that he fancied, Barnes assaulted her with a series of savage letters. Quinn, answering in her name, replied in kind, but finally was urged by Prendergast's brother Charles to give in and let Barnes have the pictures.[57]

Bryant herself soon realized that decorating, not dealing in art, was her forte. Trying to run a gallery was too much for her. "I should like to say," she told Quinn in her final letter to him, " . . . that to my mind (not to mention my purse) it has been a costly experiment." Rankled by the letter, in which she appeared to be taking him to task for her failure, Quinn replied, "I imagine that if you had re-read your letter [before mailing it], you might have become aware of the callousness of tone in certain parts of it."[58] Coming from him, this was a mild rejoinder. As a decorator, Bryant herself was eventually to discover how troublesome it can be when debtors are uninclined to pay up. In 1933 she sued the socially prominent Mrs. E. F. Hutton for $1,500 owed her for compiling a catalogue of Mrs. Hutton's collection of antiques as far back as 1927.[59]

Joseph Brummer, born in Yugoslavia, arrived in Paris in 1906 from Hungary at the age of twenty-two or twenty-three and found work as a model and shaper of marble for Auguste Rodin. A shrewd opportunist in the art world even as a young man, after being introduced to Henri Matisse by Max Weber, whom he met when both were students at the Académie de la Grande Chaumière in 1908, he offered to model for Matisse and sweep out his studio in exchange for permission to attend the artist's classes.[60] In that year he met Henri Rousseau, again through Max Weber, and was fortunate or wily enough to have his portrait painted by Rousseau in 1909. Rousseau's brush describes him as dark-haired and robust. Although he is seated and relaxed in the portrait, with a cigarette dangling from his right hand, a purposeful, inquisitive look about his eyes suggests the intelligence that would lead him to substantial success in the art trade.

Brummer quickly gave up his efforts to forge a career as an artist and opened a gallery, with Rousseau among the artists whose work he sold. So eminent did he emerge as a promoter of art that the French government made him a Chevalier of the Legion of Honor. Then, having created a name for himself, he determined in 1914 to establish himself in New York while maintaining his gallery in Paris.

In New York, on Fifty-seventh Street, he offered a series of exhibitions of such modernist artists as Brancusi, Derain, Duchamp-Villon, Matisse, Seurat, Vlaminck, and Villon (the first in the United States for Villon), among others. But Brummer was equally in love with the art of Greek and Roman antiquity, Near Eastern art, and the art of the Middle Ages, and all this held as prominent a place in his gallery as modernist paintings and sculptures. In this range of his dealing he had not only individual collectors but many institutional clients as well, including the Boston Museum of Fine Arts, the Art Institute of Chicago, the Detroit Institute of Fine Arts, the St. Louis Art Museum, and the Metropolitan Museum, which bought heavily from him and, perhaps for doing so, reaped a rich reward of works from his estate on his death in 1947.[61]

Quinn, always on the prowl for modernist art, was one of his clients and developed a genuine liking for him as well as respect for his knowledge. When Brummer wrote to request a loan of paintings by Derain from his collection for an exhibition in 1922, Quinn began his reply with a characteristically heated paragraph in which he declared that he had made up his mind to lend nothing more for at least two years and added, "The number of applications that are made to me to loan paintings have become a damn bore." Yet he went on, cordially, to say that Brummer could have the Derains and invited him to his apartment for a look at them.[62] In 1924, when Rousseau's monumental *Sleeping Gypsy,* now in the Museum of Modern Art, arrived from Paris, where Henri-Pierre Roché, one of Quinn's advisers, had found it for him at the gallery of Daniel-Henry Kahnweiler, he organized a small dinner party to show it off and included Brummer among the guests.[63] This, as it happened, was the last of Quinn's acquisitions; in that same year he succumbed to cancer. Acting in accordance with his instructions, his executors asked Brummer to organize the sale of the collection, then much the largest and most important hoard of modern art in the United States.[64]

In February 1927 a test of the tariff act of 1913 permitting the duty-free entry of works of art came about when the severely abstract metal sculptures of Brancusi, who had exhibited his work at Brummer's gallery in the previous year, were declared by F. J. H. Kracke, a U.S. Customs appraiser, not to be art and therefore dutiable. Since seven or eight of Brancusi's sculptures had sold for a total of about $10,000, Kracke demanded that $4,000 be paid by the artist. This very large figure, 40 percent of the purchase price, was justified in the eyes of Customs officials by the Underwood Tariff Act of 1922, which placed high levies on many commodities, including metals. At the center of the storm was another work, the artist's *Bird in Flight,* which Edward Steichen had purchased in Paris and sent to New York. On this particular sculpture, in which Customs could find nothing resembling a bird, the government claimed a duty of $229.35, or 40 percent of the price Steichen had paid. "After a long inquiry and a report from this inspector," said Kracke, referring to himself, "it has been decided that Brancusi's work is not art. Several men high in the world of art were asked to express their opinions for the

Government. They were unanimous in their decision." The appraiser did not vouchsafe the names of the men he had consulted, but he soon heard from many others "high up in the world of art" who disputed his judgment. Among them were Duchamp; the sculptor Jacob Epstein; Forbes Watson, editor of *The Arts;* and Frank Crowninshield, editor of *Vanity Fair.* Not until November 1928 was the case decided, when the Federal Customs Court found that *Bird in Flight* was indeed a work of art. But, said the presiding judge, whose jumbled words read like an attempt at saving face, "without the exercise of rather a vivid imagination it bears no resemblance to a bird, except, perchance, [that] with such imagination it may be likened to the shape of the body of a bird. It has neither head nor feet nor feathers portrayed in the piece." Still, this was a landmark decision. It paved the way for the importation of abstract works without their submission to the esthetic standards of Customs employees.[65]

Brummer plied his trade vigorously and lucratively through the Depression and beyond. Operating since 1929 at 53 East Fifty-seventh Street, he purchased the adjoining property, a five-story brownstone town house, in 1941, and remodeled it to accommodate two tenant galleries on the upper floors and an expansion of his own gallery on the ground floor. There he remained until his death, in 1947.[66]

Of all the galleries for which 291 formed a precedent, the only one that can described as its offshoot was the Modern Gallery, formed by Marius de Zayas, Agnes Meyer, Francis Picabia, and Paul de Haviland in 1915 with financial assistance from Eugene Meyer Jr., Agnes Meyer's investment-banker husband. Although in creating this new locale for modernism the founders were not showing disrespect to Stieglitz, a degree of rebelliousness was plainly evident in their activity. Close to him though they were, they had begun to be impatient with his seeming lack of concern for the placement of the art he exhibited in collections and museums. What they hoped to do was to sell art by those artists shown by Stieglitz and thus to become a kind of arm of 291. Something had to be done, as Agnes Meyer declared to Stieglitz, "to keep us all from getting into a deep gulf of inactivity and aimlessness, to keep 291 from dying an involuntary death."[67]

The new entrepreneurs chose rooms in a building at 500 Fifth Avenue, across Forty-second Street from the New York Public Library. This put them twelve blocks north of 291, a location rather far uptown for a modernist gallery. The opening took place on October 7, 1915. Stieglitz was helpful at first, even to the extent of taking over for his protégés at midday when they dashed out for lunch. But he eventually found the Modern Gallery's commercialism more than he could stomach, and after three months, late in December 1915, he put an end to the connection between it and 291.[68] The new gallery continued in business through the 1917–18 season, showing modernist French painting, African sculpture, and the work of a few Americans, including Charles Sheeler and Morton Schamberg. Sheeler became one of de Zayas's scouts abroad.

In 1919 de Zayas opened another gallery, this time under his own name. With backing from Walter Arensberg, he maintained it for two seasons. Like all other dealers, he suffered the galling, senseless wrath of John Quinn. When de Zayas offered Quinn an Ingres whose authenticity was in doubt but which the dealer believed to be genuine, Quinn was more than slightly annoyed, but the real explosion occurred a year after the closing of the gallery. De Zayas had delivered two Brancusi sculptures to Quinn in June 1922 and near the end of the year was still awaiting payment for them. At last on December 22 he notified Quinn that he had engaged a packing company to come to Quinn's apartment and retrieve them. Quinn responded in fury on December 30 at the length of four pages, but paid up. The amount was $1,200. He had simply been his usual quixotic self, delaying payment for no better reason than to make trouble.[69]

With the closing of his second gallery, de Zayas began a new career in which he developed exhibitions to be staged at other galleries in New York and Europe. In 1923, hard-pressed for money, he took the sad but necessary step of selling his personal art collection at auction.[70] In that same year Gertrude Vanderbilt Whitney, the wealthy sculptor and arts patron behind the Whitney Studio, a venue for exhibitions of American art, decided to offer shows of European art at the studio as well, and asked de Zayas to develop them.[71] (Of Whitney, her lieutenant Juliana Force, the Whitney Studio, and the Whitney Museum, we will hear more in a later chapter.) De Zayas continued in this post until 1927 but then abandoned the New York art scene altogether. In his later years he produced documentary films and wrote on the introduction of modern art to New York as witnessed by himself.[72] He died in 1961, the last survivor among the many dealers for whom Stieglitz and the organizers of the Armory Show cleared the path.

9

GROUNDBREAKER

The first of many American women to make a strong impact on the art trade, although not the first to operate a gallery, was Edith Gregor Halpert, who persevered in business for more than forty years. She was born Edith Gregoryevna Fivoosiovich in Odessa, Russia, in 1900. Her father, who died in 1905, was a grain broker, but also conducted a wine-and-spirits business with his wife. In 1906 Edith, her mother, and her sister left Russia for New York. There her mother shortened the family name slightly to a more pronounceable Fivisovitch. In 1914 Edith began to attend painting classes at the National Academy of Design. Accounts of her next few years are murky and contradictory. It appears, however, that in 1916 she changed her name to Fein and, while continuing to study painting, took a job as a comptometer operator at Bloomingdale's department store. By 1917 she had shown sufficient talent to become an assistant to the advertising manager of Stern Brothers,

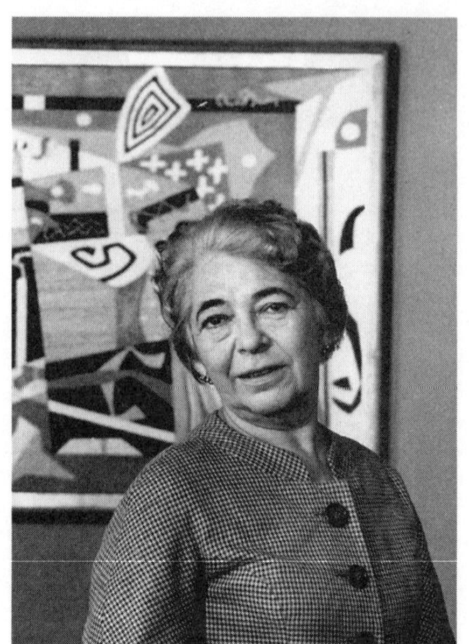

Edith Halpert.
Behind her is a painting by Stuart Davis.

another department store. In that position she not only created sketches for advertisements but also wrote copy.[1]

While at the National Academy, she frequented art galleries and was particularly impressed not by Stieglitz's 291 but by the gallery of Newman E. Montross, where, once Montross was sufficiently stirred by the Armory show to turn away from Impressionism, she could see modernist American and European art. She also became active in the People's Art Guild, the organization founded by John Weichsel that from 1915 to 1918 staged exhibitions for the underprivileged in settlement houses and churches.[2] At the age of eighteen she married the artist Samuel Halpert, whom she had met as a child. From Stern's she moved on to other managerial positions in New York. From 1921 to 1925 she served as personnel manager and head of correspondence for S. W. Straus and Company, an investment-banking house. While in France in the summer of 1925, she accepted an offer to reorganize the Galeries Lilloise, a department store in Lille.[3]

Up to this time, nothing in the records of her life provides evidence that young Edith Halpert had been thinking of opening an art gallery. But on her return to New York, she realized that her true interest lay in fine art, not the world of big business. In 1926 with her husband and a partner, Berthe Kroll Goldsmith, a sculptor and the sister of the painter Leon Kroll, she opened a gallery in Greenwich Village on West Thirteenth Street, a venue far to the south of the heart of the trade, which had shifted to Fifty-seventh Street.

Halpert's determination to succeed as a businesswoman on her own may be seen as at least in part an effect of the cultural climate of the 1920s. Like all major wars, the First World War brought about far-reaching social and cultural changes. With the war's end, in 1918, at long last the double sexual standard that decreed a distinctly inferior place for women began to wither away. Moreover, the pervasiveness of Sigmund Freud's theories of personality and the causes and nature of its responses to sexual stimuli led to an openness of discussion of previously taboo subjects. In literature, the premier spokesman for this new freedom was Eugene O'Neill, whose plays, most notably *Anna Christie* (1921) and *Strange Interlude* (1928), offered dialogue of a frankness previously unheard on the American stage. O'Neill's heroines in these two plays were women capable of determining their destiny, not puppets whose views were controlled or shaped by men. In real life, this progress toward female independence was spurred in 1920 when a long-sought and hard-won amendment to the Constitution granted women the right to vote. Always vigorous, alert, and very much her own woman, Halpert had no difficulty succeeding in a trade dominated by men.

Her decision, to which she held, was to exhibit contemporary American art. Although her tastes were very different from those represented by the Macbeth Gallery, Halpert was nevertheless one more of the countless dealers in the long line of Macbeth's followers who specialized in or emphasized the native product. A decade after his death they were everywhere, and in even greater numbers than during his lifetime. All around the San Francisco Bay Area, for example, galleries and gift shops of the 1920s and beyond showed the work of the Society of Six—William Clapp, August Gay, Selden Gile, Maurice Logan, Louis Siegrist, and Bernard von Eichman—East Bay Impressionist creators of lavishly colorful canvases—and the dealer Beatrice Judd Ryan of San Francisco showed the work of such local modernists as Eduardo Piazzoni and Maynard Dixon in her Galerie Beaux Arts, which flourished from 1925 to 1933.[4]

Another and perhaps more unlikely venue was Oklahoma City, which to the blinkered eyes of the Eastern art establishment might seem even more distant than San Francisco. From the teens to 1925 that city could boast of an American gallery owned and operated by one Sam Yunt. Seeking as wide a territory as he could cover, Yunt not only dealt in his premises at home in Oklahoma City but now and then traveled with his stock to other centers in the Midwest and to Texas and Louisiana as well. In 1925 he relocated in Kansas City, where he maintained his gallery until hard times closed him out in the 1930s. Like many other dealers, he took art on consignment from Macbeth's, whose proprietors he addressed as "you folks." He also bought from Macbeth's on credit—and had trouble paying his bills. His associate in business was his sister, always "Miss Yunt" when mentioned in his correspondence. When feeling proud or embarrassed, he would draw himself up (one imagines) and sign himself "S. McClellan Yunt."[5] He differed from the many others in the Macbeth Gallery's network only in his down-home manner.

In New York when Halpert and Goldsmith opened, the city harbored many other galleries specializing in American art besides Macbeth's own establishment and Stieglitz's Intimate Gallery. Among them were three that were destined to outlast both: the Milch Gallery (1912-81), the Ferargil Gallery (1915-63), and the Rehn Gallery (1918-78). All these galleries showed American artists of distinction, some in the mainstream of realism, some more daring. Milch, founded by the brothers Albert and Edward Milch, showed many American greats, both living and deceased, including the American Ten, the Eight, Homer, and Whistler. Like those nineteenth-century art-market pioneers before his time, Albert Milch, the elder of the brothers, came to the trade after first practicing the craft of gilder and framer.[6] Frederic Newlin Price, the owner, with Thomas H. Russell, of Ferargil, was an admirer of the art of Thomas Eakins, the eminent nineteenth-century Philadelphia painter and teacher. Price also championed the regionalists Thomas Hart Benton, John Steuart Curry, and Grant Wood. Perhaps his greatest effort as a seller of art was in marketing the paintings of Albert Pinkham Ryder—along with, the available evidence very clearly suggests, paintings reported to be by Ryder that he was quite aware were forgeries.[7] Frank Knox Martin Rehn, the son of an artist of the same name, had worked for the Milches before establishing his own gallery. On his own, he developed a roster that included such American realists as Edward Hopper, Elsie Driggs, Reginald Marsh, George Luks, and Charles Burchfield. Late in the 1920s Rehn was introduced to Burchfield's watercolors by the upstate New York collector Edward Root and took him on, enabling the artist to give up his dull job as a wallpaper designer and devote himself entirely to painting.[8] Rehn gave Hopper his first one-artist exhibitions, in 1924.[9] The gallery continued to represent Hopper for the remainder of his career. Rehn himself died in 1956, but the gallery continued in business under John Clancy, his assistant, for another twelve years.

It was not long before Halpert and her partner became as prominent as their contemporaries in the American field. The original name chosen by the two women for their enterprise was Our Gallery, but after the first year it became the Downtown Gallery, a name well suited to its out-of-the-way location at 113 West Thirteenth Street, in Greenwich Village. Although in 1940 Edith Halpert relocated at an uptown site at 43 East Fifty-first Street and in 1965 to the basement of the Ritz Tower Hotel on Park Avenue at Fifty-seventh Street, her gallery remained the Downtown Gallery. In his memoirs the sculptor William Zorach, a sometime member of Edith's group of artists, maintained that the change of name was made at his suggestion. He also wrote that behind Edith's decision to open the gallery was her conviction that she could do a better job of selling her husband's work than Charles Daniel, then his dealer.[10] In 1929, however, only three years after the opening, she initiated divorce proceedings against Samuel Halpert. He died in 1930, with Edith at his side. Edith and Goldsmith continued to own the Downtown Gallery jointly until 1935, when Halpert bought her partner out. She would never have another.[11]

One variety of American art that was to be excluded from the new gallery was Impressionism. It might still have appeal for the Macbeth family, but it had none at all for young, modern-minded Edith Halpert. Her first artists were Peggy Bacon, Alexander Brook, Stuart Davis, Yasuo Kuniyoshi, Reuben Nakian, Charles Sheeler, Niles Spencer, Dorothy Varian, and William Zorach, all in the realist tradition, to be sure, but with an up-to-date outlook. They were members of the Whitney Studio Club, the group founded by Gertrude Vanderbilt Whitney and her associate Juliana Force in 1918 for the fostering and promotion of American talent. Samuel Halpert had been a member of the club from its inception, and Edith herself had shown work there a few times.[12] Her idea of what the gallery ought to be promised well for the future, and the promise was kept, at least through the 1930s. Even as early as the 1920s she had developed a coast-to-coast reputation as a dealer of sound judgment. San Francisco's Beatrice Judd Ryan began early on to take etchings and watercolors—easily transportable works—on consignment from her.[13] Although she complained in later life of having been "dead broke" in the middle of the Depression, she ran a prosperous business to the very end.[14]

In 1931 Halpert expanded her trade to include American folk art, which she gathered with the assistance of Holger Cahill, then a specialist in the field who in the previous year had organized a folk-art exhibition for the Newark Museum. For her dealings in this field, she established a separate business, the American Folk Art Gallery, which she ran in the same space as the Downtown Gallery. At the suggestion of Ben Shahn, one of the most eminent painters on her roster, Halpert hired the rising photographer Walker Evans, with whom Shahn shared a studio, to record her folk-art inventory with his camera.[15] Among her clients for this art, and probably the most dedicated collector among them, was Abby Aldrich Rockefeller, whom Halpert met during the gallery's first years. Through an architect who worked for the Rockefeller family, Halpert borrowed a watercolor by Winslow Homer to surround with contemporary watercolors in a show, not knowing that it belonged to Mrs. Rockefeller. Happily for Halpert, Mrs. Rockefeller visited the show and bought all the other works.[16] Thus was a productive dealer-client relationship formed, and soon other members of the family became her clients as well. An exhibition of American folk art that Cahill organized for the Museum of Modern Art in 1932 was composed entirely of works that had entered the Rockefeller collection from the Downtown Gallery.[17] The Modern would have been an unlikely venue for an exhibition of that kind had it not been for the fact that Mrs. Rockefeller was one of the museum's founders. In later years, Halpert repeatedly declared that her folk-art dealings comprised the most profitable part of her business.[18]

Although the field of collectors of means was severely narrowed by the stock market crash of 1929 (*crash* having displaced *panic* as the preferred means of describing a precipitous drop in market values), Halpert, secure in her self-confidence, moved blithely on. In 1934 she conceived the notion of promoting art and artists and herself as well by staging a huge exhibition of contemporary works, including, of course, those of several of her own artists, in a large public space. According to William Zorach, Halpert hoped to duplicate the success of the Armory Show.[19] Mayor Fiorello LaGuardia agreed to let her install the exhibition in one of the city's armories, but when she found that the armory he had in mind was not suitable, she accepted the suggestion of young Nelson Rockefeller, by that date another of her collectors, that the show be presented in Rockefeller Center.

With Holger Cahill as the show's director, almost a thousand works in all media were made available to the public gaze on February 26, 1934.[20] Although Halpert herself did not select the works on view, she was in the process of developing what Charles Alan, her associate from 1945 to 1953, would call "a 1930s eye."[21] She developed a taste for the "American

Scene," a term that had recently come into broad use. It was a label for paintings of landscapes, mining, and manufacturing that represented the nation at this period in its history. The landscapes, in particular, revealed nostalgia for a less stressful age, without crowds of the unemployed in the streets, without race riots, and without the threats posed by Hitler, Mussolini, and Japanese militarism. When the Federal Art Project of the Works Progress Administration (WPA) came into being in 1935, Halpert helped to secure the directorship of it for Cahill and assisted him as the project got under way. She snapped up several WPA artists for the Downtown Gallery, including such future stars as Jacob Lawrence and Jack Levine, painters whose work was inspired by social causes: for Levine, right-wing politics; for Lawrence, racial conflicts.[22]

With Ben Shahn in the lead, Halpert's phalanx of painters of the American Scene formed a major component of her stable. Shahn's emotionally powerful paintings, such as his series on the tragedy of Sacco and Vanzetti, formed a secure base on which his fame quickly grew; with such renowned works a part of his background, he became a member of the social and academic establishments in the post-Second World War years, with honorary degrees from Princeton and Harvard and Nelson Rockefeller as an occasional dinner companion.[23] Among other works for which he was noted were the stark photographs he shot in the 1930s for the federal government's Resettlement Administration (later the Farm Security Administration).

The Downtown's most important rival in American Scene painting was the ACA Gallery (the initials standing for American Contemporary Artists), founded by Herman Baron in 1932. Among Baron's artists were such social realists as Philip Evergood, Robert Gwathmey, Anton Refregier, Joseph Solman, Moses Soyer, and William Gropper. Baron was the managing editor of the short-lived journal *Art Front* (1934–37), which was sponsored by the Artists' Union and the Artists' Committee of Action, organizations in the forefront of efforts to secure federal assistance for artists such as was soon made available through the WPA. In 1935 Baron participated in the formation of the Artists' Congress Against War and Fascism, which under the leadership of the noted painter Stuart Davis was held in the following year, with the purpose of establishing a united front of left-wing and liberal artists for the furtherance of social action against the increasingly menacing power of the far right at home and abroad, but with the additional purpose, to be sure, of agitating to protect their security under the WPA and other government agencies. After Baron's death, in 1961, the ACA continued in operation but gradually took on artists of a wider spectrum of interests than those of his choice, as it continues to do. Terry Dintenfass, a member of Baron's staff with a similar interest in figurative art, left ACA in 1960 to open her own gallery and was still in business as the new century began.

At the same time that she daringly plucked new artists from the WPA, Halpert cleverly evened her chances of avoiding financial disaster by cultivating an acquaintance with Stieglitz and securing paintings by his regulars, O'Keeffe, Marin, Demuth, and Hartley. In 1939 she persuaded Stieglitz to let her have several small Marin watercolors to sell for $500 each. Concurrently with her show, Stieglitz held an exhibition of major Marin works that, in a gesture typical of the dealer, were "not for sale at any price," unless someone was willing to buy the entire group of them.[24] After Stieglitz's death, in 1946, O'Keeffe, Sheeler, and Marin joined Halpert's roster, Marin having been granted a room all his own at the gallery.

Halpert's "1930s eye" never widened its range. Although she was enough of a modernist to reject all the increasingly pallid descendants of the American Impressionists, she also rejected Abstract Expressionism when it burst spectacularly onto the scene in the 1940s. She was, however, always on the lookout for new talent of the sort she could sanction—abstract, perhaps, but not nonobjective—and in the 1950s took on a group of younger painters whose oils could be sold for as little as $200. Many of her collectors had such faith in her judgment that they bought something by each of these new artists. Their work and minor pieces by her major artists could be had for very little money at the annual Christmas shows in the gallery, when every year treats no less covetable for being small were brought out of the gallery's storeroom to find their way under the trees of lucky recipients on Christmas morning. In the 1950s a small O'Keeffe oil could be had for a mere $350, a smaller, luminous O'Keeffe pastel for $100. As late as 1961 the Christmas show included a William M. Harnett drawing of a cast of the Venus de Milo that was offered at only $600.[25] Halpert was always troubled by the need to raise her artists' prices and equally troubled by any visitor to the gallery whom she took to be a speculator in art. On one occasion she ordered a man to leave the gallery after he asked the price of a painting by Charles Sheeler and then inquired what it would be worth the next year.[26] She was also impatient with bargainers. Once when the celebrated actor and collector Edward G. Robinson, a notorious bargainer, inquired about a painting, she quoted an outrageously high figure and then let him bargain his way down to the price she had actually put on it.[27] "Hard-boiled" was

William Zorach's phrase for her "a hard-boiled business woman—and I mean hard-boiled."[28]

Like virtually all other dealers, Halpert herself was a collector. But it was a point of pride with her that she would not skim off the best work of her artists for her personal collection. She was pleased to say that she would wait until an exhibition closed and then choose a work for herself from those that had not been sold.[29] Even though limited by this policy, she amassed an enviable gathering of works of art. In 1973, three years after her death, the collection was sold at Sotheby's. So large was it that four separate sessions had to be scheduled for the sale. The first and most important of them brought in $3.6 million, more than a million over the estimate.[30] The Harnett drawing of Venus went for $2,500, more than four times the figure she had originally set on it. A Japanese collector bought Yasuo Kuniyoshi's *Little Girl with Cow* for $220,000, setting a record price for an American painting. Elie Nadelman's carved-wood *Tango* fetched $130,000, then a record for an American sculpture.

Halpert did more for her artists than sell and buy their work. Witnesses to her life in the early years of the Downtown Gallery and on through the 1930s describe not merely a shrewd businesswoman, such as she undoubtedly was, but a contented, good-natured person with a motherly interest in the welfare of her artists. She soon learned that it took a new artist an average of five years to find a public, and she was quite happy to subsidize him until his sales provided him with a comfortable income.[31]

She owned a vacation house in Connecticut but made her home in an apartment above the gallery on East Fifty-first Street, living "over the shop" like many other turn-of-the-century immigrants. There were, inevitably, some visitors to the gallery who did not share her conviction that all the artists were geniuses, and said so. One such was Sidney Janis, author, collector, and dealer, who remarked a decade after her death, "From time to time she would let me know that I was looking at a masterpiece, and I knew damn well it wasn't."[32] But from all accounts, in those years of her growth and maturation she was a pleasure to be with. Because her friends were artists and collectors, whatever she spent on entertainment became a business write-off. "Her whole life," said Charles Alan, "was somehow tax deductible."[33]

But as the years passed, what endeared Halpert to her acquaintances and clients gradually slipped away. She began lose her talent for friendship. Dorothy C. Miller, Holger Cahill's wife and the chief associate of Alfred H. Barr Jr., the director of the Museum of Modern Art, remarked in the year of Halpert's death, "Edith [was] a very curious enigma as a personality. . . . She was such a good person at the beginning, and in the end she didn't have a friend or a person who would work with her, and it was some sort of self-destructive element in her personality as I analyze it." When young, she was very good-looking, Miller observed, "and she could tell marvelous stories on herself. . . . Then in the middle '40s something began to happen. First she started dropping various artists from her gallery in a rather abrupt way. The gallery had been sort of a family group, as it were, and so these were battles. . . . In other words, the atmosphere began to be cloudy and very difficult. . . . We weren't friends anymore. And she slowly did this with everybody." Artists, Miller said, no longer liked her. She quarreled bitterly with one of her best-selling artists, Ben Shahn. Peggy Bacon, who departed for the Kraushaar Galleries, said of the Downtown, "It was an awfully nice gallery. I can't say nice things about Edith Halpert." Max Weber and Stuart Davis, also among her most respected artists, left the gallery.[34]

What started Halpert on her downward spiral was a flaming controversy over the works of William M. Harnett, the greatly talented nineteenth-century genre painter whom she, with only a little stretching of the truth, could be said to have discovered. Her promotion of Harnett began in 1935 when a young man from Philadelphia showed her a painting by the then forgotten artist with the thought that it might sell in her folk-art division. But Harnett was no folk artist. He was a highly skilled "magic realist" delineator of miscellaneous objects hanging from walls or heaped together on tables, and his ability was immediately apparent to Halpert. This first Harnett that she saw was titled *The Faithful Colt* and showed a pistol hanging from a nail on a rustic door. Halpert paid $75 for it, sold it to the Wadsworth Atheneum in Hartford, Connecticut, and looked for more paintings by the same artist. She was sensible enough to know, as she later said, that anyone who could paint so well must have painted more than one picture.[35] Supplied by runners (crafty freelance agents who make finds and bring them to the attention of dealers), a substantial number of works with the artist's signature made their way to the Downtown Gallery. In 1939 Halpert offered a special exhibition of them, which she called "Nature-Vivre." Presumably what she meant by this phrase was *nature vivante,* as opposed to *nature morte*, French for "still life."

Nelson Rockefeller, Alfred Barr, and the noted restorer Sheldon Keck were buyers, and through Rockefeller's generosity the Museum of Modern Art acquired one of the paintings. Halpert could not have imagined that she would eventually become a victim of her own success. That, however, is what happened. After the Second World War, Alfred Frankenstein, the art critic of the *San Francisco Chronicle,* made the discovery that many of the paintings signed with Harnett's name were in fact not his at all. Those with a painterly technique that Frankenstein described as "soft" proved to be the work of John Frederick Peto. Among them, embarrassingly, was *Old Scraps,* Rockefeller's gift to the Modern.[36]

Halpert could not accept Frankenstein's findings, despite the fact that they were backed by solid evidence, including Peto's genuine signatures hidden under the forged signatures of Harnett. According to Dorothy Miller, Halpert believed that Frankenstein's intention was to attack her personally. Holger Cahill tried to convince Halpert that if she had sold the Peto paintings innocently, the fact that they were not by Harnett scarcely mattered, since Peto was an equally impressive artist. He believed—correctly as it turned out—that the owners would elect to keep the paintings if she offered to take them back and refund what had been paid for them. Of the effect of this sorry affair on Halpert, Miller later said, "I think she [went] a little bit crazy progressively, slowly, very slowly, as she went on living."[37] Halpert went so far as to try to persuade the Guggenheim Foundation to rescind the fellowship under which Frankenstein had conducted his research. Eventually Frankenstein came to believe that Halpert herself had been a party to the covering over of some of Peto's signatures, but he was wise enough not to express that libelous opinion publicly in her lifetime.[38]

Charles Alan, whose tenure at the Downtown began after the Second World War, for years entertained the hope that Halpert would make him her partner. When it became clear to him at last, in 1952, that this would never happen, he broke away to found a gallery of his own. So did another member of her staff, Lee Nordness, in 1958. Alan took many of Halpert's artists with him, including Lawrence, Levine, and George L. K. Morris. Several of the young crew of artists she had recently gathered also defected eventually to his gallery.

But along with all these dark and stressful events, the postwar years brought Halpert some moments in the sun. In 1946 the State Department spent $49,000 on American art with the intention of sending two traveling exhibitions abroad, one to Europe and the other to Latin America. Twenty-three of the seventy-nine works came from the Downtown Gallery. This endeavor went under the name "Advancing American Art," a phrase that might be interpreted in two ways. The participle "advancing" suggested that American art was continuing to develop in both technique and the variety of its themes, but it could also be taken to mean "advertising" or "promoting," which is surely what the shows would have done for American art had the State Department's plans proceeded as intended. But in the cold war climate of the late 1940s, this high-minded wish to display the products of American creativity in the capital cities of less fortunate nations was doomed to fail.[39]

The first stops on the tour, Prague and Port-au-Prince, Haiti, were as far as the exhibitions went. Cries of outrage against the expenditure of public funds on modern art, which was perceived as being tainted with communism, echoed through both houses of Congress, and the conservative press was quick to join in the shouting. General George C. Marshall, to whom was credited the plan for the rehabilitation of Europe through infusions of American cash and credit, promised that there would be "no more taxpayers' money for modern art." In turn, the art community protested heatedly. Halpert, cleverly tossing the ball back into the opponents' court, declared, "We will have communism in art if Congress can control what we paint, and free and individual expression is stifled." But such arguments got nowhere. Even Harry Truman inveighed against them. He had no more liking for modern art with its distorted, out-of-drawing figures than did Congress. The art was sold off at bargain prices. None of the show's disparagers seems to have cried out against the loss to public funds created by the sale.

Thirteen years later, in 1959, under a Republican administration and without Congressional complaint, the United States Information Agency sent Moscow an American exhibition that included art both old and new along with much other evidence of native enterprise and inventiveness, including a model home with a kitchen in which Vice President Richard Nixon and the Russian premier Nikita S. Khrushchev held an impromptu "debate." Halpert selected the art and traveled to Moscow with the show. Although she received official praise, her effort initially did not meet with favor on all sides. Eisenhower had expressed disapproval of Jack Levine's *Welcome Home,* a satirical imaginary portrait of a general returned from the wars. Nevertheless, Halpert insisted that it be included, and through the intervention of Nelson Rockefeller and C. Douglas Dillon she succeeded in preventing its removal. Halpert's conservative Connecticut neighbors, however, were incensed by her daring to contradict the wishes of the President. She felt so threatened by them that she asked the local police to set up a guard around her house.[40]

Halpert's personal collection also won kudos for her. Selections from it were exhibited at Washington's Corcoran Gallery in 1960 and at the Santa Barbara Museum of Art in 1963. Although this confirmation of her judgment can only have given her pleasure, it could not stem the downhill drift of her life. Toward the end, Frankenstein made an effort to see her. She agreed to a meeting, but let him cool his heels so long that finally he gave up and walked out.[41] In her last five years as she conducted her business in the claustrophobic atmosphere of the basement of the Ritz Tower, Halpert became ever more difficult and remote. She would be remembered as a potent force in American art, but the lustrous image she had once projected was lost.

10

PAST MASTERS AND OLD MASTERS

The death of Uncle Henry Duveen in January 1919 left total control of Duveen Brothers in the iron grip of his eager nephew Joe. Henry's principal heir was his son Geoffrey, who was then working in the New York gallery. Seeking to avoid liquidation of the firm's assets, Joe, with the concurrence of his brother Louis, bought him out.[1] That same year, 1919, saw Joe on the royal honors list; he was knighted by George V, as his father had been in 1911. Joel died shortly after receiving the honor; Sir Joseph—still plain Joe to most of the art world—had in store two more decades of hyperactive salesmanship after receiving his. Toward the end of his inaugural year as chief, Duveen Brothers became the first firm ever to transport a work of art by air, from London to Paris.[2] This daring act dramatized the optimistic outlook of the new leader, who was already on his way to becoming a living legend.

A part of that legend was the measureless well of energy that sustained him. A *New Yorker* profile from 1928, when he was at the peak of his physical power, says much in little:

> This patron of monarchies and republics is of middle height and sturdy build, with black hair, scintillating black eyes and a ruddy complexion. He is quick in movement and speech and has a quick, hearty laugh. Sir Joseph has, too, the faculty of charging up other people with his own excess vitality. Some people resent being loaded up with energy without their consent, but this is not the fault of Sir Joseph. It is something that he cannot help.[3]

Along with his vitality, Joe possessed a rough-edged kind of affability, and he knew how to use it. Kenneth Clark, who, as director of the National Gallery in London, saw much of him in the 1930s, described him as "irresistible."[4] Clients found him bubbly and amusing. With flattery and cajolery and an unmatched ability to supply just the art that a client desired—and also the ability to create that desire—Joe had no trouble ingratiating himself with some of the wealthiest and most art-avid millionaires in the world.

In winning or keeping his clients, Duveen often showed little respect for the integrity of works in his inventory. He sometimes would order so far-reaching a "restoration" of a canvas that little of the original remained. Nor did he balk at having a painting prettified if in a portrait, say, a wrinkle or a double chin deprived the subject of the youth and beauty that a prospective buyer might be presumed to require in his acquisitions.[5] But he knew his clients and knew, too, that it was far less difficult to deal in the beautiful than in the grotesque—as it still is, although no longer will a self-respecting dealer alter an original image. But Joe wanted to be, and indeed was, the leading art salesman of his age, and in his stride toward that goal he took whatever means suggested themselves. When hopeful of snaring a buyer, he would occasionally forgo his usual sky-high markup and sell a work at cost. By such tactics are addictions created.

There were, of course, dissenters to the prevailing favorable opinion of him held by collectors. One dissenter was Paul Mellon, whose father, Andrew W. Mellon, was one of the nation's leading patrons of the arts, as Paul himself would become in time. "Duveen was thought to have great personal charisma," Paul Mellon wrote in his memoirs,

> but I regarded him with distaste and thought of him as an impossibly bumptious and opinionated ass who took advantage of any opportunity to burnish his image and further his own interests. I have never been entirely able to undestand how Father, normally a sound judge of character, should have fallen under his spell, although I suppose one must bear in mind that Duveen had by that time made himself one of the very few sources of fine pictures.[6]

Another individual with a profound distaste for Joe was Bernard Berenson. Berenson, as we have seen, commenced an association with Duveen Brothers with his cataloguing of the Hainauer collection and his examination of the Italian items in the Kann collection. That the association proved lucrative to Berenson could be observed in the high style of living that he and his wife, Mary, enjoyed. The close relationship between him and the firm began in 1909, when Berenson was called on by Joe to lure Benjamin Altman, whose taste in art was largely confined to the Dutch school, into the market for the art of the Italian Renaissance. Despite personal doubts and the advice of two acquaintances, John Graver Johnson of Philadelphia and Henry Walters of Baltimore, to shy away from the house of Duveen, Berenson accepted the challenge. Altman bought two sculptures and five paintings, and Berenson pocketed a quarter of Duveen Brothers' profits on the sales. These negotiations with Altman lasted through the first half of 1912, after which the association was formalized with a contract allowing Berenson a quarter of the profits of all items of Italian origin sold by the firm.[7] All sales of works bought by the firm on his advice were recorded in a ledger known as the "X" book. Despite the fact that he and Joe disliked and distrusted each another their arrangement lasted, with modifications as to Berenson's fees, until 1937, two years before Joe's death.[8]

Born in the Jewish pale of Lithuanian Russia, Berenson was brought to the United States in his boyhood by his father. He was educated at Harvard, where he proved to be a scholar of such distinction that in his senior year, 1886–87, he could entertain a legitimate hope of receiving a grant that would enable him to visit Europe after graduation. It was his vague notion at that time to pursue a career in literature, as either a critic or a historian. His application was supported by a number of his professors, but was unsuccessful for lack of an endorsement by Professor Charles Eliot Norton, with whom he had studied art history. Nevertheless, with $700 provided by generous friends and acquaintances—

including among the acquaintances Isabella Stewart Gardner, an art enthusiast indulged by her wealthy husband, Jack—he was able to make the journey abroad. Once in Europe, he found himself drawn to art, especially the art of the Italian Renaissance, and in its seductive glow the thought of becoming a bellettrist faded from his mind.[9]

Drawing on fresh sums of money raised for him by his favorite sister, Senda, or lent to him by admirers or given outright by Mrs. Gardner, the young Berenson could manage a life abroad considerably above the poverty level when the original purse of $700 was gone. And soon there was another way of making ends meet: by acting as adviser to Mrs. Gardner as she built an outstanding collection to fill her palatial Boston dwelling, Fenway Court. Berenson found it possible to live in modest comfort by taking commissions on sales of paintings that he ferreted out for her. In time, he would have other clients as well as "Mrs. Jack." With the publication of six books on Italian art between 1894 and 1901, along with a sheaf of essays, he established himself as a foremost connoisseur while still a young man. Other books and essays were to follow in a seemingly endless flow. Although he frequently returned to the United States for visits during his long life, he became a confirmed expatriate while still in his twenties. The great art was abroad, the great wealth was at home; by channeling European paintings and sculpture into eager hands back in the States, he could do quite well for himself. The "squillionaires," as he and his wife called the very rich, were ever eager to buy.

Yet because both Berensons lacked self-restraint when it came to spending money, their lives were never free of anxious moments until the Duveen offer came along. But the arrangement, although it provided liberation from financial constraints, was morally and intellectually punishing. It was, in fact, a Faustian agreement with ultimately a heavy price: a loss of self-esteem as Berenson began to recognize that assisting a dealer, in effect becoming a dealer himself, compromised his integrity as a connoisseur. Armand Lowengard, Joe's nephew and a member of the firm, resembled Joe in having no illusions about Berenson's character. With apparent pleasure he told another of his uncles, René Gimpel, that Berenson once remarked to an antique dealer named Bauer, "A man as scholarly as yourself shouldn't be a dealer; it's horrible to be a dealer," only to be told in reply, "Between you and me there's no great difference. I'm an intellectual dealer and you're a dealing intellectual."[10] Berenson was stung.

Although Berenson's activities on behalf of Duveen Brothers troubled him and have frequently been called into question, he could be pressed just so far. One occasion on which he refused to be manipulated occurred in 1922 after the death of William Salomon, a collector who had made many purchases from the firm, although even here Berenson's motives may have been mixed. Salomon's heirs decided to put the collection, which included many Italian paintings, up for auction, but Maurice Brockwell, a critic who was formerly Berenson's secretary, disallowed the firm's attribution of two paintings, one supposedly by Bernardino Luini and the other, about which he had been in touch with Berenson, supposedly by Botticelli. The Botticelli had been purchased by the firm on the recommendation of Osvald Sirén, a Swedish expert whom Berenson distrusted and loathed. Joe, foreseeing trouble, dispatched his associate Edward Fowles to Berlin, where at the moment Berenson was staying with Nicky Mariano, his secretary-companion. Fowles's mission was to wring a confirmation of the "Botticelli" from him. Berenson made it clear that he had had only a fleeting glance at the painting while at dinner in Salomon's house. He would not go beyond a statement that, as he wrote to his wife, it was "not by Botticelli but might be by Jacopo del Sallajo, whose better works, until not long ago, were frequently ascribed to Botticelli himself." When Duveen, not willing to give up hope of a better attribution, wrote to Berenson, Mary replied bluntly that it was "close to Sellajo" and that the "Luini" was "obviously a Giampietrino." Fowles, who perhaps was not aware of the depth of Berenson's contempt for Sirén, believed that Berenson held back on the "Botticelli" only because it had been bought on Sirén's advice and that therefore Berenson had received nothing from the sale. Although that may not have been true, Fowles in his history of the firm very firmly declares that Berenson, after writing his letter about the painting, told him, "Don't forget to put it in the 'X' book." One way or another, Berenson would get something out of the painting. In fairness to the firm, it should be pointed out that Salomon's Italian paintings, although perhaps not the products of the hands to which Duveen Brothers had assigned them, were of more than passable quality. Hoping to avoid the embarrassment of the exposure that might arise from an auction, Joe bought them back en bloc from the heirs. Eventually they found homes in museums and private collections.[11]

Berenson's break with the firm in 1937 was precipitated by Joe's heavy-headed attempt to persuade him to identify as a Giorgione an *Adoration of the Shepherds* whose authorship had vexed him for years. He viewed it as conceivably an early Titian and was enraged by the pressure put upon him, in the form of urgent telephone calls and letters from

Fowles, to pronounce it anything else. Joe had bought the painting from Lord Allendale for the equivalent of $300,000 and knew, of course, that as a Giorgione, it would command a much higher price than it would as a Titian, whose works were in greater supply. In 1938, without Berenson's collaboration, it went to Samuel Kress as a Giorgione. Two decades later, Berenson, having second or perhaps third or fourth thoughts, declared it *partially* a Giorgione, but completed by Titian.[12] It is now in the National Gallery, Washington, where it is exhibited as a Giorgione.

The Duveens were not the first dealers with whom Berenson did business, nor were they the last. Before 1912 he either had been consulted by or had bought art for clients from the Agnew, Colnaghi, and Dowdeswell & Dowdeswell galleries of London; Eugene Glaenzer and Company of New York and Paris; and Böhler and Steinmeyer of Munich. After signing the agreement with Duveen Brothers, he took fees from most of these dealers and also from the Kleinberger, Knoedler, Seligmann, and Wildenstein galleries of New York and Paris; René Gimpel of Paris; and Arthur Sulley of London.[13] After his death, I Tatti, his villa near Florence, went to Harvard as a center for the study of the art of the Italian Renaissance.

Before Joe became its undisputed leader, Duveen Brothers had already sold to Henry Clay Frick for his Fifth Avenue mansion eight panels by Boucher depicting the arts and sciences, four works by the same artist depicting the four seasons, Fragonard's *The Progress of Love* in eleven panels (for $1.25 million, the price Joe paid for them), four Gainsboroughs, a Frans Hals from the Kann collection, portraits by Reynolds and Romney, and much more, including costly furnishings.[14] Joe's attempt to sell Frick a van Dyck failed, however. It was a portrait of two young men with, as René Gimpel, Joe's brother-in-law reports, "strongly curved noses." Mrs. Frick told her husband that she couldn't bear to look at those Jewish noses, not knowing, apparently, that the two young men were the nephews of Charles I of England.[15] The painting might have made an honorable companion to the eight van Dycks Frick bought from other dealers.

Benjamin Altman remained a constant buyer, as did Henry E. Huntington and his wife Arabella. Among Joe's other steady customers were the financiers Jules Bache and Andrew Mellon, the industrialist P. A. B. Widener, and Samuel Kress, the founder of a chain of five-and-ten-cent stores. Once these possessors of great wealth were shown the firm's rich holdings, they were in Duveen's hands for life. To Bache alone Joe sold forty masterpieces.[16]

But soon after acquiring his position of dominance in the firm, Joe, in what may have been a foolish effort to establish himself as a connoisseur as well as a salesman, found himself in a legal battle. Andrée Hahn, a woman born in France but living in the United States as the wife of a First World War serviceman, owned a painting, *La Belle Ferronnière* (the beautiful headband), which she believed to be by Leonardo da Vinci. The Louvre, as it happened, also owned a canvas representing the same image and exhibited it as a Leonardo, although not all authorities agreed with that identification. When Hahn let it be known that she had had an offer of $250,000 for her painting from the Kansas City Art Institute, the New York *World* asked Joe for his opinion of it. He had not seen it, but that did not stop him from pronouncing it a copy of the painting in the Louvre. As might have been expected, Hahn and the museum's board were alike troubled by Joe's statement, Hahn so much so that she determined to sue for $500,000 on the charge of slander. Her lawyer, the memorably named Hyacinth Ringrose, confided to Edward Fowles, who then was in charge of the Duveen firm's Paris branch, that the suit was not to be taken too seriously. Nevertheless, the hostilities dragged on for years, with S. Lawrence Miller, a sharper lawyer than Ringrose, ultimately in charge of Hahn's affairs. As usual, Joe was represented by Louis S. Levy. With Joe's contention that the Hahn painting was a copy supported by a battery of eleven experts, including Roger Fry, the former director of the Metropolitan Museum, and the inevitable Bernard Berenson, the suit came to trial in New York in February 1929. Hahn hoped that by proving the Louvre's painting to be a copy, she could establish the legitimacy of hers. Matters were uneasy from the start because of the fact that although Berenson had earlier questioned the authenticity of the Louvre's painting, in an examination of the witnesses in Paris in 1923 he declared that he now took it to be the work of the master. Under questioning by Ringrose at that time, he was forced to admit that he was being paid by Joe.[17]

Miller, an aggressive litigator, told the courtroom at the outset that Duveen had a "stranglehold" on art. From that point on, the behavior of the opposing attorneys and Duveen himself became increasingly unrestrained. The judge, naturally offended by the verbal free-for-all taking place in his courtroom, tried to hold matters in check, but with little success. The truth, according to Fowles, was that Duveen enjoyed lawsuits. He had at least ten of them over the years, including two others for $500,000, and was having a good time with this one.[18]

The trial dragged on for a month and ended unsatisfactorily for both sides when the jury split nine to three in Hahn's favor. The judge ordered a new trial, but in 1930 Duveen, made anxious by the Wall Street crash and perhaps foreseeing defeat, circumvented the order by making an out-of-court settlement of $60,000.[19] Meanwhile, in the middle of the charges and countercharges, he had been spared another trial when Joseph Demotte, a restorer and authority on Gothic art, was accidentally shot and killed in a wood by a hunter in 1923 before his $500,000 suit for libel against Duveen could commence. Duveen had declared that an enamel claimed by Demotte to date from the thirteenth century was a modern creation. Expert opinion had mounted against Duveen's assertion, and much later, in 1929, the enamel was indeed proved on metallurgical evidence to be genuine.[20]

The Huntingtons, Henry and Arabella, were among Duveen's favorite clients, as, considering the number of their acquisitions from him, they deserved to be. With his great fortune gathered from railroads, streetcar lines, and Los Angeles real estate, and with the credit gladly extended to him by Duveen, Huntington could afford virtually whatever works of art suited his fancy. Included among them was Thomas Gainsborough's *Blue Boy,* then and now one of the most famous of all British paintings, which he bought from Duveen in 1922. Huntington had long admired Gainsborough's art. In 1901 he bought from the Schaus gallery prints after three of the artist's paintings: *The Blue Boy, The Pink Boy,* and *Mrs. Siddons as the Tragic Muse*. But these reproductions of the master's work did not satisfy him for long. He was in search of the real thing on canvas, and in 1911 he found it at Duveen Brothers in the form of three great Gainsborough portraits: *Edward, 2nd Viscount Ligonier, Penelope, Viscountess Ligonier,* and *Julia, Lady Petre.* In 1912 he added a fourth: *Anne, Duchess of Cumberland*.[21] But *The Blue Boy,* that prize of prizes, remained for another decade in the hands of its longtime owner, the Duke of Westminster.

Huntington had talked about the painting with Duveen. He was not the first American collector to covet it. In 1896 Berenson, acting as adviser to Isabella Stewart Gardner as she built her collection at Fenway Court, apprised her of a rumor that the duke might be willing to part with it. She told him to try for it in her behalf. Her top figure, $150,000, proved inadequate, however, and the painting remained in its ducal home.[22] But years later, in 1921, Joe heard another rumor, that the duke was in need of cash. Knowing of Huntington's admiration for *The Blue Boy,* he made a successful bid for it along with two other Gainsboroughs: *The Cottage Door* and *Mrs. Siddons as the Tragic Muse*. Huntington rose to the bait. The price he paid for *The Blue Boy* was $728,000; it was the costliest painting in his collection. Before sending it to its new home in California, Joe had the painting cleaned and revarnished, returning the youth's raiment to its original blue, which smoke and grime had long since rendered green.[23] With Huntington's permission, he exhibited it at London's National Gallery and at Duveen Brothers in New York. Later *The Cottage Door* and *Mrs. Siddons* followed it to San Marino.

Twelve years after his death in 1939, Joe became a celebrity all over again when the *New Yorker* published a series of biographical essays about him by S. N. Behrman, the popular author of glossily mounted, star-studded comedies of manners. This came about after Behrman mentioned to William Shawn, the *New Yorker*'s editor, that he had seen a foolish panegyric on Duveen written by Louis S. Levy,[24] perhaps to make use of the time on his hands provided by his disbarment from practice in the federal courts in 1939 and the state courts in 1940.[25] Shawn, amused by Behrman's comments on Levy's writing, commissioned Behrman to write on Duveen for the magazine. Duveen was a natural subject for Behrman, whose dramatic protagonists were almost invariably rich, independent, well connected, and in happy possession of Duveen-like panache. In 1952 the essays were gathered into a book, *Duveen,* and published by Random House. It would be a pleasure to say that this brief, delightful volume, which reads like light fiction, provided an accurate portrait of its clever and influential subject. The trouble, however, is that parts of the book *are* light fiction. To get closer to the truth, although not always down to bedrock, it is necessary to turn to the reminiscences of Edward Fowles, who, strangely enough, is not included among the twenty-eight men and women whose recollections of the dealer Behrman sought.

According to Behrman, once when Huntington and Duveen were sailing to Europe on the same ship, Huntington looked at a reproduction of *The Blue Boy* in his suite and asked Duveen what it might cost if it were for sale. Duveen, Behrman tells us, replied that it might never be available at any price. But when Huntington, obviously interested, asked what Duveen thought it would cost if ever it were for sale, he offered the opinion that it might go for about $600,000. Although this was more than Huntington had ever paid for a painting, he told Duveen (according to Behrman), "I might see my way clear to paying that much."[26] Not so, says Fowles, who knew that Duveen, having heard of Westminster's financial worry and aware of Huntington's ingrained admiration for Gainsborough, had all along hoped to arrange a transaction between the two.

Another Behrman tale refuted by Fowles concerns an effort supposedly made in 1920 by a consortium of dealers including Duveen, Wildenstein, Seligman, Stevenson Scott, and the Knoedler gallery, whose head then was Charles Henschel, to persuade Henry Ford to become a collector. As Behrman tells it, the group, hoping that Ford would make a selection of works from their inventories, bankrolled the publication of three handsome volumes illustrating their finest wares in full color, took them to Michigan and offered them to Ford as a gift. The Master of Dearborn was delighted to receive so sumptuous a present and thanked them courteously for it. But to the astonishment and sorrow of the dealers, he saw no difference between the illustrations in the books and the paintings themselves. With the books to look at, he said, why buy the paintings? But Fowles, always the wet blanket, insists that Joe had no part in such a scheme and that if any dealer had ever tried to woo Ford in so extravagant a manner, it was Francis Kleinberger, the Paris-based dealer in old masters who had opened a New York branch in 1909.[27]

There is more. In his memoirs, Fowles recalled that in 1921 the Paris office of Duveen Brothers received Monet's *The Japanese Fan,* a full-length portrait of the artist's wife, from the collection of Philip Lehman, whose dining room it had graced. Since Duveen Brothers did not deal in such recent art, Fowles did not understand why Joe had shipped it to him. Not until visiting Lehman some time later did he learn that Joe had swapped a fifteenth-century French tapestry for it. Why? Fowles does not say. The firm was stuck with the painting for some thirty years, presumably because collectors did not go to Duveen Brothers for Impressionist art. It went finally to the Boston Museum of Fine Arts, where, a gloriously rich painting, it was to become a favorite of visitors. In Behrman's *Duveen,* the story takes a different tone. Duveen, Behrman says, was disturbed to discover the Monet when dining in the house of a client (not named)—disturbed because its presence suggested that this collector might be moving away from the old masters to more recent art. But, according to Behrman, Joe quickly came up with a solution to the problem: He offered to buy it for himself. The sum he mentioned satisfied the collector, and the two cut a deal. Duveen then took the Monet home and put it in his basement, from which—again, according to Behrman—it never emerged. "I didn't want that fellow buying modern pictures," Behrman says that he said. "There are too many of them." Although we are obliged to accept Fowles's tale and reject Behrman's, the Duveen bag of tricks could well have included such a ploy.[28]

In his fifties and sixties Duveen made several coups as grand as the

Hainauer and Kann buys of his early years in the trade. The first of these was his purchase of the collection of Robert H. Benson, a merchant banker of London. This was thought to include the finest group of Italian paintings, 114 of them, in private hands in Europe. The price paid by the firm was $2.5 million.[29] At the outset of the Depression Joe made an even more costly purchase: the collection of Gustave Dreyfus of Paris, for which the asking price was reported to be $5 million. This collection also consisted of Italian works, including a terra-cotta bust ascribed to Leonardo da Vinci.[30] Both collections were shipped to New York. No works from either were earmarked for specific buyers or had been requested by them; Joe knew that eventually his collectors would sweep them away. Andrew Mellon took many works from the Dreyfus collection, and others went to John D. Rockefeller Jr.[31]

Undercutting his pleasure in these successes was a severe disappointment that Joe suffered in 1931. The Soviet Union, acutely in need of foreign money to implement its massive effort at industrialization, had let it be known to the West in 1928 that certain of its national treasures, some from collections amassed by Russian rulers in the distant past and some from private collections confiscated after the revolution, could be had for prices matching their distinction, provided the transactions were handled discreetly. An agency, the Antikvariat, was established, and foreign offers were considered. Joe, Edward Fowles, and Armand Lowengard traveled to Leningrad and Moscow in 1931, taking along a list of desirable Italian paintings prepared for them by Berenson.

Although the journey itself was pleasant enough, at least as described by Fowles, and the Russians were polite, the trio came away with only furniture and art objects formerly belonging to the Romanovs. Andrew Mellon had preempted five of the items on Berenson's list, Botticelli's *Adoration of the Magi,* a Perugino *Crucifixion,* Raphael's *Alba Madonna* and *St. George and the Dragon,* and Titian's *Venus with a Mirror,* and the Antikvariat was apparently unwilling to allow them to purchase any of the others. In his memoirs, John Walker, the first chief curator of the National Gallery in Washington and later its director, described this debacle as the worst failure of Duveen's career. He surmises that it was Joe's love of publicity that set the Russians against him.[32] Here, however, the not always reliable Colin Simpson, writing with access to the Duveen papers in the Metropolitan Museum, may be a superior source. According to his account, Duveen made an offer of $25 million for nine paintings before Mellon made his purchase but rescinded it on being informed that he was to be appointed a trustee of Britain's National

Gallery. The reason, again according to Simpson, was that he had been advised that the royal family and the government would not be pleased if he were to deal with the Soviets, who had assassinated the royal family's relations, the Romanovs.[33]

It was with Mellon that Joe experienced his last great triumph. Since the early 1920s the voracious collector had entertained the notion of establishing a national gallery in the United States on the order of England's National Gallery, one of the great museums of the world, and Duveen was determined that it should house works from his inventory. Mellon and Duveen met in 1919 at the home of Frick, but saw nothing more of one another until 1921, when they met again, this time at Claridge's in London, where Mellon was staying and where Duveen had a suite. Duveen had enlisted—for a fee, and no doubt a substantial one—the aid of Mellon's valet for information on Mellon's comings and goings. When informed by his own valet, who had had the word from Mellon's, that Mellon was about to go out, Duveen moved quickly and managed to pop into the elevator that was carrying Mellon to the ground floor. After an introduction, or reintroduction, Duveen suggested that the two visit the National Gallery, with the intention of reminding Mellon that he had in his stock paintings equal in greatness to those on view.[34]

That, at any rate, is Behrman's story, and the fact that it is accepted by John Walker lends it a degree of credibility. Duveen was ready with a similar trick up his sleeve when plans jelled for the National Gallery. As secretary of the treasury under Harding, Coolidge, and Hoover, Mellon maintained an apartment in Washington, and kept it after leaving that post. Duveen, bold and wily as ever although suffering from the colon cancer that would soon end his life, took an apartment in the same building and filled it with works he was hopeful of placing in the National Gallery when the plan to erect it should become a reality. It was a venue not only for paintings but for sculptures, which Duveen intended to convince Mellon were as essential to the gallery as paintings; never mind that England's National Gallery collected paintings only. He entertained Mellon in the apartment, gave him a key, and let him know that the works of art and the rooms were there for his enjoyment.[35] Acceptance of Mellon's great gift to the nation was authorized by Congress and President Roosevelt in 1937. Duveen's sculptures joined the paintings in Mellon's collection and went with them into the National Gallery when it opened to the public in 1941.

In addition to the triumphs of salesmanship that Duveen achieved in his last years, he also received new honors from Britain. In 1927 he was made a baronet, and in 1933 he was elevated to the peerage as Lord Duveen of Millbank, London's Millbank being the location of the Tate Gallery. These honors came to him because of his benefactions to his native country in the form of additions to its museums: a gallery for Italian art at the National Gallery, an extension of the National Portrait Gallery, a gallery at the British Museum to house the Elgin Marbles, galleries for modern art at the Tate, and a sculpture wing also for the Tate. In London he served on the board of the National Gallery from 1929 to 1936, but a second term, which he fully expected, was denied him at the intervention of Kenneth Clark, then the director. Clark had been put off by Joe's hostility toward works submitted by rival dealers and also believed that when he looked at works submitted for sale by private owners "his professional instincts were aroused"—in other words, that he would like to sell them to the National Gallery himself.[36] But other prestigious appointments came his way. Although much of Duveen Brothers' trade was in portraits, from 1933 until his death Joe was a trustee of the National Portrait Gallery, with no problems arising over a possible conflict of interest. He also served on the board of the Museum of Modern Art in New York. With the Modern, conflict of interest could not possibly become a problem, since Duveen did not deal in the art that the museum collected.

Duveen succumbed to his illness in 1939, having kept it at bay for twelve of the busiest years of his life. He left 45 percent of Duveen Brothers to Fowles, 45 percent to his nephew Arman Lowengard, 10 percent to his aide Bertram Boggis, and 10 percent to the firm's comptroller, John Allen. With the expiration of the forty-year lease on the Fifth Avenue land in 1952, Fowles and Boggis transferred the business to a town house on East Seventy-ninth Street. At the deaths of the other owners (Lowengard died in 1944, Boggis in 1958) Fowles negotiated the purchase of their shares.[37] He maintained the firm until 1964, when, still hardy at seventy-eight and with another seven years remaining to him, he sold his entire inventory to Norton Simon, the California manufacturer. Thus was brought to an end the most successful, most publicized, most envied, and most notorious art firm of its time.

11

MASTERMINDING THE TRADE

When Lord Duveen of Millbank was in his prime—a prime that he sustained even after a severely debilitating illness overtook him—his firm was the unquestioned leader in the old-master trade. He knew it, and so did his rivals, to whom, as to everyone else, he was "Joe." But the rivals, of whom there were many, not only in New York, London, and Paris, but in Amsterdam, Berlin, Munich, and elsewhere on the continent of Europe, also prospered in Joe's golden age, and it does not seem to have occurred to him to wish them harm.

In at least one way, competition benefited Duveen, because if a rival firm introduced a rich man or woman to art, he could step in and supply works from his own inventory to feed the new collector's addiction. When his free-spending client Henry Clay Frick introduced him to Andrew W. Mellon in 1919, and told him, "This man will some day be a great collector," Joe knew that the time would come, even though from the onset of his collecting habit in 1899 until the day of his first purchase from Duveen, Mellon had bought art only from M. Knoedler and Company.[1] Of all the rivals of Duveen Brothers, Knoedler's was the most powerful. But close behind was Wildenstein, a firm of immense wealth and power that outlasted Duveen Brothers and was still dealing in the old masters long after Knoedler's abandoned them in favor of contemporary art.

In 1946, in celebration of the centennial of the Knoedler firm, Charles Henschel, its head since the retirement of Roland Knoedler, his uncle, in 1927, published a pamphlet recounting its history.[2] He was proud of the firm's past and very pleased with its circumstances of the moment. The New York premises (there were others, in London and Paris, and for a short time in the 1930s there had been one in Chicago) were located just off Fifth Avenue on East Fifty-seventh Street, the street that had become the center of the art trade. The gallery had shifted gradually to sites farther and farther uptown, following the progression of the city's mercantile enterprise: to Fifth Avenue and Twenty-second Street in 1869, to Fifth and Thirty-fourth in 1895, to Fifth and Forty-sixth in 1911, and to 14 East Fifty-seventh in 1925.

Along the way, the firm's clientele had steadily increased, and so had the prices of the art it sold. Among the firm's customers in its first quarter century were John Taylor Johnston, the first president of the Metropolitan Museum; Collis P. Huntington, head of the Union Pacific Railroad; and the philanthropist Catherine Lorillard Wolfe, whose substantial collection went to the Metropolitan after her death in 1887. Through his patronage of the gallery, Johnston formed a close friendship with Roland Knoedler and not only bought from him for his own collection but saw much of him socially in both New York and Paris.[3] In 1895 the firm opened its Paris branch and followed this with a London branch in 1908. In between, in 1897, Knoedler's opened another American branch, in Pittsburgh, to take advantage of the collecting desires of Henry Frick, Andrew Mellon, and other local magnates. This branch remained in business for ten years, under the guidance of Charles S. Carstairs, who came to the firm in 1895 from the Philadelphia gallery of Charles Haseltine. For a time, these optimistic moves gave the Knoedlers four venues to the two, in London and New York, of the Duveens. Not until 1912, when Joe built his new gallery in the Place Vendôme, were the firms even again.

But Roland Knoedler waited a while before emulating Duveen Brothers in the important matter of dealing in the old masters. Until the turn of the century, under his guidance the inventory of the firm had been made up of contemporary American and European art, as it had been under his father. According to Henschel, it was with the arrival of Carstairs that Knoedler's began to widen its trade to include older art. Given the wealth and the keen collector's instinct of Mellon, Frick, and P. A. B. Widener, to name only three of the wealthy art enthusiasts of the turn of the century, it was inevitable that Knoedler's should tap into that market. The firm's first sale of an old-master painting was not, however, to a private collector, but to the Boston Museum of Fine Art, which bought Velásquez's *Don Balthazar and His Dwarf* in 1901.[4]

For the next seventy-five years, old-master paintings were a Knoedler staple. The chocolate-brown plush decor favored by the firm provided a luxurious foil for the costly works on view. In 1907 the gallery achieved its first major coup in the old-master field by acquiring seven superb Van Dyck portraits from the Cattaneo family of Genoa. Questions arose in the press over the means whereby these great works, which might have been declared national treasures had their existence been known to the Italian government, were spirited out of Italy (allegedly in an automobile by night), but the matter remained at the level of a mere to-do, not a scandal. Three of the paintings went to P. A. B. Widener, who paid for them in part with twenty-three Barbizon paintings from his collection. Two others went to Frick.[5] Old-master drawings and prints were also available at Knoedler's. In the latter category, the firm's only serious rival was Frederick Keppel and Company.

After Colnaghi's of London landed Frick as a client in 1903, Otto Gutekunst and E. F. Deprez of that firm initiated an alliance with Knoedler's that enriched both firms by establishing Knoedler's as Colnaghi's principal contact with American collectors, among whom were (in addition to Frick) Benjamin Altman, Jules Bache, Charles Schwab, Widener, and the investment bankers Otto H. Kahn, Philip Lehman, Andrew Mellon, and J. P. Morgan, along with many other men of great wealth. This arrangement remained in force for the next forty years.[6]

As his father had been, Roland Knoedler was a good-natured, well-liked man. Measures of his popularity, along with the prestige of the firm, are evident in the frequent mentions of him in the press. It was front-page news in 1907 when a reporter discovered that for many years Roland had been secretly married to a French actress.[7] Since his father's death Roland had been the sole owner of the firm. After his retirement, the firm was bought by Henschel, Charles Carstairs, his son Carroll Carstairs, and the personable and talented Carman Messmore, who in

1898, at age sixteen, had taken a temporary job as a mailroom worker and before long found himself assisting in the development of the collections of some of the firm's most valued clients. At the time of the restructuring, Charles Carstairs and Henschel were named chairman of the board and president, respectively.[8] Carstairs died only months after assuming the chair, in July 1928. Henschel continued to head the firm until his death in 1956.

Henschel's single greatest achievement, and the most remarkable of the firm's entire history, was brokering the sale to Andrew Mellon of some of the greatest prizes among the paintings collected by the rulers of Russia from Catherine the Great to Alexander III—that is, from 1763 to 1894. Being an American, Henschel could not be daunted by the fear (such as reportedly possessed Duveen) of being passed over for a peerage for dealing with the Soviets.

The USSR had been conducting a mating dance with American collectors for over two years before Henschel's negotiations got under way. In 1927 a delegation of Russians approached the international dealer Germain Seligman in the firm's Paris gallery with an invitation to visit their country and examine its art, some of it confiscated from the collections of private owners after the revolution. Encouraged by the French government, Seligman made the difficult journey to Moscow. After a tedious interval during which he was shown minor items, he was taken to see a wealth of great paintings, sculptures, furniture, and rare objects of art, but was not told that this treasure was for sale.[9]

The following spring he was again visited by a group of Russians. To his astonishment, they proposed to send him the magnificent works of art and craft that he had seen in Moscow, and much more besides—trainloads of it, in fact. What to do with these holdings, whether to have them sold at auction or to display and sell them in his gallery, would be left entirely to his discretion. Although Seligman was excited, nothing came of this jaw-dropping proposition. The French government balked at the difficulty of providing the Soviets with legal protection from the suits for the repossession of their confiscated belongings that were certain to be instituted by the many Russian émigrés then residing in France.[10]

Next, in 1928 at roughly the same time as the grandiose offer made to Seligman, a syndicate of American dealers, whose composition is not known but may have included Duveen, was hopeful of taking advantage of the Russians' need for capital. The syndicate asked Dr. Armand Hammer, an American highly esteemed in Russia, to investigate the report that some of the holdings of the Hermitage, the museum that was the pride of Leningrad and indeed of the entire USSR, might be for sale. Although he possessed a medical degree, Hammer had abandoned the notion of practicing medicine after botching an abortion and causing the death of the patient, an act for which his physician father took the blame and the prison sentence.[11] But the title *Doctor* itself conferred prestige, of course, and he hung on to it all his life.

Hammer's brothers, Victor and Harry, were also involved in the projected deal with the Soviets. Hammer had become something of a hero to them for undertaking in 1921, when their country was gripped by famine, to ship them a million bushels of wheat in exchange for goods. But hero though he may have been, he was also a shrewd businessman who saw that the swap would pay him very well. By 1928 he had become a major figure in the business life of the USSR, as both importer and exporter and the representative there of Ford Motors and thirty-seven other American corporations, as well as the possessor of profitable concessions in asbestos mining and the manufacture of pencils in Russia. Since 1924 the Hammers had resided in Brown House, a vast Moscow mansion, which a grateful government made available to them.[12]

With his brother Victor, Hammer called on a man named Shapiro, the head of Antikvariat, the Soviet art-export commission, to inquire whether the report on the Russians' willingness to sell some of its treasures was true. Shapiro uttered a vehement denial but coyly added, "If your friends in America want to make offers, we are obliged to submit them to the proper authorities, and then whatever happens, happens."[13] In the hope that the syndicate would buy the *Benois Madonna* of Leonardo da Vinci for the Russians' price of $2.6 million, from which they would of course receive a commission, the Hammers had been in touch with Max Steurer, a New York lawyer who spoke for the syndicate. When Steurer could not come up with more than $2 million, the deal collapsed.[14]

But the Hammers profited nicely from other sources. They bought rare icons, tsarist china, examples of the products of Fabergé, the famed goldsmith and enamelist, and other works of applied art that, if not masterpieces on canvas, were nevertheless of value. In 1928, having been permitted to take their purchases out of Russia, they established a gallery, now the Hammer Gallery, in New York at which these collectibles were available to the public. Later the gallery would become a venue for the exhibition and sale of humdrum decorative paintings.

Interestingly, Steurer also had told the Hammers that if the $2 million offer were accepted, he would dispatch Berenson to Russia to examine the painting. This provided a hint or at least a suggestion that Duveen was involved. The Hammers failed, but their failure, along with the successful efforts of Calouste Gulbenkian, the head of the Iraq Petroleum Company and a passionate collector, to buy from the Hermitage smoothed the way for Knoedler's. In late 1929 and through the fall of 1930, the Antikvariat sold silver and major works of art by Giorgione, Rembrandt, Rubens, and others to Gulbenkian, who had won favor in Russia by arranging the marketing of Soviet oil abroad.[15]

Henschel heard of Gulbenkian's purchases and sensibly recognized that more might be forthcoming from the Hermitage. The head of Berlin's Matthiesen Gallery, M. Zatzenstein, who had an agent in Moscow, was his chief informant. Zatzenstein would have bought directly from the Antikvariat had he had the necessary capital. Without it, he turned first to Otto Gutekunst and Gus Meyer of Colnaghi's. But they too were short of funds, hence the move to bring Knoedler's into the negotiations. Henschel did not intend to be used by the Antikvariat. Even at the beginning of 1930, when these negotiations began, the Wall Street crash of late 1929 was already causing a downward slide of the economy. It was no time for speculation. On January 30 Henschel notified George Davey, his European representative, by letter that he had told Gutekunst "that we were prepared to buy a number of [works] provided we got the pictures that we wanted and not necessarily the pictures that they wanted to sell. My idea was that if we purchased about £500,000 [$2.5 million] worth, it would tempt them, and we could get some other pictures on assignment."[16] Mellon, as Knoedler's most eminent client, was the obvious target of these purchases. They could not have been made without his participation by way of a loan. Carman Messmore, the firm's frequent representative in negotiations with him, masterminded an agreement whereby Mellon authorized the firm to buy a group of paintings but did not promise unconditionally to take them all. On those he decided to keep he would pay the firm a commission of 25 percent of the price paid to the Antikvariat; those he might refuse were to be sold by the firm, and he was to be given 25 percent of Knoedler's profit on them.[17]

Henschel visited Leningrad, and, like other dealers who made the same journey, found his patience taxed by delays, discomfort, and hunger, but came away with an agreement to buy twenty-five paintings for something over $7 million. The transaction was completed in June 1930. Between April of that year and April 1931 Mellon bought twenty-one of the works for $6,654,053. Among them were four Rembrandts, two

Raphaels, four Van Dycks, a Botticelli, a Rubens, a Titian, and a Veronese. Henschel had bargained sharply, knowing of the Russians' need for dollars, but had paid a good price even so. As John Walker, the second director of the National Gallery, has suggested, Mellon himself may have had an ungenerous hand in the bargaining, not understanding that from no other source in the world could he acquire such great works of art as those taken from the walls of the Hermitage.[18]

Both Henschel and Mellon were reluctant to inform the press of the purchases, perhaps out of fear of a hostile reaction on the part of the public to a report of such a huge personal expenditure at a time of dire national distress. But rumors spread, all of which Mellon denied. *Art News* quoted him as saying that he had bought "no pictures whatsoever from Russian collections."[19] In 1934 the *Times* was moved to print on its front page the rumor that Mellon had paid $1.5 million for Raphael's *Alba Madonna* (in fact, he had paid more: $1,710,558), and to editorialize against such self-indulgence.[20] As usual, Mellon denied the charge. To a German art historian who wrote to congratulate him, he tersely replied, "I am not the owner of the painting in question."[21] Always taciturn, he took naturally to stonewalling when he himself was up against a wall.

Mellon's collection became a matter of national debate in the anxiety ridden 1930s. Three Republican presidents had honored him with the post of secretary of the treasury, but with the election of Roosevelt in 1932, he was no longer a power in Washington. Even before the election, in 1931 and again in 1932 Congressman Wright Patman of Texas attempted to bring impeachment proceedings against him on the grounds that in his appointed office he had been responsible for conditions that created the Depression. This was doomed to fail, but it resulted in Mellon's resignation. Immediately after he left the Treasury, President Hoover, not one to let a friend down, appointed him ambassador to England, a post that gave him a pleasant year abroad.

Mellon, as he may have expected, did not fare quite so well under the New Deal. The Internal Revenue Service sued him for somewhat more than $3 million allegedly owing on his 1931 income tax. He issued a stinging denial, but the IRS was not to be deterred. When the suit came to trial in 1935, he declared that the disputed monies had paid for paintings he had turned over to a trust for the national museum that he hoped eventually to create on the Mall in Washington. He had all along, since 1931, poured money into the trust and assigned many of his paintings to it. Henschel, Messmore, and Duveen testified in his behalf, with Duveen's testimony putting on the record the fact that he, too, had tried to buy art from the Soviets. With help from these men, his lawyer, and his staff, Mellon's arguments succeeded; in 1937 the Board of Tax Appeals found him innocent of any attempt at tax evasion. He did, however, owe money in back taxes and paid the government $668,000. *Art Digest* reported that during the trial he chewed gum "agitatively."[22]

Henschel made still other purchases from the Hermitage. In 1933 he bought Renoir's *A Waitress at Durval's Restaurant,* Cézanne's *Madame Cézanne in the Conservatory,* van Gogh's *Night Cafe,* and Degas's *Chanteuse Verte.* He first offered them to Albert Barnes, who was not interested. He next tried Stephen Clark, who took all four.[23] Henschel also bought the van Eyck diptych composed of *The Crucifixion* and *The Last Judgment,* which the firm then sold to the Metropolitan.

Another of Henschel's well-publicized transactions in the old-master trade was Knoedler's sale of consigned canvases from the estate of J. P. Morgan in 1935. One, a Ghirlandaio, went to Edsel Ford. The Metropolitan took two: a Rubens and a triptych by Lippo Lippi.[24] But Knoedler's was never without a stock of American, Barbizon, and French Impressionist art on hand also, along with items from most other schools. In the first two decades of the twentieth century the gallery offered, along with much more, the Pre-Raphaelite paintings of Edward Burne-Jones, pastels by Everett Shinn, sixteenth- and seventeenth-century miniatures, watercolors by John Singer Sargent and John Lafarge, the western art of Henry W. Ranger and Frederick Remington, the colorful, idiosyncratic oils of the American *saloniste* Florine Stettheimer, and even, in 1915, early Chinese paintings. And so it went; well beyond the midcentury mark, the gallery's offerings were a wide-ranging assortment of periods and styles. The exhibitions had in common only the fact that until the 1960s, no matter the school, all the art was representational. An exception was the memorial exhibition in 1918 of the work of the American Dadaist Morton L. Schamberg, who had died in the flu epidemic of that year. Yet Schamberg's art, abstract renderings of machinery for the most part, had at least a toe-hold in the realist tradition, as in fact did virtually all the creations of the Dada artists.

The Knoedler inventory was never without this rich mixture; under Henschel and his staff the firm sought what it considered to be the best art available, regardless of its period. In the season of 1929–30, for instance, just as Henschel was huddling with the Antikvariat, the firm bought such diverse products of the creative spirit as a Cézanne from the collection of Louisine Havemeyer and, at a price reported to be $1 million, the Thomas B. Clarke collection of American portraits.[25]

Henschel died in 1956, after fifty-two years of service with the firm. He had brought it successfully through the Great Depression and the years of the Second World War and had reopened the branch in Paris in 1944 soon after that city was liberated by the Allies. One of the most curious events in Knoedler's long history occurred in the year immediately preceding his death. At the trial in November 1955 of John G. Broady, a lawyer and private investigator who was accused of wiretapping, a former employee of the New York Telephone Company testified that under Broady's direction he had tapped many lines in the city, including Knoedler's and that of another dealer, Rudolph Heinemann, with whom Knoedler's often conducted business. It further appeared that Emanuel J. Rousuck, a vice president of Wildenstein's, had authorized the tapping of Heinemann's line and paid Broady a fee of $2,000. When Rousuck himself was asked whether he had spoken to Broady about other dealers, he replied, "Well, I mentioned Knoedler for one."[26]

There could be no question that the line had been tapped by Broady; Henschel and his staff had the evidence in the form of tapes. In March 1956 Knoedler's filed a suit against the Wildenstein corporation, Georges Wildenstein, Daniel Wildenstein, and Rousuck for $500,000. Wildenstein's lawyer immediately issued a disclaimer on behalf of his client. "It would appear," he said,

> that Knoedler has instituted this action for selfish business reasons, hoping thus to obtain an unfair competitive advantage. The Wildenstein Galleries, established over eighty years ago, have a reputation which is unequalled in this field. The Wildenstein Galleries welcome this opportunity to prove, in open court, that Knoedler and certain persons associated with them have deliberately perverted the testimony in the recent Broady trial.[27]

The affair rocked the art community. Wiretapping itself was hardly a new threat to privacy; a federal law against it had existed since 1934. But no dealer was known to have resorted to it before. The upshot, however, was anticlimactic: Knoedler's dropped the suit in August 1956. The Wildensteins declared their innocence but recognized that Knoedler's privacy had been invaded and that "a Wildenstein employee" had in fact paid Broady to tap the line.[28] That "employee" was, of course, Rousuck, although the Wildensteins' apology did not name him. Other dealers speculated that the Wildensteins made an out-of-court monetary settlement with Knoedler's, but no such exchange was reported.

Henschel was succeeded in the presidency by Roland Balay, a cousin of Roland Knoedler and therefore a relation of Henschel as well. In the 1950s and 1960s the firm turned increasingly to contemporary art. Among the artists it acquired were the sculptors Henry Moore and Tony Smith and, to the amazement of the art community, the Abstract Expressionist painters Willem de Kooning and Barnett Newman. De Kooning held one-artist shows at Knoedler's in New York in 1967 and Paris in 1968; Newman was included in a group show of American art in the Paris gallery in 1967 and held a one-artist show in New York in 1969.

These artists were not to remain with the firm for long, however. Two dramatic changes in Knoedler's occurred in rapid succession at the start of the 1970s. IBM, planning an expansion along Fifty-seventh Street, bought the firm's building. Roland Balay found suitable if somewhat smaller quarters in the form of a town house on East Seventieth Street, and late in 1970 the firm was installed there. Since the late 1950s many new galleries had established themselves on the Upper East Side, and several older ones had relocated there; this move put Knoedler's at the center of the action, and a short distance up the block from the Frick Museum. The *Times* reported that the new gallery would have walls "high enough to hang a full-blown painting by Barnett Newman."[29] And those walls were to be covered in brown plush.

Only a year later, however, Newman—and Moore, Smith, and De Kooning as well—withdrew from the gallery. A flurry of denials in the press notwithstanding, Knoedler's was changing hands, no longer to be in the control of a descendant of the original owner. The sale, which occurred late in 1971, was to Armand Hammer, by that date the CEO of Occidental Petroleum; his brother Victor; Dr. Maury Leibowitz, a clinical psychologist; and Bernard Dannenberg, a young dealer. This shift of ownership was to result in a drastic change in the image and temperament of the gallery. The new Knoedler's soon became a leading contemporary-art gallery, no longer a plush-clad sanctuary where one might find a Titian, a Rubens, a Veronese. The plush was stripped away and the walls were painted white, after the new, postwar fashion. The place of the old masters was taken by such venerable contemporaries as Adolph Gottlieb and Robert Motherwell and such cutting-edge younger men as Frank Stella, Richard Diebenkorn, and Robert Rauschenberg. Not all of these popular artists would stay, however, and there were further changes in management in the 1980s and '90s. In 1996 the firm celebrated its sesquicentennial with an exhibition of some of the great art of the past that had passed through its hands. Trade in such art was left to other firms, however, of which none was more prominent worldwide than Wildenstein's.

For the Wildenstein gallery, or, more properly, Wildenstein & Company, to be spotlighted in the newspapers for anything other than a great sale or a great purchase was of course profoundly embarrassing to the family. But the Rousuck-Broady affair was not merely an embarrassment. It gave the public a glimpse into the firm's behind-the-scenes activities such as the family had always been at pains to guard against. Nathan Wildenstein had insisted on secrecy in all matters pertaining to the firm, and the generations of Wildensteins who followed him into the business adopted his code. In the end, however, there was nothing to worry about. A mere incident of wiretapping could not prevent the Wildenstein juggernaut from achieving dominance in the field.

After René Gimpel ended his association with the firm in 1919, Nathan continued to head the Paris branch of the gallery. Having developed an uncanny visual memory en route to becoming a connoisseur, he encouraged his son to do the same. "Now, is that beautiful or is it ugly?" he would ask Georges as they viewed a work of art.[30] These exercises had the desired effect. With a discerning eye the equal of his father's, Georges became a well-reputed scholar. Although inclined to rule the firm autocratically, Nathan made room in it for Georges. Thus began a tradition, with succeeding generations of Wildensteins unquestionably accepting their fate: They would be merchants of art. Guy Wildenstein, Nathan's great-grandson, once remarked,

> When I was a boy at the Lycée Français, the teachers asked you what you wanted to be when you grew up. All the other children in my class said, "I want to be a fireman," or "I want to be a doctor," and so on. But I said, "I *am going* to be an art dealer." The teachers were outraged. They called my father and said, "You are not allowing the child any free will." But that's the way it was for my father, that's the way it was for us. And we will do the same for our children. They won't be asked, they'll be told.[31]

After the First World War, Georges developed a taste for the Impressionists, despite his father's disapproval of them. But Georges persisted, and with Nathan's grudging permission their works entered the already bulging inventory.[32] This infusion of relatively recent art, so unlike the eighteenth-century works and old-master paintings that composed

Wildenstein's principal stock, resulted before long in a massive increment in the firm's net worth. The paintings were also helpful in seeing it through the Depression of the 1930s. Another unexpected turn in the firm's direction also occurred at this time. With the Paris dealer Paul Rosenberg, Georges entered a partnership to promote and sell the paintings of Picasso. This arrangement lasted until 1932. Of particular interest to the firm were the products of Picasso's rose and blue periods, the most handsome of his works and the least difficult to read. In the partnership's dealings with Picasso, the Wildensteins usually stayed in the background, although on one occasion, in 1923, they made the New York gallery available for a Picasso exhibition staged by Rosenberg.[33]

In 1928 Georges, scholar as well as dealer, bought the *Gazette des Beaux-Arts,* a journal of art history founded in 1859, and edited it until his death in 1963. In 1930 he began the publication of *Beaux-Arts,* a weekly newspaper. Demonstrating an eclecticism of taste that distressed some conservative members of the art community, he allowed an international Surrealist exhibition to be held in the Paris gallery in 1938 and followed this with the publication of a dictionary of Surrealism.[34] He was also the compiler of catalogues raisonnés of the works of Lancret, Fragonard, Ingres, Chardin, Manet, and Moreau that are recognized as major contributions to scholarship, although it should be noted that the merit of a Gauguin catalogue, Georges's last, has come under heavy attack on grounds of incompleteness.[35]

With business booming in Paris and the inventory constantly growing as Nathan bought collections outright from their owners and still more paintings at auction, the firm opened a branch in London in 1925. A Buenos Aires branch soon followed. Meanwhile, the New York gallery was managed by Felix Wildenstein, who had been associated with it since its founding. In 1934, in the depth of the Depression, this branch moved from 647 Fifth Avenue and resettled in a new, elegant, travertine-clad building at 19 East Sixty-fourth Street, which the firm had commissioned of the Philadelphia architect Horace Trombauer. There it remains. After the death of Felix in 1952, Georges's son Daniel oversaw the workings of the New York branch. From the death of Nathan to his own death, Georges was the leader and the decision maker in all major matters. The Paris branch closed in 1964, but the Wildenstein Institute, its scholarly arm, remains there. Recognizing the economic power of the Japanese, in 1973 the firm set up a shop in Tokyo. As the twenty-first century begins, Daniel's son Guy presides over the firm and manages it in association with his brother Alec.

His all but total dedication to the firm notwithstanding, Nathan was a convivial man. Clients and dealers were welcome to drop in for afternoon tea at the Paris gallery, and did so in crowds. Georges, however, canceled teatime when he took over.[36] He was reputed to have little interest in social life, devoting his attention almost completely to the firm and his scholarly writings. Knowing himself well, he could without hesitation compare himself to another master of secrecy, Joseph Stalin, as he did during the Korean War, when he heard associates express fears that the war would spread. He and the Russian dictator were alike, he said, because they both knew how to take risks and also when to hold off, and Stalin would not risk the loss of his empire by extending the war.[37] Georges's only outside interest was horses, as it was for his father and as it has continued to be for his son and grandsons. The Wildenstein stables at Chantilly receive the family's careful attention and the attention of the press as well.

Georges was believed to know the location of every work of art in the world that the firm might take an interest in. Like Joe Duveen, he organized a battery of paid informants to let him know if the owners of important works were showing signs of possibly wishing to sell. In addition, Georges supervised the growth of a gigantic library, with new books coming in, it is believed, at the rate of as many as a thousand a year. In 1959 it was reported that the library contained 300,000 books, 100,000 auction catalogues, and 100,000 photographs. The firm also owns the Durand-Ruel archive, another of Georges Wildenstein's purchases.[38] This massive accumulation of reference materials continues with the current generation. The purpose, of course, is to ensure the growth of the inventory. Eight paintings by Rembrandt, eight by Rubens, twenty-five by Corot, and ten by Seurat—to name only four artists—were said to be housed in the Wildenstein vaults in 1959, out of a total of two thousand works. Writing in 1994, Michael Lewis, a former employee, estimated that in 1982, when he worked for the firm, the total came to three thousand. Daniel Wildenstein, however, told a reviewer in 1981 that the holdings then numbered ten thousand paintings.[39]

Thus a collector with sufficient funds to buy a work of art of any period from the Italian Renaissance to the era of the Post-Impressionists need only inquire at the New York branch. His search will be rewarded, at a price. Or, as frequently happens, a dealer whose gallery is located in another city will ask for paintings on consignment to satisfy the needs of a client. One such, who serves as a suitable example, was the Los Angeles dealer Earl Stendahl, art purveyor to the stars in the 1930s, '40s, and beyond. When Hollywood mogul Jack Warner and his wife needed suitable decorations for a new house in 1940, Stendahl became the intermediary between the couple and Wildenstein's. What especially was required was a work of the right size to fit a panel over the living-room mantel.[40] Felix Wildenstein dispatched a Degas to Stendahl from New York, but it proved to be too small. He had intended to deliver a Gauguin himself on a planned visit to Los Angeles in the summer, but as the Second World War raged across France after the calamitous failure of the French army to turn back Hitler's Wehrmacht, he was too anxious about the future of both his country and his gallery to make the trip and canceled it late in May. He sent the painting to Stendahl, who delivered it to the Warners. A Brittany scene, it depicted pigs in a farmyard. Mrs. Warner liked it, but her husband refused to have it in the house. "Mrs. Warner phoned for me to pick up the Gauguin," Stendahl wrote to Wildenstein. "Her husband objected to it immediately because of the two pigs, in spite of the fact that he eats pork. Somehow he does not want the pigs in the parlor." Wildenstein replied that had they known that, they could have told Gauguin to paint cows.

Their next try was a small Seurat, a study painted on wood for the great *Grande Jatte*. Here too they were unsuccessful, although for a much different reason: no sooner did Jack Warner have the panel in his hands than he dropped it. Broken in two, it went back, was repaired, and was eventually sold to David O. Selznick, who may or may not have known about Warner's clumsiness and the fact that the panel had been restored. When the panel was on view at Sotheby's, New York, before the sale of works from the estate of Irene Mayer Selznick on May 7, 1991, the crack in the panel was clearly visible, as it is also in the sale-catalogue photograph.

These mercantile efforts, trivial at best, to satisfy art-hungry Hollywood took place on a peaceful continent three thousand miles from the turmoil of the war that had begun in September 1939. On June 14, 1940, Hitler's blitzkrieg reached Paris, and eleven days later, at Compiègne, the Republic of France ignominiously surrendered, the victim not only of its enemy's superior strength but of the moral weakness of its premier, Henri Pétain. Along with other dire consequences, this catastrophe posed a threat to the safety of the Jews of France, including, to be sure, the Wildenstein family.

Among the art dealers of Paris, many of the most prominent were Jews, including Daniel-Henry Kahnweiler, René Gimpel, Paul Rosenberg, Léonce Rosenberg, Jacques Seligmann, and Gaston and Josse Bernheim-Jeune, as well as Georges Wildenstein. Their inventories and their lives were in jeopardy. The Nazi dictatorship had caused the removal from German museums of all modernist art, which, because of its distortion of the figure, often to the point of unreadability, as in Cubist art, was branded *entartete* (degenerate), as though the product of madmen hoping to subvert the taste of the public. Equally intolerable to the Hitler regime was all art created by Jews, the realistic landscapes and genre pictures of Max Liebermann no less than any vividly colored *entartete* Expressionist scene by Ludwig Meidner. But this art, degenerate or not, had an unquestioned monetary value beyond Germany's borders, and the Nazis had begun to sell it in the months before the outbreak of war. That they would confiscate and sell the holdings of the Jewish dealers of Paris and all other conquered cities was a certainty, provided the dealers could not find the means of protecting them.

René Gimpel died a hero's death during the war. Although fifty-eight when it broke out, he joined the Resistance, as did his sons. When the Vichy government got wind of his underground activities, he was arrested. In 1942 he was released, only to be arrested a second time, by the Germans. He was sent to the death camp at Neuengasse, where although very ill he set an example of fortitude to his fellow prisoners by facing death serenely.[41]

Paul Rosenberg, who had a gallery in London as well as in Paris and was Picasso's principal dealer between the wars, left Paris in the summer of 1939, before the Second World War broke out, and settled near Bordeaux. After the fall of France, he sailed for the United States, but without most of his inventory of contemporary masterpieces, which had been seized by the Germans, and also without his gallery's records, which were permanently lost. Ironically, his gallery and home on the rue La Boétie were taken over by his namesake, the notorious German anti-Semite Alfred Rosenberg.[42] With as much art as he could salvage, he established a gallery in New York, on East Seventy-ninth Street. He was no stranger to the United States; in 1923 he had arranged Picasso exhibitions at the Wildenstein gallery, as noted, and for the Arts Club of Chicago in the Art Institute of Chicago, and in 1934 at the Wadsworth Atheneum in Hartford, Connecticut. In 1934 he also staged two exhibitions at the Durand-Ruel Gallery in New York. His son, Alexandre, joined the Free French forces. In August 1944, shortly before the liberation of Paris by the Allies, Alexandre Rosenberg was the commanding officer of a detachment of troops who captured a train on its way to Germany with a treasure of modern art confiscated from museums and private owners, including the Rosenberg family.[43] At the war's end, he joined his father in New York. On the senior Rosenberg's death in 1959, he became director of the gallery and remained with it until his own death in 1987.

Léonce Rosenberg, Paul's brother, managed to survive in Paris during the occupation. Unable to deal in art and having lost his gallery and his personal collection to the Germans, he quietly monitored the activities of dealers who had no scruples about doing business with them. After the liberation of Paris, he offered testimony on those dealers' activities to the French authorities briefed to investigate thefts of art and to examine claims made for the recovery of the stolen items.[44]

Georges Wildenstein had dealt openly with a member of the Nazi Party before the war. The virulently anti-Semitic Karl Haberstock, a Berlin dealer in nineteenth-century German art of the sort approved by the party, very early saw the possibility of increasing his wealth by purchasing works stripped from German museums and reselling them to dealers or collectors abroad. In 1937 he bought Gauguin's *Riders to the Sea* after it was removed from the Wallraf-Richartz Museum in Cologne and, his zeal for profits momentarily sanctioning the suppression of his hatred of Jews, sold a share in it to Wildenstein. Wildenstein sent it to New York, where it was purchased by Edward G. Robinson.[45]

Lynn H. Nicholas in *The Rape of Europa,* her invaluable study of the Nazis' systematic looting of art during the war, informs us that along with works from other Jewish-owned collections, some but not all of the holdings of the Wildensteins were taken by French museum authorities to Sourches, a town southwest of Paris, in the days before the city fell to the Germans. Georges Wildenstein placed 329 others in the vaults of the Banque de France in Paris, while the Louvre took in 89 more. This, it was hoped, would prevent their confiscation. But still others remained in the firm's gallery in the rue La Boétie and in Wildenstein's house outside Paris. With his family, Georges fled to Aix-en-Provence, leaving the gallery in the charge of Roger Dequoy, a longtime employee.[46] Dequoy had only recently returned to Paris after a visit to New York, having been called back hastily, it would seem, because of the emergency at home.[47]

After the French surrender, Hitler decreed that all art objects in the occupied zone, which of course included Paris, should be safeguarded—that is, taken from museums or their private owners and sequestered. Alfred Rosenberg created an art-gathering agency, the Einsatzstab Reichsleiter Rosenberg (ERR), for that purpose—with Paul Rosenberg's commandeered premises as his office. Some infighting or at least sparring occurred between this organization and various German officials over what exactly should be done or could be done without violating international laws regarding the spoils of war, but the upshot was that the entire artistic patrimony of France was in danger of being transported to Germany. Much did make its way there, either to decorate the castle of Hermann Göring or in the expectation that it would eventually hang in the museum Hitler intended to build in the Austrian city of Linz. Everything was confiscated that the leading Jewish art dealers of Paris had not found a means of either hiding, shipping abroad, or transporting to the unoccupied zone set up by the Germans in 1940. The part played in these and subsequent events by Georges Wildenstein has been the subject of discussion ever since.

At this moment in the history of the firm, Haberstock reenters the scene. A time would eventually come when the Nazi regime took complete control of the Unoccupied Zone, but in 1940 and 1941 Jewish dealers resided in comparative safety there, and some Jews, Gertrude Stein and Alice Toklas among them, remained in it, leaving only after the liberation of Paris in 1944. In November 1940 Haberstock journeyed with Roger Dequoy to Aix-en-Provence, where Georges Wildenstein was staying until he could get away to New York with the paintings he had taken on his flight from Paris. In effect, Haberstock was in competition with the ERR for as much Jewish-owned art as he could get his hands on. His immediate purpose was to secure any or all of Wildenstein's holdings that would not offend Nazi tastes, in exchange for which he would send "offensive" works to Wildenstein in New York. Haberstock also suggested that Wildenstein buy works from other refugee dealers for him. Although Wildenstein later said that Haberstock had with him a high-ranking German officer, thus suggesting an atmosphere of menace that left him defenseless, he found these arrangements suitable. Business, it seems, was business. Haberstock also said that he had a buyer for *Beaux-Arts,* which, if not sold to a German, might be confiscated or "Aryanized"—that is, assigned to the control of a non-Jewish French national.[48]

With Dequoy, a non-Jew, already in charge of the Wildenstein gallery, Haberstock was able to prevent its being taken over. This meant that the works taken to Sourches and desired by the ERR could be returned to the gallery. An accountant, one Gras, was appointed Wildenstein's administrator by the French, but Dequoy continued to run the gallery. Eventually he and two partners received permission to buy the gallery outright. To make this possible, he swore that he had had no contact with Wildenstein since 1939—patently a lie, but one not detected by French or German officials.[49]

It should be pointed out the Wildenstein gallery was not alone in making an advantageous arrangement during the occupation while the holdings of the galleries of the Rosenbergs, the Bernheim-Jeune brothers, and other prominent Jewish dealers were confiscated. Daniel-Henry Kahnweiler was able, although not easily, to shift the management of his gallery to his sister-in-law Louise Leiris, a Catholic, under whose name it still exists. André Weil, also a prominent dealer, gave control of his gallery to Louis Carré. Neither Kahnweiler nor Weil made a deal with such a nefarious character as Haberstock, however, and both remained in France, hidden in the country, until Paris was free.[50] But Georges Wildenstein, now living in New York, was determined to mastermind the operations of the family's gallery from abroad. In this he was frequently foiled. His hope of receiving pictures from Haberstock was unsuccessful; an attempt, the only one known to have been made by the firm, to ship French eighteenth- and nineteenth-century paintings to New York ran into a British blockade.[51]

Meanwhile Dequoy, selling, buying, and reselling, did good business in Paris. When the paintings from Sourches arrived at the gallery, Haberstock bought seven of them from him and then sold them to Hitler's projected museum at Linz. In 1942, after buying back two major Rembrandts, *Portrait of Titus* and *Landscape with Castle*—works that earlier had hung in the Hermitage—from a client to whom the gallery had sold them in 1933, Dequoy then sold them to Haberstock, also for Hitler's museum. The new German owner of *Beaux-Arts* gave him a discount on advertisements. All this was thanks to the arrangement between Georges Wildenstein and Haberstock. When in January 1944 the Germans took over the gallery space in the rue La Boétie for an Institute of Franco-German Cultural Exchange, Dequoy moved to the rue du Faubourg St.-Honoré. His premises there remained the location of the gallery after the Allied victory in Europe and the resumption of its business under the Wildenstein name. For his dealings with the enemy, Dequoy paid a fine in 1947. An effort on the part of French officialdom in 1949 to bring charges against the Wildensteins for voluntarily trading with the enemy was thrown out of court, however, for lack of proof.[52]

In the postwar years, the firm continued to grow in wealth and, correspondingly, power in the international market. Guy Wildenstein told an interviewer in 1991 that when the Metropolitan bought Rembrandt's *Aristotle Contemplating the Bust of Homer* at auction in 1961 for $2.3 million, the report that this was the highest price ever paid for a work of art was incorrect; the Wildensteins had just sold a Leonardo for $10 million and, protecting the purchaser and observing their code of secrecy, had said nothing publicly about the sale.[53] In 1971, when the Metropolitan went for even bigger game than the Rembrandt, Velásquez's *Juan de Pareja,* which was to be auctioned at Christie's in London, Thomas Hoving, then the Metropolitan's director, asked the Wildenstein firm to do the bidding on behalf of the museum. The firm itself had tried repeatedly, and unsuccessfully, to buy the painting from its English owners, the Radnor family, but consented to act as agent with no commission, although with two provisos. First, if the Metropolitan authorized a bid beyond $4 million, then the Wildensteins would take the assignment, but—and with this second proviso they bared their economic muscle—if the Metropolitan failed to score with its top figure, they reserved the right to bid for themselves above that amount. Happily, the museum won the painting at its price: 2.2 million guineas or, in the rate of exchange at the time, $5.7 million.[54] How high the Wildensteins were prepared to go on their own behalf is known only by the family.

In the same 1991 interview in which he revealed the sale of the $10 million Leonardo, Guy Wildenstein remarked that he and the firm were "interested" in contemporary American art. "We will not be trying to discover a new artist," he said. "It has to have some relation to what we do now, what we know. That's why Jasper Johns might be the most understandable for us."[55] On October 28, 1993, an article in the *Wall Street Journal* revealed that the Wildensteins had acted on this interest by buying a 49 percent share in the Pace Gallery, a leader in contemporary American art. The price cited by the *Journal* was vague: between $50 million and $100 million, for which it was said to have acquired approximately half the Pace inventory. The following day the *New York Times* also reported on the event. The article did not mention the financial terms, but noted that the merger would be effective for the Wildenstein firm's worldwide operations and quoted Alec Wildenstein's disclosure that his family had known and worked with Arnold Glimcher, Pace's president, for thirteen years. The artists did not include Jasper Johns, the capture of whom might have been the greatest coup of all, but nevertheless constituted a vast roundup of blue-chip painters and sculptors, among whom were Chuck Close, John Chamberlain, Jim Dine, Agnes Martin, Claes Oldenburg, Robert Ryman, Julian Schnabel, Richard Serra, and Joel Shapiro, along with the equally blue-chip estates of Joseph Cornell, Louise Nevelson, and Mark Rothko. The artists on Pace's roster would not be the first contemporaries whom the Wildensteins had deigned to show in recent years. Works of several American artists, including some members of Glimcher's stable, had been on view at the gallery on Sixty-fourth Street, but only in loan exhibitions. Now the firm had a hefty financial investment in them. Pace, founded in 1960, became PaceWildenstein. But, as might have been predicted, Wildenstein and Company remained Wildenstein and Company.

An ugly late chapter was added to the Wildenstein saga on September 3, 1997, when the *New York Times* reported the difficulties faced by the lateral descendants of Alphonse Kann, the noted French-Jewish collector, to retrieve eight fragile illuminated manuscripts believed to have been looted by the Germans in October 1940 along with all other Kann holdings in art. A man without children of his own, Kann, who died in 1948, left his holdings to his five nephews. In November 1996 Kann's great-nephew, Francis Warin, discovered that these perishable treasures were in the possession of the Wildensteins. It was known that the Germans had marked all works taken from Kann with the letters *ka* and had given them serial numbers. These eight works were similarly inscribed and numbered.[56]

When Warin claimed them as part of his great-uncle's collection, the Wildensteins dismissed the claim and insisted first that they were bought from Kann before the Second World War (but without providing an exact date), then that the works had been looted from their inventory by the Germans and returned to them after the war. Their lawyer somewhat later, in response to a further claim from Warin, said that they had been bought from Edouard Kann, Alphonse Kann's cousin, in 1909. Warin did not yet know that the Wildensteins had recently placed the manuscripts on the market. This effort was futile, however, because the London dealer in rare books, Sam Fogg, with whom they had been in contact as a possible buyer, would not accept them when the firm proved unable to offer evidence of ownership and refused to indemnify him against claims of any legitimate owners.

In response to a query from the *Times,* Daniel Wildenstein replied that the firm could prove ownership, but he did not come forward with the papers. As for the letters *ka* he insisted that they had no significance. "I can't understand the claim," he said, naively unaware of the naked arrogance of his remark. "It's an absolutely crazy thing, 100 years after an object was bought to come with a claim without any paper whatsoever. They claim it 50 years later? They had no claim for 50 years? I tell you something. If tomorrow someone steals a picture from me, I make a declaration to the police that it's stolen. After 30 years, the man who stole it owns it."[57] Warin was prepared to sue for recovery of the property. To him, the letters *ka* were in no way insignificant. They seemed to provide a clear indication that the manuscripts belonged to Alphonse Kann's heirs.

12

NEW DIRECTIONS

As the 1920s raced toward their disastrous conclusion in the Wall Street crash of October 29, 1929, the world of art also moved rapidly along. The avant-garde art fostered by Stieglitz, collected by Quinn, and purchased (slowly, to be sure) by the Metropolitan Museum began to lose one of the qualities that it had so noticeably projected at the Armory Show: the power to offend. The general public for fine art was not, and would never be, as large as the public for film, jazz, or vaudeville—the "lively arts," as Gilbert Seldes, the 1920s' leading advocate of popular culture, designated these robust sources of pleasure—but its members were gradually becoming comfortable with modernism; if they had not admired the new art enough to pay good money for it, fewer exhibitions would have been mounted.[1] Stieglitz, as noted, could not afford to keep 291 open after 1917, and Marius de Zayas closed his gallery in 1921 for the same reason, but other galleries kept the faith and made a profit until the crash drained away most of their clients. From 1920 through 1930 New York dealers offered literally scores of exhibitions of modernist art.[2]

Attempting to aid in the appreciation of new creative directions in the 1920s and beyond were two museums: the Société Anonyme, established at the beginning of the decade, and the Museum of Modern Art, established at its very end. Both were the creations of redoubtable women with the courage and the means to act on their assumption that the best of the modern needed fostering. The Société Anonyme came into being somewhat too early to make a major impact on the art life of the nation. The Museum of Modern Art, on the other hand, not only thrived and inspired imitators in other cities but acquired such prestige that dealers vied with one another to place work by their artists in its collections. It should be noted, however, that preceding these efforts was the establishment in 1918 by the collector Duncan Phillips (1886–1966) of the Phillips Gallery (now the Phillips Collection) in Washington, D.C., where he exhibited his own substantial, growing collection of Impressionist, Post-Impressionist, and contemporary art, with inclusions also of older notables, among whom were Daumier, Delacroix, Goya, El Greco, and Ingres. After his marriage in 1921, his wife, the artist Marjorie Phillips, was his partner in the development of the collection.

The Société Anonyme was the brainchild of Katherine S. Dreier, a collector with substantial means and an artist herself who had exhibited two paintings at the Armory Show. Its complete name, although the second half was seldom used, was Société Anonyme—Museum of Modern Art. Joining with her in the development of the museum were the two pillars of New York Dada, Marcel Duchamp and Man Ray, the artist and inventor of the rayograph, a means of making art by placing objects on a photographic plate, exposing them to light, and thus creating a picture. Dreier's close friendship with Duchamp, already of several years' standing in 1920 when the Société Anonyme was formed, had survived her vote as a member of the Society of Independent Artists to bar R. Mutt's *Fountain* from the 1917 exhibition.[3] With missionary zeal to advance the education of the public in art, she leased rooms in a town house on East Forty-seventh Street and opened her museum on April 29, 1920. Man Ray was involved only because Duchamp brought him along to Dreier's apartment for the first planning sessions. It was he who suggested that the organization be called Société Anonyme, the familiar French term for "corporation," which he, not understanding its meaning, translated literally as "anonymous society."[4] Duchamp was named the museum's treasurer and Man Ray its secretary.

In 1921 the museum could boast of eighty-six members, but it soon lost most of them.[5] It also lost Man Ray and (temporarily) Duchamp in 1921, when both men left New York for Paris. Dreier was not daunted by the decline in membership or the corresponding decline in financial support. She organized exhibitions, lectured year after year, and made frequent additions to the collection of the Société. In 1923 she relocated the museum from East Forty-seventh Street to West Fifty-seventh but kept it there only one year, after which it was entirely peripatetic, with exhibitions in such diverse venues as the Daniel Galleries, the Colony Club, and the Brooklyn Museum. But in 1941 the Société Anonyme ceased to exist, and its holdings were turned over to Yale University.[6] The Museum of Modern Art had put it in the shade.[7] Dreier's own very large personal collection was dispersed to several museums after her death, in 1952, by Duchamp, one of the executors of her estate. To the Museum of Modern Art went 102 works, including two by Duchamp himself.[8]

The Modern, as in time the Museum of Modern Art would be nicknamed by its friends, or MoMA, as the museum eventually came to refer to itself, was founded in 1929. It was the creation of three wealthy and intrepid women: Abby Aldrich Rockefeller (Mrs. John D. Rockefeller Jr.), Lillie P. Bliss, and Mary Quinn Sullivan (Mrs. Cornelius J. Sullivan). All three were collectors with a strong interest in the new art. Under the guidance of Arthur B. Davies, Lillie Bliss had attended the Armory Show and brought works from it. Her collection eventually included over a hundred paintings and drawings. Mary Quinn Sullivan also bought from the Armory Show. Her mentor there was John Quinn. The two Quinns, Mary and John, were not related, but, as it happened, John Quinn was the Harvard Law classmate of her future husband, Cornelius Sullivan, whom she married in 1917. With her Armory selections as the basis of their collection, she and her husband acquired works by such modern masters as Cézanne, Picasso, and Van Gogh. Abby Aldrich Rockefeller, the unofficial leader of the group, and in her personal tastes perhaps less advanced than her friends, collected works by American artists of her time, including George Bellows, Georgia O'Keeffe, and Edward Hopper.[9]

The women recruited an organizing committee headed by A. Conger Goodyear, a wealthy businessman and collector with a pronounced taste for modern art. Formerly he had been president of a museum, Buffalo's Albright Gallery. The other members of the committee were Frank Crowninshield, the editor of *Vanity Fair* and champion of the arts through its pages; Paul J. Sachs, professor of fine art at Harvard and connoisseur of drawings; and Mrs. W. Murray Crane, an intimate friend of

Mrs. Rockefeller and, although not a collector of modern art, well-known for her intense interest in cultural matters.[10]

The key figure within this group was Sachs, who, although a collector of old-master drawings, was no enemy of modern art and its enthusiasts. He had recently made this clear when in 1928 three Harvard undergraduates, Lincoln Kirstein, Edward M. M. Warburg, and John Walker, bearded him in Harvard's Fogg Museum and reproached him with the fact that no modern art was to be seen on the campus. He recognized the rightness of their grievance and encouraged them to remedy the situation themselves. Spurred to act by this advice, they founded the Harvard Society for Contemporary Art, engaged two rooms over the Coop (the university store), and began to mount a series of spectacular exhibitions: contemporary American art, recent and contemporary French art, the wire sculptures of Alexander Calder, and still more, amounting to twenty-one exhibitions in two years. With a board of distinguished trustees and funds supplied by the young men's wealthy families, the Harvard Society attracted attention far beyond Cambridge. After graduation Walker went on to study with Bernard Berenson at the Villa I Tatti, Warburg became a trustee of the Modern, and Kirstein a donor to the Modern and sometime organizer of its exhibitions.[11]

At the suggestion of Sachs, Alfred H. Barr Jr., a young associate professor of art history at Wellesley, was invited to be the museum's director.[12] It was an astute choice, with far-reaching effects. Barr's intelligence, his knowledge of art, and his fervent belief that the new museum should interest itself not only in fine art but in architecture, film, photography, and industrial and graphic design was to create in the Modern a model for countless museums of the future, both at home and abroad. His own model was the Bauhaus, Germany's ultraprogressive school of the arts, established in Weimar in 1919 but relocated in Dessau in 1925. At the Bauhaus attention was given to every category of art, as it would be at Barr's museum. Touring Europe on a travel grant in 1927, Barr paid the Bauhaus a visit he had long anticipated.[13]

The Modern was organized at a time that could hardly have been less auspicious for its future. It opened to the public, in rooms in a building at 730 Fifth Avenue, just ten days after Wall Street's shattering fall. Yet the wealth of the three women was such that their museum was in no danger of collapsing at its birth. At first no funds were available for acquisitions, but gifts, including many from the women themselves, formed the nucleus of a collection to come, and loans from collectors, dealers, and other museums were sought for exhibitions. In 1939, after two and a half years on Fifth Avenue, six in a town house on West Fifty-third Street, and two in the Time-Life building in Rockefeller Plaza, the Modern returned to West Fifty-third Street and triumphantly opened the doors of its own newly constructed building. At that site it has remained ever since, with expansions to its right, its left, and its back, and with further expansions always under consideration.

For some of the dealers who sold second- or third-generation Impressionism, the arrival in their midst of a museum dedicated to art that was modern not merely in being newly or recently produced but also in being revolutionary was downright alarming. The Modern threatened the stability of their emotions at the same time that, coming just when the stock market debacle was beginning to wreak havoc in their own market, it seemed to threaten their financial stability as well. The wealth of the Modern's backers ensured its permanence. The now-you-see-it-now-you-don't Société Anonyme had not frightened the dealers to such a degree; nor had the ongoing exhibition at New York University, beginning in 1927, of the ultramodernist collection of A. E. Gallatin, which included masterpieces by Mondrian, Seurat, Cézanne, Picasso, Miró, and others.[14]

One dealer, Robert Macbeth, with a heavy inventory of American Impressionism on his hands, was beside himself with worry over the Modern. In November 1930, one year after the opening of the museum, Macbeth revealed his resentment of its program in his gallery's *Art Notes*. Whereas his father had been urbanely humorous in expressing disapproval of some of the exhibits in the Armory Show, the younger Macbeth wrote heatedly and defensively. Although willing to accept Cézanne, Van Gogh, and even the early Picasso, he was outraged by Barr's praise of Paul Klee in the catalogue of the Modern's fourth exhibition, which included works by Klee, Wilhelm Lehmbruck, Aristide Maillol, and Max Weber. Picking up Barr's observation that "[t]he child, the primitive man, the lunatic, the subconscious mind, all these artistic sources . . . offer valuable commentary on Klee's method," Macbeth pleaded for "sane" American art, which he thought of as "our kind" of art. That, of course, meant American Impressionists and such recent realists as two that he names, George Bellows and Eugene Speicher. This issue of *Art Notes* turned out to be the last, although the Macbeth Gallery itself managed to survive. Presumably the costs of printing the little bulletin were too great to be sustained after the sharp downturn of business. In the early 1930s, not a great many people could afford to buy Macbeth's kind of art or any other kind.

In Chicago a newly organized conservative group called Sanity in Art was just as anxious as Macbeth about an infusion of what it deemed madness into museums and galleries. Katharine Kuh, a dealer from 1935 to 1942 in the work of Kandinsky, Klee, Léger, Miró, and other modernist artists, suffered invasions of her premises by members of the group, who created havoc by disrupting sales and disturbing the serenity of her patrons. Kuh took direct action: she called the police and had them thrown out.[15]

Two decades after Macbeth published his screed, Charles Daniel complained in much the same fashion, as we have noted, accusing the Modern of trafficking in "decadent and degenerate art." But such complaints had no effect on the Modern's fortunes; within a decade of its birth it was to become a major contributor to New York's, and the nation's, cultural life. As such, it has had little difficulty in attracting major gifts of money and seemingly no difficulty at all in attracting major gifts of art. Not the least of them were the 102 works from Dreier's collection. Nor did Sanity in Art destroy the fiscal health of the Art Institute of Chicago, which it shortsightedly chose as another of its targets.

The 1930s saw the arrival of still two more museums in New York: the Whitney Museum of American Art and the Museum of Non-Objective Art(later the Guggenheim Museum). As with the founders of the Museum of Modern Art, the financial anxieties that gnawed at most Americans during the Depression did not touch the backers of these institutions. Their fortunes may have contracted somewhat during the decade, but not to the point of shaking their commitment to art and their ability to collect it.

The Whitney Museum was the creation of Gertrude Vanderbilt Whitney, a sculptor and art patron who was born to wealth and provided with access to even more by her marriage in 1896 to Harry Payne Whitney (a marriage to which neither partner was faithful). Having developed an extensive personal collection of American painting and sculpture, she conceived a plan to subsidize artists as early as 1904. After ten years of generous responses to the financial needs of talented artists, she and her assistant, Juliana Force, began to show contemporary work in her studio at 8 West Eighth Street. For their first two exhibitions, she and Force enlisted the aid of William Macbeth in the choice of works to be shown. In 1915 she helped to form the Friends of Young Artists and in 1918 the Whitney Studio Club, the latter with dues of $5 and a policy of welcoming any artist who cared to join. These endeavors and the shows resulting from them led to the founding of the Whitney Museum in 1930 in expanded quarters at the same address. Its doors opened to the public in the following year.[16]

Modernist art surrounded Gertrude Vanderbilt Whitney in the intellectual circles of New York which she frequented, but it was not the art that she preferred, as was made clear by her recruitment of Macbeth to assist with the first Whitney Studio shows. In 1913 she was aware of the plans under way for the Armory Show and responded to an appeal to pay for the decoration of the hall with a $1,000 check, but was not invited to exhibit in it. Although she traveled abroad during its entire run, depriving herself, perhaps deliberately, of an opportunity to visit it, she did not hesitate to express disapproval of the advanced art it included. Accepting the opinion of the critic Royal Cortissoz, whom she cited in a speech prepared some time after the closing of the show, she joined him in a condemnation of the products of Matisse and the Cubists.[17]

But the Whitney Museum did not confine itself rigidly to representational art. As the creative energies of increasing numbers of American artists responded to the modernist movement in its various branches, including Cubism, so too did the Whitney respond, if within limits. In 1935 the museum held an exhibition of abstract painting, and it continued to show and to buy such art. Chiefly, however, the abstract art collected by the Whitney in the '30s was based on natural forms. Not until much later did the museum begin to collect hard-edge, geometrical abstraction. With the arrival of the Abstract Expressionists in the late 1940s and the firm establishment of their fame in the 1950s, the Whitney as a matter of course bought their art as well. By 1954, when the Whitney moved from Eighth Street to a new building on West Fifty-fourth Street behind the Museum of Modern Art, its holdings and its exhibitions had begun to reflect all the latest trends as accurately as those of its neighbor.

In the early 1960s the Whitney secured a lot at the corner of Madison Avenue and Seventy-fifth Street, where a hole had already been dug for an apartment house whose developers abandoned the project. Marcel Breuer was commissioned to design the new museum building and arrived at an inverted ziggurat, resulting in an unconventional structure whose spacious stories were tall enough to accommodate the huge canvases favored by the Abstract Expressionists. The Fifty-fourth Street building was bought by and incorporated into the Modern as space for education, storage, and conservation.

The Museum of Non-Objective Painting was established in 1939 by Solomon R. Guggenheim in a town house at 24 East Fifty-fourth Street, after three years of offering exhibitions in temporary venues. The original director was Hilla Rebay, Baroness von Ehrenwiesen, whom Guggenheim had met in 1927, at which time she herself was an artist, one of a group who showed at a Berlin gallery, Der Sturm.[18] Although opinionated and irritatingly stubborn, she impressed Guggenheim with her knowledge of art and with what might best be described as her spirituality, a quality that led her to a mystical conviction beyond rational analysis that abstract art was more conducive than realist art to the expansion of the soul. "Abstract art," however, was not the phrase she chose to describe the works she admired. To her mind, "non-objective art" was preferable because the term *abstract* suggested that the art to which it was applied had a basis in something tangible. The increased usage of the phrase (but without the hyphen) following her adoption of it perhaps constitutes her most lasting contribution to art history. The late paintings of Wassily Kandinsky, with their hard-edge circles and polygons seemingly floating or whirling in space, exemplified her taste. She admired even more the work of Rudolf Bauer, a would-be Kandinsky of minimal talent whom she had known in Berlin and who had become her lover.

With money provided by a foundation established by Guggenheim, she bought scores of the paintings of both men. In the art community, eyebrows rose over the sums laid out by Guggenheim for their work. Kandinsky commanded respect, but Bauer emphatically did not. Karl Nierendorf, a Berlin dealer, reported to his colleague J. B. Neumann in New York the rumor that Guggenheim had given Bauer 25,000 marks for a Kandinsky that Bauer had bought for only 2,500 marks. Nierendorf had plenty to say:

> This *Kandinsky-Imitator* (with no style of his own) obviously made a good deal with G[uggenheim]. . . . Bauer now has rented a huge villa in Herrstrasse, completely furnished it, and hung a show of his and Kandinsky's paintings. Only a little while ago he was hanging around . . . and borrowing money from everyone. Now he drives a big Packard, has a servant, and plays the big shot. He must have made at least $100,000 from Guggenheim.[19]

Happily for the public, Rebay also added paintings to Guggenheim's collection by such respected artists as Chagall, Klee, Modigliani, Picasso, and Seurat, among others, whose work was based on objective reality. Sculptures of any sort, however, were banned, because no matter how abstract, they inevitably were concrete objects that could be viewed in the round.

Despite her success in drawing Guggenheim into her sphere, Rebay's career did not run smoothly. In 1942, during the Second World War, she was arrested by federal agents and officials of the Office of Price Administration who claimed to have found Nazi propaganda materials in her possession as well as fourteen hundred pounds of coffee and sugar, commodities then closely rationed. After being held for two months by the Federal Bureau of Investigation, she was released and the charges were dropped.[20] Much later, in 1963, after she had left the museum, she was newly charged by the federal government, this time with incorrectly reporting the market value of eight paintings from her personal collection that she had donated to colleges. In between, however, she achieved a personal triumph: in 1944 Frank Lloyd Wright, whom she had long admired, accepted a commission to design a new building for the Guggenheim collection.

This would be the renowned architect's first (and, as it happened, his only) building in New York.[21] Guggenheim, pleased by Rebay's notion of making the offer to Wright, acquired a lot at Fifth Avenue and Eighty-ninth Street in 1944, then bought up the rest of the stretch along Fifth to Ninetieth Street, ensuring that Wright's plan would be adequately accommodated.

The war delayed construction, and when the building at last opened to the public in 1959, Hilla Rebay was no longer in charge. Solomon Guggenheim had died in 1949, leaving his nephew Harry Guggenheim in control. Realizing that the inflexible Rebay was not the best person to direct the new museum, which would be renamed for its founder and would no longer be a haven primarily for nonobjective art, he forced her to resign in 1952. The alternative would have been outright dismissal. She was furious and, having held in a well of anti-Semitic contempt for Solomon Guggenheim over the years, released a full flow of Teutonic invective against his nephew.[22] With as much strength as she could muster, she fought against the museum board's attempt to have returned to it the many paintings—almost 250—that Solomon had lent her. "Why," she rhetorically asked, "should I take down the precious paintings from the wall of my house and give them to a pigsty?"[23] The house itself and the fourteen acres of land surrounding it had been given to her by Solomon in happier times. The paintings were still in her possession on her death in 1967. Finally in 1971, after four years of litigation, the Guggenheim Museum secured the paintings in an out-of-court settlement.[24]

In Rebay's place, Harry Guggenheim appointed James Johnson

Sweeney, who had headed the Department of Painting and Sculpture at the Museum of Modern Art from January 1945 to November 1946 but had resigned in November 1946 over several grievances, including the decision of the Modern's board to deny him the right to veto proposed acquisitions.[25] Still, he was a recognized scholar and collector with wider tastes than Rebay's, and therefore suitable in Harry Guggenheim's eyes. But, finding himself in constant disagreement with Wright over how pictures should be displayed in the museum, he remained only one year after the Guggenheim opened its doors.

Wright's design evolved into a bowl-like structure with a spiral ramp along which the art was to be exhibited. The result was less successful as a place for hanging and viewing art than as a gigantic and photogenic sculpture, a heaven-sent subject for the museum's postcard racks. Nevertheless, the Guggenheim's holdings in modern art would come to place it among the most written- and talked-about museums in the world.

Although the 1930s were a time of efflorescence for museums, the art market itself suffered. Art, which one can neither eat nor wear nor use as shelter against winter winds, held a low priority among those whose funds were wiped away in bank failures or stock speculation, or whose business failed. With an estimated fifteen million people left unemployed at the depth of the Depression in 1932, how could the art trade survive? And yet it did. Despite the worst possible miscalculations that optimistic pundits of economics (Herbert Hoover among them) had made, the very rich remained very rich, and there were more of them than the Whitney, Rockefeller, and Guggenheim clans. Marie Harriman, the first wife of the politician and railroad magnate W. Averell Harriman, opened a gallery on East Fifty-seventh Street on October 1, 1930, eleven months after Wall Street's fall, with an exhibition of paintings by Cézanne, Derain, Gauguin, Matisse, Renoir, and Van Gogh—costly goods even then. Whatever the number of sales from the show may have been, they were sufficient to encourage her to keep the gallery going, as she did until America's entry in the Second World War, at which time she thought her energies might be better spent on the war effort.[26]

Harriman was not alone in having the courage to enter the trade in the 1930s. Early and late during the Depression years, other would-be merchants of art opened their doors. All the arts, not painting and sculpture alone, held on throughout the decade. Hollywood, having learned to talk in 1927, provided inexpensive and sometimes provocative entertainment, whether depicting the nation's ills or, conversely, offering glimpses of the great wealth of a fortunate few in the so-called white-telephone movies. Broadway, at a $3.30 top for tickets, was expensive but survived; Clifford Odets, the most talented of the decade's new playwrights, became a spokesman for the young and disadvantaged as his short but powerful *Waiting for Lefty* was performed by theaters across the nation. Radio, the cheapest entertainment of all, increased the public for classical music with broadcasts of Metropolitan Opera performances and concerts conducted by such revered masters as Arturo Toscanini.

Some of the new dealers looked for ways around the economic difficulties and found them by selling art so inexpensive that the hopeful collector with only a few dollars for discretionary spending could afford it. In 1934 a young man named Reeves Lowenthal founded the Associated American Artists Gallery, or AAA, for the sale of prints for only $5. With his partner, Maurice J. Liederman, he secured work from such recognized artists as, to name only two, Grant Wood and Alexander Archipenko. Although the gallery sometimes held exhibitions of paintings, its mail-order print business was its financial mainstay.[27] At about the same time, an acquaintance of Lowenthal's named Samuel Golden conceived the notion of commissioning prints and selling them at an even lower figure: $2.75. These were issued in unsigned, unlimited editions, but many of the artists who created them were as distinguished as those who made prints for the AAA, such as, again to name only two, Thomas Hart Benton and John Marin. Golden's company was called the American Artists' Group, or AAG. Both AAA and AAG published Christmas cards as well; Golden issued many cards that reproduced the prints commissioned by Lowenthal and Liederman. Under Hugh Stix, the Artists Gallery, a cooperative venture, opened in 1936 for the sole benefit of the artists who showed in it. Subsidized by generous donors, the gallery took no commissions. All these business outlasted the Depression. The AAA, the longest-lived of all, continued through the twentieth century and, after many changes of management and with prints no longer its principal stock, headed confidently into the twenty-first.

A young woman named Marian Willard approached the problem of disseminating art in hard times from still another angle. In her East River Gallery, which opened in 1936 at 358 East Fifty-seventh Street, four very long blocks east of the Knoedler and Durand-Ruel galleries, she allowed art lovers to rent pictures by the month for as little as $4 or $5. If after looking at their borrowed art and finding that they could not bear to part with it, the renters could then buy it, subtracting the paid rental fee from the purchase price. Two years later, giving up her rental business, she joined the émigré dealer J. B. Neumann in his gallery, the New Art

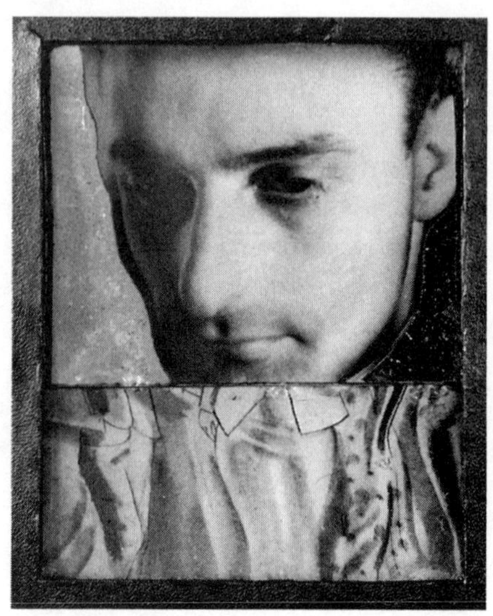

Julien Levy, in a collage by Joseph Cornell.

Circle, at 543 Madison Avenue. In 1940 she was back on her own with a gallery that eventually exhibited such eminent artists as David Smith, Morris Graves, Mark Tobey, Richard Lippold, Norman Lewis, and Charles Seliger. In 1970 she retired, handing control of the gallery to her daughter, Miani Johnson, who maintained it until 1986, when, having tired of the trade, she closed it down.[28]

In a class of its own among the new galleries of the 1930s was that owned by Julien Levy. A young New Yorker who had lived briefly in France in the late 1920s and had married there, Levy returned shortly before the crash and courageously opened the Julien Levy Gallery of Modern Art on November 2, 1931. Like Alfred Barr, Levy had studied with Paul Sachs at Harvard. But quite unlike Barr, he had taken up art history only because he did not know what else to do. His wealthy father was a developer of apartment buildings, and when he and his wife suggested that art might be a good academic major for their son, Julien acted on the suggestion *faute de mieux*. As so rarely happens in such situations, his parents were right.[29] But, failing in an attempt to get paternal backing for the making of an experimental film, he left Harvard in 1927 only three months short of graduating and went with Duchamp to Paris in the hope of producing a film there. Nothing came of this plan, but Levy maintained a lifelong interest in film.

In Paris he met Joella Loy, a young woman whose mother, Mina Loy, a poet, novelist, painter, collagist, and maker of artistic lampshades, had been a member of the Arensbergs' New York circle. The two young people fell in love and were married, with the blessing of Levy's father, who had made inquiries as to the suitability of the match. Julien was halfway enamored of Mina as well as her of daughter. He remained close to her even as his marriage to Joella floundered in the 1930s. Mina voiced no objection when he entered into an extramarital affair under her very nose; on the contrary, and oddly enough, she defended him in his philandering. Once he established a New York gallery, Mina became his Paris representative.[30]

On his return to New York Levy worked briefly for the family firm but soon realized that assisting in the construction of expensive housing did not constitute his métier. Although a job in the small but bustling gallery and bookshop of Eberhard Weyhe on Lexington Avenue suited him better, it too left him unsatisfied. He was driven to be his own employer, and when he received the capital of a trust fund created for him by his mother, he used it to found his gallery.[31]

Having become interested in photography at Harvard, Levy devoted his debut exhibition to the work of Stieglitz, Steichen, Sheeler, Paul Strand, and other masters of the medium. This familiar material, excellent of its kind though it was, added nothing new to the scene. Nor did it sell well; Stieglitz's heroic efforts notwithstanding, collectors of fine-art photography were still few in number. Although Levy would offer photography exhibitions frequently over the eighteen years of his gallery's life and would occasionally show films as well, he had an eye to the future, as the art-conscious public soon learned. The gallery became famous for its innovations, including its cocktail party openings, which soon became standard procedure for leading galleries in the city.

Levy's fourth exhibition, which opened in January 1932, was devoted to Surrealism, a mode of art conceived in France and at that time unfamiliar to the American public. Shortly before the opening, a similar exhibition had opened at the Wadsworth Atheneum in Hartford, Connecticut. Levy had known A. Everett "Chick" Austin, the director of the museum, at Harvard. In his memoirs he maintains that he had planned and gathered the works for the exhibition himself and allowed Austin to offer it first. This claim has been called into question, however; although some of works appeared in both shows, the available evidence suggests that each man worked on his own.[32] Austin billed his exhibition *The Newer Super-Realism,* a designation rejected by Levy. Among the artists shown by both Austin and Levy were Salvador Dalí, Marcel Duchamp, Max Ernst, Man Ray, and Levy's own discovery, Joseph Cornell, to whom we will return in a moment. Levy's gallery being very much smaller than Austin's museum, the show, announced as *Surréalisme* (the French spelling), was considerably the smaller of the two, but, being in New York, it drew greater attention from the press. One of the most striking works on view, and the most talked about, was Dalí's *The Persistence of Memory,* a small painting of drooping pocket watches which would become a prime icon of the Surrealist movement once it entered the collection of the Museum of Modern Art in 1934. Levy himself was the original owner of the painting. He had bought it in Paris for $250; his asking price at the exhibition was $450.[33] After closing in New York, this much talked about show went to Cambridge under the auspices of the Harvard Society for Contemporary Art.

The French poet André Breton, who in 1924 got the Surrealist movement under way with his *First Manifesto of Surrealism,* defined the new development, then only a literary movement, not yet one that embraced painting, as "[p]sychic automatism in its pure state, by which one proposes to express—verbally, by means of the written word, or in any other manner—the actual functioning of thought. Dictated by thought, in the absence of any control exercised by reason, exempt from any aesthetic or moral concern."[34] Had it been applied to art, this definition would have gone a step beyond Dada, whose products, whimsical as some of them might seem, were closely calculated, not arrived at by automatism, which implies an absence of calculation. But Surrealist art, when it arrived, could depict scenes of a sort—dreamscapes—as did Dalí's paintings or those of Max Ernst, or could be utterly nonobjective, as in the paintings of Matta (Roberto Matta Echauren), although neither Breton and his circle nor Levy approved of such work. To Levy, Surrealist painting was an art that projects "the world of dream, myth, metaphor, the subconscious."[35] Thus it might be said that the watches of *The Persistence of Memory,* detailed as they were, issued from Dalí's subconscious and were beyond rational control, beyond calculation, no matter how carefully rendered on canvas.

Dalí's paintings were less baffling than simply entertaining, as later was the fur-lined coffee cup of Meret Oppenheim, created in 1936 and eventually acquired by the Modern. This work was included in the exhibition *Fantastic Art, Dada, and Surrealism,* assembled by Alfred Barr for the Modern in 1936. In that same year appeared Levy's *Surrealism,* a volume of surrealist writings that he edited and for which he provided an introduction. Although Barr's exhibition was undoubtedly viewed by more people than attended the Surrealist shows in Levy's little gallery, to Levy belongs the credit for publicizing the movement in America. In addition to those Surrealist artists previously mentioned, Levy also offered shows to Yves Tanguy, Alberto Giacometti, Paul Delvaux, and Peter Blume. Although Mina Loy, unlike these artists, was not in the avant-garde, he admired her work also, and herself as a person, enough to schedule an exhibition of her paintings in 1933.

Among Levy's major discoveries was Joseph Cornell, a young man from Queens who had frequently drifted in and out of the gallery during the opening exhibition. One day Cornell showed him some collages of his own making. These were composed of pieces of steel engravings and bore a resemblance to collages made by Max Ernst, the German Surrealist. Levy writes that he at that time urged the artist to work in three dimensions, inciting him then and there to construct the fantasy boxes that became his signature pieces. But, as Cornell's biographer points out, this is at best an overstatement.[36] Such constructions came five years later, in 1936, when Cornell was invited to submit a work to Alfred Barr's *Fantastic Art, Dada, and Surrealism*. Before that, his work in three dimensions was confined to pillboxes and glass bells filled with beads, spangles, and other oddments.

Levy claimed as well to have suggested to Alexander Calder that he give up motorizing his mobile sculptures and let them drift in whatever currents of air were available.[37] A hint, nothing more, is offered in his memoirs that he also was responsible for the shift in Arshile Gorky's art away from the Cézannesque landscapes and Picassoid portraits of his early years to the abstract paintings for which he would be best known.[38] All these claims are subject to question, but Levy must be credited, along with Berenice Abbott, with saving the negatives of Eugène Atget, which after the photographer's death had come into the hands of the concierge of the building in Paris where he had lived. At a cost of $1,000 Levy and Abbott purchased the negatives and then spent another $1,000 to preserve them.[39]

Along with his admiration of surrealism and photography, Levy developed an enthusiasm for Neo-Romantic painting. Pursuing this vein, he frequently held exhibitions of the paintings of Pavel Tchelitchew, Christian Bérard, Christians Bonny, and the Berman brothers, Eugène and Leonid. These artists, whose works projected a certain dreamy, ethereal atmosphere, sorted well with those of the Surrealists. Especially akin to Surrealist art were the deep-perspective imaginary landscapes of Tchelitchew. But distinctly a misfit among Levy's refined collection of Europeans and the Americans inspired by them was Ben Shahn. After one show with Levy, Shahn was gone. A more sympathetic milieu awaited him a few blocks south at Edith Halpert's Downtown Gallery.

Sharing in Levy's regard for the Surrealists was Pierre Matisse, the son of the celebrated artist. Lacking his father's genius with brush or pencil, the younger Matisse (born in 1900) hoped for a career in art dealing and in December 1924 came to New York with that goal in mind. As Levy would do a few years later, he first went to work at the Weyhe Gallery, where Eberhard Weyhe proposed that he prepare an exhibition of works on paper by his father. After briefly trying to deal on his own, he went on to the Dudensing Gallery, where he organized an exhibition of French painting that included canvases by Bonnard, Braque, and his famous father. Soon the proprietor's son, Valentine Dudensing, left his father to deal on his own, and Matisse went with him.[40] At last in 1931 he set up his own gallery.

Matisse started out as a dealer on his own in an aerie high up in the Fuller Building, at Fifty-seventh Street and Madison Avenue, a building that was (and is) a prime location in the art trade. He was soon able to afford larger rooms, on the fourth floor, where he remained until his death in 1989. With plenty of space and funds enough to subsidize artists in exchange for their work, he attracted several from Levy's roster. Among those who left were the Surrealists Yves Tanguy and Alberto Giacometti, along with Calder and the Mexican artist Rufino Tamayo. In his memoirs, Levy describes his relationship with Matisse as one of "friendly rivalry" and writes as though he did not mind the departure of his artists, finding himself "becoming too crowded to do them justice."[41]

Matisse also, and perhaps more memorably, showed the work of masters of the School of Paris, including that of his father, to whom he gave one-artist exhibitions in 1934, 1936, 1943, and 1945. Others of this school whom he exhibited were Balthus (Balthus Klossowski de Rola), Marc Chagall, Jean Dubuffet, and Joan Miró. In 1942 he staged an *Artists in Exile* show that brought together fourteen Surrealists, Cubists, Neo-Romantics, and one lone representative of De Stijl, Piet Mondrian.

After the Second World War, Pierre Matisse presented, as his friend and biographer John Russell has written, "a whole new cast of characters."[42] These included, among many others, the Americans Sam Francis, Loren MacIver, and Theodore Roszak. At his death he owned an inventory of some twenty-three hundred works by modern masters. Sotheby's, the largest of the auction houses, and William Acquavella, a dealer in nineteenth- and twentieth-century European masterworks, took over the entire collection for $142.8 million, a record purchase. The auction house supplied the financing, and Acquavella assumed the task of marketing the works.[43]

Offsetting Levy's losses to Matisse were several outstanding replacements. Rico Lebrun, Kay Sage (the wife of Yves Tanguy), and Paul Delvaux were among the artists whom he took on as they came to the fore in the 1940s. With Arshile Gorky, whose paintings and drawings he exhibited in the last years of the artist's life, he had an especially close relationship. After the Second World War, a series of calamities befell Gorky. He was operated on for colon cancer. In a severe automobile accident with Levy at the wheel, he suffered a broken collarbone and two fractured vertebrae in his neck. He became so violent that his wife, having been struck by him more than once, left and took their children with her. On top of it all, he was in pain from the cancer. The problems mounted beyond endurance, and in 1948 he hanged himself.[44] He left a body of painstakingly executed, frequently somber nonobjective oils and drawings that would be recognized as a bridge between Surrealism and Abstract Expressionism.

Although Levy's artists were among the most talented men and women on the scene, he never made much money from them (or for them). But if great financial rewards eluded him, it was not for want of trying. He was a hardworking salesman of art who had the Depression to contend with. One of the factors in the success of Edith Halpert in the 1930s was that she, unlike Levy, dealt in the kinds of art that were fancied by the public of the time: reminders of a happier past in the form of American folk art along with contemporary depictions of the American landscape and American city life. In a valiant effort late in 1941, Levy tried something new: he took a boxcar of his artists' work to San Francisco and Los Angeles and set up temporary quarters in both cities. The results were disheartening. His only important sale was of a Dalí painting, *Accommodations of Desire,* to the Santa Barbara collector Wright Ludington. John Barrymore was one of the visitors to Levy's exhibition. Drunk and disorderly, he expressed his opinion of the show by urinating on a Max Ernst canvas. Levy returned to New York on December 7. Stepping off the train, he was greeted by reports of the Japanese attack on Pearl Harbor.[45]

Levy closed his gallery in 1942 and entered the army but was soon mustered out with a medical discharge. For one year before reopening, he showed his artists at the New York branch of Durlacher's, a London-based firm specializing in old masters. R. Kirk Askew Jr., the director of the firm's New York gallery (and later its owner), had known Levy at Harvard. From the early 1930s until America was drawn into the war, members of New York's cognoscenti of the arts assembled on Sunday evenings at the East Sixty-first Street home of Askew and his wife for drinks and conversation, with Levy often in attendance. Entrée into this charmed circle was considered a mark of distinction among New York's upper-class bohemians. One had to be well schooled in the technique of making smart chatter to enjoy the Askews' gatherings. Also, an undercurrent of unspoken sexual inquiry and invitation was always a part of the evenings, particularly among the men. One man who delighted in the gatherings was Virgil Thomson, whose account makes them seem the very center of New York's intellectual life.[46] But to another, younger man, Gray Foy, an artist on Askew's roster who was frequently present, they were chilling and, to make matters worse, the refreshments were less than adequate.[47] Levy, although heterosexual to the core and an increasingly heavy tippler as the years passed, was very much at home in this environment.[48]

In 1943 Levy rented new space, this time on Fifty-seventh Street, the heart of the market, and tried again with his familiar mix of Surrealists, Neo-Romantics and other contemporaries. Tchelitchew, Blume, and others among the artists who had shown earlier with Levy stayed on with Askew. Max Ernst went to the gallery of Valentine Dudensing, much to the dismay of Levy, who blamed Peggy Guggenheim, then Ernst's wife, for his defection.[49] But with Gorky, Lebrun, and Kay Sage, he had a roster to equal any other New York dealer's collection of modernists. Yet in 1948 he decided to quit for good; the constant cash-flow problem had at last taken the fight out of him. His final exhibition, of sculptures by David Hare, closed in April 1949. Had he not wanted to prepare a Gorky retrospective, he would not have remained open for that last season. Simple fairness requires an observer to comment that Levy was no match as a dealer to his "friendly rival" Pierre Matisse when Matisse's vast inventory of art by international stars and his meticulously prepared catalogues for every exhibition are taken into consideration. But he could say for himself, and did so in his memoirs, that to him belonged the credit for introducing Surrealism to the American public—no small matter—and to keeping it on view despite the odds.

13

FLEEING THE WHIRLWIND

Imperiled as the Jewish dealers of France knew themselves to be when the threat of a new global war intensified in the 1930s, those in Nazi Germany had an even graver reason to fear for their lives: once Hitler came to power, they witnessed the rapid intensification of anti-Semitism throughout their country. It became all too clear that they had been mistaken in thinking of Germany as their fatherland. But it was not the Jewish gallery owners alone who felt threatened; the officially sponsored attacks on modernist art provided a warning to all dealers, regardless of their religion, that control of their destiny was no longer in their own hands.

The new émigrés from Germany had been preceded for more than a decade by J. B. Neumann, a dealer who took up residence in New York in 1923 at the suggestion of the American artist Oscar Bluemner. His presence there provided a kind of beacon to those other Germans who after the advent of Hitler had to find a new locale in which to ply their trade. By that date Neumann, although still in his thirties, had become a well-known figure in the international art world. Others who had urged him to make the move were Katherine S. Dreier, Scofield Thayer, owner-publisher of the prestigious magazine *The Dial,* and Wilhelm R. Valentiner, the director of the Detroit Institute of Art.[1]

Neumann, born in 1887 in Galicia, then a part of Austria, moved at the age of seventeen to London, where he learned English as an employee of Mudie's bookshop and as an apprentice librarian at the British Museum. In 1906 he left London for Berlin and found a job at a bookstore that specialized in works on art and architecture but also dealt in original prints. At this time he discovered the graphic work of Edvard Munch, the Norwegian artist whose proto-expressionist style made a strong impact on German artists. At the young age of twenty-three, Neumann took the bold step of opening a gallery, the Graphisches Kabinett, in Berlin, where he dealt in prints and books. Only a year later, in 1911, he opened a new and larger gallery. His marriage to a young woman with a substantial dowry made this possible. At his new location he offered, among other exhibitions, the first showing of work by Die Brücke, the Expressionist group composed of Erich Heckel, Ernst Ludwig Kirchner, Otto Müller, Max Pechstein, and Karl Schmidt-Rotluff. At this time, too, many other artists came into his life, including those in Der Sturm and Die Blaue Reiter, the latter a group whose principal members were Kandinsky, Alexei Jawlensky, Franz Marc, August Macke, and Paul Klee. Still another new acquaintance was Max Beckmann, whose prints he began to publish. As Neumann became well-known and increasingly involved with the latest movements in art, including Cubism and Dada, his operation began to expand. In the early 1920s he opened branches in Bremen, Salzburg, and Munich. The Bremen and Salzburg galleries were short-lived, but the Munich branch of Graphisches Kabinett remained in business long after Neumann moved to New York, as did his Berlin gallery. Along with Beckmann's prints, he also showed those of Lovis Corinth and Georg Grosz, among others.

In 1921 Neumann met Paul Klee and gave him an exhibition, the Swiss-born artist's first in Berlin. This raised the hackles of Beckmann, who did not admire Klee. But no amount of criticism on the part of Beckmann could persuade Neumann to ignore Klee, whom Neumann liked as both an artist and a person. He once remarked that Klee was the most modest of all the artists he had ever met. No other artist figured so importantly in his career.

The sale of a painting by Franz Marc provided Neumann with the financial security necessary for the move that Bluemner and others had urged him to make. He appointed his colleague Karl Nierendorf to be director of the Berlin gallery, which was renamed the Neumann-Nierendorf Gallerie, and put Günther Franke, another colleague, in charge of the Munich gallery. In New York he found space at 19 East Fifty-seventh Street, in the heart of the art district, and opened the J. B. Neumann Printroom. Bluemner, who had previously been shown by Stephane Bourgeois, was one of his first artists. Through him Neumann met Stieglitz. As easygoing as Stieglitz was cranky, Neumann at first got on well with him—so well that Stieglitz, stepping out of character, permitted him to exhibit John Marin's prints. But when Stieglitz opened his Intimate Gallery in the Anderson Galleries in 1925, he recalled the Marins, and that put an end to the friendship. Abraham Walkowitz and Max Weber, who had shown with Stieglitz, came to him, however. Among the many other Americans whose work he exhibited in New York over the years were Lee Gatch, George Overbury "Pop" Hart, Ernest Fiene, Walt Kuhn, and Charles Sheeler. But he also showed his German artists and other Europeans, as well as African sculpture, Mexican and American Indian crafts, and the prints of Thomas Rowlandson (1756–1827), the English satirist, of which he owned about a thousand.

As he had done in Berlin, Neumann was quick to give up his first gallery space for more suitable premises. In 1925 he opened at 35 West Fifty-seventh Street with a new name for the gallery: the New Art Circle. He inaugurated a magazine, *Art Lover,* issued irregularly, as he had also done in Berlin. Intending to make his gallery a home for all the arts, not graphics and painting alone, he brought in a piano and persuaded such luminaries as Walter Gieseking, Otto Klemperer, and Paul Robeson to perform there. In his long career in New York, he made many other moves and changes of the gallery's name. In the late 1930s, as we have noted, he teamed briefly with Marian Willard. In 1941 he took space in the Fuller Building. He remained at this prestigious address until 1953. After the closing of his gallery, he lectured widely on art and served as a consultant to other dealers.

Luck, more than financial acumen, guided his hand. In the late 1920s (1927 or 1928) he was offered Van Gogh's *Landscape with Setting Sun* for $10,000 and had the wit to buy it. That same day he sold it to Julius Oppenheimer, the father of the physicist J. Robert Oppenheimer, for $30,000, a fine coup for Neumann, but one of very he few managed to achieve.[2] Among his other dealings, a few stand out. He received a number of Picassos on consignment from Leo Stein in 1930 and bought fifty works by Paul Klee from the German dealer Alfred Flechtheim in the same year. Instead of exhibiting the Klees, he suggested to Alfred Barr that the Museum of Modern Art should buy them, and Barr accepted for the museum. In 1935 Neumann became Klee's American agent and Kandinsky's representative on the Atlantic seaboard. But his lack of business acumen cost him heavily; debts to Karl Nierendorf and Curt Valentin ate severely into his profits from sales of the work of these and his other artists.

Among his clients was Duncan Phillips, to whom Neumann frequently sent works on approval for inclusion in the Phillips Gallery. Phillips continually claimed to be short of funds, and Neumann obligingly cut his prices for him. "I simply cannot buy everything I like at this time as our funds are so low we are obliged to sell some good paintings at a sacrifice," Phillips complained in 1926. Returning some Klees a few months after the Crash, he wrote, "The financial problem involved in purchasing these pictures remains unsolved and the prospects of funds being available inside of a year are very poor indeed." But when Neumann, hard up as usual, appealed to him for help in 1932, Phillips responded generously. "Funds are extremely short," he wrote, "but we have managed to send you the check for five hundred dollars which you say you so urgently need."[3]

Neumann's closest dealer-client relationship was with Clifford Odets. The two were introduced in 1941 by the stage designer Boris Aronson, who had been commissioned to design Odets's *Clash by Night,* a play that Billy Rose was bringing to Broadway. The playwright and the dealer went with Aronson on the designer's research trip to Staten Island, where the play was set. The meeting resulted in a strong bond of friendship between the two men. Odets found Klee's work irresistible and bought many of the artist's intimate abstractions from Neumann. Neumann also supplied him with works by Louis Eilshemius, Delacroix, Lee Gatch, George Grosz, and Rouault, among still others. The German Expressionists, however, artists whom Neumann had long championed, provoked his wrath. When W. R. Valentiner, who had left Detroit for the Los Angeles County Museum, gave him a work by Ludwig Meidner, Odets wrote explosively to Neumann:

> My God, these German painters are to be pitied. They are all so raucous, so obsessive, so strained and screaming, so without repose, finesse or lightness, without humor, something so dishonest in

> them, so forced, so full of hurly burly, so bigger than they really are, so emotionally dishonest, so hysterical, etc., etc. . . . What unadulterated crap!![4]

Harsh as this typically vigorous Odetsian tirade may have seemed to the eyes and ears of Neumann, it did not ruffle their friendship.

Odets was useful to Neumann by providing him with introductions to many potential clients in Hollywood, among them Charlie Chaplin, Burt Lancaster, and the film colony's most respected collector, Edward G. Robinson. He was also helpful in another way: knowing that the dealer had offered subsidies and outright gifts of money to needy artists, Odets magnanimously continued these benefactions when Neumann no longer could afford to keep them up. Neumann was grateful for the playwright's patronage. "Listen, dear boy," he wrote in 1947, ". . . you must make big money. It is paramount . . . one of us has to do it. I just can't." Later that year his request to Paul Mellon for financial assistance elicited a polite rejection.[5]

In the 1930s reports on the depravity of the Nazis reached Neumann regularly. As early as 1930 Nierendorf, although not Jewish, wrote of his concern over the Nazi-fostered anti-Semitism that had begun to create a sinister, repressive atmosphere throughout the country. But in fact Neumann needed no one to inform him of this. On his annual travels in Germany he could see for himself. In 1933 he took his name off the Berlin and Munich galleries; it had become all too clear that no business obviously operated by a Jew had a chance of survival once Hitler was firmly in power.

Soon many of Neumann's acquaintances, Jewish and non-Jewish alike, began to leave Germany for safer shores. Nierendorf sailed for New York in 1936, where he established himself first on West Fifty-third Street, across the street from the Museum of Modern Art, and then at 18 East Fifty-seventh Street. A far shrewder businessman than Neumann, he soon had Neumann in his debt, with paintings by Klee as collateral. When Neumann could not pay up, he of course kept the Klees. As a Swiss national, Klee remained popular during the war years, whereas German artists, whether or not they were scorned by the Nazis, did not sell and were infrequently shown. A few months after the end of the war in Europe, however, Nierendorf felt confident enough that the tide would turn to offer an exhibition of *entartete Kunst* as *Forbidden Art in the Third Reich*. His gallery continued in operation until his death in 1947. Albert Flechtheim, who had galleries in Berlin, Cologne, and Düsseldorf, left first for France and then for England. Well liked by artists, he had made a name for himself with exhibitions of Impressionists and Cubists.

Curt Valentin, who when very young had worked in Flechtheim's Berlin gallery, sailed for New York in 1937. For the previous three years he had been associated in Berlin with Karl Buchholz, a dealer in books and modernist art. A member of the Nazi party and also of the Reichskammer der Bildende Kunst (Imperial Ministry of Fine Arts),[6] Buchholz in 1938 was deemed sufficiently eminent to be chosen, along with three other German dealers, by Hitler's government to sell the "degenerate" art pulled from the museums of Germany.[7] On his arrival in the United States, Valentin had $75 in his pocket and enough art to set up a gallery, which he named the Buchholz Gallery—a gesture obviously intended as an act of homage to his mentor, but somewhat puzzling, nevertheless, in view of Buchholz's complacent attitude toward the status quo in Germany.[8] Valentin's opening exhibition, in rooms he took on West Forty-sixth Street, was composed of sculpture and drawings by Ernst Barlach, Georg Kolbe, Wilhelm Lehmbruck, Gerhard Marcks, and others. Many of his other early exhibitions before the outbreak of the war also consisted of German art.

In June 1939 Valentin traveled to Switzerland to attend an auction held in Lucerne for the disposal of modern masterworks confiscated by the Nazis. His purpose was to bid on behalf of museums and private collectors. To be sure, the auction posed a moral dilemma to all potential buyers; this art, after all, had been public property, owned by Germany's leading museums. Did anyone else have a right to it? One answer to the question—or perhaps one rationalization—was that by buying it the new owners were saving it from possible destruction. In fact, the Nazis did destroy some of the confiscated art. But one museum director, Alfred Barr, on the other hand, refused to attend the auction, believing that his museum should have nothing to do with this looting of Germany's patrimony.[9]

Because so much of the modernist art of Germany had been exported by dealers and collectors to other European countries, Valentin had no great problem securing as much of it as he cared to add to his inventory even after the war began. To Galka Scheyer, Klee's representative on the West Coast, he wrote on December 20, 1939, "By the way, it is not too difficult to get pictures from Europe. I received shipments from Switzerland, from France, from England and even from Klee himself."[10]

Like Nierendorf and other dealers, Valentin could not easily sell German art during the war years, but with a program of exhibitions that included other European art as well as work by contemporary Americans, he developed the admiration of critics and collectors. In 1951 he capitalized on his popularity by renaming the gallery for himself. His list of clients included such wealthy collectors as the four Rockefeller brothers—David, John D. III, Laurance, and Nelson—and the prominent St. Louis collectors Morton D. May and Joseph Pulitzer Jr. There was, moreover, scarcely an American museum with which he did not do business, with the Museum of Modern Art preeminent among them.[11] Valentin maintained his gallery until his death in 1954, after which it remained open for one last year.

Valentin's former employer, Buchholz, did not fare so well. After the war, he relocated in Madrid, where he opened the Libreria Buchholz. Eventually he settled in Bogotá, Colombia, leaving the Madrid shop in the hands of his staff. In 1946 he had a credit balance of $6,473.15 with Valentin, but he was never able to collect it. Valentin had had to turn this sum over to the American government's alien-property custodian in 1946, along with all the art from Buchholz's inventory that was on consignment with him. The custodian then disposed of these works at auction.[12]

Justin Thannhauser, another German dealer in masterpieces created by the pantheon of modern European artists, arrived in New York in 1941. He had been born to the trade; his father, Heinrich Thannhauser (1859–1935), had successfully operated galleries in Munich, Berlin, and Lucerne. In 1937 the younger Thannhauser traveled on business to Switzerland from Berlin, only to find on his return that the contents of the Berlin gallery had been seized by the Nazis. With the heat of Hitler's regime on his neck, he left Germany and opened a gallery in Paris. But after the fall of France in 1940, he could no longer stay in Paris. Making his way to Portugal with some of his holdings, he sailed to New York from Lisbon on Christmas Eve 1940. In New York he quickly built up an inventory of remarkable quality and opened a gallery at 165 East Sixty-second Street. Grateful, like other refugees, for his sanctuary in the New World, he presented a collection of seventy-five masterpieces, including thirty-four works by Picasso, to the Guggenheim Museum, which created a new wing to house them.[13]

Equally at risk were Jewish dealers in the smaller lands occupied by the Nazis in the blitzkrieg. Among them was the Amsterdam dealer Jacques Goudstikker, one of the Continent's most renowned dealers in old masters. He and his wife, the Austrian-born concert singer Désirée "Dési" Halban, were accustomed to living comfortably, even lavishly, as the owners of three residences, the grandest of which was Castle Nyenrode, near the city. But they were well aware of the danger they faced from Hitler as war threatened. In May 1939 they traveled briefly to London with some the firm's inventory, which they stored. They also sent $50,000 of their funds to a New York bank, obtained visas for the United States valid until May 10, 1940, booked passage for New York for the fall, and then, these precautions taken, returned to Amsterdam. But they were reluctant to leave Holland even when the threat of war became a reality, and their ship sailed without them. This turned out for both the best and the worst. The ship was sunk by the Germans, and there were no survivors. Although they were spared that watery death, another horror awaited them.[14]

The German army invaded Holland in May 1940—ironically, on the tenth, the very day their American visas expired. Unable to renew the visas, on the fourteenth the Goudstikkers, their infant son, and a Belgian couple, the director of the Belgian museums, Leo van Puyvelde, and his wife, managed to secure a booking on a Dutch ship bound for Dover. The little group drove to the ship in the Goudstikkers' Rolls-Royce, abandoned the car on the road, and boarded the ship. They survived a bombing attack en route to Dover, but when the ship docked, the Goudstikkers were not permitted to disembark, their papers, unlike those of the van Puyveldes, not being in order, and were told that they must proceed with the ship to Liverpool. On the first night aboard the ship in Dover, Goudstikker fell into an open hold, broke his neck, and died. His wife, who made her way to London with her son, was coolly denied a new visa to the United States; Austria having been annexed to Germany, she was looked upon as a German national and told that the quota of Germans was filled. She was, however, able to secure a Canadian visa, her next-best choice. From Canada eventually, but with difficulty, she and her son reached New York, where she established herself as a singer.

Meanwhile, through a series of wheelings and dealings the massive inventory, 1,208 paintings, that Goudstikker had left behind in Amsterdam fell into the hands of his employees. Hermann Göring, building a collection to be displayed at Carinhall, his baronial estate, bought 779 paintings for 2 million guilders, a substantial sum, but well below the paintings' true value. Alois Miedl, Göring's agent, bought the rest and all other personal property of Goudstikker, including Castle Nyenrode. Miedl invested a share of the money for Dési Goudstikker, perhaps not fully convinced that she would ever return to claim it. Although she recovered these funds after the war, she eventually wearied of the effort to reclaim the art itself. She had remarried and was creating a new life for herself. She was aware that many paintings from the Goudstikker inventory had entered the collections of Dutch museums, probably through sales instituted by Miedl, but did not attempt to reclaim them. Nothing from the firm's inventory was restored to her. Nor, although she was far from destitute, could she afford to keep Castle Nyenrode or most of the other Goudstikker properties. She and her son, who had taken his stepfather's name, both died in 1996. In 1997 Marei von Saher, her daughter-in-law, never having heard much from her husband or Dési about the disposition of the paintings, learned with astonishment about the museum holdings from the Goudstikker inventory. She had no wish to have the paintings handed over to her, but asked for compensation for herself and her daughters. Rebuffed in this effort, in 1998 she brought suit against the Dutch government.[15]

Artists, of course, had as much to fear from Nazi policy as did the dealers. Beckmann, although not Jewish, was under pressure for having allowed his work to be exhibited by Jewish dealers. The Surrealist artist Max Ernst, who also was not Jewish, had left Germany for France in 1922 but was on the German blacklist for having created paintings as early as 1933 that made manifest his conviction that the Nazis were the potential destroyers of civilization. Moreover, his wife was Jewish. Bearing no resemblance to the art approved by the New Order, the work of both Beckmann and Ernst was reviled as *entartete*. Both artists would eventually emigrate to the United States. Among the many other persons of international fame in flight from Hitler who came to the United States were several of the artists, architects, and graphic designers associated with the Bauhaus—the Bauhaüsler, as they have come to be called. The first, in 1933, was Josef Albers, whose wife, Anni, was Jewish. He was followed by Herbert Bayer, Marcel Breuer, Walter Gropius, Lyonel Feininger, László Moholy-Nagy, and Ludwig Mies van der Rohe. The exodus would continue through the decade and beyond, a massive gain of talent for the New World.

14

THE FUTURE BEGINS

Out of the turmoil of the Second World War was born Abstract Expressionism, the daring new nonobjective art painted as often as not on huge canvases that, like unfurled banners, were the American artists' means of claiming the independence of their work from that of any other artists in the world. The nonobjective art created in the early decades of the century was hard-edged and geometrical, resembling Abstract Expressionism only in its lack of concrete images. Efforts have been made to establish precedents for Abstract Expressionism in even earlier works—most questionably, perhaps, in the Museum of Modern Art's J. M. W. Turner exhibition of 1966. In this exhibition the museum implied that some of the artist's streaky late watercolors, which are only barely perceptible as seascapes, offered the suggestion that even in the nineteenth century an artist might have been inching toward the kind of abstract art created in the mid-twentieth century by such painters as

Mark Rothko and Clyfford Still. Among the earliest artists to be identified with the new movement were the young men whose work was first shown at the gallery of the confessed "art addict," Peggy Guggenheim.[1]

The artists had not yet arrived at this daring style while showing with her but were rapidly moving toward it, and she was capable of appreciating the innovative quality of their work. A true source of the new style, as opposed to the sketches of nineteenth-century realists, could be found in Surrealist art. Peggy Guggenheim, as both a collector and a dealer, especially with her second gallery, Art of This Century, provided a bridge between the two movements. A notoriously flamboyant sexual adventuress, she was also the possessor of more than adequate wealth, a good eye, an open mind, and the generosity of spirit to promote and protect the artists whom she admired.

"Peggy," as she seems to have been called by everyone who knew her (and as she will be called here to avoid confusion with all other Guggenheims), was a nickname; at her birth, in 1898, she was named Marguerite. The daughter of Benjamin Guggenheim and Florette Seligman, she was the product of two of New York's most prominent and most prosperous German-Jewish families. The fortune of the Guggenheim family originated in mining. After successful forays into the ore-rich fields of Colorado and Mexico—efforts that provided great yields of silver, lead, and copper—in 1889 the patriarch Meyer Guggenheim and his seven sons formed the Guggenheim Exploration Company, or Guggenex, to search the world for still more profitable lodes.[2]

Their next step was a hostile takeover maneuver in 1900 against the American Smelting and Refining Company (ASARCO), a giant backed by members of the Rockefeller family. Their success in this endeavor put control of the mining and smelting industry firmly in their hands. Peggy's father, Benjamin, and his brother Will, however, resigned from the company, apparently alarmed by the very dimensions of the takeover and unhappy with the possibility that outsiders would be called in to help run the business as it grew beyond the capacity of the Guggenheims to manage it alone.[3] The two defectors received a share of the profits on leaving the firm, however, and Ben had sufficient wealth to set up a business of his own, the International Steam Pump Company, with headquarters in Paris. If not so rich as his brothers, he was nevertheless a wealthy man who could provide an opulent domestic environment for his wife and children. But he was also a philanderer, and sadly lacking in the ability to conceal his affairs.

It was Benjamin's misfortune in 1912 while on a business trip abroad to book return passage at the last minute on the ill-fated *Titanic*. He and his valet went down with the ship, as did most of the men aboard. His French mistress, who was traveling with him, survived.[4] After his death, his family found their income considerably reduced, but still ample enough to provide the three girls an expensive upbringing at private schools and social gatherings where they could meet young men of their own standing. In 1919 on turning twenty-one, Peggy came into the income of a trust fund set up after her father's death with the $450,000 he had left her. Her wealth was minuscule compared to the riches of her Guggenheim cousins, but a substantial fortune nevertheless, and enough to secure her independence. Later she would receive an equal amount in trust from her mother, as well as still more inheritances. Florette was a notorious penny pincher, and—like mother, like daughter—Peggy despite her wealth and her charitable impulses was always careful with money.[5]

Peggy had visited Europe frequently with her parents and sisters in her childhood. In 1920 she went again, accompanied by her mother, to Paris. Thereafter, although she returned to New York on occasion, Europe—Paris, Venice, the south of France, London—would be her home until the outbreak of the Second World War. In Paris she met James Joyce and Marcel Duchamp, among other leaders in the arts, and there in 1922 she married the handsome writer and artist Laurence Vail.

A son and daughter, Sinbad and Pegeen, came of the marriage, but not much happiness. Peggy frequently found herself attracted to other men and saw no reason to resist their advances. She was not a beautiful woman; her legs were too thin, and her nose was an unattractive blob, the result of botched plastic surgery. But what she lacked in looks she made up in persistence and accessibility. Vail, too, had his failings, but of another kind. One of them was a disposition to violence.[6] While the marriage lasted, Peggy, perhaps stimulated by its frenzied atmosphere, found an outlet for her energies in entrepreneurship. The American avant-garde poet Mina Loy, whom she met through Vail, was the creator of delicate collages as well as verse. Peggy took a liking to her well-made lampshades and other decorative products. She backed a workshop in Paris where Loy could work and also rented a store where her wares could be sold. To Julien Levy, the husband of Joella, Loy's daughter, this was a "madcap and ridiculous enterprise," and one not likely to succeed, but for Peggy it provided training of a sort for her later career as an art dealer. After the business closed, Levy's father paid off Loy's debt to her.[7]

Peggy and Vail ended their loveless marriage in 1929, but were frequently drawn together because of the children. Until the war years, when the cost of maintaining her art gallery in New York forced her to economize, Peggy paid Vail an allowance.[8] In time, after his marriage to the writer Kay Boyle, he became a good friend and confidant to her. Once she was free of him as a husband, Peggy looked for other male companions, and had no difficulty finding them. She settled in England and enjoyed two lengthy liaisons there. The first was with an intelligent but unaccomplished writer, John Holms.[9] His death in 1934 was a devastating blow, yet not so emotionally crippling as to render her incapable of further romance. The second affair was with Douglas Garman, a communist activist. After her breakup with Garman, she plunged into an intense, frustrating relationship with Samuel Beckett, not yet the world figure he would become with the production of his *Waiting for Godot* in 1953.[10]

Emotionally adrift in 1937 with Garman out of her life and Beckett not yet in it, she felt the need of an occupation. When a friend suggested that she open either a publishing house or an art gallery, she decided on the latter, even though at the time, as she admitted in her memoirs, she "couldn't tell one thing in art from another."[11] Nor was she then a collector. Behind her decision to choose art over literature was the mistaken conviction that an art gallery would be less expensive to run. Another friend suggested that she call the gallery Guggenheim Jeune. This echoed the name of the prominent Paris gallery, Bernheim-Jeune, owned by the brothers Josse and Gaston Bernheim-Jeune, dealers in Post-Impressionist art. They had added "Jeune" to Bernheim, their family name, to distinguish their gallery from that of their father, Alexandre, who dealt in the Barbizon school and other earlier art of the nineteenth century. In view of the fact that at thirty-nine Peggy had passed well beyond her *jeunesse,* it was a curious choice, although undeniably arresting. She found a vacant second-story space on Cork Street, in the heart of London's gallery district, and with the help of Duchamp, who had become a close friend, began her education in fine art.

Although the London art community responded favorably to Guggenheim Jeune, one American resident of note was infuriated. When Peggy wrote to her uncle Solomon regarding the availability of a Kandinsky that he had admired, Hilla Rebay, seemingly moved by the conviction that only she could link the name Guggenheim with art, wrote in part to Peggy,

> It is extremely distasteful at this moment, when the name Guggenheim stands for an ideal in art, to see it used for commerce so as to

give the wrong impression, as if this great philanthropic work was intended to be a useful boost to some small shop. Nonobjective art, you will soon find out, does not come by the dozen, to make a shop of this art profitable. Commerce with real art cannot exist for that reason. You will soon find you are propagating mediocrity; if not trash.[12]

In the two seasons of the life of Guggenheim Jeune, from January 1938 to June 1939, Peggy offered a very mixed lot of art and artists. She began with drawings by Jean Cocteau and then moved on to works in several mediums by Kandinsky. A group show running from June 21 to July 2, 1938, included a heavy representation of Surrealists: Dalí, Ernst, Magritte, and Masson, along with Joan Miró, Henry Moore, Oskar Kokoschka, and still others, some of whom have dropped from sight. This was followed by an exhibition of the Surrealist paintings of Yves Tanguy, an artist who was yet another object of Peggy's affections. The second and final London season included, along with much more, a collage show and an exhibition of children's art. Mindful of her artists' needs, Peggy bought a painting from every exhibition. In this fashion she became a collector.

Although Guggenheim Jeune was well attended and did enough business at least to appear prosperous, in fact the gallery lost about £600 in each of its two seasons.[13] Yet it yielded Peggy much; her education broadened, and her circle of acquaintances in the art world expanded to include such stellar artists as Piet Mondrian and Henry Moore. She also came to know Herbert Read, the widely published English art critic who was then editor of the prestigious *Burlington Magazine* and an enthusiastic proselytizer for modern art. Peggy was attracted to Read, as, in fact, she was to all presentable males, but—perhaps because he was an older man—had no desire to bed him, or so she intimates in her memoirs.[14] The two developed a close, long-lasting friendship in which sex played no part.

With the realization that she could not make the gallery pay, Peggy decided to close it. A new enterprise, one that she knew from the start would be not only costly but unremunerative, suggested itself: a museum of modern art for London. New York's Museum of Modern Art was of course the model. Such a museum had been talked about for years in London's art circles, but no strong effort had yet been made to achieve it. As the second season of Guggenheim Jeune was drawing to its close, Peggy approached Read with an offer of a five-year contract to become the museum's director. The making of her plans coincided with an unexpected problem: Peggy's liaison with an English sculptor whom in her memoirs she identifies only as Llewellyn resulted in pregnancy and an abortion.[15]

Read accepted the offer, giving up the *Burlington* despite the security the magazine offered, and asked only for an advance of one year's salary, which he used to buy shares in the Routledge publishing house. Her idea was to make use of her own burgeoning collection as the base on which to develop exhibitions of works borrowed from established museums and private collectors. A general survey of modern movements in art was to open the new museum. Read gave her a list of artists whose work should be included. Her income at the time was sizable for the 1930s—roughly $50,000—but obligations to old friends and the upkeep of her children cut deeply into it.[16] Always cautious about money, she had to maintain a close watch on her expenses if her plans for the museum were to be realized. But in the 1930s everything was cheap to a person as well off as Peggy, including even the art she would soon begin to buy.

Meanwhile, she formed a close friendship with Nellie van Doesburg, the widow of the Dutch artist Theo van Doesburg, a founder, with Mondrian, of De Stijl, the Dutch movement in geometric abstraction. Peggy allowed Nellie, whose knowledge and understanding of modern art surpassed her own, to revise Read's list. With the list in hand, she set off with Nellie for Paris with her new car, an inexpensive Talbot. It has been suggested that the relationship of the two women, whose intimacy ended only with Nellie's death in 1975, included an element of sex, and Peggy herself admitted to a few sexual episodes with women. These were of little moment in her life, however, compared with her countless affairs with men, which she pursued even beyond middle age.[17]

In Paris, Peggy sought out her friend Duchamp, who looked over the list and made further revisions. But these preparations came to nothing. Peggy, like millions of others, was to suffer an alteration of her plans and in fact of her entire life with the outbreak of the Second World War.

She was slow to grasp the fact that war was inevitable. Like virtually the entire population of France, she was equally slow, once the war began, to realize the fierce power of the German military. But with the joint French and English declaration of war against Hitler on September 3, 1939, she at least understood that her dream of opening a modern museum in London would have to be postponed. She was, however, prevented from returning to London by the refusal of the English to provide her with a visa unless she would bring her son and daughter with her.[18]

But not until the German troops were advancing on Paris in June 1940 did she leave that city. In the fall and winter of 1939–40, lulled by the peaceful atmosphere of the "phony war," she enjoyed life in Paris. She began to collect art on, literally, a daily basis, buying, as she was proud to say, a picture a day. In addition to the income her trusts continued to provide, she had on hand the cash that she had put aside for the development of the museum.[19]

With her checkbook at the ready, Peggy soon realized that she had the pick of what Paris offered, and usually at a very low price. With a war on, even a "phony war," other collectors were holding back, and the market was down. "My total purchases, for about ninety works," she later reported, "did not exceed forty thousand dollars. That is all I had, so that is all I spent."[20] True, she did not get everything she sought. She was rebuffed by Picasso, whose studio she visited in the hope of snaring a recent painting. He had nothing but contempt for this rich American upstart. "Now, what can I do for you, madame?" he asked. "Are you sure that you are in the right department? Lingerie is on the next floor."[21] And the sculptor Constantin Brancusi, who had been her friend for many years, staged a row with her when she tried to buy his sleek *Bird in Flight.* His price was $4,000, which in her opinion was scandalously high. She bought another Brancusi bird, *Maiastra,* from another collector for $1,000, but still longed for *the* bird. Eventually she got it. Brancusi proved willing to accept payment in francs rather than dollars, and cannily, by buying the francs in New York, Peggy saved $1,000 on the exchange.[22]

At this time, a short, ungainly, epileptic, inarticulate man named Howard Putzel stumbled into her life. Putzel, who was the same age as Peggy, had owned a modernist gallery in Los Angeles in the 1930s. Before that, he had worked at the East-West and Paul Elder galleries in San Francisco, where he spent his early years. Surrealism had then and later a strong appeal for him. In 1934 at East-West he staged an exhibition of Joan Miró's paintings, and exhibitions of the work of Dalí and Ernst in the same year at Paul Elder's. A year later he accepted a position as director of the Stanley Rose Gallery in Los Angeles; there he continued to favor the Surrealists with one-artist exhibitions of Miró, Tanguy, and Dalí, and a group show that included those artists and others. Going into business for himself in 1936, he continued in much the same vein.[23]

Peggy became aware of Putzel when he sent good wishes on the opening of Guggenheim Jeune and told her that he was leaving the art trade. Art was his passion, but he lacked the business acumen necessary for dealing in it. A few months later he lent her some Tanguy paintings for the exhibition of the artist's work that she held in the summer of 1938. After closing his gallery, he moved to Paris, where in the winter of 1938–39 he and Peggy met face-to-face for the first time. He was not much to look at; according to Jimmy Ernst, Max Ernst's son, he "resembled a well-worn teddy bear"; according to Peggy he was "a big, fat blond." But she also noted that he was "a man of great force of character" and acknowledged that he was in large part responsible for the development of her eye for art.[24] He was as passionate about art as she, and, fortunately for her, acquainted with the elite corps of Paris artists. Until both he and she left Paris in 1940, he escorted her to studios where she could view and purchase what he took to be the best work of the moment—with a commission, of course, for himself. He talked her into buying a number of works that in fact she did not care for, but hunted down others by artists whom she was eager to include in her collection and could not locate on her own.

One of the artists to whom Putzel introduced her was Max Ernst, who for many years had been living in Paris. Although his first wife, Lou Straus, whom he left in 1927, was Jewish, Ernst himself was not a Jew but was nevertheless on the Nazis' enemies list. Such paintings of his as *The Petrified City, Europe after the Rain I, The Barbarians March West,* and *The Angel of Hearth and Home,* allegorical visions of the horror of a world conquered by fascism, had made clear beyond question his hatred of what the Nazis stood for.[25] Yet after the fighting began he was interned as an enemy alien by the French, then released, and later interned twice again. He managed to escape from the third camp, a farm that offered plenty of lice and no sanitation facilities. Peggy, although she had long admired his work, did not buy from him on their first meeting. Later, however, during his first internment, she bought three of his paintings.[26]

The Wehrmacht's rapid conquest of Holland and Belgium in May 1940 was followed by an assault on France. With the Germans at the approaches to Paris in the spring of 1940, Peggy at last understood the precariousness of her situation. She was mainly concerned for the safety of her collection, which included works by almost all the leading European modern artists, painters and sculptors alike. When the Louvre refused to give the collection shelter on the grounds that, being modern, it had no value, she sent it to her friend Maria Jolas, who was then conducting a bilingual school near Vichy. Jolas had a barn in which she hid the collection. Peggy, however, did not accompany it. Romance, this time with a married man whom she identifies in her memoirs only as Bill, held her to Paris. Her biographer supplies his family name, Whidney.[27]

When at last she came to her senses and left the metropolis, she drove with Nellie to the town of Mégève, where Vail lived with their children. Taking a house in Le Veyrier on Lac d'Annecy to be with the children for the summer, she had her collection shipped from Vichy. From Le Veyrier it went on to Grenoble, where the director of the local museum housed it in the museum's basement. Peggy had hoped that he would exhibit the collection, but, expecting a visit from Marshal Pétain, the Germans' puppet head of the unoccupied zone, he would not do so for fear of a reprisal. Finally an old acquaintance who was a partner in a Paris shipping firm arrived in Grenoble and suggested that Peggy ship the art to the United States with other belongings, including her car, as household objects.[28]

That done, she had now to worry about transporting herself, her children, and Ernst, with whom she had fallen in love, to New York. Fortunately, Kay Boyle had made reservations for them, herself, Vail, their four children, and yet another child who was a friend of her children's, on the Yankee Clipper, which flew regularly from Lisbon to New York. Nellie, sadly, was left behind; although the two women had quarreled, Peggy tried to help her, but found she could do nothing for her.[29] Not until after the war, when Nellie at last reached New York, were the old friends reunited. Ernst, despite the miseries of his internments, was still painting vigorously and vigorously conducting an affair with the artist Leonora Carrington. Peggy easily managed to draw him to her bed, but found it much more difficult to replace Carrington in his affections.[30]

Although so far as one can surmise from her memoirs Peggy never looked upon herself as a heroine, that in simple truth is what she became. It was Kay Boyle who booked the seats on the Clipper, but it was Peggy who organized their hegira from France to Spain, from Spain to Portugal, and, at last on July 13, 1941, after an anxious five weeks of waiting to board a plane, from Portugal to the United States.

Yet when the weary passengers, made irritable by their thirteen hours in the air and the head-throbbing effect of too much Scotch whisky, arrived in New York, they faced another obstacle to peace of mind. Immigration authorities, alert always to the possibility of spies landing on American shores, were not pleased to see that Ernst was traveling with a German passport. Peggy explained that, being German, he had been unable to obtain a passport from the French. Unsatisfied, they put him under the surveillance of an airline detective but allowed him one evening in New York with Peggy before transporting him to Ellis Island for a hearing. With help from Nelson Rockefeller, John Hay Whitney, and Alfred Barr, who brought the prestige of the Museum of Modern Art to bear on the matter, and after an anxious wait of three days, Ernst was released into the custody of his son, Jimmy, a mail room worker at the museum who had resided in the States since 1938 and aspired to a career as an artist.[31]

During Ernst's ordeal, Peggy had hired a launch and chugged to Ellis Island every day to see him and provide what assistance she could. Accompanying her on the first of these suspenseful outings was Julien Levy, who had exhibited Ernst's paintings off and on since the first season of his gallery and hoped to do so again, now that Ernst had crossed the Atlantic. Peggy quashed this hope aboard the launch, making it clear to Levy that she expected to deal in art herself and of course to show the work of the artist she had every intention of marrying.[32]

Always in Peggy's mind was the plan of establishing her own museum. In the fall of 1941 on a cross-country trip with Pegeen and the two Ernsts, father and son, she considered both New Orleans and San Francisco as possible sites for it, but eventually realized that New York, with its overwhelming abundance of talent, was her best choice.[33] After a sojourn in California and a drive back to New York in a new car, Peggy rented three floors of a house on East Fifty-first Street near Beekman Place. The tenant on the top floor was another art lover, Clifford Odets. Jimmy Ernst had been offered and had accepted a position as Peggy's secretary, and he settled to the task of cataloguing her collection, which had arrived safely from France. On December 30, Peggy and Max Ernst were married. But as in her marriage to Vail nearly twenty years before, Peggy had been blind to the character flaws of the man she loved, and perhaps blind to her own flaws as well. The marriage was doomed from the start. Nature had not programmed either Ernst or Peggy for monogamy. As soon as she had the chance, in the autumn of 1942, Peggy realized an ambition of twenty years' standing: to have an affair with Duchamp, or at least so she claims in her memoirs. The record of Ernst's life with Peggy clearly shows that it was not for love that he succumbed to her persistent urging to marry, but for the opportunity to bask in the comfort her money provided. It was true as well that without her wealth and her circle of powerful acquaintances, he might have had no American career.[34]

The FBI harassed Ernst again in 1942 in the hope that he might help to nail the Surrealist artist Roberto Matta Echauren as a spy, an absurd charge based on the knowledge that Matta possessed a short-wave radio and the suspicion, quite unjustified, that he might have been supplying fuel for German submarines.[35] With the help of the collector, lawyer, and accountant Bernard Reis whom Peggy summoned and who had a friend in the Bureau of Enemy Aliens, the FBI backed off.[36] In spite of such difficulties *and* his marriage to Peggy, Ernst painted steadily and by the spring of 1942 had enough new canvases to justify an exhibition; also on hand were earlier paintings of his that Leonora Carrington had brought with her from Europe. With Levy in uniform and his gallery closed for the time being, Ernst's first New York exhibition of the war years was held at the gallery of Valentine Dudensing.

In her rented house Peggy entertained on a large scale. Invited to her parties, and happy to accept, were émigrés and the native-born alike: artists, dealers, and critics, along with other assorted intellectuals from outside the art community. As a hostess, she was positioning herself better than she knew for a second career in the art trade. When she was fully of a mind to reemerge as a dealer, she went on an art-shopping spree in New York that secured for the collection two Picassos, a Mondrian, two de Chiricos, several Mirós, and other works by Archipenko, Giacometti, Klee, Lipchitz, Ozenfant, and Tanguy, a Malevich for which she traded the Museum of Modern Art an Ernst, and pieces by two Americans, John Ferren and Alexander Calder—artists who were on Read's list as amended by Duchamp and Nellie van Doesburg. Accompanying her as she made her purchases were Putzel, Ernst, and André Breton.[37] She had generously provided passage to New York for Breton and his family. Shortly after his release from custody, Ernst had had a brief exchange of heated words with Breton over Breton's suggestion that Paul Eluard might have collaborated with the Germans in Paris, but the quarrel did not create a permanent rift.[38]

Before the gallery was ready to open in October 1942, Peggy published the catalogue of her collection, *Art of This Century,* a title suggested by Laurence Vail. Breton, Mondrian, and Hans Arp supplied prefaces to it. Breton, not surprisingly, seized the occasion to present Surrealism as the ultimate movement in art to which all other modern movements had led. Arp and Mondrian, in brief essays, discussed abstraction. The book also had a Surrealist design element: photographs of each artist's eyes. This was the suggestion of Breton, who had examined the catalogue in manuscript at Peggy's request and thought it needed a visual spark.[39] The dedication was to Peggy's old love, John Holms.

Less than a week before the scheduled opening of Peggy's museum-gallery on October 20, 1942, there occurred another major art-world event, the opening of *First Papers of Surrealism,* an exhibition planned to celebrate the presence in New York of the European Surrealists and to benefit the Coordinating Council of French Relief Societies. With Breton as director and Elsa Schiaparelli, the famously high-spirited couturière, as sponsor, the exhibition ran from October 14 to November 12 in the Madison Avenue mansion of Whitelaw Reid. Duchamp was recruited to design the catalogue and the decor. With very little to spend on the exhibition, Duchamp bought sixteen miles of string to use for the creation of a sort of web that would hang from the mansion's structural elements and chandeliers down to the floor, allowing it to crisscross in front of the works of art on exhibit. In the end, he needed only one mile to complete his design, but had to hang it twice because the first installation caught fire from the chandeliers. Aiding him in constructing his web were Breton and his wife, Alexander Calder, Ernst, and the sculptor David Hare. To further the Surrealist effect, Duchamp persuaded the eleven-year-old son of the writer and future dealer Sidney Janis to bring friends to the opening and play boisterous games among the exhibits all through the evening.[40] Janis himself provided an introduction to the catalogue.

Peggy fretted that the Breton-Duchamp-Schiaparelli event would so exhaust or divert the public that her own opening, planned as a benefit for the American Red Cross, would be little noticed. But she had no real reason to fear; members of the art community were agog over her enterprise. Only Hilla Rebay withheld an endorsement. Envious of the attention Peggy could command, and doubtless worried, as she had been about Guggenheim Jeune, that any institution owned by Peggy would somehow adversely affect the future of her Museum of Non-Objective Art, she had gone so far as to ask real-estate management firms to refuse to rent space to Peggy for the gallery.[41] But her efforts were in vain; Peggy found a good spot, on the seventh floor of a building at 30 West Fifty-seventh Street; the ground floor was occupied by a grocery store. By way of an official disclosure to the public of what it might encounter within her walls, she named it Art of This Century, after the title of her catalogue. The first exhibition consisted solely of works from her own collection.

From the beginning, Peggy had planned to create more than just a gallery; Art of This Century was originally intended to be a museum in which she could present her personal collection, a fulfillment of the scheme she had developed in her London years. But even before the opening she resolved to provide space in which to show and sell works by Ernst and younger avant-garde artists. Despite wartime restrictions on materials and the close financial calculation that usually figured in her business affairs, the gallery offered a spectacular sight, whether or not one was an aficionado of art. On the advice of Howard Putzel, the architect Frederick Kiesler, a native of Vienna who had lived in the United States since 1926, was invited to design the rooms. Thwarted in his chosen profession, he had derived his livelihood mainly as director of the design laboratory at Columbia University's School of Architecture and as director of scene design at the Juilliard School. He took to his assignment with gusto.[42]

Peggy gave Kiesler carte blanche, with the happy result that his plans turned the place into something more than a gallery, just as she wished; it became, in itself, a work of art. There were four exhibition rooms, of which the most talked about was the Surrealist gallery. Here the paintings, left unframed at Peggy's insistence, were mounted on baseball bats projecting straight out from the walls, which were curved concavely to form a tunnel. The bats were hinged so that they could be tilted, and each painting was given its own spotlight. The tunnel effect was heightened by sound effects: at intervals, visitors heard the whoosh of a speeding train. Chairs placed in the room were of such ingenious design that they could be turned seven different ways, so as to function not only as seats but also as stands for art. In the beginning the spotlights turned on and off at three-second intervals, illuminating first one side of the room and then the other. This lighting effect, however, proved so troubling to viewers that ultimately, at Putzel's suggestion, Peggy abandoned it.

The room for Abstract and Cubist work was equally dazzling. Paintings were hung by strings at right angles to walls covered by an ultramarine curtain. More paintings were suspended from strings in the center of the room, as were sculptures. In another room a wheel on which were hung paintings by Klee began to revolve when a visitor stepped through a beam of light. In the fourth room, fronting on Fifty-Seventh Street, the walls were painted white, and light from the windows was muted by a nylon curtain. This area was reserved for changing exhibitions. Kiesler also provided a small office, but Peggy was seldom in it. She preferred to sit at a desk near the main entrance, where she could observe the action and also collect 25 cents from visitors. The office was usually left to her secretary, a post filled first by Jimmy Ernst, later by Putzel, and later still by Marius Bewley, who was to become a distinguished critic and professor of literature at New York University. In kind-hearted Jimmy Ernst's period as secretary, students and artists were allowed in free during

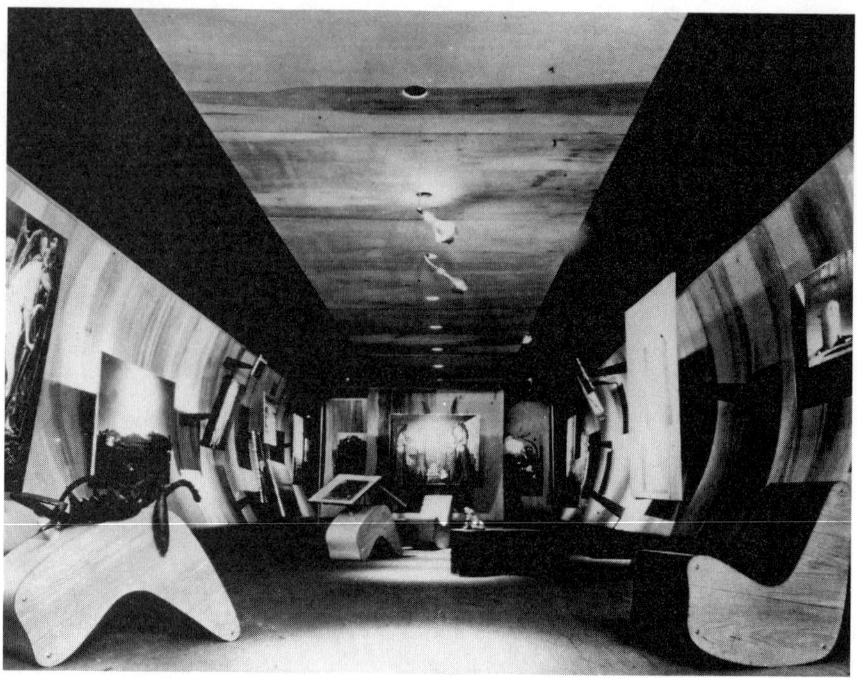

Peggy Guggenheim's Art of This Century "Surrealist Gallery," designed by Frederick Kiesler.

Peggy's lunch hours.[43] She was considerably less than pleased when she found out about it.

The cost for the curving walls, the blinking lights, the strings, the electric eye, and the other embellishments of Peggy's rooms came to approximately $7,000, a sum that she found outrageously high. She paid the bills, but did not hesitate to let Kiesler know that she was unhappy with what she viewed as gross extravagance. But Kiesler also had a grievance: Peggy, he believed, had paid him too little for his contributions. "Oh! foolish youth," he later wrote, "whose payment is in enthusiasm and postmortem gossip."[44]

Peggy's collection of classic modern art remained on view and in itself offered a sound reason for visiting the gallery. But the monthly shows of new work provided gallery goers with an additional incentive for parting with a quarter. Most, if not quite all, were of high quality. The series began with a three-artist exhibition consisting of Joseph Cornell's boxes, bottles decorated by Vail, and Duchamp's *boîte en valise*, a well-made leather case filled with miniature replicas of his major paintings and readymades. Peggy, who made a practice of buying from each of her shows, kept two of Cornell's boxes. The most sumptuous work in the show, and possibly the most mysterious and glowing of all Cornell's boxes, his *Medici Slot Machine,* went to Bernard Reis and his wife.[45]

Although Peggy offered one-artist shows by such recognized masters as de Chirico, Arp, Giacometti, and van Doesburg, along with group shows including works by Braque, Picasso, Léger, and others of nearly equal eminence, the most talked-of exhibitions at Art of This Century were those which brought forward young artists of uncommon talent. A collage show in the spring of 1942 was the first of its kind to be held in the United States. This provided William Baziotes and Robert Motherwell, artists then virtually unknown, with their first sales.[46] Jackson Pollock also had a work in the show, but no sale. These artists were then at a point between Surrealism and the still unborn Abstract Expressionism. Hints, sometimes extremely vague ones, of the human form could be seen in their productions, as, for example, in Motherwell's *Pancho Villa, Dead and Alive,* which the Museum of Modern Art purchased in 1944.

The *Spring Salon for Young Artists,* a juried exhibition that followed the collage show, included Baziotes, Ilya Bolotowsky, Jimmy Ernst, Morris Graves, Motherwell, and Jackson Pollock. Similarly, in her fourth season, 1945-46, Peggy's *Autumn Salon* featured works by twenty-nine artists, including, in addition to some of the artists from her *Spring Salon,* Adolph Gottlieb, John Ferren, Richard Pousette-Dart, Mark Rothko, Charles Seliger, and Clyfford Still. Seliger was a mere nineteen years old at the time. In the abstract paintings of many of these artists, including Gottlieb, Pollock, Rothko, and Seliger, could be found references to myths in the form of symbols, although seldom were they easy to read as such. In the work of Rothko and Baziotes as shown by Peggy were abstract references to creatures of the sea. For some of these artists, their new work revealed a startling shift in style from the work of only a few years before. In the 1930s Pollock had studied with Thomas Hart Benton and turned out work revealing the influence of Benton's regionalist style. Also in the '30s, before Rothko had shortened his name from Marcus Rothkowitz, both he and Gottlieb, as we have noted, had been members of a group calling themselves the Ten whose realist art served the purpose of furthering the decade's liberal agenda.

Peggy could also be credited with staging the first one-artist shows of Pollock, Baziotes, Rothko, Seliger, and Still, and the first one-artist show in New York of Hans Hofmann, and only the fifth of his life, although in 1944 he was sixty-four years old. It was through Putzel, whose eyes were always open to new talent, that Peggy met most of these artists. Although Putzel also offered one-artist shows at Art of This Century to Willem de Kooning and Adolph Gottlieb, neither exhibition was held; de Kooning declined because he felt he was not yet ready for such exposure.[47] Peggy also offered Jimmy Ernst a one-artist show, but, sensing that it would smack of nepotism because of her relationship with his father, he decided against it.[48]

Of all of Peggy's emerging talents, the temperamental, hard-drinking, rough-and-ready Pollock was the artist whose work made the greatest impact on Peggy herself as well as on the public. She was hesitant, even reluctant, to show his work, however, and had included him in her *Spring Salon* only on Putzel's relentless urging. Putzel's persistence and Mondrian's thoughtful endorsement of the canvas Pollock submitted to the exhibition resulted in Peggy's decision to give him a one-artist exhibition early in her second season.[49]

This was the first of four exhibitions that Pollock would have with Peggy. Before the first show, she offered him a one-year contract that provided a monthly subsidy of $150 against sales. If his sales for the year came to $2,700, her third of the take would pay off his debt. If not, she would receive paintings to make up for the difference. As a consequence, she came into possession of much of his output for the year.[50] Nevertheless, Pollock was grateful for the independence the contract gave him and pleased when Peggy renewed it after the first year. Ironically, he had been working as a carpenter and general handyman for the Baroness Rebay. It was a job he was happy to give up. Moreover, he soon had a commission, also at the prodding of Putzel, to provide a mural for the apartment Peggy had taken when her rented house was sold by its owner. This was a huge undertaking, almost eight feet high by twenty feet long, and Pollock in a burst of energy completed it in one fifteen-hour stretch. When he attempted to install it in the apartment, he found it was too long to fit the space and rang up Peggy in the gallery in despair. She then called Duchamp and Hare, who went to the apartment and simply cut eight inches off the canvas. Relieved—and drunk—Pollock did not object.[51]

The mural, like most of Pollock's art of the early 1940s, may best be described as Surrealist. It is abstract, but not Abstract Expressionist. Examined closely, the mural reveals parts of human and animal forms in great swirls and loops of paint, as much the product of automatism as any work by André Masson, Matta, or Dalí. Pollock's art was not the sort that found many takers. Nevertheless, some of his paintings did sell to museums and private collectors committed to the avant-garde. There were, for example, two important sales to museums, *The She-Wolf* to the Museum of Modern Art and *Guardians of the Secret* to the San Francisco Museum of Art, and a few to such eminent private collectors as Joseph Hirshhorn and Edward Root, owners of massive collections of contemporary art.[52]

Peggy and her circle were not the only art enthusiasts of the day who found something to admire in Pollock's output during this transitional period of his career. In his path-breaking study *Abstract and Surrealist Art in America,* published in 1944, Sidney Janis wrote confidently of the talents of many young Americans, including Pollock, whom he categorized as a Surrealist and whose *She-Wolf* he described as "hallucinatory" and "the product of furious slashing of pigment"—words intended as praise. But, more importantly, in this book, written before the term Abstract Expressionism had been invented, Janis himself came within a hair's breadth of inventing it by bringing the words *abstract* and *expressionist* into close proximity. An untitled painting of 1944 by Hans Hofmann he describes as "both abstract and expressionist," and in the next paragraph he notes that the "[m]erging of abstract and expressionist streams is also apparent in the painting of other artists," Motherwell among them.[53] Included in the book is a kind mention of Art of This Century; Janis was a sympathetic observer of Peggy's career, and at least once shared her bed.[54] The book gave him an opportunity to develop an exhibition, *Abstract and Surrealist Art,* for the Mortimer Brandt Gallery, at 15 East Fifty-Seventh Street, until then mainly a milieu for the old masters.

During the first years of her gallery, Peggy's personal life was tormented. Max Ernst was increasingly unresponsive to her emotional needs. In the winter of 1943 he met a young artist, Dorothea Tanning, and embarked on an affair with her. Neither Ernst nor Tanning made an effort to conceal the affair from Peggy, and when finally she could no longer endure the situation, she moved Ernst out of the house on East Fifty-First Street and out of her life. Knowing that German aliens were not allowed access to short-wave radios, she installed one in the house; had Ernst not left, or had he tried to come back, the FBI would doubtless have made serious trouble for him.[55] He and Peggy were divorced in 1946, and in that same year he married Tanning.

André Breton also ceased to be a part of Peggy's life in 1943. He expected her to pay for an ad in *VVV,* the magazine that he, Ernst, and Duchamp were publishing, and she, close-fisted as ever, refused. In her opinion, her contributions to the cause of Surrealism, including paying for the Breton family's passage from Europe, deserved this small consideration of a free advertisement. "But," she later wrote, "Breton maintained that all his life he had sacrificed to truth, beauty, and art, and he expected everyone else to do as much."[56] As it happened, Breton's stubbornness in another matter, his insistence on publishing much of the contents of *VVV* in French, brought the magazine to an end after only three numbers.

Troubled and unhappy, in 1943 Peggy began a relationship of sorts with Kenneth Macpherson, an expatriate Englishman.[57] Although she knew when they met that he was homosexual and that any arrangement she formed with him would be sexless, that somehow did not matter; she was too deeply drawn to his looks and his intelligence to care. Nor did she mind that they could not marry; in 1927 Macpherson had entered a marriage of convenience, and riches, with Bryher (Winifred Ellerman), an English lesbian writer whose father, a shipping tycoon, was one of Great Britain's richest men. As with all of Peggy's affairs, this one with Macpherson was not destined to last. A row instigated by a friend of his so weakened the relationship after its first year that, although they continued to live together for a while, matters between them were never the same. She soon entered an intimate friendship with another homosexual, Dwight Ripley, scion of a wealthy Connecticut family. Ripley was a sometime painter; Peggy included him in a group show and allowed him to help hang exhibitions at her gallery. This relationship, such as it was, came to an abrupt close when Peggy found him in bed with a good-looking cab driver.[58]

In 1944 Peggy received and accepted an offer from Dial Press to publish her memoirs. When the book, which she titled *Out of This Century,* appeared in 1946, it offered revelations of a frankness that readers in that rather circumspect age were unused to seeing in print. To protect the privacy of her lovers and friends, she invented a new name for each of them. Duchamp, for example, became "Luigi," Beckett "Oblomov," Kay Boyle, rather unappealingly, "Ray Soil," and so on. No one was fooled, of course, and some of her cast of characters were far from pleased, Max Ernst most notably. Reviews on the whole were not favorable; one printing was all that Dial hazarded. Nevertheless, Peggy was happy. She had wanted to stir things up, to create a sensation, and in that she had succeeded.

She had succeeded well enough in her gallery also, if success could be measured by the attention it received from the press and the effective launching of her young artists. But at the end of the war, with neither Ernst nor Macpherson at her side, she was eager to return to Europe. The season of 1946–47 was her last. Because she could afford to provide a contract for Pollock only, many of her most promising artists had already left her for the galleries of two new dealers, Samuel Kootz and Betty Parsons. Jimmy Ernst and Putzel in turn had left to set up galleries of their own. To the puzzlement of many of her friends, Peggy chose to establish

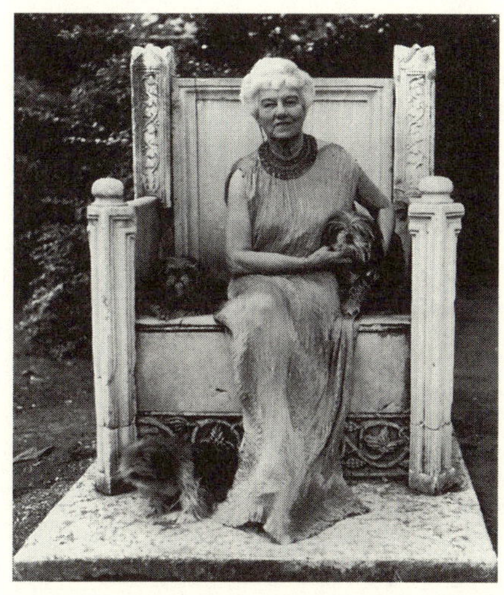

Peggy Guggenheim enthroned in Venice.

herself in Venice and bought a palazzo on the Grand Canal. There for the rest of her life she lived with her collection, to which she continued to add. She also began to give works from it to American museums, along with more than thirty to the Tel Aviv Museum; the most impressive of these gifts, perhaps, was Pollock's huge mural, which went to the museum of the University of Iowa. In 1960 she published another book, *Confessions of an Art Addict,* and in 1979, the year of her death, she published a combination of the two; for this volume she provided the true names of her friends and lovers. Impressed by the grandeur of her life, the Venetians dubbed her the *ultima dogaressa.*

One sorrowful event of her late years was the death of Pegeen, her daughter, in 1967. "I felt all the light had gone out of my life," she later wrote.[59] Yet she recovered and resumed the essentially bohemian existence she had always known. As she aged, her looks improved, if one may judge from photographs. The bulbous nose, which had always been an embarrassment to her, became less noticeable as it settled into the increasingly puffy geometry of her face. To the end, she enjoyed shocking the public. On the canal side of the palazzo she placed a hefty nude equestrian sculpture by Marino Marini on which the erect phallus of the rider was eminently noticeable. It amused Peggy to watch the reactions of her guests to this spectacle, but she detached the phallus when she knew dignitaries or nuns would be passing by on the canal. The sculpture is still on view in Venice, as is her collection. At her death the collection became the property of the Solomon R. Guggenheim Museum, which maintains the palazzo as an auxiliary branch.

15

A PROBLEM FOR CRITICS

Surrealist art was still alive in 1945 and would be produced as long as its famous adherents, the émigré artists, were able to apply paint to canvas. But as a movement, it began to lose its luster when, as we have seen, Peggy Guggenheim's young Americans stepped tentatively toward something new: the still unnamed Abstract Expressionism. A phalanx of dealers scanned this new art and seized the opportunity to promote it. A path had been cleared for them, not only by Peggy Guggenheim, but by Howard Putzel and, to a lesser extent, by Jimmy Ernst.

Very much under the shadow of his famous father, but rapidly growing up in the environment created by Peggy, Jimmy Ernst achieved a degree of emotional independence from Max in 1943 when he met a young woman named Elenor Lust and fell in love. She was enrolled at the Art Students League and had also enrolled her dog as a student, so as to be allowed to keep it with her during the day. Such extravagance and eccentricity naturally gave rise to amused chatter among other young art devotees. But Lust had a serious side and a serious ambition. Not content to be only an artist, she also wished to operate an art gallery. Giving up his job at Art of This Century and pooling his small savings with hers, Jimmy Ernst set about turning a run-down second-story loft on West Fifty-sixth Street into a respectable-looking showcase for art. This space, in a building without an elevator, was the best they could get for their money. Charles Seliger, who had met Ernst at Art of This Century, assisted him in painting the walls.[1]

The opening of the Norlyst Gallery, as Lust chose to call her enterprise, took place on March 15, 1943. The gallery's name was made up of the last syllable of her first name and a variation on her last. (As a painter, she originally called herself Elenor List.) The debut exhibition, which consisted of fifty works in a variety of styles, proved to be the best that the young entrepreneurs ever mounted. In it were paintings by Baziotes, Motherwell, Gottlieb, Rothko, Seliger, Milton Avery, John Ferren, and Boris Margo, a sculpture by Louis Nevelson, and one of Joseph Cornell's boxes. All the artists were on the threshold of fame. But one other artist, Jackson Pollock, whose fame would outstrip even theirs, was absent from the show. Ernst had tried to obtain something from him, but had not been sufficiently persuasive.[2]

Of the exhibitions that followed, the most exotic was a "circus" show for which the walls were decorated with nineteenth-century circus posters and the floor covered with glass marbles on which were placed twenty-four of Louise Nevelson's assemblages. These were composed chiefly of scraps of wood collected from a furniture factory, a lumberyard, and carpentry shops. Although hardly literal, they represented circus figures: the trapeze artist, the juggler, and so on. Karl Nierendorf, Nevelson's dealer at the time, authorized the show, having no desire to exhibit the works himself. He claimed to prefer her drawings, but added that "there isn't much you can say for them, either." Nothing sold, and Nevelson, not yet the self-possessed woman of heroic aspect she was to become two decades later, was so despondent that she destroyed most of the sculptures as well as some two hundred of her paintings.[3]

Later exhibitions included the abstract paintings of Jimmy Ernst, who was beginning to develop a following. The Museum of Modern Art, his employer of old, bought a canvas in 1943. But apart from the sculptor Louise Bourgeois and Esphyr Slobodkina, a highly talented constructivist collagist and painter, the other artists who showed at Norlyst have remained obscure; the breakaway painters of the opening exhibition were attracted to dealers more mature than Lust and Jimmy Ernst. Norlyst's last exhibition, a group show in June 1949, was composed entirely of work by men and women now forgotten.

In the meanwhile, Putzel, with backing from Kenneth Macpherson, had opened a gallery. He numbered many New York artists among his acquaintances, including Baziotes, Pollock, and Rothko; it was through his powers of persuasion that Peggy Guggenheim scheduled their first one-artist shows at Art of This Century. Many reasons for his leaving her have been mooted; it has been conjectured that he believed Peggy's standards were slipping, that he knew she would leave New York for Europe at the war's end, and that, having been her impresario and gained little to show for it, he decided to employ his talent-spotting skill to make some money for himself.[4] The last is the most likely, despite the fact that he was notoriously lacking in business sense.

In October 1944 Putzel set up his gallery in the building at 67 East Fifty-seventh Street, where he was then living, and named it the 67 Gallery. Somewhat curiously, in view of what was soon to come at the gallery, he opened with an exhibition of the ballet designs of Eugne Berman, the Neo-Romantic painter who had shown with Julien Levy and at Durlacher under Kirk Askew. Putzel followed this with European moderns and then, in December, mounted a show of forty American moderns, including, among many others, Gottlieb, Hofmann, Motherwell, Pollock, Rothko, Seliger, David Smith, and Mark Tobey. These were artists whom he knew personally and of whose future stardom he was certain. But as the chronicler of his brief life points out, Putzel's most important exhibition took place in June 1945 under the title *A Problem for Critics.*[5]

The problem was how to define, and what to call, the new movement in contemporary art. Although its roots were in surrealism, it clearly had departed from that movement and arrived at . . . what? Late in 1944 Robert M. Coates, critic for *The New Yorker,* had noted that it "is neither Abstract nor Surrealist, though it has suggestions of both, while the way the paint is applied—usually in a pretty free-swinging, spattery fashion, with only vague hints at subject matter—is suggestive of the methods of Expressionism."[6] There were the two words, *abstract* and *expressionism,* but even farther apart than *abstract* and *expressionism* had been in Sidney Janis's *Abstract and Surrealist Art in America.* Putzel's term for the movement was "new metamorphism," and in it he saw "real American painting beginning now." To stress his point, he included not only Hofmann, Rothko, Seliger, and Lee Krasner, Pollock's wife, in the exhibition, but also, by way of contrast, Arp, Miró, and Picasso, artists whom the new Americans admired but, as he said in effect, did not take as models.

Putzel's exhibition had been preceded by a similar one in the Washington, D.C., gallery of David Porter. Titled *Personal Statement: Painting, Prophecy, 1950,* it included most of the same artists. But because Putzel's gallery was located in New York, his exhibition drew attention on a broader scale. Putzel's "problem" remained a problem, for none of the reviewers knew quite what to make of the art or were inventive enough to give it a name while his exhibition was on view. But the show was one on which to build, as was demonstrated by the intense interest taken in the artists by other dealers.

Putzel, however, derived no benefit from the publicity given his show. He had planned a two-artist exhibition for the fall consisting of the prints of William Stanley Hayter, the British founder of the prominent print workshop Atelier 17, and drawings by Charles Seliger. But the poor health from which he had suffered all his life suddenly worsened; moreover, Macpherson withdrew his support. On August 7, 1945, a month and a week after the closing of *A Problem for Critics,* Putzel died. Peggy Guggenheim was convinced that he took his own life, but in view of the fact that he had long suffered from heart problems as well as other illnesses, a heart attack would seem the more likely cause.[7]

Finally, some eight months after Putzel's death, Robert M. Coates, reviewing an exhibition of paintings by Hans Hofmann, put adjective and noun together and coined the phrase that eventually would stand as the new movement's name. Hoffman, wrote Coates, "is certainly one of the most uncompromising representatives of what some people call the spatter-and-daub school and I, more politely, have christened abstract Expressionism."[8] The critic Harold Rosenberg frequently wrote of this new art as "Action Painting," as apt a name for it as any in view of the broadly gestural technique with which the artists put paint on canvas, but, despite the generally high regard in which Rosenberg's criticism was held, the phrase never achieved quite the currency of Coates's term.

Keener by far than Putzel when it came to making money out of art was Samuel M. Kootz, a suave southerner who had been a sympathetic viewer of the exhibitions at Art of This Century. After Putzel, he was the first dealer of influence and prominence to champion the challenging new trend in art. He had had several careers before setting up as a dealer. In 1921 he earned a law degree at the University of Virginia, but, it would seem, did not enjoy the practice of law. After only one year at it, he quit. In 1923 he took a post with an advertising firm as an account executive and remained in it until 1934, when he entered the silk business. For many years he had been a steady observer of American art and while still a student had visited New York to see the exhibitions staged by Stieglitz and Charles Daniel.[9] In 1930 he published *Modern American Painters,* a book in which he decried the conservative art preferred by reactionary critics. As an executive in a firm manufacturing silk yardage, he seized the opportunity to commission fabric designs by Stuart Davis, Yasuo Kuniyoshi, and Arthur Dove.[10]

In 1941 Kootz wrote a letter to Edward Alden Jewell, art critic of the *New York Times,* in which he vigorously complained against stagnation in American art. He found little to admire and, with Paris under German occupation and therefore unable to provide leadership, he insisted that it was up to America to invent a fresh art. In essence, this was an attack on the "American Scene" and watered-down Impressionism, although he used neither term in his letter. Jewell was impressed enough to describe the letter as "a truly shattering bomb."[11]

Clearly intended for publication, which it achieved, the letter in its tone is close to the breathy style that in the 1930s could be found in gossip columns across the broad spectrum of journalism from the *Daily Worker* to the *Daily Mirror*:

> Subject matter! That's the only thing the galleries are showing. Poor Cézanne fought a losing battle, didn't he? To give birth to this pleasant, harmless, dispirited series of anecdotes.
>
> True, some years ago we had a rash of class-struggle painting; but the boys didn't have their ideas straight, and they killed what they had by shamelessly putting those ideas in the same old frames. They made no effort to invent new techniques to express their thoughts.
>
> And the old-timers, those who were at the top ten years ago: What do they report? They're still there, resting on their laurels. Rigor mortis has set in and they don't know it. Yet no new talent has come forward to challenge them. And the old boys are not good enough for us to rest our hopes upon. The spirit isn't there. The questing has gone. . . .
>
> Anyhow, now's the time to experiment. You've complained for years about the Frenchmen's stealing the American market. Well, things are on the up and up. Galleries need fresh talent, new ideas. Money can be heard crinkling throughout the land. And all you have to do, boys and girls, is get a new approach, do some delving for a change. God knows you've had a long rest.

The letter led to an invitation to Kootz from Macy's department store to organize an exhibition of contemporary American art. Seventy artists were represented, including Milton Avery, Ilya Bolotowsky, Adolph Gottlieb, Arshile Gorky, Carl Holty, Ralston Crawford, Jan Matulka, and Mark Rothko. Prices were low, ranging from $24.97 to $249. Two paintings by Rothko, *Oedipus* and *Antigone,* were available at $200 apiece.[12] The store issued a press release optimistically concluding that "Macy's presentation of this important exhibit to a larger-than-usual audience, combining the regular gallery visitors with the department store public, constitutes an experiment which may very well determine the future of exhibits of this sort."[13]

Following up the success of this exhibition and the excitement generated by his letter to the *Times,* Kootz wrote a second book, *New Frontiers in American Painting,* published in 1943, in which such directions as were apparent in the exhibitions at Art of This Century came under his gaze. The Museum of Modern Art took notice of his interest and offered him a place on its advisory board.

In 1944 Kootz provided subsidies for Baziotes and Motherwell, who had asked Peggy Guggenheim, in vain, for such help. She protested that she could not afford to honor their request, and in view of the commitments she had made to friends and hangers-on, along with the expense of running Art of This Century and providing for her children, that was very probably the truth of the matter. Kootz gave the two men money and sent them off to Florida to paint.[14] In the next year, 1945, he officially became a dealer. Baziotes and Motherwell were among the first to join his gallery, much to Peggy's dismay.

Kootz opened at 15 East Fifty-seventh Street, across the hall from Mortimer Brandt, who held the lease on the entire floor. At that time Betty Parsons, who until recently had organized exhibitions of contemporary art at the small Wakefield Gallery, was developing exhibitions of contemporary art for Brandt. In 1946 when Brandt decided to give up on the contemporaries and transfer his old masters to another building, Parsons took over the lease, and Kootz stayed on in his half of the floor. For about three years, until Kootz left the building in 1948, this move put two dealers in very advanced art within whispering distance of each other. In September 1946 *Fortune,* the monthly devoted to the ups and downs of big business, offered an article titled "57th Street" whose anonymous authors noted that along Fifty-seventh or nearby were some 150 dealers "who control the art market of the country in an apparently unbreakable bottleneck." The article provided the names and addresses of the best of them.[15] But of all these dealers in art at that moment in the history of the trade, only Kootz, Guggenheim, Parsons, and Charles Egan, a newcomer, showed and tried to sell the newest of the new.

Ever mindful of American artists on the current New York scene, Kootz inaugurated his gallery with a show that included his protégés Baziotes and Motherwell, and also Carl Holty, Fritz Glarner, and one French artist, Fernand Léger, who had spent the war years in New York. Kootz's stable soon included Byron Browne, Romare Bearden, and the sculptor David Hare as well. But he did not for long keep Glarner, whose geometrical art in the Mondrian-De Stijl tradition of limiting the palette to the primary colors plus black and white may have been too classical for his taste.

Kootz sought to take advantage of the postwar boom and its accompanying baby bull market by designing exhibitions meant to attract young collectors, such as his 1946 show *Building a Modern Collection,* which consisted of paintings small enough in size and low enough in price to appeal to those whose fortunes were still in the making. At the same time, he had no intention of ignoring collectors in the upper brackets. Earlier in the year he held an exhibition of works from the collection of the stockbroker Roy R. Neuberger and his wife. The collection consisted of American art, some of which Kootz himself had sold to the Neubergers.

Other collectors of established wealth were the audience targeted by Kootz for his Picasso exhibition of 1947, the artist's first postwar show in the United States. While this was a personal triumph, if not an absolute success from the critics' point of view, it was offset by a disastrous exhibition of six artists from Kootz's stable, Baziotes, Bearden, Browne, Gottlieb, Holty, and Motherwell, at the Galerie Maeght in Paris late in March. The exhibition was savaged by the French press. Kootz tactfully refrained from providing the artists with copies of the reviews, but of course they understood that the show had failed. Each artist was represented by five paintings, none of which sold. But the artists had not expected sales. For a few days before the opening, it was reported, mistakenly, that all the paintings had been lost in Iceland en route to Paris. That was good news to the artists, who would have received insurance money had the report been accurate. None of the artists could afford to travel to Paris for the show.[16]

Kootz had worked his way into Picasso's favor by presenting him with a copy of Harriet and Sidney Janis's *Picasso: The Recent Years, 1939–46* (1946), as Kootz was pleased to tell Sidney Janis on his return.[17]

Apparently Picasso had not already seen the book. Why the Janises themselves had not given him a copy is a mystery. Persistent rumor had it that Kootz gave Picasso another, considerably more costly present: a white Cadillac, sent on to the artist in advance of their meeting as a "calling card."[18] After the meeting, Kootz, at Picasso's suggestion, planned to deal exclusively in the artist's work. At the end of one year, however, finding that he missed the daily contact with the public (and embarrassed to be discovered in his pajamas one lazy morning when the wealthy collector Stephen Clark came to call), Kootz took space at 600 Madison Avenue, near Fifty-seventh Street, and resumed his practice of dealing in the work of a number of artists, many of whom he had not exhibited before. This move did not mean that he gave up Picasso or that Picasso gave up Kootz. For the first ten years of the new gallery's existence, Picasso's art was its mainstay.[19] It was not until the mid-1950s that Abstract Epressionism, despite its endorsement by such influential critics as Clement Greenberg, Thomas Hess, and Harold Rosenberg, began to sell at good prices.

The move to Madison Avenue caused Kootz to rethink his position and to review the talent of his artists. Three, Browne, Holty, and Romare Bearden, were found wanting and were dismissed in 1949. Over the next six years the sculptors Ibram Lassaw and Herbert Ferber joined the gallery, but accompanying these gains were serious losses: when he put the French abstractionists Georges Mathieu and Pierre Soulages under contract in 1953, Motherwell and Gottlieb left.

In 1949 Kootz offered a group exhibition of Abstract Expressionists that was larger in scope than Putzel's *A Problem for Critics,* but with the same underlying premise: that these artists represented a school. His term for them was "intrasubjectives," a clumsy word that proved no help to the exhibition. The catalogue was a broadside printed in rich black and decorated with lively drawings by Adolph Gottlieb. It included statements by Harold Rosenberg and Kootz himself. Rosenberg, constructing an apologia for art then not well understood by much of the public, wrote in part,

> Space or nothingness . . . that is what the modern painter begins by copying. Instead of mountains, copses, nudes, etc., it is his space that speaks to him, quivers, turns green or yellow with bile, gives him a sense of sport, of sign language, of the absolute.
>
> When the spectator recognizes that nothingness [that is] copied by the modern painter, the latter's work becomes just as intelligible as the earlier painting.

In his own remarks, Kootz struck again at his old bogey, American Scene painting, and went on to observe that the intrasubjective artist "deals with inward emotions and experience." He also stressed the importance to the movement of the diversity of the styles of its adherents: "Intrasubjectivism is a point of view in painting rather than an identical painting style." Thus one could exhibit together, as Kootz did, paintings by Mark Tobey, Pollock, Baziotes, Bradley Walker Tomlin, Gorky, Ad Reinhardt, Motherwell, Gottlieb, Willem de Kooning, and Hofmann. But, oddly, Morris Graves's *Joyous Young Pine,* a representational work now in the collection of the Museum of Modern Art, was also included. Loans for the exhibition came from the Egan, Levy, Parsons, and Willard galleries.

Kootz built his gallery on a combination of Abstract Expressionists and modern European masters. In the announcement for a Hans Hofmann exhibition in 1949, he let it be known that he had not only paintings by Americans but also "important examples" of the work of Picasso, Braque, Léger, Arp, and Jean Dubuffet. Yet it was the Americans for whom the gallery was noted and who made up most of his exhibitions, although not with a strong financial return in the gallery's early years. Only one painting sold from his innovative 1949 exhibition of black-and-white paintings, a de Kooning that was a steal at a mere $700.[20]

Contributing to his success, and attesting to his fervent endeavor to promote American art, was an exhibition called *New Talent* that he staged in 1950. Twenty-three artists were chosen for the exhibition by Meyer Schapiro, an eminent art historian who taught at Columbia University, and the equally eminent Clement Greenberg, whose influential columns on art appeared in *The Nation* and *Partisan Review*. These were men whose knowledge and understanding of the contemporary scene guaranteed an audience. Among their choices were Elaine de Kooning, Robert de Niro, Robert Goodnough, Grace Hartigan, Alfred Leslie, and Larry Rivers. In 1954 Greenberg selected eleven artists for an exhibition titled "Emerging Talent" at Kootz's gallery. The color-field painters Morris Louis and Kenneth Noland, who would achieve eminence in the 1960s, were included.

Kootz's intention was only to introduce these artists, not to add them to his roster. Goodnough, Hartigan, Leslie, and Rivers were taken on by John Bernard Myers at the Tibor de Nagy Gallery, which opened in December 1950 with backing from Dwight Ripley, Peggy Guggenheim's erstwhile friend. Myers, who received advice on choices for his gallery from Jackson Pollock, Lee Krasner, and Greenberg, later added Kenneth

Noland and Helen Frankenthaler.[21] En bloc, these young artists made up a "second generation" of Abstract Expressionists.

Although Kootz's love of art might never be questioned, he was a practical businessman with a businessman's eye on the balance sheet. He had bought scores of paintings by Byron Browne and Carl Holty as an advance against sales, but in 1951, two years after he had dropped the artists from his roster, many of the paintings were still on his hands. In a bold effort to recover his investment, he offered them in a sale at the gallery. There were, however, few takers. His next move was to take the paintings—forty by Browne, fifty-nine by Holty—to Gimbels department store, then Macy's great rival on Thirty-fourth Street, where they were to be sold along with other household items.

Readers of New York's newspapers were informed of the sale in advertisements whose tone was a far cry from the measured prose of a respectable gallery's press releases:

> Gimbels loves modern art (we like the Mona Lisa too, but she's 450 years old), but we don't spell art with a capital A. The mention of the word doesn't send us into awe-struck silence. We think fine paintings are just as logical in a department store as they are in a hushed, plushed gallery. . . . But are our prices the same as the uptown galleries'? The answer is 'not very likely!' Gimbel's doesn't see any reason why we can't save you money on a fine original painting as on a pot, or a pan, or a pair of nylons.[22]

Although Kootz claimed that the artists were informed of his plan in advance and approved of it, in truth they had no choice, for the paintings were his personal property, to be disposed of as he pleased. Had they not consented, the works would have been sold at auction, in which case, as the artists believed, they would in all probability have been knocked down for only a few dollars each.[23] Although it is true that the dismissal of an artist from a gallery is not unethical (or unusual), since no dealer is morally obliged to support an artist for whom there is at best a limited market and perhaps none at all, Kootz's decision to dump the paintings on the mercy of Gimbels was at least questionable. The bargain prices at which they were offered drastically undercut the value of *all* work by the artists wherever it might be found and threatened their market in perpetuity. Gimbels, moreover, sold very few of the paintings.

It may be said that Kootz got away with it—that is, did not receive a general condemnation for such harsh treatment of two respected artists—but the artists themselves were gravely affected. As a result of the sale, Browne suffered a heart attack. He lived to 1961 and had a successful career as a teacher at the Art Students League, but the sale so flattened the regard of the art-conscious public toward his work that not until the 1980s was interest in it renewed on the part of dealers and collectors. Holty accepted a teaching post at Brooklyn College in 1956 and continued to teach until his death, in 1973. Although he was no less talented than Browne, his work did not begin to fetch good prices until the '90s.

In 1953 Kootz opened a gallery in Provincetown, Massachusetts, the village on the tip of Cape Cod that had been a thriving artists' colony since the turn of the century. After two years, however, he turned it over to Nat Halper, a James Joyce enthusiast who renamed it HCE, after H. C. Earwicker or Here Comes Everybody from Joyce's *Finnegans Wake,* and maintained it until 1967.

In the fall of 1957 Kootz instituted the bold policy of closing his gallery on Monday. Until then, it had been the general practice of the trade to maintain a six-day schedule. It was not long before most other gallery owners in major cities across the nation adopted Kootz's plan, and museums also began to close one day a week, although not always on Monday. Kootz received his colleagues' heartfelt thanks for this comforting innovation. "At last we could have a day off!" the dealer Eleanor Ward joyfully recalled many years later.[24]

In 1966, after twenty-one years in the profession, Kootz retired. Although a boom was under way for dealers who, like himself, had a stable of popular, cutting-edge artists, he had had enough of it—and had earned enough—to see no reason to go on. "I feel sad about giving it up," he said, "because of my friendships with the artists. But there are enough merchants in the market—they don't need me."[25]

16

POWER PLAYS

Kootz had it right: there were so many galleries in New York by the time he left the scene that visitors who wanted to look into the best of them could not complete their rounds in less than two full days unless they intended nothing more than a quick glance from the doorway. But in 1946, twenty years before the Kootz Gallery closed, the number of dealers showing art on the cutting edge were fewer than even a fifteenth of the 150 galleries that *Fortune* claimed to have spotted. Kootz, of course, was one of them. Others were Betty Parsons and Charles Egan, and two years later Sidney Janis would enter the field.

These four, to be sure, were not the only men and women who promoted Abstract Expressionist art in the 1940s, the '50s, and beyond. Marian Willard, who opened her gallery in 1936, successfully showed paintings by Mark Tobey and sculptures by David Smith, two major figures in the pantheon of nonobjective art, along with the mystical but

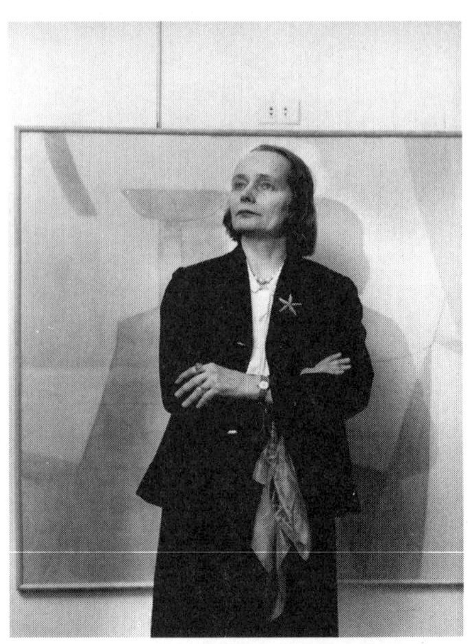

Betty Parsons. Behind her is a painting by Kenzo Okada.

essentially realist paintings of Morris Graves. But the movement's extraordinary success, and the subsequent transfer of supremacy in the art trade from Paris to New York, was largely due to the efforts of Parsons, Egan, Janis, and Kootz. Kootz was the first of them to open a gallery, but on the rosters of the other three could be found the most striking of the new modern masters. The four dealers formed a cluster whose careers were inseparable, although not always to their pleasure. Janis's first location was the space that Kootz had previously rented, across the hall from Parsons. When Kootz moved out, Janis moved in, under a sublease that Parsons gave him.

Betty Parsons, who became a dealer in a somewhat roundabout way, differed from her colleagues in the social standing of her forebears. She was born Betty Bierne Pierson in 1900 to parents then living in a dream world in which money, and plenty of it, was always at hand. The family firm manufactured heavy machinery. Betty's father was originally a member of the firm, but later switched careers to become a stockbroker. This proved to be a costly error. As a businessman, he was singularly lacking in talent. According to Betty, "if he had never worked he would have been a very rich man."[1] Eventually his inability to earn an income large enough to pay for his wife's extravagant ways brought an end to the marriage. Neither Pierson nor his wife was pleased by Betty's fascination with art, which she dated from her visits to the Armory Show at the age of thirteen. There amid the avant-garde exhibits she was struck with the desire to become an artist herself. While a student at Miss Chapin's School in New York, she expressed a wish to continue her education at Bryn Mawr, where she thought she might get instruction as an artist. Her parents, however, had other plans for her. They expected her to remain within their social milieu and to that end intended to expose her to only so much education as would prepare her for the conventional life of an upper-class matron. A finishing school, the sort of institution for proper young ladies where not much was demanded of students and not much given by way of instruction, was what they had in mind. Betty's tomboyish behavior was also a matter of concern to them. A compromise was reached: she would go to a finishing school, but would also receive instruction in the making of art.[2]

Betty attended classes in art conducted by Gutzon Borglum, who was to receive the nation's notice two decades later with his gigantic portrait heads of Washington, Jefferson, Lincoln, and Theodore Roosevelt gouged and blasted out of what had been the ruggedly beautiful escarpment of Mount Rushmore, South Dakota. His classes were not a success; Betty objected to his method of instruction, which consisted in the main of requiring students to make drawings of bones from other drawings, not from the bones themselves.[3] Later she studied sculpture with Mary Tonetti in a happier studio environment. But in the meanwhile, at the age of twenty, she married. Her husband, Schuyler Livingston Parsons, ten years her senior, was rich and well connected and, like herself, a rebel against the constrictive standards of behavior thought appropriate for persons of their social background. But the marriage was a mistake. Betty had been aware ever since her teens that her sexual orientation was toward her own sex, and her husband also was homosexual. After more than two years of trying to put a good face on an impossible situation, in 1923 they divorced amicably on grounds of incompatibility. Like many divorced women of her time, Betty elected not to resume her maiden name. For the rest of her life she was Mrs. Parsons.[4]

The divorce took place in Paris, and there Betty, whom we will now know as Parsons, remained for ten years. She studied sculpture with Antoine Bourdelle and Ossip Zadkine and painting with Arthur Lindsey, a little-known English artist recommended to her by Adge Baker, a woman ten years her senior who had become her lover. But in 1933, after the crash, an event that deprived her ex-husband of the means to keep up his alimony payments, she returned to the States and headed for California. Her parents had lost virtually everything, and her rich grandfather Pierson was so incensed over her divorce, the first in the family, that he cut her off completely.[5] For the rest of her life a group of wealthy women who had long been her friends, some from as far back as her Chapin years, helped out with gifts and loans of money as well as lunches, dinners, and vacations. It is clear from the selfishness that she sometimes displayed in later life that their attentiveness spoiled her. But in her brief Hollywood period she was fiercely independent. She paid her bills by giving art lessons, painting portraits, and, for a time, working in a liquor store, where her knowledge of French wines proved useful.[6] At this time, her principal medium was watercolor, as it would be for several years. In 1934 the Stendahl Galleries gave her a one-artist exhibition.

Parsons's social charm, her intelligence, and her seeming lack of interest in accumulating personal wealth were important assets. Many of her friends, including some of the women who protected her, were of her own sexual persuasion. One such was the sometime actress Hope Williams, who in 1928 became famous for creating the role of Linda Seton in Philip Barry's *Holiday*. In Hollywood, Parsons knew Greta Garbo well, and her remarks about the actress's liking for women, as quoted by Parson's biographer, suggest that the two may have had an affair.[7] But Parsons also had friends, including men, in many other circles who cherished their relationship with her. Her biographer tells us, somewhat surprisingly, that one of the men in her life was the comic essayist and screen comedian Robert Benchley. Another close friend was Alexander Calder.[8]

Still another was Stuart Davis (not the well-known artist of the same name), a New Yorker of means who had pursued her in California and whom she had agreed to marry. Parsons returned to New York in 1935 as an engaged woman. Soon, however, her common sense asserted itself and she drifted out of the engagement. In 1936 Benchley suggested that she take a portfolio of her watercolors to the Midtown Gallery, founded by Alan Gruskin in 1932 as a venue for representational art. Gruskin looked through the portfolio and immediately signed her on for a show. It was success, with fourteen pictures sold. Among the purchasers were Wright Ludington, an important California collector who was her friend, and Lee Ault, a New York collector. Other buyers were Benchley himself and his old-time *New Yorker* colleague and drinking companion, Dorothy Parker.[9] Nine more exhibitions followed at the gallery until 1957, when Parsons came to believe that her current work, abstract sculpture, was out of place at the Midtown.

In addition to offering her a show, Gruskin, aware that she had a coterie of wealthy acquaintances and a great deal of charm, offered Parsons a job. She was delighted to accept; the fact that she was not expected to show up for work until two-thirty in the afternoon made the offer especially alluring. At the Midtown she sold art on commission and helped in the hanging of exhibitions. After a year and a half she moved on to the Park Avenue gallery of Mary Quinn Sullivan, one of the three courageous founders of the Museum of Modern Art. There the emphasis was on realist art. But in Sullivan's inventory were paintings by Lyonel Feininger, Mondrian, Cézanne, Modigliani, and the Irish artist Jack Yeats. Among her clients was the Museum of Modern Art, which, according to Parsons, bought several Modiglianis.[10]

A more challenging offer came Parsons's way in 1940, when the owners of the Wakefield Bookshop, on East Fifty-fifth Street, decided to open a gallery in their store and asked her to serve as its director. Here, too, she would sell on commission, but the choice of works to exhibit was to be entirely up to her. Among the artists whom she invited to show at the Wakefield were Saul Steinberg and his wife, Hedda Sterne, Theodoros Stamos, Adolph Gottlieb, Joseph Cornell, Alfonso Ossorio, and three whom she would later show in her own gallery: Walter Murch, Rothko, Hans Hofmann, and Ad Reinhardt. With advice from the artist Barnett Newman, who became her counselor and friend, she also staged an exhibition of pre-Columbian sculpture.[11]

Late in 1944 the Wakefield's owners closed the gallery. Parsons was not long out of work, however. It was at this time that Mortimer Brandt invited her to take charge of the contemporary section of his gallery at 15 East Fifty-seventh Street. At last she would have a salary: forty dollars a week.

After two years, when Brandt concluded that his experiment with modern art had not brought a sufficient financial return to justify going on with it, he moved to another building and left the space at 15 East Fifty-seventh to Parsons to develop as she pleased. She had been happy as a dealer, especially in discovering new talent, and decided to establish a gallery under her own name. Having only a thousand dollars of her own to invest, she borrowed $4,500 from friends, including Steinberg and Sterne.[12]

Fifty-five hundred dollars was a very small capital with which to undertake such an enterprise. But, as Calvin Tomkins has written, her real capital was in artists.[13] In addition to the many artists she had shown at the Wakefield and Mortimer Brandt galleries and who were happy to continue to show with her, she took on Pollock, Rothko, and Still when Peggy Guggenheim closed Art of This Century and departed for Venice. Barnett Newman came along with them. These four men, soon to be recognized, along with Willem de Kooning, Franz Kline, and Motherwell as the nuclear core of Abstract Expressionism, were the central figures of the Betty Parsons Gallery for as long as they remained in it. With the exception of de Kooning, who had sailed from his native Holland in 1926 as a stowaway, all had been born in the United States.

Parsons had had doubts about Pollock's stability, but added him to her roster out of admiration for his work. Peggy, who had contracted to pay him a $300 monthly stipend through February 1948, offered him to Parsons with the stipulation that Parsons would take over the contract. During the period it covered, Peggy would continue to own all of Pollock's new work with the exception of one painting chosen by him for himself. Parsons, however, was permitted to sell the works at prices that she determined and to keep the commissions. On older works, on the other hand, the full sales price would go to Peggy, and she alone could price them.[14] After this contract expired, Pollock signed a new one with Parsons.

As designed by Parsons, the look of her gallery set the style in such rooms for decades to come. The walls were painted white. Not only was there no plush, there was no color except that supplied by the art. Nor was there furniture to accommodate the weary visitor, such as the ottomans that graced the rooms of Knoedler's. This simple, stripped-down decor she thought essential to showing off the large and increasingly larger works produced by her artists. Nothing was present to distract a viewer from the swirls and skeins of paint on Pollock's canvases or the clouds of color that seemed to have floated onto Rothko's. Except at openings, Parsons herself could seldom be seen in the exhibition room. The first show, for which she sent out an announcement with notes by Newman, consisted of Northwest Coast American Indian art. Although the preponderance of the exhibitions that followed were of the work of living artists, most of whom were Americans, examples of the art of primitive peoples were often to be seen here and there about the gallery.

As a dealer, Parsons, courageous as she was in championing the avant-garde, was not lacking in faults. One was her tendency to overestimate the talent of some of the young artists whose work she saw. Moreover, she occasionally booked exhibitions of mediocre work merely because the artists were her friends. She developed so lengthy a roster that she could not give adequate attention to all the men and women on it. This gave rise to complaints among her artists of recognized ability, who resented the presence in *their* gallery of persons they considered inferior to themselves.

In the winter of 1951 Robert Rauschenberg, then an ambitious unknown, brought some canvases to Parsons without an appointment or a prior introduction. In the previous year, lacking a reputation, but with his energy, cockiness, and youthful good looks creating a magnetic field around him, he had talked Willem de Kooning into giving him a drawing, not so that he could sit and admire it, but so that he could assert his independence and, it may have been, his manhood by erasing it. His approach to Parsons was equally effective. She looked at his canvases and simply said, "Well, I can't give you a show until May."[15] He had the show, his first name rendered informally as "Bob" in the advertisements. (His true given name was Milton.) But this time his luck ran out; none of the seventeen paintings, all in white, found buyers.

Some time after the closing, Rauschenberg wrote cryptically to Parsons from Black Mountain College in North Carolina, where he was then a student, to ask for a second show of more white paintings: "Have felt that my head and heart move through something quite different that this hot dust the earth threatens. They bear the contradictions that deserve them a place with other outstanding paintings and yet they are not Art because they take you to a place in painting art has not been."[16] Nothing came of this request, however, and Parsons never offered him a second exhibition. He believed this slighting of his talent was due to Barnett Newman's disapproval of his work.[17] Although Newman had only two one-artist shows with Parsons, along with appearances in five of her group shows, he was her staunch adviser as well as an intimate associate of Pollock, Rothko, and Still. She may well have backed away from Rauschenberg on his advice.

A problem as grievous to her prominent artists as her tendency to load the gallery's schedule with immature artists or those of questionable ability, a problem rarely heard of in the art world, was that Parsons was afflicted with a patrician reluctance to involve herself in the details of trade. Although, as a search through her papers makes clear, she frequently sent personal notes to clients, these in the main were friends or other persons who had often bought from her, such as Wright Ludington, Burton and Emily Tremaine, Duncan Phillips, and Susan Morse Hilles. The act of picking up the telephone and informing collectors of the presence in the gallery of a certain desirable work of art was something she could not bring herself to do. "Most artists don't think I'm tough enough," she said. "That I don't go out and solicit, call up people all the time. I know how people hate that sort of thing, because I hate it myself, so I don't do it."[18] It is true, to be sure, that some collectors do have an intense dislike of telephone solicitations, those from art dealers no less than those from stockbrokers. Nevertheless, since her artists were aware that sales are frequently initiated over the telephone, they could hardly be blamed for their impatience with her quirkiness.

Parsons often spoke of Pollock, Rothko, Still, and Newman as the "Four Horsemen," a curious phrase if with it she had intended to evoke the Four Horsemen of the Apocalypse. What she meant, however, was that they were the giants of her gallery. The four artists were often at odds with one another, but offered a show of solidarity in order to create a group identity for the "first generation" of Abstract Expressionists.[19] Parsons was slow to grasp the fact that of these artists, Pollock, Rothko, and especially Still, expected more attention and more publicity than she was prepared by nature to manufacture for them and that they had begun to resent the presence in the gallery or artists whom they judged to be greatly inferior to themselves. As their fame grew, so grew their frustration.

Their activities, both social and more directly pertaining to their art, strengthened the appearance of a bond among them. At San Francisco's California School of Fine Arts under the direction of Douglas MacAgy, Still taught from 1946 to 1950 and Rothko in the summers of 1947 and 1949. In the summer of 1950 Ad Reinhardt also was on the faculty. The artists' influence on young men back from the Second World War and eager for a career in art gave rise to a Bay Area coterie of Abstract Expressionists. In 1948 Still and Rothko organized a school of their own in New York, which they called the Subjects of the Artist. Still did not stick with the plans for the school, and Pollock did not participate, but with Rothko, Motherwell, Baziotes, and David Hare in on it from the start and Newman shortly joining in, the school, in a loft at 35 East-Eighth Street, provided for the single year of its existence a fertile ground for discussion and, as Rothko's biographer suggests, also provided publicity for the artists.[20] Their sessions were held on Friday evenings. In 1949 three members of the faculty of the New York University School of Art Education took the loft and maintained the Friday evening meetings as Studio 35 until April 1950, by which time the questions asked by the public in attendance had become so repetitious that there seemed no reason to go on with it.[21]

But in the meanwhile, a number of artists of exceptional talent banded together as a club, which they referred to as simply the Club, and rented a loft at 39 East Eighth Street at which to hold meetings. They were friends who for years had held informal discussions in cafeterias and coffee shops in Greenwich Village.[22] Among the founders of the Club were Willem de Kooning, Kline, Reinhardt, Ibram Lassaw, Landes Lewitin, Conrad Marca-Relli, Philip Pavia, and Jack Tworkov. Charles Egan was also a founding member. Originally the Club was to be open to men only, and, cold-war politics being what they were, Communists were also kept out; this was, after all, the age of Senator Joseph McCarthy, and, more to the point, it was the age of Representative George Dondero of Michigan, who was convinced that all creators and promoters of abstract art were subversives intent on destroying traditional values.[23]

The second wave of members, invited by the founders, included the first woman, Elaine de Kooning, along with Leo Castelli, Harold Rosenberg, and, among other artists, Philip Guston and Esteban Vicente. Still others were brought in by successive votes. On Wednesday evenings roundtable discussions open only to members were held, but at gatherings held on Friday evenings, collectors, critics, and dealers were frequently present as guests. Alfred Barr attended very often.[24] Parsons, who came to some early meetings, quickly lost interest; the carryings-on were too rowdy for her taste.[25]

Debate at the Club did indeed sometimes lead to shouting matches, but despite these occasional bursts of vocal violence the Club served to brace its adherents to face a world still not attuned to their talents. Nearby, at Ninth Street and University Place, was a friendly saloon, the Cedar Tavern. There the artists could drink themselves into oblivion or aggressive displays of machismo leading to fist fights. Good customers, the artists won a place in the owners' hearts despite the fisticuffs. After all, they turned up night after night and bought round after round.

In the spring of 1950 the Metropolitan Museum announced a painting competition to open in December, with four prizes ranging from $3,500 down to $1,000, good money at the time. At what proved to be the last sessions of Studio 35, April 21-23, 1950, the artists in attendance took up the matter of this show, its jurors, and its prizes, and were troubled that Francis Henry Taylor, the director of the Metropolitan, Robert Beverly Hale, the Metropolitan's associate curator of American art, and the jurors were too conservative to give advanced art fair play in the show. Adolph Gottlieb, with the aid of others in the Abstract Expressionist camp, drafted a letter to the *Times* addressing the issue. Nearly a

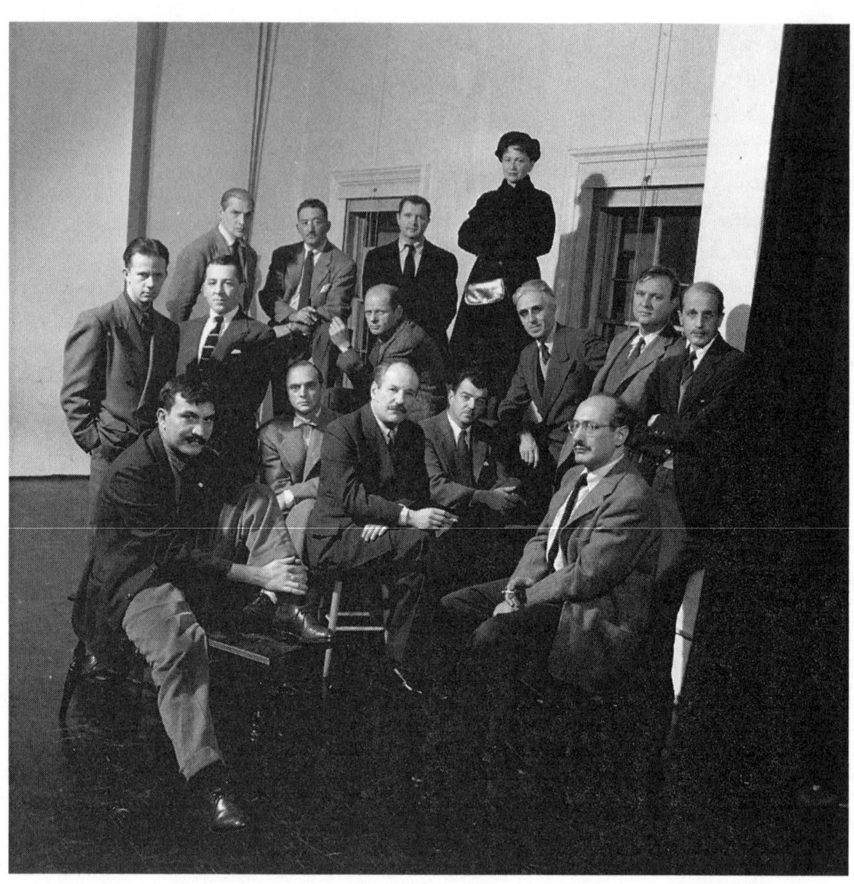

The Irascibles. Seated, left to right: Theodoros Stamos, Jimmy Ernst, Jackson Pollock, Barnett Newman, James Brooks, Mark Rothko. Standing, left to right: Richard Pousette-Dart, William Baziotes, Willem de Kooning, Adolph Gottlieb, Ad Reinhardt, Hedda Sterne, Clyfford Still, Robert Motherwell, Bradley Walker Tomlin. Missing: Fritz Bultman.

month passed before the final version was ready. Eighteen artists and ten sculptors then signed it, and Barnett Newman delivered it to the newspaper, which published it on May 21.[26]

Two days later the *New York Herald Tribune* editorialized on the letter under the heading "The Irascible Eighteen." The adjective stuck, and Kootz briefly entertained the notion of presenting a show of the eighteen artists who had signed, only to have the offer spurned by the artists on the grounds that Kootz's gallery was too small to display their paintings effectively.[27] The editors of *Life* also became interested. Planning a pictorial essay on the exhibition with publication to follow the announcement of the prize winners on December 5, they gathered fifteen of the signatories to the letter for a group photograph as "the Irascibles." The essay appeared in the issue of January 15, 1951. Dressed in their best, many of the artists resembled bankers or lawyers, as was their intention. The winners of the Metropolitan's competition, it should be noted, were impressively talented artists, but, as the "Irascibles" expected, hardly in the avant-garde. In descending order, the prizes went to Karl Knaths, Rico LeBrun, Yasuo Kuniyoshi, and Joseph Hirsch.

New sources of support for Abstract Expressionism developed in the '50s and into the early '60s as the Tanager, Brata, Area, and March galleries sprang up on Tenth Street, and opening close by were the Jane Street, James, and Hansa galleries, the last named to recall the medieval Hanseatic League and to pay homage to Hans Hofmann.[28] Taking heart from what seemed to be a gathering public curiosity about their art, in 1951 some of the original members of the Club staged an exhibition in an empty store on East Ninth Street, a memorable display of art that was to go down in history as simply the Ninth Street Show. Leo Castelli, not yet a dealer but a friend of the artists, helped to organize it and spent $450 of his own scant funds to set it up. His generosity was amply repaid by Willem de Kooning, who gave him a drawing that he later sold to Ben Heller for $10,000.[29] Because no artist could be trusted to hang the works to anyone's satisfaction but his own, he took on that task as well, a grueling one because of the complaints of many of the artists over the positioning of their paintings. Sixty-five artists were represented by one work each. Rothko, Still, and Newman refused to take part, presumably thinking that to be represented in such a milieu was beneath their dignity, but Pollock asked Parsons to send down one of his canvases. Kootz, disapproving of the show, forbade his artists to participate and succeeded in intimidating all of them with the exception of Motherwell.[30]

Because attendance went well beyond the artists' expectations, they looked for a midtown space in which to stage annual invitational exhibitions. When an offer came from Eleanor Ward in 1953 to make use of her newly established Stable Gallery, they quickly accepted it. The Stable was located on West Fifty-eighth Street in what had once been an actual stable, of which the odors rising from its floor on humid days provided all too clear a reminder. Ward liked to have it believed that she came from a wealthy, socially prominent family, when in truth she was the product of a middle-class upbringing in a Pennsylvania hill town.[31] Before becoming a dealer, she had had two unsuccessful marriages and two unsatisfying careers, the first in advertising in New York and the second in fashion in

Paris, at the house of Christian Dior. Knowing of her passion for art, Dior suggested that she return to New York and open a gallery, sage advice on which she acted profitably.[32] The Stable annuals took place over five years, to 1957. Among the many artists whom she was to show in advance of their fame and public acceptance were Rauschenberg, Andy Warhol, and Cy Twombly. In the early '50s Rauschenberg, hard up and in need of a job, was the Stable's janitor. The gallery remained in business until 1970, by which time it had moved to the less odiferous environment of East Seventy-fourth Street.

In the meanwhile, Charles Egan had begun his rise as a major figure among dealers in the avant-garde. He made his start in the trade in 1935 as a salesman in the art gallery of Wanamaker's department store. From this employment he went on to the Ferargil Gallery and then to J. B. Neumann's New Art Circle.[33] All three posts offered him exposure to modern art. He had received no training in art, and his formal education had come to an end when he dropped out of high school.[34] In 1945, a young man in his early thirties, he opened a gallery of his own in a cramped space at 63 East Fifty-seventh Street. At the outset he showed older Americans, but he soon developed a preference for the newest of the new: Abstract Expressionism. The artists enjoyed his company; he possessed an abundance of "Irish charm," according to the dealer John Bernard Myers, who knew him well.[35]

Like Pollock and Willem de Kooning, Egan was a heavy drinker, quite able to hold his own with them or anyone else at the Cedar Tavern. If bored while an exhibition was under way, he would ask the elevator man to monitor the gallery while he went out for a drink or two. Myers once visited the gallery during a Joseph Cornell show, saw that Egan was missing, and thought for a moment of purloining a Cornell box and holding it for ransom to teach Egan a lesson.[36] Joan Peterson, who operated a gallery in Boston in the '60s and '70s and occasionally called on Egan to borrow works for her exhibitions, was startled and amused to find his lips flecked with white foam, perhaps from antacid pills he chewed to relieve alcohol-induced dyspepsia.[37]

In 1948 Egan gave de Kooning his first one-artist exhibition, a momentous event in the art community. It was a striking show of black-and-white paintings. The art-press critics were enthusiastic, and the Museum of Modern Art bought a large untitled canvas, the first of many works by the artist to enter its collection. Yet with prices ranging from only $300 to $2,000, the show was a financial failure. Egan kept it going for two months beyond the scheduled closing, although whether out of hope or inertia one cannot be sure. De Kooning's wife, Elaine, who was having an affair with Egan at the time, later recalled, "But nothing sold and we all got a little embarrassed." When Egan did manage to sell a de Kooning, he was impossibly slow to pay the artist. On one occasion the artist, hard up as he usually was in the '40s and '50s, confronted Egan, who was in his cups, and demanded payment, only to be charged with disloyalty to the gallery. Incensed over the absurdity of the accusation, de Kooning threw a punch at him.[38] He needed a dealer less like himself—that is, someone who drank less, if at all, and who knew how to keep accounts—and found one in Sidney Janis.

Franz Kline, the painter of huge black-and-white abstractions, also had his first one-artist show with Egan, in 1950. Their relationship was no less problematic than Egan's had been with de Kooning. When Kline eventually demanded that Egan pay him what was due him from sales, Egan suggested that they have a drink together. They had more than one, but not so many as to muddle Kline's thoughts. He insisted heatedly that Egan hand over the money. Egan, perhaps invoking the charm for which he was famous, replied that he couldn't, because they had drunk it up.[39] Like de Kooning, Kline went to Janis. Esteban Vicente, who was briefly in Egan's stable, was present in the gallery one day when a woman mentioned her intention of buying one of his works. At his request she sent her check to him, not to Egan; he banked it and turned Egan's share over to him.[40] This time, at least, an artist got what was due him.

Egan showed the work of Cornell from 1949 to 1953. Although Abstract Expressionism had become the standard fare of the gallery, where in addition to de Kooning and Kline, Jack Tworkov and Philip Guston were also on the roster, Egan made room not only for Cornell's Surrealist boxes but also for the photographs of Aaron Siskind, whose abstract black-and-white images of weathered boards and slashes of paint were akin to the black-on-white paintings of Kline. Cornell had joined when, at his invitation, Egan visited his home in Queens and admired his work.[41] His departure from the gallery was for the usual reason: Egan was holding back on the money due him. He moved on to the Stable in New York and the Allan Frumkin Gallery in Chicago, a bustling place founded in 1952 whose genial owner did good business with contemporary American paintings and modern European master prints. Late in 1954 Egan gave Rauschenberg a one-artist exhibition of red paintings and the artist's earliest neo-Dada assemblages of found objects, which he called "combines." Rauschenberg, too, eventually found another dealer: Leo Castelli, who opened his gallery in 1957.

Raoul Hague and Reuben Nakian, impressively talented sculptors, remained with Egan until late, but his other heavyweights left him one by one. Guston went to Janis, and Tworkov, briefly, to Leo Castelli. Dorothy Miller and Holger Cahill offered succinct remarks on Egan halfway through his career as a dealer. Miller observed, "The Egan Gallery, Charles Egan, promoted painfully and long the work of Bill de Kooning, Franz Kline, Jack Tworkov, and Philip Guston. . . . They'd come through and were just ripe to sell, and now everything they are painting [sells]." Cahill replied, "That's true. But you can't have much sympathy for Egan, because Egan owed every one of those artists thousands of dollars."[42] The gallery closed in 1971. By that time, Egan had moved it to the Fuller Building, at 41 East Fifty-seventh Street, where it was in the expensive company of Pierre Matisse and the New York branch of the international Marlborough Gallery.

As a dealer, Egan obviously posed no threat to others in the trade. On the contrary, his losses benefited Sidney Janis and Eleanor Ward substantially. Sadly, Parsons's mishandling of her artists also proved beneficial to other dealers. The defections from her gallery were many, and most of the departing artists went to Janis. For almost forty years Janis held a commanding position in Abstract Expressionism while also doing business on a large scale in the work of modern European masters. He was fifty-two years old in 1958 when he opened his gallery, a somewhat advanced age for the commencement of a new career.

But Janis's early years had not been wasted. For thirteen years he had owned and managed a successful business as a manufacturer of shirts, and although the technique required for the selling of shirts may differ from that required for the selling of art, this experience provided him with a valuable understanding of marketing.[43] His other strengths, which he developed as an ardent collector of modern art, lay in his keen eye for quality and his knowledge of the psychology of the collector and the artist.

Janis (the family name was originally Janowitz; it was shortened in 1936) was born in Buffalo on July 8, 1896, the son of a traveling salesman who was also well-known as a cakewalk dancer and champion roller-skater. Young Sidney attended Buffalo's Technical High School, but dropped out in his senior year. An enthusiastic and talented ballroom dancer, he seized an invitation from the Palais de Danse in Buffalo to dance professionally. His performances there gained him an offer from the vaudeville impresario Gus Sun. After a stint of touring with Sun, he moved on to slightly more elevated employment in nightclubs, where he taught patrons the newest steps. He earned his living as a dancer for only three years, but danced for the pure pleasure of it all his life.[44] He especially enjoyed the beat of Latin music, and at the ninetieth birthday party given him by the Museum of Modern Art in 1986 he found a willing partner and showed the crowd assembled in his honor that he was still adept at the tango.[45]

During the First World War Janis joined the navy; as a sailor he studied and taught aeronautical mechanics. After his discharge he returned to Buffalo and went to work in his brother's shoe business. It was during these years, from 1919 to 1924, that he developed his interest in art. On trips to New York he began making the rounds of the galleries and museums but was not yet ready or, it may have been, not yet financially secure enough to make his first purchase of a work of art. Gallery-going, he later observed, "was a nice, free diversion that you could enjoy in the daytime."[46] In 1924, on one of his trips, he met Harriet Grossman, the woman who in the following year, when he moved from Buffalo to New York, was to become his wife. Two sons, Conrad and Carroll, would be born of the marriage.

With Harriet (Hansi to her friends) as his principal assistant, in 1926 Janis began his third career, as a shirt manufacturer. Like no other firm of its sort, the rather grandly named M'Lord Shirt Company produced only one variety of shirt. It was always white, never another color, and had two breast pockets—and it sold very well, especially in the warm South, where jacketless men found the extra pocket a great convenience.[47] In the same year as the opening of his company another momentous event occurred in Janis's life: he at last bought a work of art. This first purchase was a Whistler etching.[48] It would not remain in his possession for long, but it led to an addiction to art.

In 1927 he traded the etching, along with some money, for a small oil by Matisse. Purchases of other works by modern European masters followed in short order as Janis began, in 1928, to make annual trips to Paris. There in 1929 he bought his first Picasso, a *Head*.[49] In the next two years he acquired works by Klee, Dalí, de Chirico, and Mondrian. While in Paris in 1932, the Janises had the pleasure of meeting Mondrian and Picasso. They visited the studios of both artists and selected a painting by each. In 1933 the small Matisse oil was traded advantageously for another Picasso, the outstanding *Painter and Model*. Still more works by these artists entered the collection, and in 1934 Janis bought from the Knoedler

Gallery a masterpiece by Henri Rousseau, *The Dream*. Despite the Depression that kept a stranglehold on the American economy through the 1930s, M'Lord shirts supported these and still more purchases.[50] Among other New York galleries that he frequently visited in the '20s and '30s were those of Newman Montross, Charles Daniel, John Kraushaar, and Valentine Dudensing. Of all the dealers then operating in New York, Dudensing, a specialist in modern European art, struck Janis as the most admirable.[51]

As the collection grew, its importance became known throughout the art community. In recognition of Janis's connoisseurship, the Museum of Modern Art asked him to join its advisory committee in 1934. He accepted, and remained on the committee for fourteen years, until the opening of his gallery.[52] In those years he began a second career as a lecturer and writer. These activities and still another, as an organizer of special exhibitions at the Modern, so engaged his time and emotional energy that in 1939 he decided to sell M'Lord. Writing about art, talking about art, and buying art became his full-time occupation.

The purchase of *The Dream* in 1934 turned Janis's attention to primitive art for the first time. After studying what might be called the sophisticated primitivism of Rousseau, he began to look at American naive art. His first purchases in this field were two works by the self-taught Louis Eilshemius. He came upon the work of another primitive, William Doriani, at an outdoor exhibition in Washington Square and bought a painting.[53] In 1938, when the Marie Harriman Gallery gave Doriani a show, Janis wrote the catalogue introduction. Among other naive artists to come to his attention were Patrick J. Sullivan, a West Virginia steelworker; Patsy Santo, a Vermont plasterer; Morris Hirshfield, a Brooklyn cloak and suit manufacturer; and Grandma Moses—more formally, Anna Maria Robertson Moses—a housewife living in upstate New York. In 1939 he organized an exhibition of paintings by these and fourteen other primitive artists at the Museum of Modern Art. As a result of Janis's promotion, Hirshfield was given a one-artist exhibition at the Modern and Grandma Moses became a mainstay of the Galerie St. Etienne, founded in 1939, and developed a nationwide legion of fans, including Hollywood's Louis B. Mayer, who owned a dozen of her pictures.[54]

In 1939 Janis took the chairmanship of a committee brought together to exhibit Picasso's *Guernica* and related studies in America. The exhibition was held at Valentine Dudensing's gallery in New York and, later, at the Stendahl Galleries in Los Angeles. This large painting, Picasso's angry response to the bombing by Germans of the Basque town of Guernica during the Spanish Civil War, then went to the Museum of Modern Art on long-term loan from the artist until such time as Spain again became a democracy; at the museum, where it remained for forty years, its commanding power often seemed to overwhelm visitors. In 1941 Janis interrupted the writing of a book on American primitive art to develop an exhibition of such painting for the San Francisco Museum of Art and Stendahl. The book, titled *They Taught Themselves: American Primitive Painters of the 20th Century,* appeared in the following year. Janis also wrote articles on these painters.[55]

While exploring primitive art, Janis began to look at American Scene painting and the work of young American abstract artists. For the former, he often visited the Downtown Gallery, although always leaving without making a purchase. More to his taste was the work of Jackson Pollock, which he first looked at in 1941 at the suggestion of Lee Krasner. Although he eventually became the owner of Pollock canvases, he did not buy at first sight; later it was his boast that he was the first dealer to admire Pollock's work. According to Janis, Peggy Guggenheim, who became Pollock's dealer, went to see the artist's paintings because of Janis's recommendation to Howard Putzel.[56] In 1942 Janis was introduced to Mark Rothko and liked his work as well.[57]

The war years saw the arrival in New York of such renowned European artists as Mondrian, Fernand Léger, and Max Ernst, and, from Chile by way of Paris, Roberto Matta Echaurren. Janis befriended them, wrote about them, and acquired works by them. He offered a hint of the direction his life would take after the war in an article titled "School of Paris Comes to U.S." "New York," he wrote,

> is supplanting Paris as the art center of the world. This naturally means that the whole of America will play its part. Appreciation is gaining momentum on a nation-wide scale, but distribution . . . is still a problem of large proportions. An extensive and imaginative merchandising plan aimed to encourage a vast American public to participate by purchasing the works of their time, will be a step in the right direction.[59]

Meanwhile, he continued to direct exhibitions for museums and to write books and articles. His *Abstract and Surrealist Art in America* was published in 1944. It was this publication that persuaded Mortimer Brandt to invite Janis to put together an exhibition of the artists discussed in the book.

In 1946, as soon after the war as transatlantic steamship accommodations were available to the general public, Janis went back to Paris, where he spent nine weeks in Picasso's studio inspecting and analyzing the artist's wartime output. From this came his *Picasso: The Recent Years, 1939–46,* published late in the year.

At this time in his life, Janis began to feel a financial pinch; the publications, lecturers, and museum work had not brought in money on the scale of the profits of the abandoned M'Lord Shirts. The obvious solution, as he saw it, was to open a gallery. In 1947 he sailed to Europe again, with the purpose of securing paintings by modern masters for his first season. Kootz's rooms at 15 East Fifty-seventh Street were available to him soon after his return.[59]

Janis's first season was a mixture of one-artist and group exhibitions, with the emphasis on such familiar names as Léger, who opened the gallery, Mondrian, Kandinsky, Joseph Albers, and Robert Delaunay. Two slots in the calendar went to artists little known at the time and now forgotten, Evsa Model and Lucia Cristofanetti, and one show consisted of the work of modern French and American primitives. Taken as a whole, the season's slate was strong enough to establish the Sidney Janis Gallery as a potent claimant for attention.

The years to come would find the gallery holding to schedules balanced between group and one-artist shows, with the emphasis on well-known figures. The retrospective exhibitions of such modern masters as Léger, Mondrian, Kandinsky, Rousseau, Hans Arp, and Kurt Schwitters that he held over the years were of a quality more often encountered in museums than in commercial galleries, as were group exhibitions of the Cubist, Fauve, Futurist, De Stijl, and Dada artists. Of all the work of the gallery, it was these theme exhibitions that gave Janis the greatest pleasure. The catalogues for these and his other shows were of a quality approximating that of museum catalogues in both scholarship and design. All the gallery's publications, announcement cards and posters as well as catalogues, were admired for their appearance and content by casual gallery-goers and art-world professionals alike. During Janis's lifetime at least one exhibition was held of these ephemera, at Bennington College in 1960, unaccompanied by actual works of art. Their handsomeness by itself spoke for the taste of the gallery. One famous example was the Dada catalogue (1953), a single unillustrated sheet designed by Marcel Duchamp with a layout suggesting the outline of his *Nude Descending a Staircase.* In the spirit of Dada, the sheets were crumpled into balls. Some, however, were available in an unwrinkled state for archivists and collectors.

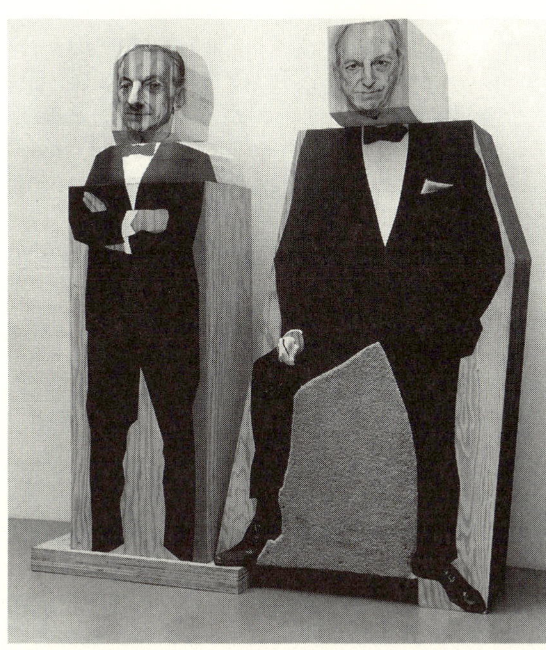

Portrait of Sidney Janis Selling Portrait of Sidney Janis *by Marisol.*

Janis had no trouble at all in reaching artists of recognized ability. Many of those whom he showed came of their own accord, without prompting from him. With some, the reason for joining the Sidney Janis Gallery was that their current dealer had decided to close, and with others it was the inadequacy of the original gallery as a space for displaying their art. For still others, and this of course was the most potent reason of all, it was the inability of the original dealer to get their work into the hands of collectors—thus the addition to his roster in the '50s of one artist after another from Parsons. Because he attracted powerful talents, Janis was viewed by some dealers as a freewheeling marauder. But Janis himself would eventually suffer the loss of artists looking for what they thought would be more effective representation.

The German-born Joseph Albers, in his young manhood a Bauhaus instructor and later a member, successively, of the faculties of Black Mountain College and Yale, was Janis's first American nonobjective painter, with an exhibition held early in 1949. His work did not sell well at first, and he always expressed amazement whenever a painting of his found a buyer. "Isn't it strange," he once said to Janis, "that someone would like my work?"[60] Before becoming regulars on his roster, Jackson Pollock (with Lee Krasner) and Willem de Kooning (with Elaine de Kooning) showed paintings at his gallery in 1949 in a loan exhibition of works by husbands and wives. In the following year Janis showed works by Pollock, Willem de Kooning, Mark Rothko, Franz Kline, and the late Arshile Gorky in a loan exhibition of young American and French painters organized for him by Leo Castelli.[61] These exhibitions of work by major Abstract Expressionists offered an indication of things to come.

Early in 1951, Betty Parsons's four giants asked her to concentrate on their art alone and abandon all others on her roster, a demand to which she could not accede.[62] When in the spring of 1952 the Museum of Modern Art included Pollock, Rothko, and Still in an exhibition entitled *15 Americans,* it was clear that at least these three, if not Newman as well, were destined for art-world stardom. In view of her well-known inability to market her artists aggressively, they would probably have left Parsons anyway, for some other dealer if not for Janis. Unlike the others, Newman did not go to Janis, but, gravely demoralized by the failure of his second show with Parsons, held in the late spring of 1951, he withdrew his paintings from her gallery. Although he allowed a retrospective of his work to be held at Bennington College in 1958, he showed with no other dealer until 1959, when he was offered the opening exhibition at the gallery of French and Company.[63]

The first of Parsons's artists to march across the hall to Janis was Jackson Pollock, in 1952, after the close of *15 Americans.* Furious with Parsons's limp efforts to market his work, he had already made it clear to her that he intended to find other representation after the expiration of his contract with her. He would have preferred Pierre Matisse above all other dealers, but his was not the sort of art Matisse favored. Kootz, whose regard for Abstract Expressionism might have made his gallery seem a suitable berth for Pollock, did not admire his work and had no patience with his alcoholism. Shortly before the *15 Americans* opening, Pollock had come into Kootz's gallery blind drunk and shouting obscenities, and Kootz had told him to leave. Although Charles Egan would have been pleased to represent him, his gallery was too small to accommodate Pollock's huge paintings. Janis clearly was much the best of the possibilities open to him, yet Janis too had some doubts about taking on an artist so unpredictable and emotionally unstable.[64] Parsons had also had Lee Krasner on her roster and, under pressure from Pollock, had given her an exhibition in 1951 in tandem with Anne Ryan, whose small and delicate collages provided a sharp contrast with Krasner's Pollock-sized paintings. But with Pollock's departure, Parsons dismissed Krasner from the gallery. She could not look at her paintings without thinking of Pollock's perfidy, as she saw it, in leaving the gallery.[65]

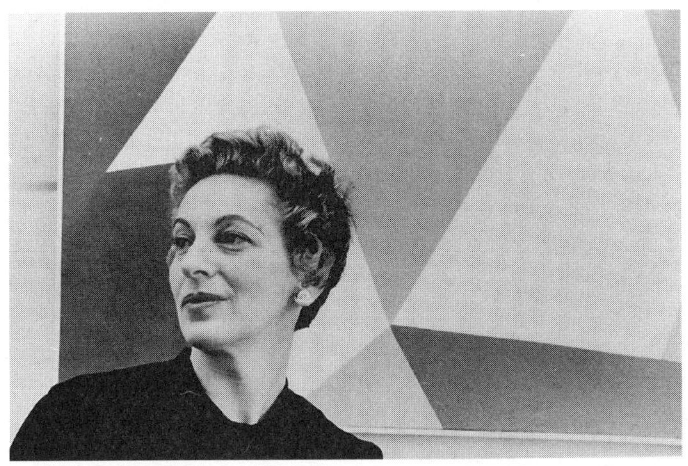

Grace Borgenicht

Pollock's dissatisfaction with Parsons, enhanced by his consumption of alcohol, affected his view of the gallery scene in general. In 1955, a year before his death, he persuaded his friend James Brooks to leave the Grace Borgenicht Gallery, where Brooks had been given a one-artist exhibition in 1954 and at whose opening Pollock had turned up drunk. Although the gallery's roster included the Abstract Expressionists Jimmy Ernst and Edward Corbett and the abstract sculptor José de Rivera, Pollock declared it to be not progressive enough for such a painter of boldly gestural canvases as Brooks. Brooks acted on Pollock's suggestion and went to the Stable. To Grace Borgenicht, who had faith in Brooks, this was a serious disappointment. Pollock's true motive may have been spite. He had made an unsuccessful effort to interest Borgenicht in his own work when she opened her gallery in 1951.[66]

Pollock profited greatly by his move to Janis. In no time at all, one of his paintings went for $1,500, and prices escalated quickly to $2,500. Parsons had never been able to do so well for him. Employing his well-honed skill as a salesman, Janis not only succeeded in raising Pollock's net worth but convinced him that for the easier identification of his canvases he should title them rather than merely numbering them, as had been his custom.[67] Janis gave Pollock a second one-artist show in 1954 and a third in 1955, *15 Years of Jackson Pollock,* the last in the gallery during the artist's lifetime. A posthumous show of Pollock's drawings was offered in November 1957, the first exhibition of his work in New York after his fatal automobile accident. What amounted to a memorial exhibition followed one year later. This was his last at Janis's gallery. Krasner herself became the guardian of Pollock's estate and rationed sales carefully to protect the market for them. In 1962 she put the estate in the hands of Frank Lloyd of the Marlborough Gallery in order to secure gallery representation for herself.[68] Since being dropped by Parsons, she had drifted from gallery to gallery but had never found a solid mooring. She left Lloyd in the '70s and went to the Pace Gallery, taking Pollock's remaining works with her. In her will she provided for the establishment of the Pollock-Krasner Foundation to manage the posthumous dispersal of both artists' works. The foundation's officers assigned Krasner's to the Robert Miller Gallery. They at first turned Pollock's over to the gallery of Jason McCoy, Krasner's nephew by marriage, but in 1997 assigned them to the gallery of Joan T. Washburn. By that date not much was left in the estate.

In the spring of 1953 Janis held a one-artist show of paintings by Gorky, followed by his first one-artist show of Willem de Kooning. The de Kooning exhibition included the sensational "Woman" series in which absurdly comic, overweight women with Bette Davis eyes seemed to be emerging from a background of Abstract Expressionist brushstrokes. Janis's first sale of a de Kooning was not one of these, however, but the large *Excavation,* a wholly nonobjective work, which went to the Art Institute of Chicago.[69]

Janis's first offering of paintings by Rothko and Still occurred in January 1954 in the exhibition *9 American Painters Today.*[70] Shortly before this event, Still had decided to join up with Janis. Parsons was furious when she discovered by way of the grapevine that he was leaving her. On December 4, 1953, she let him know the full extent of her wrath:

> To leave me to find out through others that you have signed up with Sidney Janis is your final act with me. I am forced to realize you are a coward, all your big talk about guts and integrity will remain to me empty chatter. It will always be incomprehensible how you could have made this decision without informing me.[71]

His response was to call her a little twerp and tell her to mind her own business.[72] Always truculent and difficult to deal with, he asked her to sell back to him some paintings she had bought outright from him. She refused: "As for the pictures I own, I consider it a closed deal, they are mine to do with as I consider best for them."[73]

Next to join Janis was Rothko, late in 1954. His departure from Parsons's gallery, unlike Pollock's and Still's, was calm. As she recalled, "Oh, we were always friends. We cried on each other's shoulders when we parted company, because as he said, 'I'm doing you no good. You're doing me no good.' "[74] Janis, unlike Parsons, was not hesitant in asking good money for good work. Whereas Parsons had asked only $900 for Rothko canvases larger than six feet in length or height, Janis demanded and received from $1,000 to $1,200. Price rose steadily, ultimately reaching a high of $18,000.[75]

Philip Guston, whose work of the 1950s was often described by critics as Abstract *Im*pressionism because of the delicacy of the brush strokes and color, had his first one-artist exhibition with Janis in February 1956. His show was followed in the next month by the large abstractions of Franz Kline, that painter's first one-artist exhibition at the gallery.

In 1957 Motherwell, who had been showing with Samuel Kootz since 1946, moved over to Janis, giving him control, for the time being, of the work of all the most outstanding Abstract Expressionists with the exception of Newman. By the start of the '60s, with a roster of these masterly artists and a growing reputation as a master dealer, Janis had outgrown his half of the floor at 15 East Fifty-seventh Street. When Betty Parsons's lease ran out in 1962, she found on trying to renew it that the landlord's agent had let the entire floor to Janis. She had waited too long before negotiating a renewal. Irate, and threatened with expulsion from the space that she had once controlled, she came to the conclusion that Janis had engineered the deal. But according to Janis, the landlord had learned that it was a violation of the fire code to permit more than one tenant to rent the floor and decided to rent it to him.[76]

Tempers flared. Who was to blame for this contretemps? The full truth of the matter has never been released to the public. But as Parsons read Janis's character, he was and would remain an out-and-out villain. "Sidney Janis did this unspeakable thing to me," she complained years later to her biographer.

> How would I know that new leases had to be settled before old leases were used up? I didn't. I thought I would *renew* that lease—it was *my* space; I had rented it to Sidney Janis. I had given it to him. My gallery was there first. . . . And it was known in *that* space. I was in that space—The Mortimer Brandt Gallery, you know—even before my gallery was there. Janis . . . went sneaking off behind my back and talked to the landlord. I don't know what kind of promises he made. I don't know how much money he offered. I just know that he *stole* my lease. A gentleman, . . . even if the law allowed, would not *do* such a thing. I've always hated Sidney Janis and I've always thought that he had very, very bad morals.[77]

Parsons sued Janis and lost, but was permitted by him to remain on the floor for one year, after which he expanded his gallery. In his view, she was "a very nasty neighbor."[78] She reopened across Fifth Avenue on West Fifty-seventh.

Nor was the loss of her space Parsons's only complaint against Janis. In 1963 Ellsworth Kelly, whose extremely stark but glowing canvases she had first shown in 1956, decided to leave her after a series of disputes. She told him that he could leave whenever he liked, but that she would terminate the friendship that had developed between them if he went to Janis. That, however, he proceeded to do, and for years she would have nothing more to do with him. In time, however, the two, according to Parsons's biographer, "again became good friends again and traveling companions"[79] In 1997 Kelly gave the Museum of Modern Art a drawing "in honor" of Parsons. Also in time, Kelly, in the fickle way of artists, moved on again, to the gallery of Leo Castelli.

Parsons endured still other losses. Agnes Martin, whose subtle grid paintings were much admired by collectors and her fellow artists, had only a single one-artist show at Parsons, after which she left for the Robert Elkon Gallery. Saul Steinberg, the cartoonist whose satirical drawings had attracted collectors ever since he arrived in the United States as a wartime refugee in 1942 and who had shown with Parsons since 1943 in her Wakefield Gallery days, wished for greater exposure than she alone could provide and began to show with Janis in 1977 as well as with her, but eventually he took most of his work to Janis. Parsons did not let this harm her close relationship with Steinberg, however.

Janis's eventual loss of Kelly to Leo Castelli was only one of many that he suffered in the course of his long career. Paradoxically, several of these came about as the result of a gain: the admittance of young creators of Pop Art to his roster. This new phenomenon came into being by spontaneous generation in 1961 as several artists working independently began to create paintings of such everyday items as kitchen gadgets, take-out food, and sports equipment. With most of the Pop artists, the style was either that of comic books or billboard advertising. The term itself was invented by Lawrence Alloway, an English critic, and caught on quickly. Pop had been in a state of formulation since the mid-1950s, when Robert Rauschenberg and Jasper Johns began to create works combining the brush strokes of the Abstract Expressionists with familiar images encountered in everyday life.

Concurrently with the rapid development of the reputations of Johns and Rauschenberg (born in 1930 and 1925, respectively) came the emergence of pure Pop, which was totally free of the influence of Abstract Expressionism. One of the first exhibitions of art that could be described as Pop took place in February 1957. It was a show at the Hansa Gallery, then on Central Park South, of George Segal's white-painted figures made of plaster that had been wrapped around the bodies of courageous sitters and removed when hardened. Soon came other more or less pioneering efforts to display this new art, the Reuben Gallery's shows in 1960 of works by Jim Dine and Claes Oldenburg being among the most notable, along with two large group exhibitions of Pop artists and others held at the Martha Jackson Gallery in the same year. This gallery, on East Sixty-ninth Street, harbored a motley lot of European and American contemporaries and held a substantial inventory of Kline and Willem de Kooning canvases. But Martha Jackson had mixed feelings about Pop. Although she admired Dine and added him to her roster, she declined to take on Andy Warhol, then a rising Pop star.[80] Oldenburg himself opened a store—called The Store—in December 1961 on East Second Street, where he sold, among other items of his making, plaster sculptures of pies, sundaes, and baked potatoes.

More shows of Pop were held in 1961 and 1962 at galleries both uptown and downtown. But it was left to Janis to mount the first major exhibition of this new, instantly enjoyable art. He planned a group show far too large for his rooms at 15 East Fifty-seventh alone; to accommodate it he looked for another space and rented an empty shop located not far away on West Fifty-seventh. The show, which he called *The New Realists,* filled both locations. Included were works by seventeen European artists and twelve Americans; among the latter were Jim Dine, Robert Indiana, Roy Lichtenstein, Claes Oldenburg, James Rosenquist, George Segal, Tom Wesselmann, and Andy Warhol. A sensation, *The New Realists* codified the Pop movement. All of a sudden these young artists found themselves counted among the most famous creative men in America.[81]

But the show bred rage, or perhaps anxiety, in the hearts of the Abstract Expressionists. They chose not to accept the fact, however reasonable it may have seemed to outsiders, that Janis could admire both schools. Gottlieb, Guston, Motherwell, and Rothko were so disturbed that they resigned from the gallery. When the Marlborough Gallery opened its New York branch the next year, 1963, all four joined it. Another artist to leave at this time was Louise Nevelson. Her departure was not voluntary, however. On New Year's Eve 1962, Janis opened his first and, as it turned out, his only exhibition of her sculptures, abstract wood assemblages in her mature style, painted in black, white, and gold.

Very soon after the opening, on discovering that she was attempting to sell pieces from the show privately, thus depriving him of his commission, he dismissed her.[82]

With the death of Kline, in 1962, Janis was left with only one Abstract Expressionist: Willem de Kooning. Yet eventually he too left, in 1967, for Knoedler's, following a disagreement that erupted when Janis found out that he was selling from his studio. Very angry, Janis thought of suing but ultimately held off.[83]

"It took me completely by surprise," Janis later said of the departures.[84] But soon the losses were offset by the gain of five stellar pop talents: Segal, Tom Wesselman, Oldenburg, Dine, and Marisol (Marisol Escobar), the creator of satiric portrait sculptures hewn from wood and treated with subtle colors. Marisol had shown at the Castelli Gallery in 1957, its first year, but had not felt comfortable there. After a two-year sojourn in Europe, she joined the Janis Gallery. She was doubtful at first about making this move to Janis but did so "because," as she later said, "they make a very nice catalogue."[85]

Although in his efforts to promote emerging talent Janis sometimes brought in artists of no staying power, as with the graffiti makers Crash, Daze, Noc, Toxic, and A-One, his roster during his thirty-eight years as a dealer remained consistently high. His list of clients was equally impressive. Major museums across the country acquired paintings from him. Janis's first sale of all, as it happened, was to Hilla Rebay for the Museum of Non-Objective Art. She bought two Mondrians and a Léger very shortly after Janis opened his doors in 1948. Adventurous collectors such as David and Nelson Rockefeller, Albert Lasker, Ben Heller, Leigh Block, Burton and Emily Tremaine, Philip Johnson, and Donald Blinken, among many others, were also his clients. Robert Scull, the owner of a fleet of taxis who avidly sought fame and social prestige through his collection, bought Abstract Expressionist paintings from Janis before discovering Pop, his ultimate passion.[86] Prices climbed rapidly for Janis's artists, and in the case of Pollock, quite dramatically.

One month after Pollock's death, Lee Krasner demanded that Janis try to sell his *Autumn Rhythm* for $30,000, a painting originally offered for $6,000. Alfred Barr had put a reserve on it for the Modern at that lower figure but gave it up when Janis told him that it would now cost five times as much.[87] The Metropolitan Museum, however, was willing to meet Krasner's demand, thereby ratcheting up precipitously the monetary value of every work Pollock had ever created. Fred Olsen bought Pollock's large *Blue Poles* (approximately seven by twelve feet) for $6,000 in 1950 and sold it in 1956 to Ben Heller for $32,000. In 1973 Heller, professing pain at the loss, sold it to the Australian National Gallery in Canberra for $2 million, at that time the largest sum ever paid for an American painting.[88] But with acclaim for Pollock and the other central artists in the movement continually spreading, by the end of the century $2 million would seem a bargain price.

In 1967 Janis and his wife presented the Museum of Modern Art with 103 paintings and sculptures from their personal collection. Among them were two works by Gorky, three by Willem de Kooning, four by Léger, eight by Mondrian, five by Picasso, two by Pollock, one each by Rothko and Still, and portraits of Janis by Marisol, Segal, and Warhol. A gift of incalculable value, it was Janis's way of thanking the Modern for the preparation its holdings and the programs in which he had taken part had contributed to his career as a dealer. In 1986, still in good health but with nearly four decades in the trade behind him, he turned control of the gallery over to his sons and retired. But during the years remaining to him he kept a watchful eye on trends in the market. At his death, in 1989, he was ninety-three. In 1999 the gallery closed.

The last years of Parsons were less placid. In 1981 a stroke deprived her of speech. The gallery remained open under the care of her staff until a second stroke in the summer of 1982 brought her life to an end. The exhibitions of her last years were very mixed, as though she had tried—and failed—to find artists comparable to the many she had lost. In 1983 seventy-seven works from her estate were auctioned at Christie's. An impressive collection, although in no way comparable to Janis's, it included, among much else, paintings and drawings by Newman, Pollock, Rothko, and Still, her Four Horsemen, along with others by Kelly, Reinhardt, Frank Stella, and Agnes Martin.

The death of Kootz, who was one year older than Parsons, followed hers by one month. Egan died ten years later, in 1993, at eighty-one. With his passing, the trade had lost the last of the four strongest links among the promoters of Abstract Expressionism. Their deaths had been preceded by those of all but one of its stars: de Kooning.

Rothko died by his own hand in 1970, after a long period of depression unrelieved by, and perhaps aggravated by, his intake of alcohol. Alcoholism is no more common among artists than among members of any other profession, but with the Abstract Expressionists it came under the glare of publicity as never before in the history of art. Not every member of the school was an alcoholic, of course; one could not imagine the dignified Barnet Newman ever becoming addicted to drink or anything else that might disturb his stoic placidity. Nor could one imagine it in Robert Motherwell, a club man with memberships in the Century Association and East Hampton's Maidstone Club. But the art world and its hangers-on were nightly witnesses to the rough and tumble sessions at the Cedar Tavern of Pollock, de Kooning, and Kline as they attempted to slake a thirst that was in fact unslakable.

When Pollock, sodden with gin, crashed his car in 1956 and died at age forty-four, the event made headline news the world over. Kline, who had been one of Pollock's drinking buddies and his sometime sparring partner at the Cedar, died at fifty-one in 1962, felled by heart disease. De Kooning, yet another heavy drinker, gave up the bottle in 1976, but only after his estranged wife, Elaine, came back into his life after nearly twenty years' absence and took him in hand.[89] The drinking problem of all these men was well known to the public. Rothko's drinking and his excessive, unsuccessful reliance on anti-depressant drugs on the other hand, did not become common knowledge until after his death in 1970, perhaps because, unlike Pollock and de Kooning, he had always maintained a low profile. That this hugely successful man should be a victim of depression and die in drink-induced suicide was both perplexing and shocking—more so, even, than Pollock's fatal spree behind a wheel that he was in no condition to control.

What followed Rothko's death, and that of his wife, Mell, seven months later, was more shocking still: a series of events involving his estate that smelled so rankly of duplicity and intrigue as to threaten the probity of the entire art trade. Rothko's executors were his accountant, Bernard J. Reis, the Abstract Expressionist painter Theodoros Stamos, and Morton Levine, an anthropologist. After Rothko's death, Reis asked the dealer Daniel Saidenberg to appraise the estate for tax purposes; its assets consisted chiefly of Rothko's 795 unsold paintings. Saidenberg had participated in deals with Frank Lloyd, the owner of Marlborough. Moreover, he and his wife had visited Frank Lloyd at his Caribbean vacation home, along with the Reises. The figure Saidenberg arrived at was an absurdly low $2,654,900.[90] That a conflict of interest existed was obvious, but was ignored by all parties. Although one half of the estate was to be shared by the two children, the executors gave Frank Lloyd of the Marlborough Gallery complete control of Rothko's studio, including the paintings stored in it, and sold a hundred of them to him outright under terms outrageously, but, as it turned out, not inexplicably, favorable to the gallery. Lloyd got the paintings for $1.8 million, or $18,000 each, well below market value. Moreover, after an initial payment of $200,000, the rest of the money was to be given out over a period of twelve years without interest. Lloyd fully expected to deal as he wished with the other 695 when the time was right. Reis was in Lloyd's pocket. His organization, Bernard J. Reis, incorporated, supervised the accounts of Lloyd's New York gallery, and, what is more, Reis had fed many of his artist-clients into the Marlborough stable. Among them were Naum Gabo, Gottlieb, Guston, Motherwell, Larry Rivers, Rothko himself, and the valuable estates of Baziotes and Kline. Making the sale even more suspect as a sweetheart deal was the fact that only five weeks after Rothko's death Reis himself became a salaried member of the gallery's staff as director and secretary-treasurer. In none of these transactions were Rothko's children consulted.[91]

But that was not all. Concerned for the protection of the works remaining in his studio after his death, Rothko had established a foundation to be backed by the other half of the estate's assets with the expectation that its directors would distribute the paintings in clusters to museums. The papers drawn up for the foundation did not specify this, however, but indicated only that it was to function "exclusively for charitable, scientific and/or educational purposes." Nor, although Rothko had at one time mentioned the possibility that his foundation might provide aid to older and underappreciated artists, did the will make mention of this. Nevertheless, the directors of the foundation, who were the three executors along with Morton Feldman, a composer, Robert Goldwater, an art historian, and Clinton Wilder, a theatrical producer, ignored Rothko's concern for the distribution of his paintings and bent themselves solely to the task of providing such aid. Thus might the sale of the paintings to Lloyd be rationalized. It subsequently became clear that the executors were the principal force behind the decision to employ the assets of the estate in this fashion.[92]

Kate Rothko, underage when her father died, soon realized that the assets were being wasted and that the executors had no intention of distributing the paintings as he had wished. Nor were they willing to turn over any of them to her and her very young brother, Christopher. At the age of twenty, she appealed to her guardian, the sculptor Herbert Ferber, to bring suit on behalf of herself and Christopher. Although reluctant to sue such important art-world figures as Reis and Lloyd, Ferber agreed to do so when she reminded him that soon she would be twenty-one and able under the law to bring suit herself.[93]

In the long and troubled years of court battles that followed and the secret attempts on Lloyd's part to sequester paintings from the studio,

Kate Rothko's claim prevailed. The presiding judge found against Lloyd and the executors and levied fines and penalties of $9,252,000.[94] Appeals by the defendants followed, of course, but were denied; when the matter came, finally, before the New York State Court of Appeals in November 1977, the original decision was upheld. Reis filed a voluntary bankruptcy petition after the decision.[95] He died in 1978, considerably poorer than when the affair began. Stamos, whose sales had always been modest, declared himself to be a ruined man. He was forced to give up possession of his New York townhouse to pay his share, but was allowed to live in it for the rest of his life, which ended in 1997.[96] Levine, unlike his fellow executors, remained silent as to the effect of the decision on his finances, but was probably the hardest hit of the three. In December 1977, the three were ousted as executors, and Kate Rothko was named administrator of her father's estate. Lloyd was at his home in Nassau when the charges were brought.[97]

The Marlborough Gallery lost many of its artists, including the Pollock estate, as a result of the trials and the bringing to light of a preposterous design of Lloyd's late in 1975 to protect his assets and avoid payment of the sums required in the judgment against him by shipping 1,750 works of art, including twenty-four Rothkos, from Toronto to Switzerland, from which they could not be recovered. This was foiled when lawyers for the Rothko children were tipped off by an anonymous source. The gallery also lost its membership in the Art Dealers Association of America (ADAA). Although the association's administrative vice president, Ralph Colin, a Marlborough client and until recently Marlborough's general counsel, was reluctant to condemn Lloyd while the trials were in process, he acted decisively when Lloyd sent the ADAA a letter of resignation. The resignation was not accepted, and the gallery was expelled from the association.[98] Lloyd remained in Nassau until 1983, when he returned to Manhattan to stand trial for tampering with evidence in the suit. In lieu of a prison sentence, he was required to provide a $100,000 scholarship fund for students in New York City public schools and to hold tours of Marlborough Gallery exhibitions for students. The prosecuting attorney described the sentence as "extraordinarily lenient."[99] Lloyd died, not noticeably lamented, on April 7, 1998.

Robert Motherwell died in 1991, leaving behind only one of the pioneers of Abstract Expressionism: Willem de Kooning. In 1997 this world-renowned artist passed away at the great age of ninety-three. Long before his death, Alzheimer's disease had deprived him of his awareness of the movement's triumph.

17

THE LION'S SHARE

In 1957, when he opened his gallery in New York, Leo Castelli was nearly fifty years old. Within ten years' time he became the most interviewed, talked about, and envied member of his profession in the United States, which, since in the 1960s New York was the world's art center, is to say that he was the most interviewed, talked about, and envied art dealer in the world. No one else since the great days of Joe Duveen could command so much attention in the press. Both men possessed seemingly limitless energy and the wisdom to give as well as take in their relations with clients, but in the makeup of Castelli's personality was a quality that Duveen lacked: grace. It could be said of him that he established the idea of the art dealer as star.[1]

Castelli, born in Trieste, arrived in New York in 1941 with his wife, Ileana, their daughter, Nina, and Frances Grundy, their daughter's English nanny. A Jewish family, the Castellis were among the countless Europeans

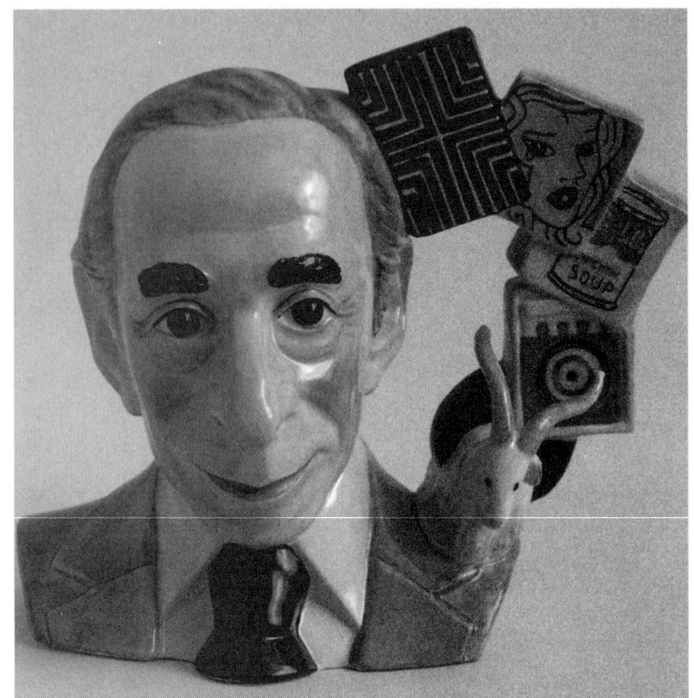

Leo Castelli, depicted as a Toby Jug by Meyer Vaisman. The handle is composed, top to bottom, of miniatures of works by Frank Stella, Roy Lichtenstein, Andy Warhol, Jasper Johns, and Robert Rauschenberg.

who in the time of Hitler sought refuge in the United States. Their life in the interwar years had been singularly free of hardships, and their life in their new country was far less troubled than that of many other émigrés in flight from the Nazis. While they could not be described as rich in their early New York years, they were never less than comfortable.

Castelli's father, Ernst Krauss, born in Hungary, was the head of an Austro-Italian bank in Trieste. After his marriage to a member of the Castelli family of Trieste, he changed his name to Krauss-Castelli and later dropped his original name altogether. With the outbreak of the First World War, the Castellis and their three children, Leo, Giorgio, and Silvia, moved to Vienna, but at the war's end returned to Trieste, where Ernst Castelli joined the leading Italian bank. Leo learned French, English, and German.[2] His fluency in these languages as well as Italian was to prove of immense value to him in later life, when European collectors stormed the Castelli Gallery in search of the exactly right Johns or Rauschenberg to round out their collections.

An eager reader in his high-school days, Castelli had come across Clive Bell's *Since Cézanne* in a Trieste bookshop and was enlightened and deeply impressed by Bell's account of Post-Impressionism. "Everything I know about art starts with that book. Just imagine!" Castelli said in 1981.[3] He studied art history in high school, but at that time did not contemplate a career in art. Instead, he appeared destined to become a lawyer. Yet although he took a law degree at the University of Milan, he never practiced. Comparative literature was then his great enthusiasm, and he entertained a wish to study and teach in that field. His father meanwhile had secured him a post in an insurance firm in Trieste. Soon finding that the job failed to engage his interest, he told his father that he would like to take a degree in comparative literature and enter the academic profession. Hearing this, the elder Castelli, although sympathetic, insisted that his son first spend some time abroad. In the spring of 1932 off he went, by his father's arrangement, to a new post at the Bucharest branch of the same insurance company. The work was no more inspiring there than it had been in Trieste, but he found compensating pleasures, foremost among them being his acquaintance, swiftly achieved, with the young woman who was to become his wife. Ileana was the daughter of a leading Romanian industrialist, Mihail Schapira. They were married in the fall.[4]

In 1934 Castelli left the insurance company for a post in a Bucharest bank, but soon moved to Paris, where Schapira had secured him a job with the Banca d'Italia. Banking, he found, had no more appeal for him than had the insurance business, but, as he later put it, "Paris was more entertaining in every respect than hanging on in Bucharest."[5] In Paris he and Ileana enjoyed the delights of the city and created a circle of close friends. One of them was an interior designer, René Drouin, who in 1938 suggested that Castelli join him in opening a gallery for art, antique furniture, and furniture designed by artists and Drouin himself. With the financial aid of Ileana's father, the two men took over the rooms on the Place Vendôme that formerly had housed the Paris branch of the Knoedler Gallery. Castelli left the bank and devoted his full time to this enterprise, the Galerie René Drouin. Through the Surrealist artist Leonor Fini, a childhood friend of his, he and Drouin and their plans "became of interest," as Calvin Tomkins has put it, to the Surrealists then residing in Paris.[6] "We will accomplish great things there!" Fini told him. "I will introduce you to all the important painters: Max Ernst, Dalí, Tchelitchew." Before the formal opening, Castelli and Drouin held a show consisting only of Tchelitchew's *Phenomena,* a very large painting (six and a half feet by almost nine feet) that ultimately entered the collection of Moscow's Tretyakov Gallery. The official opening exhibition, which took place in the spring of 1939, was made up of furniture, paintings, and sculptures created by the Surrealists, who were more than happy to have this new showcase for their work.[7]

The history of the Galerie René Drouin in this phase of its existence consists of only these two exhibitions. The partners had attracted the beau monde of Paris, a good omen for the future, but while they were on summer vacation the war broke out. They did not reopen their doors. Drouin joined the army, and Castelli thought it prudent to leave the city. He took Ileana, Nina, and the faithful Frances to Cannes, where they stayed with Ileana's father until France fell to Hitler's troops in 1940. Schapira left for New York in advance, and with money provided by him the Castellis began a long and hazardous journey that took them first to Casablanca, then to Tangier and across to Algeciras on the Mediterranean coast of Spain, across Spain by train to Vigo, on the northern coast, where, armed with American visas procured in Casablanca, they boarded a ship for Cuba and New York, which they reached at last in March 1941.[8]

With a gift of $30,000 from Schapira, the Castellis after a brief stay in a hotel first lived in an apartment on Fifth Avenue and then were installed in a town house at 4 East Seventy-seventh Street that Schapira had bought and divided into apartments.[9] This would be their home for many years and the first address of the Castelli Gallery. But Castelli had no thought of establishing a New York gallery in 1941. Once again he contemplated a career in teaching and to that end studied economic history at Columbia. After two years, however, he abandoned this plan—temporarily, or so he thought—and joined the United States Army. His value as a soldier was greatly enhanced by his skill in foreign languages. He was given special training to work behind the lines in France and presumably would have been sent there had not France been taken by the Allies before his training was completed. But the army provided him with another overseas destination: Bucharest, as an interpreter for the Allied Control Commission. His time there was largely his own, and he made the most of it, quite as he had when employed in the city ten years before, and perhaps even more, since at this time he was not burdened by tedious chores in the insurance business. His mood was darkened, however, by a message from his sister, who had survived the war years in Budapest, that their parents had died, not, mercifully, as victims of the Holocaust, but of natural causes. His brother had emigrated to the United States in 1939.[10]

The boon of automatic citizenship was available to any émigré who volunteered for service during the war. Consequently, Castelli and his family now enjoyed official status as Americans. Returning to New York in 1946 after his discharge, he intended to stay there. It would be his permanent home. Ileana meanwhile had taken a degree in psychology at Columbia. Castelli's interest in art was awakened, if indeed it had ever been dormant, by a furlough to Paris during his Bucharest assignment and his discovery there that the Galerie René Drouin was still in operation. Drouin, he learned, had given up the sale of furniture and dealt in works of art exclusively. The Surrealists were also gone, of course, mostly to America and, with few exceptions, declining in appeal to the public. Drouin's stable was composed of such notables as Nicholas de Staël, Jean Dubuffet, Kandinsky, Mondrian, and Antoine Pevsner. Castelli saw his way to a new career: he would be Drouin's New York representative. Schapira bought him an interest in a sweater factory, but whenever he was there, which was not often, his "heart and mind were elsewhere, either on East Tenth Street with the artists, or at the Museum of Modern Art," he said later. "Its incredible collection was educating my eye more than anything else."[11]

Castelli did not maintain the Drouin connection for long. Although he sold a few paintings sent to him from Paris, chiefly to Hilla Rebay for the Museum of Non-Objective Art, the arrangement was not as profitable as he might have wished. Drouin was always in need of money, and Castelli, although then not well-to-do, frequently sent funds to him.[12] When he broke with Drouin formally in 1949, he received as his share of their partnership one painting each by Kandinsky and Léger, three by Dubuffet, and a sculpture by Pevsner. These, along with a Mondrian and three Klees bought from the Nierendorf Gallery, proved to be important assets when eventually he decided to become a dealer.[13] Meanwhile his attention was drawn to the new art of America. He established friendships with the major Abstract Expressionists and saw them not only at the Club but in East Hampton, where he and Ileana bought a house in the '50s. De Kooning and his wife spent two summers there with them. "Pollock," Castelli recalled, "would come over in his model T Ford . . . , jump out of the car without turning off the motor and storm into the house, perhaps to find de Kooning or just to make a nuisance of himself."[14] Castelli also became friends with Sidney Janis and assisted him in the preparation of exhibitions. The first, in 1950, paired American and European artists, albeit rather superficially, as, for example, with the mating of Franz Kline and Pierre Soulages, who had in common only a broad brush stroke. Castelli's admiration for de Kooning and Pollock played a part in Janis's decision to add those artists to his roster, although Castelli was always quick to acknowledge that Janis was as familiar with their work as he and did not require much urging on his part.[15]

Castelli's participation in the preparation of the Ninth Street Show drew him farther into the artists' orbit. Although in these years he was urged by his artist friends to open a gallery, he held off. He bought their work with proceeds from his share in the sweater factory, which he sold in the early '50s, and occasionally teamed with Janis in investing in a painting for resale, but was reluctant to set up shop. His experience with Drouin had introduced him to the business of art, but not so appealingly as to whet his appetite for more. In addition, he was not eager to deal in the Abstract Expressionists despite his admiration for them. He was looking for something new. One evening in East Hampton, de Kooning complained to Ileana about Castelli's reluctance to open a gallery. Ileana, who recognized a questing spirit in her husband, replied, "I think that Leo will open a gallery, and that you won't be one of his artists."[16]

When at last in February 1957 the Castelli Gallery opened, Ileana was as much a participant in its operation as Castelli himself. Her prediction proved to be accurate, for although a de Kooning painting was included in the opening exhibition, a group show of modern European and American masters, Castelli did not invite the artist to be one of his regulars. Although he held de Kooning and Pollock in high regard, he knew that if he were to try to add them to his roster, he would be able to secure only their second-best work because of their commitments elsewhere.[17] As he and Ileana strove in the gallery's early seasons to develop an identity, such other talented American painters as Norman Bluhm, Paul Brach, Friedl Dzubas, Ludwig Sander, Jack Tworkov, and Esteban Vicente also came and went. Vicente, who had only one show with Castelli, of drawings in 1958, sensed that the gallery was evolving toward a state where Abstract Expressionists such as himself would be out of place. He moved on to the gallery of Rose Fried, who had been in business since 1940 and whose primary interest lay in nonobjective art.[18] The true and lasting tone of the gallery was set by Jasper Johns and Robert Rauschenberg, who were included in a group show in the first season and were given solo exhibitions in the second.

Castelli so frequently told the story of how he happened to sign up these artists as to create the impression that it was one of the most important events of his life. In the late 1950s and the 1960s the Jewish Museum, on upper Fifth Avenue, was frequently the scene of exhibitions of contemporary art chosen without regard to the religious affiliation of the artists. There in March 1957, one month after his opening, Castelli looked hard at paintings by the two men in an exhibition of young artists organized by Meyer Schapiro. Rauschenberg's work was not new to him; he had seen the artist's white paintings at Betty Parsons's gallery and his red paintings at Charles Egan's and, recognizing that this was an artist of great originality, had included one of his works in the Ninth Street Show. The Johns in Schapiro's exhibition was a green target painted in encaustic (paint with an admixture of wax) and oil on newsprint mounted on canvas. It fascinated him, although he could not say why. Castelli knew nothing about Johns, who, like Rauschenberg at that time, had no gallery connection. The two artists had survived by designing windows for Tiffany's and were involved in an intimate, highly charged relationship. They did not share living quarters, but occupied lofts in the same building downtown on Pearl Street.[19]

Two days after attending the Jewish Museum show, the Castellis visited Rauschenberg with the intention of choosing works by him for a group show to be held in May. Castelli, who knew nothing about Rauschenberg's private life, was astonished to hear him say that he was going to Johns's loft on the floor below to get some ice for drinks. Excited to hear Johns's name—and insensitive to the feelings of Rauschenberg, whose works, after all, were the supposed point of the visit—Castelli said that he must meet Johns then and there. Rauschenberg brought him up, and Castelli insisted on seeing his paintings. Overwhelmed, he offered Johns a show. Several days later Rauschenberg, deeply distressed, went to the Castelli Gallery to ask whether it was possible that he, too, might have a show. Leo was out, but Ileana talked to him, and, as she later said, "was very embarrassed . . . and suddenly aware of how much he had been hurt."[20]

Exhibitions were soon scheduled for both artists, Johns's to be held in January 1958 and Rauschenberg's in March. Johns's show sold out, with three works going to the Museum of Modern Art and a fourth, a painting of the American flag—a touchy subject for a painting in a period still tainted with McCarthyism—sold to Philip Johnson in the expectation that he would later donate it to the museum, as in 1973 he did. Rauschenberg sold only two works, one of which was made up of the paint-spattered quilt and pillow from his bed. This was bought by Castelli himself; it too is now in the Museum of Modern Art, as Castelli's gift.[21] But museums and collectors soon came to hold the two artists at equal value. In 1959 both were included in Dorothy Miller's *Sixteen Americans* at the Modern. Thereafter, although their personal relationship came to a harsh end in 1962, they were the twin stars, the Castor and Pollux, of the Castelli Gallery.

By 1959 the gallery's swift rise to eminence necessitated the recruitment of an assistant who knew the art world as intimately as Castelli himself knew it. The post was filled by Bronx-born, Brooklyn-bred Ivan Karp.[22] After a stint as the art critic of the *Village Voice,* in 1956 Karp linked up with another young man, Richard Bellamy, as codirector of the Hansa Gallery, where he received a small salary and a commission on work sold. The Hansa had a stable of young artists, many of whom were to become well-known. Among them were John Chamberlain, Fay Lansner, Jan Muller, George Segal, Richard Stankiewicz, and Myron Stout. After two seasons with Hansa he went to the Martha Jackson Gallery, where his finances improved. "I went to Brooks Brothers," he later said, "and bought a new suit."[23] An admirer of Chamberlain's sculptures, he suggested to Jackson that she take on the artist. She did, but, apparently embarrassed by his works, which were composed of the crushed bodies of automobiles, she kept them in the basement.[24] When Castelli, whom he had met at exhibition openings, approached with the offer of a salary of $100 a week, he was quick to accept.

Two men of more sharply contrasting personalities than Karp and Castelli could not be found working together anywhere else in the city's art community. Gallery-goers found that where Castelli was suave and reserved, Karp was brash and outgoing. Castelli employed a soft-sell technique with clients and, once the gallery achieved international fame, placed major works only with serious collectors, not with casual visitors to the gallery who were suddenly infatuated by art and flourished a checkbook. Karp, on the other hand, while not pressing works on new visitors, was adept at convincing them that a work overlooked by the major collectors was in fact well worth having. He also found small, inexpensive items to display and sell in the gallery's back room to art addicts of small means; among such works, which would later increase nicely in value, were Al Hansen's collages made from Hershey bar wrappers and Richard Pettibone's miniature replicas of major paintings by the gallery's regular artists.

Thanks also to Karp, the Castelli Gallery promoted a change in art-community procedures as drastic as Kootz's decision to remain closed on Mondays. Most dealers had made it a practice to open new exhibitions on weekday evenings and to enhance the celebratory air of the occasions with wine or stronger drinks. Karp saw this as counterproductive, because on such very social occasions the collectors were too busy talk-

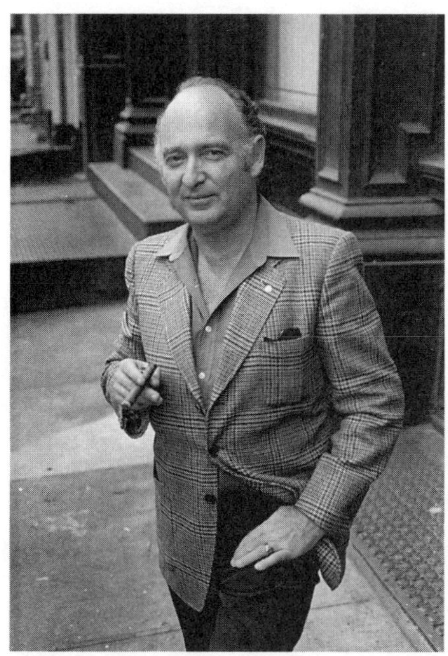

Ivan Karp

ing to friends to arrive at a decision to buy. He proposed that the gallery hold all-day openings on Saturdays, and Castelli agreed to the change. Many other dealers adopted this practice. These openings, unlike the traditional evening events, were not by invitation; everyone was welcome. In the early years of the gallery, on Saturdays when no opening was scheduled a group of collectors, including Ben Heller and Joseph Brodsky, a psychoanalyst, could be found conversing about art in the gallery's back room, with Karp presiding. Castelli, although by no means glacial, could not be imagined in such a setting.

By the mid-1960s the Castelli roster included a constellation of artists who were controversial enough to attract those collectors always on the lookout for promising shifts in the tides of art. Frank Stella, rebelling against Abstract Expressionism, offered large canvases painted in broad black stripes in geometrical patterns with thin lines of bare canvas showing in between. These, he insisted, should simply be looked at, not analyzed; in other words, "What you see is what you get." Dorothy Miller and Alfred Barr were the first to be strongly impressed. Miller included him in *Sixteen Americans,* and Barr bought a canvas, *The Marriage of Reason and Squalor,* for the museum (at the special price of $750).[25] Even so, collectors were resistant. But Castelli and Karp were confident that eventually the artist's talent would win the approval of critics and collectors, as by 1962 it did. Equally difficult to register at first were the paintings of Cy Twombly, whose early works on canvas or paper were composed of squiggles resembling the offhand "doodling" of someone engaged in a telephone conversation or listening to an uninspiring lecture. Twombly came to the gallery in 1959 through the suggestion of Rauschenberg, who had known him since the days when both were students at Black Mountain College.[26] His works also gained acceptance, although not so readily as Stella's.

Once Pop Art entered the scene, it was inevitable that Castelli, unfailingly responsive to new and promising trends, would take it up. Three of its practitioners, Roy Lichtenstein, Andy Warhol, and James Rosenquist, entered Castelli's stable in the early 1960s. Allan Kaprow, an artist best known for the invention of "happenings," nonverbal entertainments of minimal intellectual content that appealed to enthusiasts of Pop, brought Lichtenstein and the Castelli Gallery together. A member of the art department at Douglass, the women's college of Rutgers University, Kaprow told Karp in 1961 that his colleague Lichtenstein did "very peculiar work" that Karp ought to see.[27] Not having slides to send to the gallery, Lichtenstein bundled a group of his paintings together, tied them to the top of his car, and drove to New York. These works, which depicted familiar objects in the flat style of cartoon art, did not appeal strongly at first to either Castelli or Karp, although they kept some of them for the inventory. But when two of the paintings sold, it was clear that the artist deserved a permanent place in the gallery.

Warhol, who had had a successful career as a commercial artist before seeking one in fine art, came later, in 1964, after showing with Eleanor Ward at the Stable, then in its new location on East Seventy-fourth Street. She had visited his studio in 1962 and found his paintings of Coca-Cola bottles, Campbell's soup cans, and Marilyn Monroe unsettling in their novelty. With a vacancy on her schedule, she called him and offered an exhibition. "Wow," he murmured; it was his customary reply to virtually everything.[28] But he frequented the Castelli Gallery and clearly harbored the hope of moving to it one day. When Robert Indiana, who also showed with Ward, was chosen by Dorothy Miller for her *Americans 1963* exhibition at the Modern, Warhol was deeply disappointed not to be included and believed, quite without justification, the reason was that Miller would not choose more than one artist from the same gallery.[29] Rosenquist, who had previously been a sign painter and brought the bright-colored images of gigantic billboards to his paintings, had shown at the Green Gallery before coming to Castelli in 1964. Also in the Pop vein was the California artist Ed Ruscha, who joined Castelli in 1971. Well-known for his depictions of gas stations and the landmark "Hollywood" sign, Ruscha was also one of the early creators of artists' books, small paperbacks that in his case offered photographs of such scenes as thirty-four parking lots in Los Angeles and every building on the Sunset Strip.

Sculpture also figured weightily on the gallery's exhibition schedule, with showings of the crushed metal constructions of Chambelain, the boxy representations of furniture by Richard Artschwager, the "Minimal" art of Donald Judd, Robert Morris, and Richard Serra, who created nonobjective constructions in stripped down, simplified forms, works by Keith Sonnier, who chose neon as his medium, and by Lee Bontecou, who made large, heavy wall-pieces of metal and canvas. In 1963 the Minimal artist Elsworth Kelly joined them. The short-lived phenomenon of the 1960s called Op Art was briefly represented in the gallery by Larry Poons. This movement consisted of works that jarred the retina, mainly by means of moiré patterns shifting against one another on sheets of plastic or, as with Poons's paintings in his Castelli years, two or three high-intensity colors clashing boldly on canvas.

To the bewilderment of many gallery-goers, Castelli also favored the Conceptual art of Robert Barry, Joseph Kosuth, and Lawrence Weiner, works existing only in the verbal expression of an idea and offering no compensatory visual pleasure. Although these works and the artist-created videos occasionally shown at the gallery were all but guaranteed to drive the public away, Castelli did not have the heart to drop the artists responsible for them. Like most other American dealers, Castelli retained 50 percent of the sale price of works, but, unlike the others, he gave his artists monthly stipends against sales, even to those artists who sold little or nothing, which was true of the Conceptualists. With some artists receiving as much as $50,000 a month, or so it was said, Castelli's benefactions brought the gallery close to financial disaster in the early years.[30] But when Karp and others on his staff tried to persuade him to curb his generosity, his reply was simply that the artists needed the money to live and therefore he could not refuse it.[31]

Castelli's marriage to Ileana foundered in the late '50s, perhaps because of his attraction to beautiful young women, long something of a problem between them, finally became more than merely a nuisance. They were divorced in 1960. Ileana then married Michael Sonnabend, a documentary filmmaker whose film *The Titan* (1950), on the life of Michelangelo, had won an Oscar. In 1963 Castelli married Antoinette ("Toiny") Faisseix du Bost, a young Frenchwoman.

After her new marriage, Ileana moved to Paris, where she opened a gallery in 1962. Castelli's artists were among those whose works she exhibited. She came back to New York at the end of the decade and in 1970 established a new gallery at 924 Madison Avenue, a short walk from the Castelli Gallery on East Seventy-seventh Street. She and Castelli remained close after the divorce. "Leo and I are best friends," she said in 1970. "Why, I've had the same dog for 21 years and even the dog is attached to Leo."[32] Often they could be seen on a settee in her gallery or his, side by side in quiet conversation like an aging couple in a sentimental comedy. For her stable in New York Ileana took on many men (curiously, no women) whose popularity matched that of Castelli's artists; among her choices were Jim Dine, one of the original Pop artists; John Baldessari, a recycler of old photographs into new images; and the English team of satirists, Gilbert and George. She also found room, in the 1980s and '90s, for Jeff Koons, a more controversial figure by far, among whose works were basketballs floating in water and spanking-new pairs of vacuum cleaners set side by side or one atop the other in clear Plexiglas boxes. Still other Koons productions shown at the Sonnabend Gallery were voluptuously colored sculptures of the sexual embraces of himself and his wife, a star of Italian porn films.

The Sonnabend Gallery prospered under its owner's astute guidance. But into the 1980s no other dealer in contemporary art had a following comparable to Castelli's. The art community believed—mistakenly, when we consider the Conceptualists—that anything he hung on his walls would find a buyer. One evening at the Cedar Tavern in 1960 Willem de Kooning was heard to say with affection, "That sonofabitch Castelli could sell anything, even a pair of beer cans."[33] Jasper Johns, speedily responding to the challenge implicit in the remark, made a sculpture in bronze of two cans of Ballantine ale. De Kooning was right: Castelli promptly sold the piece to Robert Scull, a client willing to buy almost anything Castelli had on offer.

But that was not the end of the story. Four years later, in 1964, Johns recreated the image as a lithograph at Universal Limited Art Editions (ULAE), the print workshop of Tatyana Grosman in West Islip, Long Island, to which he, Rauschenberg, Dine, Bontecou, Larry Rivers, and other artists resorted to make prints. The edition sold out immediately. It proved too popular an image for Johns to relinquish. He used it again in prints made in 1967 and 1975 and included a single can in his large print, *Decoy,* of 1971 and the still larger painting of the same subject, also created in 1971. Johns became so adept a lithographer, and later an etcher and screen-print artist, that by the '70s printmaking had come to occupy as much of his energy and artistic consciousness as painting. In whatever form his work took, paintings, prints, or drawings, collectors clamored for it.

With Peter Ludwig, a prominent German collector, and Count Giuseppe Panza di Biumo, an equally vigorous Italian collector, eager for the output of Johns and Rauschenberg, and with Castelli's astute arrangement of exhibitions for them in Paris at the Sonnabend Gallery and elsewhere, the artists swiftly achieved a following among critics abroad, the first American artists since Pollock and de Kooning to do so. The confirmation of Rauschenberg's exalted position in the international arena occurred in 1964, when he was awarded the grand prize for painting at the Venice Biennale, a prize no other American had ever won. Alan Solomon, the director of the Jewish Museum and a close friend of Castelli's, was assigned the task of assembling the American representation at the Biennale by the United States Information Agency (USIA). This federal agency was new to the Biennale; from 1948 through 1962 the sponsor of the American representation had been the Museum of Modern Art. Solomon's choices were Rauschenberg, Johns, Dine, Chamberlain, and the Pop artist Claes Oldenburg along with the color-field artists Morris Louis and Kenneth Noland, creators of abstract works composed of bright swaths of paint on a white ground. Solomon was so much an admirer of Rauschenberg that he had given the artist a retrospective exhibition at the Jewish Museum in 1962. ("First Goy in the Jewish Museum," Rauschenberg wrote gleefully on the show's poster. This was not quite true; he was, however, the first non-Jewish artist to be given a retrospective there.) It was Solomon's great hope that Rauschenberg would win the grand prize, but the achievement of that end caused something of an uproar.[34]

Solomon was faced with the hard fact that the United States pavilion was far too small to accommodate the kind of exhibition he envisioned. The twenty-two works by Rauschenberg that he had brought over, to say nothing of all the rest, could not possibly fit into it. But he found, or thought he found, a solution: a building next to Peggy Guggenheim's palazzo, formerly the United States consulate, was available, and the president of the Biennale, Mario Marcazzan, assured him that he was free to install works there. Solomon took him to mean that the works would be eligible for prizes, but Marcazzan later insisted that he had meant only that although all the works shown there would be considered a part of the American exhibition, they would not be in the running for prizes. A poll of the jurors, one of whom, Sam Hunter of Brandeis University, was an American, had voted four to three to give Rauschenberg the prize. But because with only one exception all of Rauschenberg's works were in the former consulate, the president of the jury expressed his disapproval and threatened to resign. Castelli and Toiny were of course present in Venice from the start of the battle, as were Michael and Ileana Sonnabend. All four had a stake in the outcome of this contretemps.[35]

When a rumor floated to the effect that the jury was contemplating a compromise, with the prize going to Noland, Solomon also voiced a threat: he would remove all the American art from the competition if Noland were declared the winner. Finally a compromise of another sort was reached, and after three works by Rauschenberg were taken out of the former consulate and moved to the pavilion, the jury awarded him the prize.[36] It had been a struggle, and, perhaps understandably, the press believed that Castelli had been the prime force behind the jury's choice. The experience proved too much for the USIA, which gave up the sponsorship after this one go at it. The international politics of art, it seemed, were no less fraught with confusion, anxiety, and outrage than the international politics of trade agreements and territorial rights.

The award to Rauschenberg put a seal on the eminence of the Castelli Gallery. It was more than a matter of selling beer cans. By the mid-1960s the gallery was the world's most talked- and written-about place to view and acquire contemporary art. That its artists at that time were exclusively American may have contributed to its renown; New York, not Paris, was then the capital of the art world, as it had been from the beginning of the decade, and American art was in demand. Since the end of the war, Paris had produced only two international stars, Jean Dubuffet and Pierre Soulages, the latter, although talented, a poor second in popularity. Castelli's clients included all ardent collectors of the new in art. Among them were Burton and Emily Tremaine, Richard Brown Baker, Victor and Sally Ganz, Philip Johnson, Ben Heller, Jane and Robert Meyerhoff, Donald B. Marron, and, somewhat later, such noted Hollywood figures as the agent Michael Ovitz and the record producer David Geffen. Nelson Rockefeller, although not a regular client, commissioned a portrait by Andy Warhol.

In the 1960s the most persistent of Castelli's clients was Robert Scull, who after amassing a collection of Abstract Expressionist paintings became captivated by Johns, Rauschenberg, and the Pop artists. The owner of a fleet of taxis, Scull's Angels, Scull wanted his drivers to be known for their good manners and to that end sent them to Amy Vanderbilt, the Emily Post of her day, for instruction. He knew, of course, that the publicity this gesture received would prove well worth the price of their lessons. But although Scull and his wife, Ethel, made frequent appearances in newspaper columns thanks to their collection and rejoiced in the spotlight this cast on them, no one could seriously question the sincerity of their enthusiasm for art. From 1960 to 1965 Scull silently demonstrated this by secretly backing the Green Gallery, with Richard Bellamy as director. In its brief life this was almost as seminal a force in the art community as the Castelli Gallery. It was from this gallery that Castelli, a frequent visitor, acquired Rosenquist, Larry Poons, and the Minimalist sculptors Donald Judd and Robert Morris.

Oldenburg, who also showed at the Green, moved to Castelli in 1974, after several years with Sidney Janis. He had quietly acquired fame with the opening of The Store in the East Village at 107 East Second Street, in December 1961. There, as we have noted, he put on sale his plaster Pop sculptures of pies, sundaes, and other objects quite unfamiliar as fine-art objects. Many of these went to the Museum of Modern Art and, of course, to Scull and other collectors. At The Store the next month Oldenburg offered happenings, although he did not choose that label for them; these were presentations of what he chose to call his Ray Gun Theater.[37] He was officially accepted into the mainstream when Dorothy Miller included him in *Americans 1963* at the Museum of Modern Art.

Scull, although passionate about art, was not always gentle in his treatment of the men who sold it. He was a ruthless bargainer. Karp once remarked, "Scull would work Leo until he was a puddle on the floor."[38] And, having clinched the deal at the lowest possible price, he was slow to pay. As early as 1958 he began to buy from Castelli, beginning with a Rauschenberg. He was noisily irritated when the Tremaines saw and purchased a Johns painting, *Device Circle,* before he knew about its existence and had a chance to claim it for his collection, and furious when three large Johns paintings of the map of the United States eluded him one after the other.[39] Had he been given his way, he would have snapped up everything executed by the artist. Eventually he acquired a *Double White Map.*

To the surprise of other collectors, the Sculls sold works from their holdings at auction in 1965 and 1973. The reason given for the first sale was to raise money for a foundation whose purpose was to aid young artists. With the second sale, no such reason was offered. The couple and their collection were so well-known that the sale, held at Sotheby Parke-

Bernet, became a television event. The works fetched $2,242,000, a large figure for the time, especially in view of the small sums Scull had paid for them. The *Double White Map* went for $240,000, then a record for Johns (but a fraction of what the painting would have brought ten years later). Militant cab drivers delayed the sale by making a tumultuous scene outside the auction house. Scull, they said, was a parasite who lived off the backs of cabbies to enjoy life among the "beautiful people"—that is, well-heeled jet-setters. The artists were also displeased; the sale, in their view, represented arrant profiteering from which they themselves would get nothing. Rauschenberg, incensed, made his resentment clear in a press conference that followed the sale.[40] What remained of the Sculls' holdings after the sale was still a massive collection. When their marriage headed for the divorce court in 1975, a legal battle immediately arose over how it should be divided.[41]

In 1968 Ivan Karp, the second presence at Castelli's, began to feel restive in the gallery's very success. He became impatient with what he took to be its fixed position in art. As he saw it, the gallery's artists by that date were individuals whose development appeared to be complete, and the pleasure of seeing a talent unfold and flower was no longer to be found there. The time had come to leave. What finally brought about his determination to withdraw was Castelli's voiced intention to add Dan Flavin, another Minimalist, to the roster. Flavin took fluorescent tubes as his medium; in combinations of colors or in pristine white, these staffs of light stood at an angle in the corner of a room or were ranged in intervals along a wall. Karp saw nothing to admire in them. Moreover, he believed that Castelli also cared little for them as works of art but was impressed by Flavin only because he was doing something that no one else had attempted.[42] No sooner did word of Karp's decision circulate than his telephone began to ring with offers. He did not intend to work for someone else, however. His plan was to set up a gallery of his own.

But only one of the callers, a Castelli client, tendered a no-strings proposition. The others had hoped to play a part along with Karp in the new gallery's management. With a loan of $50,000 from his backer (whose identity he chose not to divulge), Karp looked for a suitable location. He considered sites in the preferred art districts, Fifty-seventh Street as well as upper Madison Avenue, which, thanks mainly to the Castelli Gallery's presence on Seventy-seventh Street, had become popular, but ended by renting a warehouse far downtown on West Broadway. This sizable space became the O.K. Harris Gallery. The name had been in Karp's mind since the summer of 1959, when he had chosen it for a gallery he ran in Provincetown, Massachusetts. Ten years later he thought of it as possibly suitable for the gallery being planned by Scull and Richard Bellamy. Scull rejected it, however, thinking that the name Green was preferable because it would carry the suggestion of something still unformed. "I felt O.K. Harris was a tough, American name that sounded like that of a riverboat gambler," Karp later said. "It would look good in print, and one could blame everything on the mystery character."[43] The gallery opened in the fall of 1969. In 1974 he moved to an even larger space one block farther down West Broadway.

The general location of Karp's gallery, a limbo of lofts situated between Greenwich Village and the financial district, came to be known as SoHo, for *so*uth of *Ho*uston Street—but with a nod also to London's similarly named area, a mixture of restaurants and sex shops. Only one other dealer had already settled there: Paula Cooper, who opened her gallery in 1968. Karp quickly developed a very large roster of artists, most, but not all, in the realist or, as he liked to say, hyperrealist tradition. The size of the place encouraged countless young artists to believe that there must be room in it for them, and they soon began to besiege him with their slides. Karp was prepared for them; his years with Castelli had made him a master of the graceful rejection. As the gallery evolved, it became his policy to offer four or five shows at a time. With a broad-based clientele, including a number of European collectors, the gallery prospered. Several collectors who were clients of Castelli, such as Richard Brown Baker and Sydney and Frances Lewis, bought from him. Museums, however, were reluctant to take in his artists. William S. Lieberman, curator of twentieth-century art at the Metropolitan, made some purchases for his museum in the 1980s out of the limited funds of his department, and the Museum of Modern Art bought one work, a still life by Ralph Goings, but these few acquisitions constitute only a minute fraction of both museums' total purchases. "It is not a world we have much to do with," was Karp's plaintive reply to questions about this sector of the art community.[44]

Other dealers gradually followed Karp downtown, and in 1971 Castelli himself made the move, to an entire floor of a building at 420 West Broadway. Ileana Sonnabend also took a floor. This address became a hub around which dealers clustered through the 1970s and after. Eighty-four galleries had opened in the area by 1975. Restaurants followed, and they in turn were followed by antique shops and clothing boutiques. Lofts in the area became desirable dwelling spaces, at constantly escalating prices. In time, as new galleries opened, SoHo spilled five blocks eastward to Broadway. Thus in a few short years a new commercial district was created for the city. On moving to the area, Castelli kept his floor on East Seventy-seventh Street for the sale of prints, but in 1978 he moved this part of his business down to 568 Broadway. In 1980 he took another, very large space nearby on Greene Street, two blocks east. A canny street vendor on West Broadway did good business with T-shirts bearing the message Leo Castelli Looked at My Slides.

If further evidence of Castelli's eminence were needed, it was supplied in 1970 by *Life,* whose editors were sufficiently impressed by his achievement to offer readers an article about his gallery and its offshoots.[45] These were the Sonnabend Gallery and the New Gallery, in Cleveland, which was opened as a not-for-profit enterprise in 1968 by Castelli's daughter, Nina Sundell, with a partner, Marjorie Talalay. Backing for the New Gallery was supplied by Agnes Gund, a young Cleveland collector who in 1991 would assume the presidency of the Museum of Modern Art. The *Life* essay was illustrated with a group portrait of Castelli and Toiny, the Sonnabends, and Michael and Nina Sundell, along with Ivan Karp and David Whitney, who had been a Castelli aide for two years. Nina remained as co-director of the New Gallery through June, 1973. The gallery later became the not-for-profit Center for Contemporary Art.

In the early 1960s Castelli began to assemble a network of dealers in other cities who took the products of his artists at a commission of 25 percent of the sale price, with 25 percent coming back to him and the artists receiving the remaining 50 percent, their usual share. The first American dealer with whom he did business was Virginia Dwan, in Los Angeles, the city that in the 1960s commenced its evolution into the second biggest art market in the United States. The Margo Leavin, James Corcoran, Ferus, and Ace galleries of Los Angeles soon followed Dwan into the Castelli network. Still more were to come from Los Angeles and other cities: John Berggruen and Daniel Weinberg in San Francisco, Janie C. Lee in Houston, both Ronald Greenberg and Joseph Helman in St. Louis, the Young Hoffman and Richard Gray galleries of Chicago, and the Sable-Castelli Gallery of Toronto. Castelli also made connections with dealers in Europe and with Akira Ikeda, the owner of galleries in Tokyo and Nagoya. "Everything I send to Ikeda, he sells," Castelli told a reporter in 1990. "*Nothing* ever comes back."[46]

Art that he sent to the other outlying dealers did, however, sometimes come back. The reason for the returns was the suspicion of collectors that the local galleries were getting only second-best goods. Whether

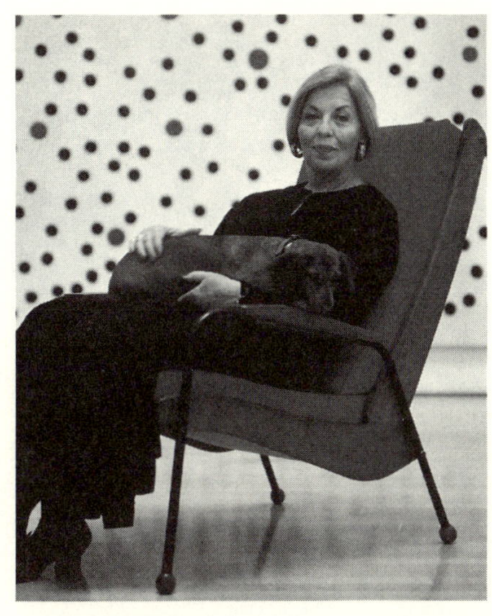

Margo Leavin, eminent Los Angeles dealer, in her gallery. Behind her is a painting by Yayoi Kusama.

true or not, it was, and was to remain, a problem for all such businesses. A client of Margo Leavin eyed an Ellsworth Kelly in her gallery in 1983 with the lust of the true art fanatic, but could not get over his nagging doubt that he would find better Kellys at 420 West Broadway. He flew to New York, asked Castelli to show him every work by the artist then in stock, saw nothing there that struck him as forcefully as the Kelly in California, flew back to Los Angeles, and wrote Margo Leavin a check.[47]

Ultimately some fifty dealers joined Castelli's web. With his widespread connections and the constant flow of publicity that his gallery generated, by the mid-1980s Castelli appeared to be the ruler of all he surveyed—that is, the worldwide market for contemporary art. But as his power grew, so did the envy of his colleagues in the trade. Despite his success, Castelli was not the richest member of his profession. Other dealers with access to more funds than he began to chip away at his roster by offering the artists such lucrative contracts against future sales that he could not begin to match them. Castelli's age was also a factor in the decision of some of the artists to leave. So were questions of his health. Troubled with an irregular heartbeat, he underwent the implantation of a pacemaker in 1975. Although this restored his energy, it also gave rise to speculation in the trade about the future of the gallery.

The first dealers to cause serious problems for Castelli were Irving Blum and Joseph Helman, who established the Blum-Helman Gallery in 1974. Both were experienced in the trade and well liked by Castelli. Blum became a dealer in 1958, when he bought a one-third interest in the Ferus

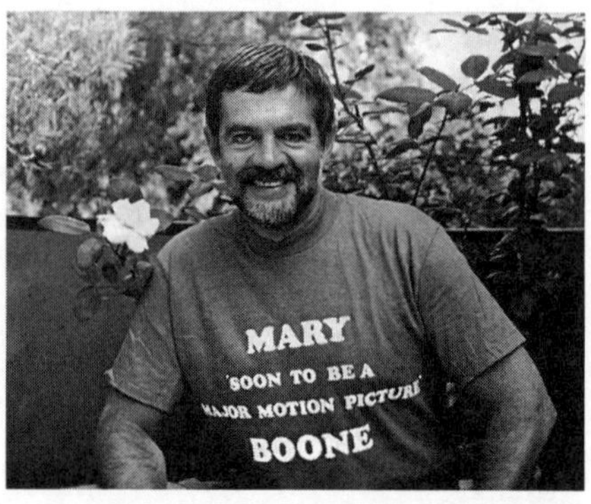

Genial Irving Blum spoofs a colleague.

Gallery of Los Angeles. A short-lived (1957–1966) enterprise, this gallery was founded by Walter Hopps and Edward Kienholz, whose idea was to provide a showcase for artists from Los Angeles and San Francisco. When in 1958 the Dilexi Gallery was founded in San Francisco by James Newman and Robert Alexander, the two galleries developed an informal alliance under which they offered exhibitions of each other's artists' work. The Dilexi, which for the most part exhibited strong local talent, grew out of the underground cultural ferment spawned in San Francisco in the 1950s, when the Beat Generation was in its first youth. It remained in business until 1970, with a roster composed of young artists whose reputations were yet to be made. Most were native Californians; among them were Jay deFeo, Roy de Forest, and Manuel Neri.[48] But Blum had a wider vision for the Ferus. On becoming its sole owner in 1960, he enlarged the gallery's scope to include exhibitions of work by Joseph Cornell, Josef Albers, and Castelli's artists as well as California artists.[49]

Before teaming up with Blum, Helman in 1970 established a gallery under his own name in St. Louis, for which he borrowed work by Castelli's artists. He and Castelli had known one another since Helman at the age of twenty-three had eagerly sought and bought a painting by Johns. A land developer in St. Louis, Helman had had no knowledge of Johns until the day when, seated in a barber's chair, he saw a reproduction of one of the artist's paintings in a magazine. After making frantic inquiries in St. Louis, he learned that Castelli was the man to see when it came to buying a Johns. He went to New York and came back with Johns's *Painting with Ruler and "Gray."*[50] Thus Helman began accumulating works by Johns and other artists from Castelli. Despite a thirty-year difference in their ages, a close friendship, in part a father-and-son relationship, developed between them.

Blum opened his gallery after ten years as a land developer. He was also a collector, of course. As much taken with Warhol as Helman was with Johns, in 1962 he showed Warhol's thirty-two paintings of Campbell's soup cans at Ferus and knew that he himself would have to possess them. Six had been sold, but he got them back and arranged with Warhol to buy the entire lot for $1,000, paying $100 a month.[51] The paintings quickly became Pop icons, and so pleased with the publicity given them was Campbell's that it advertised its products as "Mom Art." Blum held on to the paintings until 1996, when he sold them to the Museum of Modern Art. It was a profitable sale: the Modern paid $15 million for them.[52]

In 1972 Helman sold his gallery to Ronald Greenberg, one of his clients. One year later, Blum suggested to Helman that they get together to establish a gallery in New York, and Helman consented. The Blum Helman Gallery opened in 1974 on East Seventy-fifth Street with an exhibition consisting of works by four of Castelli's artists, Kelly, Lichtenstein, Oldenburg, and Stella, along with others by Morris Louis. The dealers' first one-artist show was of Richard Serra, also a Castelli artist. In 1981 they moved the gallery to West Fifty-seventh Street. Although they eventually gathered a stable of artists of their own, they continued to borrow from Castelli, on the same basis as had obtained in the galleries they had operated independently of one another. But as the Blum Helman Gallery gathered strength both financially and as a venue for major contemporary artists, the attitude of the partners toward Castelli gradually altered.

In the 1980s the gallery's announcements ceased to include a message that certain works had been borrowed from Castelli, and this was followed by the move to it of Kelly and Serra. Helman, according to reports, began to speak of Castelli as an old man, a man too old to keep in touch with the market. Castelli was both angered and hurt by Helman's sharp business practices and abrupt loss of regard for him. A sharp break occurred when Helman stopped payment on a check for the commission Castelli was to receive for the sale of work by an artist whom they shared.[53] The Willard Gallery, under its founder's daughter, Miani Johnson, also suffered a loss to Blum and Helman when Donald Sultan, a rising star, left her gallery to join theirs. Successful though it was, the partnership of the two men was not destined to last. One report had it that they quarreled over Blum's sale of a painting by Warhol without consulting Blum and, furthermore, that Helman had sent a detail of policemen to Blum's apartment to retrieve an Oldenburg sculpture that Blum had taken from the gallery.[54] Queried on his leaving the partnership, Blum would say only by that 1995 he had begun to feel uncomfortable in it.[55] After leaving the gallery, Blum, began to deal independently.

Other grave problems besides the losses of his artists arose for Castelli. Toiny, his wife of almost twenty-five years, died in 1987. Gallery visitors, noting his melancholy expression, could see how keenly he felt this loss. He gave the Museum of Modern Art a generous collection of drawings by his artists in her memory. He decided to give up the Green Street space and scheduled the last show there for October 1988. After the closing of the show, a sixteen-ton sculpture by Serra collapsed and severely injured two workmen who were dismantling it.[56]

There were still more defections by Castelli's artists in the 1980s. Richard Artschwager, who had been with Castelli since 1965, went to the young dealer Mary Boone. Both Stella and Rauschenberg moved to the Knoedler Gallery, although keeping a nominal tie to Castelli. Cy Twombly left for the Sperone Westwater Gallery. Arnold Glimcher, of the Pace Gallery, founded in 1960 in Boston but in New York since 1963, took Chamberlain, Flavin, Judd, Oldenburg, and Serra. Glimcher also captured Julian Schnabel, the much discussed young artist who had been shared by Castelli and Boone. Castelli and Boone also shared David Salle, another newcomer of the '80s, but, once launched and on his way to stardom, Salle left for the gallery of Larry Gagosian—"Go-Go" to the press—a shrewd operator in the art trade who came to New York from Los Angeles in 1979. In what appeared to be an attempt to acquire status as an aesthete who cared more about art than about money, Gagosian early on made it a practice to mount archival exhibitions in which very little was for sale. Among the artists whose works were featured in such shows were Johns and Rosenquist. Neither artist left Castelli, but when Gagosian offered Lichtenstein an exhibition at his gallery, Castelli sensed a threat and asked Lichtenstein to decline.[57] Lichtenstein remained ostensibly true to Castelli, but a year or so before his death in 1997 he began to sell from his studio.[58]

In the 1980s and '90s, meanwhile, Ileana Sonnabend had proved to be more adept than Castelli in searching out new artists. One of them, Meyer Vaisman, she soon shared with him. Castelli also forged an arrangement with the young Stux Gallery to share Doug and Mike Starns, twin brothers whose works were composed of assemblages of photographs, usually printed in sepia tones and created on a large scale. But these halfway additions to his roster could hardly compensate for the many losses.

As the century struggled to its close, Castelli's fame remained undiminished even as his roster of artists shrank. He was, however, as subject to the probing of the press as any other public figure. Reporters found good copy in his gallery's problems—and in the difficulty a man of his age might face in solving them. The image of "the lion in winter," the familiar title of a play by James Goldman (1966), was assigned to him by the press; he was Leo the lion in the winter of his years. At the time of his eighty-fifth birthday, a reporter from the *Times* queried three dealers on Castelli's position in the art community and received some blunt, unhesitant answers. Paula Cooper's response was, "He and Glimcher and Gagosian and Boone are involved in the battle of the machos, which doesn't have much to do with art. I like Leo, but he has never been very supportive or helpful to me, which colors my opinion. He's just involved with the galleries in his power axis." Both Gagosian and Glimcher were clearly offended by the reporter's suggestion that either might be the heir to Castelli's exalted position in the trade. Gagosian replied, "Succession as Leo's heir doesn't appeal to me. . . . Inheritance is not a particularly interesting form of transmission." Glimcher, the reporter noted, "bristled" at the notion. "I don't have to set myself up as the heir to anything," he said. "My gallery has been around since 1960."[59]

The sniping intensified in 1995 after Castelli married for the third time. He was eighty-eight; his bride, Barbara Bertozzi, was thirty-two. Their first meeting occurred when Bertozzi, an Italian art scholar, came to his gallery in 1994 to interview him for a book on his career. The difference in their ages set tongues wagging in ways that were unflattering to the couple, but with most of the verbal thrusts aimed at Bertozzi. To Castelli's friends, it appeared that she had somehow taken him in charge and that her influence was evident in the direction of the gallery itself. When three key members of the staff, Susan Brundage, the director of the gallery, her sister Patty, Castelli's personal assistant, and MaryJo Marks, the gallery's registrar, left in the summer of 1997, it was assumed that they had had a disagreement with Bertozzi. The conditions of their financial settlement stipulated, however, that they not comment on the reasons behind their departure, leaving the matter open to gossip and rumor. Susan Brundage had been with Castelli for twenty-five years, Patty Brundage for twenty. When queried, Castelli himself would say only, "Times change, things change."[60]

A few months after these events took place, the Museum of Modern Art gave Castelli a ninetieth-birthday party. On this occasion, he looked as fit as ever to conduct his gallery's business. But rumors floating out of SoHo had it that he was more fragile than he looked and also that the gallery would move uptown as a much smaller operation. The move came about in the spring of 1999, when the Castellis left SoHo for a smaller space on East Fifty-seventh Street. The opening exhibition was a show of monotypes by the still faithful Jasper Johns. Only a few months later Castelli died. His passing cast a wave of sadness over the art community that would be painfully slow to ebb.

In 1997 the Guggenheim Museum opened its long-awaited branch in Bilbao. The new structure was designed by Frank O. Gehry, an American architect whose distinctly individual style is marked by convex and concave curves and a pronounced absence of symmetry. One of the new Guggenheim's exhibition spaces is 433 feet long, certainly the largest museum room in the world. The twenty paintings and sculptures on view in it at the opening were huge—necessarily so, if its awesome volume was to be filled. Although this exhibition was not intended as homage to Castelli, that in fact is what it unofficially was, for of the twelve artists represented, ten had at critical moments in their past been members of his roster.

18

CENTURY'S END

The shifting fortunes of the Castelli Gallery did not constitute the only memorable events in art circles during the last decades of the twentieth century. New galleries, as always, started up. Most, in the way of such things, quickly faded from both the scene and collective memory. A few, however, made an indelible mark on the history of the trade.

One of these was the Pace Gallery. Pace was the first name of the father of its founder, Arnold Glimcher, and chosen for the gallery for that reason. Fortuitously, it carried the suggestion of pulsation and movement. The gallery's rise to the apex of prominence in the contemporary field could not have been predicted from its small-scale beginnings in Boston in 1960. When three years later Glimcher took on a partner, Frederick Mueller, the two young men moved the gallery to small quarters on West Fifty-seventh Street in New York. Mueller was a Harvard graduate of more than ample means whose wealth descended to him from a forebear who was the inventor of a mundane but indispensable product: the spark plug. In their early New York days, even with Mueller's money, the two did not have the necessary financial power to draw established artists away from their secure nests with such major players as Castelli and Janis. Their strategy was to take on a few artists of true talent who at the time seemed past their prime and whose popularity they believed could be renewed under careful management. Among them was Louise Nevelson. An artist of undoubted ability, she was at loose ends, having fallen out with Janis, when Glimcher and Mueller chose her for their stable. Once there, however, she rose to a new height in name recognition and sales. Not all others whom they picked up at the outset in New York fared so well, but gradually the roster grew. Jean Dubuffet and Lucas Samaras were other notable artists to enter it.

In 1974 Mueller left the gallery to deal on his own in oriental art.[1] As Glimcher made money, he learned how to cast his bread upon the waters. Although it has always been believed that he would not offer discounts to collectors, he wooed them successfully in other ways, chiefly by being attentive when they showed interest in his artists. The gallery moved to large quarters at 32 East Fifty-seventh Street in 1968 and eventually took over seven floors of the building as the business reached out in new directions: contemporary prints, master prints, drawings, primitive art, and photographs. In 1980 Glimcher brokered the sale of Jasper Johns's *Three Flags*, a major early work owned by Burton and Emily Tremaine, to the Whitney Museum for $1 million, then a record price for a contemporary painting.

Glimcher's approach to the market was unusual for a dealer in contemporary art. Unlike others in the field, he showed no interest in developing untried artists. He was after known talent, the tried, the true, and the expensive, which meant raiding the rosters of other galleries. About this there was nothing unusual; artists have always moved from one dealer to another, depending on where the money is and, in some instances, the prestige of the dealer making the offer. But with Castelli's artists, John Chamberlain, Dan Flavin, Claes Oldenburg, and Richard Serra, all of whom, as we have noted, left for Pace, it was also a matter of Castelli's age and health. Mary Boone lost Julian Schnabel to him. Brice Marden also left her for Pace, but found himself uncomfortable there and returned to her. From Paula Cooper's gallery Glimcher took Robert Mangold and the sculptors Donald Judd and Joel Shapiro—and also Douglas Baxter, Cooper's director. Other notable artists to come to Pace were Chuck Close, Agnes Martin, and Robert Ryman. In addition to these living luminaries, the gallery also secured the estates of Alexander Calder, Louise Nevelson, Mark Rothko, Ad Reinhardt, Henry Moore, and Picasso.

The forging of a link with the Wildensteins in 1993 braced the gallery against any future vagaries of the market. Queried as to who initiated the arrangement, Glimcher fielded the question by saying only that he and the Wildensteins had been acquainted for many years, implying that the deal had had a kind of spontaneous generation.[2] That may be so, but the highly dubious and much discussed behavior of the Wildensteins during the Second World War could well lead to reticence on the part of anyone doing business with the family, especially anyone who, like Glimcher, is Jewish.

The formation of the partnership was followed in 1995 by the opening of a branch of PaceWildenstein in Beverly Hills. Glimcher, no stranger to the neighborhood, had already established a presence in Hollywood as a producer and director of films. He first became involved in film as an actor, when he was asked in 1980 by the director Robert Benton to take a small role in his *Still of the Night* as a bidder at an auction. Among his filmmaking credits are *Gorillas in the Mist,* which he produced, and *The Mambo Kings,* which he directed. He could count such high-profile Hollywood figures as the super-agent Michael Ovits and the producer David Wolper among his clients. Men of such eminence are too mobile to have to depend on the resources of a gallery in their backyard, so to speak, to satisfy their craving for art, but unquestionably the opening of a Pace presence there seemed a shrewd move at the time. The Los Angeles area for at least three decades had been the second greatest art market in the United States, and Beverly Hills, an enclave in Los Angeles County, accounts for a major portion of the sales. Nor should the fact be overlooked that Pace's chief rival in the contemporary field, Larry Gagosian (to whom we will return in a moment), established his Beverly Hills branch within the same week that the Pace Wildenstein branch first opened its doors.

Among other new galleries of the 1960s, several stand out in the memory of collectors. Richard Bellamy's short-lived Green Gallery was one of them. Another, one of the brightest and best of the new '60s establishments, was the Bykert Gallery, the joint enterprise of J. Frederic Byers III, the owner of a real-estate company, and Klaus Kertess, an enthusiastic observer of the museum and gallery scene who had long aspired to have a gallery of his own.

Kertess and Byers had been friends since their student days at Yale.

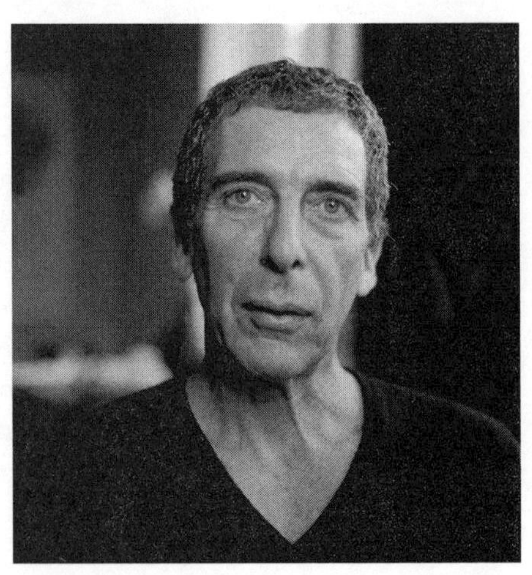

Klaus Kertess

Like Kertess, Byers, known to his friends as Jeff, also had an interest in contemporary art. A keen collector, he was on track to become a trustee of the Museum of Modern Art. He was the backer of the gallery, a silent partner who left the executive decisions to Kertess. They opened in September 1966 in rooms on West Fifty-seventh Street that had recently been occupied by the Green Gallery. Two years later they moved to larger quarters on East Eighty-first Street, where they stayed for the remainder of the gallery's brief life.[3]

Kertess admired the Green Gallery and had visited it frequently. For his opening exhibition he chose paintings by Ralph Humphrey, a young abstract painter whose work was shown by Richard Bellamy at the Green in 1965. Kertess hoped to develop a group whose talent matched that of Bellamy's artists, and quickly did so. By the end of his first year in business, the Bykert had begun to generate the same degree of excitement among collectors that Castelli had caused in 1957. But even with the backing of Byers, Kertess did not have the financial strength of Castelli. He himself did the sweeping up, and if the gallery needed painting, he painted it.

Kertess had few acquaintances in the art community at the outset. He did, however, know Henry Geldzahler, a curator of American art at the Metropolitan Museum and a man much mentioned in the art press as a talent-spotter. It was often said in the 1960s that any young artist could achieve instant renown if only he could be seen walking along Madison Avenue between Geldzahler and Castelli. Through Geldzahler, Kertess met young artists, and, as is often the way, these and other artists recommended their friends to him. Among the young men who came to him through such recommendations were Brice Marden and Chuck Close. Marden, who was a guard at the Jewish Museum and a studio assistant to Robert Rauschenberg, offered carefully brushed Minimalist panels of a single color. Close, the only figurative artist to attract Kertess, created very large portraits based on photographs. David Navros, a painter of geometrical forms and a close friend of Marden's, also joined the gallery. In 1969 Kertess added Dorothea Rockburne to the roster. She too was an assistant to Rauschenberg. Her art, in the Minimalist mode, consisted chiefly of works on paper carefully creased to form geometrical designs. Another early recruit was Deborah Remington, an Abstract Expressionist whose previous one-artist shows had been held at three offbeat San Francisco galleries: King Ubu, Six, and Dilexi. Kertess also brought in the sculptors Barry Le Va, David Rabinowitz, and Alan Saret. Eventually his stable included eighteen artists. In the early days when money was short, a crowd of young artists from the Bykert headed night after night for their favorite hangout, Max's Kansas City, a steakhouse-saloon on Park Avenue South where their credit was good and where John Chamberlain, Rauschenberg, and Warhol could occasionally be spotted. Max's to this generation of artists was what the Cedar Tavern had been to the Abstract Expressionists.

Kertess would have liked his roster to include Carl Andre, whose Minimalist sculptures of fire bricks or metal plates laid flat on the floor were attracting museums and private collectors. He had exhibitions at both the Dwan Gallery, a haven for Minimalist sculptors, and also at Tibor de Nagy. But the gallery's tight budget could not allow for the monthly stipend that Andre requested. Early on, Kertess found, with difficulty, the $300 necessary for the fabrication of an Andre floor sculpture, which he included in a group exhibition and priced at $900. This, it turned out, was the only work by Andre ever shown at the Bykert. Kertess asked Byers to buy it, but even at that low price Byers felt that he could not afford it. Kertess predicted that in five years the price for such a piece would be $40,000 and predicted also that Byers would buy one at that figure, which, in fact, he did.

Although the Bykert's never-ending cash-flow problems did not preclude loans to artists on those not infrequent occasions when they were unable to pay their rent, there was never enough money in the bank for more than one assistant in the gallery. The last of Kertess's assistants was the attractive, dark-haired, very intelligent Mary Boone, who came to him on the recommendation of his friend, the sculptor Lynda Benglis, whose student Boone had been at Hunter College. Boone was the

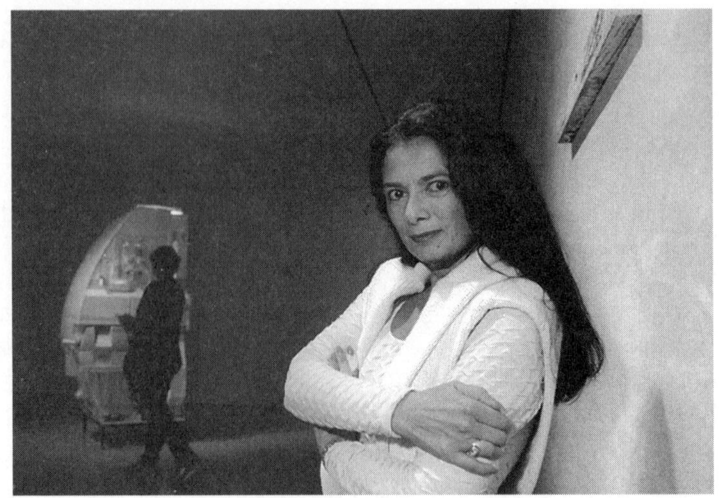

Mary Boone in her gallery. At left, one of Tom Sach's assemblages.

gallery's receptionist and watchful guardian of its accounts receivable. Her goal in taking this low-paying job was to prepare herself for the day when she would have a gallery of her own.

After six years of running the Bykert, Kertess began to think of alternative possibilities for his time and energy, among which was the writing of fiction. He kept the Bykert going until 1975 and would have left earlier had he not been concerned for the future of his artists. But leaving was not easy; it was, as he put it, "like divorcing eighteen people." At that time only Marden and Close were doing well enough not to need his sponsorship. Mary Boone also left in 1975 and began to deal in art privately from her living quarters. Two years later she opened a gallery in SoHo. The Bykert stayed open for one last year, under the direction of a young man named Frank Kolbert. The closing cost the city and the trade a fertile ground for the nurturing of emerging talent. Kertess went on to write and to serve as a curator at the Parrish Art Museum in Southampton and, later, the Whitney Museum. On the morning of December 31, 1977, Byers leapt to his death from a window in his New York apartment. Although he left a note citing business problems, his suicide has never been fully explained.

A long career in the trade awaited Mary Boone. Her first gallery was a small space on the ground floor of 510 West Broadway, the building that housed the premises of Leo Castelli and Ileana Sonnabend. She had studied Renaissance art at Hunter, but had not had opportunities to learn about contemporary art there. Her instruction in that field began at the Bykert as she became acquainted with Kertess's artists, who were kind to her. At first, after the closing of the Bykert, she had contemplated taking a job with another gallery, provided its owner was willing to add to his roster Ross Bleckner, David Salle, and Julian Schnabel, talented artists whom she had come to know and admire. She approached Max Protetch, whose gallery opened in 1970, and Robert Miller, who had just begun in the business. Both were willing to take her on, but not her three artists. Her lawyer suggested that she open on her own, which she did, in the fall of 1977. She financed the operation by selling limited partnerships, an unusual procedure in the trade.[4]

She had come to know Byers well during her time at Bykert and was in fact one of the last persons to whom he spoke before his death. In accordance with his wishes, she was allowed to sell a number of paintings from his estate, including major works by Marden, Close, and Agnes Martin. With her commissions from these sales and an overhead of only $7,000, her gallery, unlike most start-up businesses, showed a profit in its first year. Boone's stylish wardrobe, shapely legs, and piquant looks (in part the creation of a plastic surgeon who gave her a new nose) quickly drew the attention of the press, some of whose members ignored the fact that not only was she attractive in appearance but also brainy. Bleckner, Salle, Schnabel, and Eric Fischl would form the core of her original roster.

At the outset, Boone did not have the wall space to exhibit the work of Schnabel and Salle; her rooms at 420 West Broadway were too small to accommodate their huge canvases. Moreover, she did not yet have the fame that these ambitious young men demanded in any dealer who was to represent them. In order to keep them, she enlisted Leo Castelli as a partner in their work. This ploy succeeded brilliantly. Although not all critics were awed by the artists, collectors immediately took them up. Boone's success with these two made it possible for her to move to a much larger gallery space across West Broadway. With Fischl, Bleckner, and Marden also in her stable and no women as yet, Boone began hearing from feminist critics that she was interested only in gathering a circle of studs. Her response was that she was interested in talent, not gender. These complaints ceased when she brought in four highly individualistic and talented women: Barbara Kruger, Sherrie Levine, and, later, Ellen Gallagher and Roni Horn.

Not all her artists remained with her. Levine became difficult to work with and had to be let go, and, inevitably, other artists left when offered extravagant subsidies. Thus Schnabel left for the Pace Gallery after seven years with Boone, and Salle left for Larry Gagosian after twelve. Also lost to her, although with minimal regret on her part, was the talented, mercurial, drug-addicted Jean-Michel Basquiat, whose fiery, confrontational art commanded a great following of collectors and dealers. He stayed with Boone for only two shows; in 1988, at age twenty-seven, he died of an overdose of heroin.

Apart from Basquiat the losses hurt Boone in personal ways, and the departure of the best-selling Schnabel, in whom she had great confidence, threatened to create a financial problem as well. Rumors about her finances spread quite early in her career, even running to speculation that she might be facing bankruptcy.[5] They had no basis in fact, true though it was that, like all other dealers, she felt a pinch in the early 1990s when the market slumped. But by the century's end she stood out as one of the most prominent dealers in New York. She abandoned SoHo in 1996 for large, airy quarters uptown at 745 Fifth Avenue. Although the presumed heavy cost of this move and the loss to Larry Gagosian of Ellen Gallagher, whose shows with Boone turned her into a major star, were enough to start the rumors circulating again, but these, too, had no factual basis.

In the fall of 1999 Boone's customary serenity was disturbed by a brief run-in with the law. Late in September she opened an exhibition of sculptures by Tom Sachs, the creator of large and complex assemblages intended as abstract comments on human violence. Some of the works on view incorporated functioning guns, and the guests at the opening reception were offered live cartridges to take home as souvenirs of the occasion. When word of this reached New York's police, they seized the cartridges and arrested Boone. After an uncomfortable night in prison (the notorious detention center known as "The Tombs"), she was released. Soon, comforted by her colleagues in the art world, she began to look on the occasion as an adventure, and finally, on December 6, the charges against her were dismissed. "Art is the only thing I believe in," she said on hearing this good news, "and I'm glad to be arrested over it."[6] With this essentially foolish matter out of the way, no serious observer could doubt that Boone's gallery would step briskly into the twenty-first century.

In the financially heady years of the early and mid-1980s, many more galleries sprang up in New York, from SoHo to the East Seventies, with a few outposts on the West Side. But nowhere was the concentration of optimistic venturers in the trade so thick as in the East Village, an area of the Lower East Side stretching south from Thirteenth Street to Rivington Street and east to Alphabet City—Avenues A, B, C, and D. Beginning

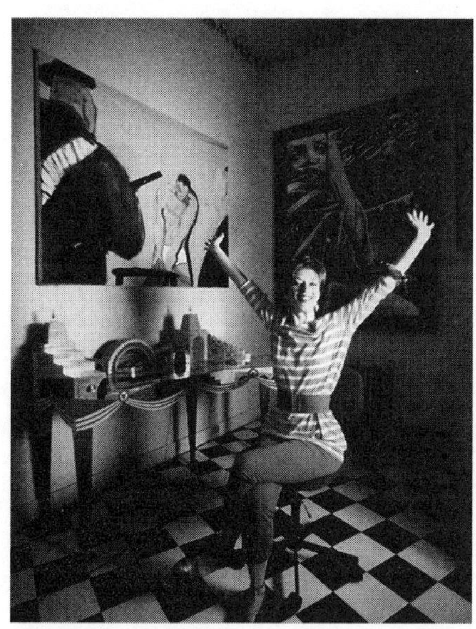

Gracie Mansion in her East Village gallery.

in 1981, a phalanx of bright young men and women moved into this blue-collar district of bodegas, decaying tenements, and crack houses with the intention of establishing themselves as art dealers. The first new East Village enterprise was set up by Bill Stelling, an artist, and Patti Astor, an underground-film actress, in Stelling's studio on Eleventh Street.[7] Next came a young woman christened Joanne Mayhew-Young, but who, looking for a more striking identity, renamed herself Gracie Mansion, after the name of the official residence of the mayor of New York. Gracie Mansion's first show was of work by Buster Cleveland, which she exhibited in SoHo in a rented limousine.[8] In 1982 she set up a gallery in the bathroom of her East Village apartment. Within a year, with larger space and exhibitions of work by the talented artists Mike Bidlo, Judy Glantzman, Al Hansen, and David Wojnarowicz, she became the most publicized figure among the East Village dealers.

Gallery names mattered very much in the East Village. At Patti Astor's suggestion, Stelling called his establishment the Fun Gallery. This set a pattern. Soon the East Village was covered with galleries bearing such names as New Math, Civilian Warfare, Ex Voto, Nature Morte, Postmasters, Vox Populi, Semaphore East, Nolo Contendere, International with Monument, and Ground Zero. Some East Village dealers—Jack Shainman, E. M. Donahue, Jay Gorney, Ellen Sragow, Pat Hearn, and one or two others—preferred to name their galleries after themselves, but they were in the minority. No matter what the galleries were called, nearly all were very small, and so neat as to give the impression that their young owners had recently left homes where their parents had frequently reminded them to straighten up their rooms.

Most of these little storefront shops were open only on weekends, including Sundays. They attracted a following among collectors, some of whom, not daring to enter this uncharted territory on foot, arrived by limousine. This was an opportunity to buy new art at low prices, and no serious collector could refuse at least to survey the scene. Among those who made the trip were Elaine and Werner Dannheisser, Adrian Mnuchin, and Eugene Schwartz, all known to have an eye for new developments in art. In truth, the art varied in quality. Much was poor, even amateurish. But on the other hand, much was good. Gracie Mansion's artists and the Starn twins, Michael Zwack, Mark Innerst, and Kiki Smith were among those who stood out. Others equally talented were Pat Hearn's artists, Donald Baechler, George Condo, Peter Schuyff, and Philip Taaffe. Ileana Sonnabend deemed Ashley Bickerton, Peter Halley, Jeff Koons, and Meyer Vaisman, all associated with International with Monument, worthy of her attention and took them on, an event, as Anthony Haden-Guest has pointed out, that played a part in the winding down of the East Village scene.[9]

In fact, the East Village boom ended as quickly as it began. Many of the dealers had set up their shops with only minimal financial backing. By mid-1987, about twenty galleries had closed, their owners having learned, as their rents increased, that more than youthful energy was required to build a successful business. "What happened," said one observer, "is that everybody grew up."[10] The sharp drop in Wall Street prices that occurred on Monday, October 19, 1987, when the Dow Jones industrial average lost 508 points, sent tremors through the art community and hastened the departure of still more dealers.

But those who had grown in wisdom as well as age saw new opportunities on lower Broadway, to which SoHo had now reached. There the rents on sizable spaces were less per square foot than the rents they had been paying in the East Village. Hearn, Shainman, Gorney, Sragow, and Penny Pilkington and Wendy Oloff, owners of P.P.O.W. Gallery, were the most prominent of those who reestablished themselves in the expanded SoHo and survived. Gracie Mansion moved to St. Marks Place, still the East Village, but not so far east as her early location. By the end of the decade the East Village could boast of many popular bars and midscale restaurants, but it was no longer a venue for art.

A cluster of new problems rose to trouble the art market as the century entered its last decade. The national debt, a drop in the value of the dollar, and the nation's weakened position in world trade conspired to create a recession that, if not the severest that the United States had ever experienced, touched most businesses. Predictably, sales of art fell off sharply. Yet it was not the recession alone that affected the art market. The boom years of the 1980s had created such expectations of success in the trade that by the 1990s there was not enough art of distinction to fill all the new galleries. In addition, dealers in the art most in demand had pushed prices to levels at which the resistance of collectors began to set in.

In 1993 a shrewd reporter for the *New York Times* made the rounds of the galleries to see how much negotiating their owners would tolerate. At his first stops, three minor SoHo galleries, he swiftly talked the owners into discounts of 20 to 30 percent. This much success emboldened him to try the big time. At the André Emmerich Gallery in the Fuller Building, an assistant allowed that the reporter might have a painting by Stanley Boxer at a 30 percent discount, bringing the price down from $19,000 to $13,300, provided Boxer agreed to the arrangement, as she thought he would. Back in SoHo at the Paula Cooper Gallery, the reporter was able to secure a reduction of $20,000 on a $115,000 painting by Elizabeth Murray, a much esteemed younger artist. His final stop was at the pinnacle: Castelli's, where he asked about a Lichtenstein. Only one painting by this most popular artist was available, and the assistant with whom he spoke was firm in limiting the discount to 10 percent. But when the reporter inquired about a Lichtenstein sculpture, *Airplane*, the assistant told him with surprising frankness that the work had come down in price by stages from $450,000 to $300,000. When the reporter asked for a further cut of 10 percent, the assistant replied, "Oh, yes."[11]

Although the early '90s witnessed the commencement, slow but more or less sure, of a boom on Wall Street, the art market remained sluggish through most of the decade. With their usual volatility, stocks went through stages of backing and filling, but the trend was definitely upward, leaving the art market far behind. Much was revealed when Grace Borgenicht, who had successfully maintained a gallery since 1951, decided in 1995 to retire. She had done everything possible to cut down her overhead, but found that no economizing measures succeeded in keeping her firm out of the red.[12] Allan Frumkin, who had opened his popular Chicago gallery in 1952 and established his New York presence in 1959, left the gallery scene in 1995 to take up a quieter career as an independent dealer, to be seen by appointment only.

Another sign of the times was the linking of two major galleries with

Sotheby's, the international auction firm. In 1990 William Aquavella joined with Sotheby's to form Aquavella Modern Art. This new entity paid $143 million for the inventory of the Pierre Matisse Gallery. Six years later, André Emmerich, who had been in business since 1954, sold his gallery to Sotheby's. The sale was initiated by Emmerich and was greatly to his advantage. It provided him with a substantial sum of money (undisclosed) for the goodwill attached to his name, an annual salary, and an office in Sotheby's building on First Avenue. Sotheby's took over the cost of running the gallery and was to receive a commission on any works Emmerich sold from his inventory, whether privately to clients or as consignments at auction. Renamed Emmerich/Sotheby's, the gallery would remain in its old home in the Fuller Building, but in only one of the two suites, on different floors, that it had formerly occupied. This proved not to be the dream situation that Sotheby's expected, however, and in 1998 the auction house decided to close the gallery.[13]

Still, most longtime dealers persevered. Of those who dealt in contemporary art, the leaders at the century's end were the Larry Gagosian, Pace, and Mary Boone galleries. Castelli, once at the very peak of the profession, could no longer be described as a major player.

With the decline of the Castelli Gallery in fin de siècle gloom, Glimcher and Gagosian had become the foremost dealers in contemporary art, with Boone not far behind.[14] Gagosian's career was slow to get under way. It began in Los Angeles, the city of his birth, in 1977, when he opened a poster shop. Two years later he established a small gallery for original art. He moved up to larger premises in 1982 and maintained them until 1987. There in 1984 he introduced Los Angeles to East Village art with a show of new painting and sculpture from the district's galleries. But he had been attracted to New York as early as 1979. He bought a loft in the city and with the dealer Annina Nosei did business in it until badgered by other tenants who complained of the traffic he had created. In late 1985 he opened a gallery in New York's Chelsea district, an area of small businesses and large lofts in the far west teens and twenties, where rentals on commercial space were relatively inexpensive. Three years later he found large quarters at 980 Madison Avenue, a building well known to the collectors as the former home of the Parke-Bernet auction house and its successor, Sotheby's. A busy man who enjoyed the rough-and-tumble of business, he next bought a building on Wooster Street in SoHo for exhibitions of large-scale works such as the sculptures of Richard Serra. For five years in partnership with Leo Castelli he operated another SoHo gallery, on Thompson Street.

In his Chelsea gallery Gagosian began the practice of offering exhibitions of art-historical importance, such as the very early work of Frank Stella and selections from the collection of Burton and Emily Tremaine. On Madison Avenue, he continued the practice of historical exhibitions with, among other such shows, Johns's paintings of the map of the United States, Jackson Pollock's black enamel paintings, Sam Francis's blue-ball paintings, and early work by James Rosenquist, each accompanied by a sumptuously illustrated catalogue. The historical shows have also included works by such Europeans as Augusto Giacometti, Egon Schiele, Max Beckmann, Constantin Brancusi, and, decidedly a stretch for a dealer with tastes so rooted in the twentieth century, Peter Paul Rubens. Few of these works were for sale; nevertheless, Gagosian realized a financial profit from most of them. Only in the exhibition of Brancusi's sculptures, in which all the works were on loan from Romanian museums, was nothing for sale. Apart from such financial returns as the shows provided, they also brought Gagosian publicity and the thanks of historians.

In 1995 Gagosian opened his Beverly Hills branch, a white cube of a space designed by Richard Meier, who was then at work on the new hilltop building of the Getty Museum in Los Angeles. The first exhibition gave the public a look at the extremely massive metal sculptures of Frank Stella. Plans were under way in 1998 for an expansion of the gallery, with new storage and office space, also designed by Meier.

In spite of the hard work known to be required to present the historical exhibitions and the regard for the public that they seemed to demonstrate, Gagosian has had a bad press ever since his arrival on Madison Avenue. Not a developer of talent, he, like Arnold Glimcher, made his way by offering lucrative contracts to artists nurtured by rival dealers. In 1998 his stable included Cy Twombly, Eric Fischl, Mark di Suvero, David Salle, Ellen Gallagher, Walter de Maria, Richard Serra, Anselm Kiefer, and Francesco Clemente, and he managed to stage several shows of works from the Warhol estate. Arnold Glimcher's press has also included some barbs over perceived marauding tactics, along with his wish to be known familiarly as Arne, with its cool suggestion of Scandinavia, rather than as Arnie, which recalls his Jewish background. But criticism of Glimcher has been mild compared to the going-over that has been Go-Go's lot. Not only his frenetic wheeling and dealing but even the look of his New York galleries and his Beverly Hills branch has been subject to criticism,[15] and rumors about his solvency have been floated repeatedly despite the planned expansion in Beverly Hills and the appearance of prosperity that he projects.[16] His opulent way of life—expensive restaurants, expensive grooming, expensive cars, expensive dwellings—has also come under attack, as, curiously, with such dealers as Castelli and Glimcher it never has. Queried on this, he put it down to envy of his success and his California origin. "I'm certain," he said, "that if you held a microscope up to any of my colleagues, as vanilla as their reputations may be, you'd reveal at least as much color." Whatever the truth of the matter, an unfavorable press has not hurt his business. Like Glimcher, he was quickly able to secure a high-profile clientele, including the Hollywood figures David Geffen and Steve Martin, the television producer Douglas Cramer, the Los Angeles real-estate magnate Eli Broad, and the British advertising magnate and megacollector Charles Saatchi. In 1999 Glimcher closed the his Beverly Hills outpost, although he maintained an office there. In a sense, Gagosian could consider himself the winner in this battle of titans. On the other hand, there could be no doubt that Glimcher could continue to do good business with his Hollywood clients without the expense of running a store in the neighborhood.

As should be clear by now, the building of a successful gallery requires hard work and a good head for business. But in such an age as the late twentieth century, publicity is also of enormous avail. An extreme instance is the fate of Tony Shafrazi, an isolated artist of Armenian extraction who long harbored the desire to operate a gallery, sought a way to make a name for himself, and found it at the Museum of Modern Art. On April 30, 1974, Shafrazi entered the museum with a spray can of red paint and ascended to the gallery that housed Picasso's *Guernica*, possibly the most famous painting in the museum at that time. Mindless of the fact that many museum visitors were in the room, Shafrazi walked up to the painting and with his can wrote on it an obscure message: "Kill Lies All." Guards immediately apprehended him, and he was jailed, but only briefly. Soon he was out on $1,000 bail. The Modern's conservators were summoned at once to remove Shafrazi's handiwork. No permanent damage was done; the painting had been protected by a heavy coat of varnish.

In accordance with Picasso's wishes, after the death of Franco *Guernica* went to Madrid, where it is now on view at the Reina Sofia Museum and protected from assaults by Shafrazi imitators by a barrier that keeps the public a good ten feet away. As for Shafrazi himself, the punishment he received for his act of vandalism amounted to a mere slap on the hand: five years' probation and the exaction of a promise not to do it again.[17] In 1981 he opened a gallery that quickly prospered as host to exhibitions of work by Keith Haring, Warhol, and Basquiat.

Shafrazi set up his business in trendy SoHo, which by the time of his arrival had become home to almost as many boutiques and restaurants as art galleries. The Saturday crowds strolling its narrow streets could shop not only for art but for clothes, antique furniture, tableware, bed linens, gourmet foodstuffs, and books, just as in midtown, and rentals were steeply on the rise. In the 1990s the situation had almost reached the point at which art was a secondary presence in the neighborhood. Troubled by the change, many dealers began to search for another area, one uncluttered by shops, which they might claim for art; they found it in Chelsea, a district on the far West Side.

Some of the newly nomadic dealers took over garages and warehouses, which were plentiful in the area, and some converted these large spaces into airy showrooms for contemporary art; others chose brownstone houses. One of the first to make the move was Paula Cooper, whose SoHo gallery was the earliest in that area. Pat Hearn, who had come to SoHo from the East Village, was also one of the first. As interest in Chelsea grew, uptown dealers such as Matthew Marks and Jason McCoy found suitable lofts. Gagosian, while maintaining his uptown premises and, at least for the time being, a SoHo venue, also took space there. Rents crept upward, of course, but Chelsea was still cheap, and, at least for the time being, free of coffee bars and all the other businesses that had begun to diminish the importance of art in SoHo. At the century's end, as an art district it rivaled not only SoHo but Fifty-seventh Street as well. The remaining SoHo dealers, of whom, to be sure, there were many, went on the offensive. Refusing to give up without a fight, they took out full-page ads in the *Times* listing current exhibitions. The unanswered question implicit in this new problem had to do with the boutiques, not the galleries. If all the art dealers were to leave, how many shoppers would make their way down to SoHo to buy a dress, a carving knife, or a duvet?

19

NEXT?

With relocation of many New York dealers to new territory in the late 1990s, we come almost to the end of our story. How much more is there to say? The art market, like the market for anything else, has its highs and lows, but since the end of the Second World War the highs have prevailed. They have taken the prices of art to distances beyond the imagination of earlier generations. Yet the business of art is tricky, and dangerously so for the unsophisticated man or woman who hopes for success in it. Galleries come and go with alarming speed. In 1971 *Arts Magazine* sent a questionnaire to the proprietors of some eighty galleries on their policies and published the replies. Of these dealers, only twenty were still in business as the century came to its close, and most had given up long before. A period of five to twenty years is the usual length of a gallery's life. Those few extant galleries that date from the nineteenth century, such as the Vose in Boston (founded 1850) and the Knoedler

(1846), Babcock (1852, as Snedecor), Graham (1857), Kennedy (1874, as Wunderlich), and Kraushaar (1885) galleries in New York, are outstanding exceptions.[1]

Of the new trends in collecting observable in the late twentieth century, one of the most durable centered not on a mode of painting or sculpture but on photography. Ever since the days of Stieglitz's 291, photographs had been exhibited and purchased, but only in limited numbers. Rarely in the time of 291 did other galleries show them, although one prominent dealer, Newman E. Montross, offered an exhibition of Edward Steichen's photographs (and paintings) in 1910 and a roundup exhibition of the work of thirty photographers in 1912. But the market was slow to develop.

The most avid collector of photographs in the interwar years, and in fact the only early collector of note in this art form apart from Stieglitz himself was David H. McAlpin, an investment banker whose passion for photography first manifested itself when he bought several works by Ansel Adams in the 1930s. In 1936 he paid $100, then an exorbitant price, for Adams's *The White Tombstone*. He made this purchase at Stieglitz's An American Place with a check made out to Adams himself. Then, at Stieglitz's insistence, he made out another check, for $49, to benefit the gallery's "rent fund." In Chicago, Katharine Kuh, the first dealer in that city to show photography, was selling the identical print for $25.[2]

In the 1950s and '60s photographs by distinguished Americans could be had for very little money in the Museum of Modern Art's penthouse gallery. There one might buy, for example, Frederick Sommers's iconic *Circumnavigation of the Blood* for $15, a work that in the 1990s could bring as much as $13,000.[3] But not until the 1970s were photographs sought by more than a few collectors. This new enthusiasm, which escalated into a full-scale boom midway through the decade, was largely due to the enthusiasm of Lee D. Witkin, a young man who opened a gallery for the exclusive sale of photographs in 1969. His schedule of exhibitions included one-artist shows not only by such renowned photographers as Adams, Steichen, Margaret Bourke-White, W. Eugene Smith, Ralph Steiner, and Edward Weston but by newcomers as well, including George A. Tice and Jerry Uelsmann. Witkin's success was of such magnitude that after seven years in the business he could afford to move from small quarters on East Sixtieth Street to the Fuller Building on Fifty-seventh Street. Once his gallery was established, other photography galleries soon sprang up. So popular did this art form become that photographers were sought after by the Castelli, Paula Cooper, O. K. Harris, Robert Miller, Pace, and

Zabriskie galleries, among others in New York, and other dealers nationwide. By the century's end, the directory of the Association of International Photography Art Dealers (AIPAD), founded in 1979, listed 114 galleries, 29 of which were located in New York and 24 in Los Angeles, San Francisco, Carmel, and other California cities. But the year 2000 list would not include the Witkin. On the death of Witkin in 1984, Evelyne Z. Daitz, his associate, took over the directorship of the gallery, but retained the original name. After managing it successfully for fifteen years, she decided to close it in the summer of 1999. Behind her decision was a wish to deal privately from her home, without the burden of running a gallery, and her dismay over the fact that photography had become big business, with some images by masters of the medium fetching six-figure prices at auction.[4]

Along with the rise in the popularity of photographs came a similar movement in the print market. Dealers had always stocked prints by the artists on their rosters, but a potent boost to the trend of print collecting occurred in the 1950s and '60s with the founding of many new, expertly staffed and managed print workshops such as ULAE, Gemini GEL, and Tamarind. With the dynamic rise in the price of paintings, prints have provided a more affordable opportunity to collectors to acquire work by major artists, although the prices of prints have also climbed. It was not uncommon in the 1980s and '90s to see some of the ULAE prints rise in value from a few hundred dollars or even less to five figures. Print fairs are now held annually in New York, Chicago, Washington, and Los Angeles.

Other trends abound. In the 1970s a renewal of interest arose in American art of the first half of the twentieth century, with enterprising dealers in New York and Los Angeles scouting the auctions to snap up the works of such neglected artists as I. Rice Pereira, Attilio Salemme, Norman Lewis, Knud Merrild, Leonard Edmundson, and Jean Xceron. Interest was evident also in "outsider art": primitive paintings from rural areas, prisons, and insane asylums. Late in the 1990s New York was host to fairs of such art. Of greater interest, and also the subject of annual fairs, was the work of black artists, including the painters Romare Bearden, Jacob Lawrence, and Norman Lewis, the sculptor Richard Hunt, and the photographer Roy de Carava, all of whom had long since been represented by mainstream galleries.

Avoiding the mainstream, some young New Yorkers have established galleries in outposts of the city where they sell works of art by men and women as young as or even younger than themselves. Their enterprise is best exemplified by Pierogi 2000, a small gallery owned by Joe Amrhein in the Williamsburg section of Brooklyn. The pierogi being a Polish edible, humble but satisfying, the gallery's name celebrates the district itself, which includes a large population of Polish origin; "2000" refers, obviously, to the new century. At the gallery, the viewer can pull out the drawers of flat files to examine portfolios of works on paper by some four hundred artists. To its owner, Pierogi is a way station for artists who may (or may not) move on to greater glory across the East River.

Not to be overlooked is the ongoing market for Old Master, eighteenth-century, Impressionist and other nineteenth-century art, and the art of the Post-Impressionists. Although great works of the distant past had become increasingly difficult to locate at the century's end, the market persisted. The leader, as it had been for a least the past thirty years, was the Wildenstein Gallery. Among its rivals in the United States as the century neared its close—if indeed any dealers could rival the Wildenstein family—were the Richard Feigen, Rosenberg & Stiebel, and Eugene V. Thaw galleries. But with museums always on the search for works of the masters and never releasing them once they are acquired, would-be dealers in these rarefied fields are aware that to enter them takes not only massive capital but massive courage. Massive generosity was displayed by Eugene V. Thaw and his wife, Clare, in their gift to New York's Morgan Library of their collection in 1995 of some 250 outstanding master drawings ranging in date from the fifteenth century to the twentieth.

Nineteenth-century American art is also in demand. For such art, the leading firm is the Kennedy Galleries. Originally the Wunderlich Galleries, its name was changed during the First World War, when sentiment against anything German—German music, German food, German-sounding names—ran high. The new name was that of a partner in the firm. In 1966 the gallery was taken over by Lawrence A. Fleischman (d. 1997) of Detroit. Until then, the market for works of the Hudson River school and others among America's oldest masters had been in sharp decline. Virtually single-handedly, Fleischman strengthened this market. He also deserves credit, and the fervent thanks of historians, for founding, with E. P. Richardson, the Archives of American Art, now an arm of the Smithsonian Institution. Mention should be made as well to the gallery of Frank S. Schwarz & Son (Philadelphia), which has made something of a specialty in collecting work by the extensive family of Charles Willson Peale.

In sharp contrast to the creators of traditional art and the dealers who promote their work are the young artists who break away from easel painting and the art-world supporters of their nontraditional creations. Artist-designed videos, which arrived in the 1960s and evoked little enthusiasm from the public at the time, surfaced again in the 1990s, with wider promotion from museums of contemporary art than from dealers. Yet another new way to distribute art arrived with the latest of technological wonders: the Internet. In 1997 the artist Peter Halley initiated a new means of getting art to the public. His hard-edged geometrical paintings (Neo-Geo) had been in demand at high prices since 1986, when Ileana Sonnabend showed them with the work of other East Village artists awaiting their first big break. Eleven years later in an exhibition at the Museum of Modern Art and on a website, Halley provided the general public with easy access to his art. The outlines of a print appeared on a computer screen, and with a few clicks of a mouse the viewer could choose from a range of colors to tint it as he or she thought appropriate and then download it with one click more. Presto: a new work of art signed by Halley and with space beside his name for that of the mouse manipulator as his collaborator. Collectors desiring an instant Johns or Rauschenberg from the Net are likely to be disappointed, but there can be little doubt that other artists will adopt Halley's means of distributing their work, and, unlike the generous Halley, charge for it. Nor was Halley's generosity of long duration; in 1998 and 1999 the magazine *On Paper* advertised that it could supply the MoMA print at a price: $350 for subscribers, $500 for others.

Dealers, of course, have boarded the Internet bandwagon. Many have e-mail addresses to which collectors can send inquiries about the availability of work by their favorite artists. (Not that a telephone call would fail to secure the same information.) Some dealers, and no doubt many more will join them, have websites to notify clients about their exhibition schedules. Technology has taken the trade and its marketing devices a long way from Michael Paff and his modest advertisements, which, it may be remembered, informed collectors that at his gallery they could find pictures "worthy of their attention . . . at the smallest expense, with the most extensive gratification."

NOTES

Chapter 1

1 *Boston Gazette,* April 4–11, 1720.

2 Advertisements quoted in James Thomas Flexner, *First Flowers of Our Wilderness* (New York: Dover, 1969, rpt.), 310–11.

3 "The Editor's Attic," *The Magazine Antiques,* July 1931, 11–12; Mabel M. Swan, "The American Kings," *The Magazine Antiques,* April 1931, 178–81.

4 William Dunlap, *A History of the Rise and Progress of the Arts of Design in the United States* (New York: Dover, 1969, rpt.), I:290–91, II:134; Edward Biddle and Mantle Fielding, *Life and Works of Thomas Sully* (Philadelphia: Wickersham Press, 1921), 28n, identify the institution referred to by Dunlap as "the old museum and theatre" and add that Sully's painting was later removed to the Boston Museum of Fine Arts. Sully was also the proprietor of a gallery, which he opened in 1819 in Philadelphia with James Earle, a framer, as partner. This served primarily as an exhibition hall and was let to painters for a share of the proceeds from paid admissions to viewings of their work; see Dunlap, I:22, 288–89, 423.

5 Anna Wells Rutledge, "Robert Gilmor, Jr., Baltimore Collector," *Journal of the Walters Art Gallery* XII (1949): 21–22. In the records of the American Academy, Flandin was designated a "merchant."

6 Rutledge, 31, 39.

7 A note, no more, should be given to David Longworth, another dealer of whom little is known in a personal way. He was the publisher of *Salmagundi,* the *American Almanack, New-York-Register, and City Directory,* prints, and plays. In 1796 Longworth opened the Shakespeare Gallery in New York, where he showed John Boydell's engravings of scenes from Shakespeare, as well as other prints, including his own publications, and plays. He maintained the gallery until 1818. See Jacob Blanck, "*Salmagundi* and Its Publisher," *Papers of the Bibliographic Society of America* XLI (1967): 1-10.

8 Matthew Hale Smith, *Sunshine and Shadow* (Hartford: J. D. Burr and Co., 1868), 114.

9 John Paff is identified as Michael's brother in Harry Dichter and Elliott Shapiro, *American Sheet Music: Its Lure and Its Love, 1869–1889* (New York: R. R. Bowker, 1941), 219.

10 Rita Sussman Gottesman, *The Arts and Crafts in New York,* vol. I (New York: New-York Historical Society, 1959), entries 87, 596–600, 1257, 1260; vol. II (1965), entries 109, 116, 151, 895-97, 1094, 1135, 1213, 1223, 1232.

11 Kenneth Wiggins Porter, *John Jacob Astor: Businessman* (Cambridge: Harvard University Press, 1931) I: 110-11.

12 Elizabeth L. Gebhard, *The Life and Ventures of the Original John Jacob Astor* (Hudson, N.Y.: Bryan Printing Co., 1915), 262.

13 Theodore Sizer, introduction to Mary Barlett Cowdrey, *American Academy of the Fine Arts and American Art-Union, 1816–1832* (New York: New-York Historical Society [henceforth NYHS], 1953), I: 24.

14 C. L. Beaumont, "The Picture Sales of New York—A Retrospective History," *New York Times* [henceforth *NYT*] *Saturday Review of Books and Art,* Dec. 11, 1897, 10.

15 This dealer was not the only member of the trade named Beaumont. More prominent was Charles Beaumont of Roxbury, Massachusetts, who was active at midcentury. Referring to him as "Mr. Beaumont," C. L. Beaumont, apparently no relation, recalls (11) that he and his father called on him to see the Stuart presidential portraits, which Charles Beaumont had bought from Doggett for resale. See also "The Editors's Attic," *The Magazine Antiques,* July 1931, 11.

16 Beaumont, 10.

17 Ibid.

18 John Durand, *The Life and Times of A. B. Durand* (New York: Charles Scribner's Sons, 1894), 68.

19 *A Century of Baltimore Collecting: 1840-1940* (Baltimore Museum of Art, 1941), 10.

20 Mrs. Jonathan Sturgis, *Reminiscences of a Long Life* (New York: F. E. Parrish, 1894), 198-99. The author was the widow of Reed's partner.

21 Tuckerman, *Book of the Artists* (New York: Putnam, 1867), 20.

22 John Durand, 159.

23 Beaumont, 10.

24 On April 17, 1833, Paff wrote to James Herring, secretary of the American Academy of the Fine Arts, "Your very polite letter of the 28th inst is at hand—in reply I would observe that I have no particular picture at hand which I believe will be suitable for your coming Exhibition—being at this time on friendly terms with both Academies—it is my wish so to continue. I am pleased to find I have your good wishes and hope we shall remain friends" (Collection NYHS). Three years

earlier he had responded favorably to a similar request from the National Academy of Design with the loan of a painting by Gilbert Stuart Newton; Mary Bartlett Cowdrey, *National Academy of Design Exhibition Record: 1816–1860* (New York: NYHS, 1943), II:50.

25 J. P. Whittlesey to Jonathan Sturges, Oct. 6, 1858, Asher B. Durand Papers, New York Public Library (henceforth NYPL).

26 Reed to Durand, March 13, 1835, Asher B. Durand Papers, NYPL.

27 Daniel Huntington, *Asher B. Durand: A Memorial Address* (New York: Century Association, 1887), 14.

28 Beaumont, 10.

29 Dunlap, II:386. Dunlap also offers (II:388) a story by Weir that may or may not cast suspicion on Paff. Weir copied an Annibale Carracci so successfully that an artist friend, identified only as "Tom," took it for the real thing. He had borrowed it from "Mr. P.," who assured him of its genuineness and said that he had paid $300 for it. Did Paff know better, or had Weir tricked him?

30 Sizer, in Cawdrey, 25.

31 Philip Hone, *The Diary of Philip Hone,* ed. Allan Nevins (New York: Dodd, Mead, 1936), 331.

32 John Trumbull, *Autobiography,* ed. Theodore Sizer (New Haven: Yale University Press, 1953); 374; Roger Hale Newton, *Town and Davis, Architects* (New York: Columbia University Press, 1942), 70-72.

Chapter 2

1 For a brief but adequate account of the Columbianum and the Pennsylvania Academy of the Fine Arts, see Nathaniel Burt, *Palaces for the People* (Boston: Little, Brown, 1977), 34-36. A very full account of the rise and fall of the American Academy is provided by Theodore Sizer in Mary Bartlett Cowdrey, *American Academy of Fine Arts and American Art-Union* (New York: New-York Historical Society, 1953), 3-93. On the Boston Athenaeum's early effort to promote art, see Mabel Swan, *The Athenaeum Gallery, 1827–1875* (Boston: Boston Athenaeum, 1950).

2 Sizer, in Cowdrey, 60-61. The first 125 years of the National Academy of Design (NAD) are covered in Elliot Clark, *History of the National Academy of Design, 1825–1953* (New York: Columbia University Press, 1954). Until 1863, persons who did not reside in New York were granted only honorary membership, and a few important persons in other fields were also given honorary membership.

3 Louis L. Noble, *The Course of Empire, Voyage of Life, and Other Pictures of Thomas Cole, N.A.* (New York: Cornish, Lampert, 1853), 56-57; William Dunlap, *A History of the Rise and Progress of the Arts of Design in the United States* (New York: Dover, 1961, rpt.), II: 359-60; Howard S. Merritt, *Thomas Cole* (Rochester: University of Rochester Press, 1969), 21-22. Merritt reproduces two of the paintings and gives their dimensions.

4 Dunlap, II: 60.

5 T. B. Thorpe "New York Artists Fifty Years Ago," *Appleton's Journal,* May 25, 1872, 572-75; William Dunlap, *Diary of William Dunlap* (New York: NYHS, 1930) has forty-seven entries on Clover and two on Paff.

6 On the tradition of the "Great Picture," see Gerald L. Carr, *Frederic Edwin Church: The Icebergs* (Dallas: Dallas Museum of Fine Arts, 1980), 24-30.

7 John Trumbull, *The Autobiography of Col. John Trumbull,* ed. Theodore Sizer (New Haven: Yale University Press, 1953), 319; Horace E. Dickson, "Artists as Showmen," *American Art Journal* V (May 1973): 11, 15-16.

8 Dickson, 13-15; John Russell, "Samuel Morse Painting Sold for $3.25 Million," *NYT,* July 30, 1982, Al, C14; Gerald Carr, "Icebergs Worth $2.5 Million," *Country Life* 26 (Nov. 22, 1979): 1919-20.

9 Kevin J. Avery, "*The Heart of the Andes.* Exhibited: Frederic E. Church's Window on the Equatorial World," *American Art Journal* XVIII, 1 (1986): 52. Before being put on view at the Studio Building, the picture was shown for two days at Lyric Hall on Broadway.

10 Daniel C. Huntington, *The Landscapes of Frederic E. Church* (New York: George Braziller, 1963), 1-9; Worthington Whittredge, "Autobiography," ed. John I. H. Bauer, *Brooklyn Museum Journal* I (1942): 28-29; Avery, "*The Heart of the Andes* Exhibited," 52.

11 Kevin J. Avery, *Church's Great Picture "The Heart of the Andes"* (New York: Metropolitan Museum of Art, 1993), 32.

12 Avery, "*The Heart of the Andes* Exhibited," 54.

13 Avery, *Church's Great Picture,* 37, 40. Another benefit to Church from the exhibition was that at it he met Isabel Carnes, the woman who the following year would become his wife.

14 Except where otherwise indicated in notes or text, the account of the American Art-Union and the career of James Herring is taken from Charles E. Baker, "The American Art-Union," in Mary Bartlett Cowdrey, *American Academy of Fine Arts and American Art-Union* (New York: NYHS 1952), 95-241. A brief commentary on Herring and Longacre's publication may be found in Robert G. Stewart, *A Nineteenth-Century Gallery of Distinguished Americans* (Washington, D.C.: Smithsonian Institution Press, 1969), 1-9.

15 *New York Mirror,* Sept. 17, 1836, 95. For a more sharply satiric comment, see the mock letter in *Yankee Doodle,* Oct. 10, 1846, 5, in which a newly rich New Yorker sends his son, who is traveling in Italy, a draft of $150 for Teeshuns, a Michael Ann Gelo, Gueedoes, and much more, adding, "As I want the real originals out of the palaces I don't mind making the draft $200 instead of $150."

16 *The Literary World,* Jan. 26, 1850, 87.

17 John Durand, *Life and Times of A. B. Durand* (New York: Charles Scribner's Sons, 1894), 169. Versions of these paintings are in the collections of two museums: the National Gallery of Art, Washington, D.C., and the Munson-Williams-Proctor Institute, Utica, New York.

18 Quoted by Baker, 152-53, source not cited.

19 Neil Harris, *The Artist in American Society* (Chicago: University of Chicago Press, 1966), 261-62.

20 Charles Henry Hart Autograph Collection, Archives of American Art (henceforth AAA).

21 *Crayon* I (1855): 91; III (1858): 158.

22 See Goupil, Vibert's 1848 catalogue *Exhibition of Works of Art.*

23 Helen M. Knowlton, *Art-Life of William Morris Hunt* (Boston: Little, Brown, 1899), 10-25; W. G. Constable, *Art Collecting in the United States* (London: Thomas Nelson and Sons, 1964), 72; Robert C. Vose Jr., "Boston's Vose Galleries: A Family Affair,"

Achives of American Art Journal (henceforth AAAJ) XXXI, 1 (1981):8.

24 Unless otherwise indicated, information on the Düsseldorf Gallery is taken from R. L. Stehle, "The Düsseldorf Gallery of New York," *NYHS Quarterly* LVIII (1974): 305–14.

25 Whittredge, 23–24.

26 *Cosmopolitan Art Journal* (henceforth *CAJ*) II: 135.

27 Among its triumphs was the bestowal, in 1852, of Hiram Powers's celebrated sculpture *The Greek Slave* upon one of its subscribers in the annual lottery. The winner, Mrs. Kate Gillespie of Brady's Bend, Pennsylvania, sent it on a moneymaking tour and then put it up for auction in 1857. The Cosmopolitan Art-Union, bending a rule against repurchasing a work that had once passed through its hands, bought it back. See the *Cosmopolitan Art Journal* I (Sept. 1857): 162.

28 Durand, 193.

29 Elihu Vedder, *The Digressions of V.* (Boston: Houghton, Mifflin, 1910), 105-6.

30 Durand, 192-93.

Chapter 3

1 *NYT,* Nov. 9, 1859, 1.

2 John Durand, *Life and Times of A. B. Durand* (New York: Charles Scribner's Sons, 1894), 193.

3 *NYT,* April 8, 1866, 5.

4 *Crayon* VII (Oct. 1860): 298. For a description of some of the artists' quarters in the building, see Thomas Bailey Aldrich, "Among the Studios," *Our Young Folks,* Sept. 1865, 594–98.

5 Aldrich, "Among the Studios," *Our Young Folks,* Dec. 1865, 776.

6 Garnett McCoy, "Visits, Parties, and Cats in the Hall: The Tenth Street Studio Building and Its Inmates in the Nineteenth Century," *AAAJ,* Jan. 1966, 1–8; Aldrich, "Among the Studios," *Our Young Folks,* 596–97.

7 Annette Blaugrund, *The Tenth Street Studio Building* (Southampton: Parrish Art Museum, 1997), 22.

8 Aldrich, "Among the Studios," *Our Young Folks,* July 1866, 395.

9 *Crayon* VI (Nov. 1859): 349.

10 *Crayon* V (May 1858): 148.

11 "The Artists' Reception in the Tenth-street Studio," *NYT,* Jan. 19, 1859, 4.

12 McCoy, 8.

13 *Crayon* VII (Oct. 1860): 298.

14 *NYT,* Oct. 12, 1860, 2.

15 Inness's relations with both firms were somewhat troubled. See George Inness Jr., *Life and Letters of George Inness* (New York: Century, 1917), 81–82, 86–88.

16 The shortening of the firm's name to Goupil from Goupil, Vibert occurred in 1850, after the death of Vibert.

17 Knoedler obituary, *New York World,* Apr. 18, 1878, 5.

18 *NYT,* Dec. 12, 1863, 4.

19 "House of Knoedler Marks 100th Milestone with Reminiscent Show," *Art Digest,* April 1, 1946, 6.

20 Alfred Frankenstein, *William Sidney Mount* (New York: Harry N. Abrams, 1975), 49; Mount, diary entry, Dec. 1849, quoted in Frankenstein, 159-60.

21 William Schaus, autobiographical press release, in Frankenstein, 153.
22 *Crayon* III (Nov. 1856): 344.
23 Charles R. Henschel, foreword to *A Catalogue of an Exhibition of Paintings and Prints of Every Description on the Occasion of Knoedler One Hundred Years 1846–1946* (New York: M. Knoedler, 1946), unpaginated. Henschel was Michael Knoedler's grandson.
24 About 25 percent of Stewart's collection was comprised of American works. For a complete account see Earl Shinn (Edward Strahan, pseud), *Art Treasures of the United States* (Philadelphia: George Barrie, 1879), I: 24-64.
25 Henschel.
26 *NYT,* March 16, 1859, 4; March 17, 1859, 4; March 18, 1859, 5.
27 *Crayon* VII (Nov. 1860): 323. Stebbins later created the sculptures for Central Park's Bethesda Fountain.
28 *Crayon* VII (Nov. 1860): 323; Lois Marie Fink, "French Art in the United States, *Gazette des Beaux-Arts* XCII (Sept. 1978): 89. Knoedler assisted Gambart with two later exhibitions that opened at the Tenth Street Studio Building in 1865 and 1866.
29 Gerald Carr, *Frederic Edwin Church: The Icebergs* (Dallas: Dallas Museum of Fine Arts, 1980), 28.
30 *NYT,* Nov. 12, 1863, 4.
31 These artists were represented by one work each in Knoedler's 150th anniversary exhibition in 1996, with brief commentary on their relation to the firm.
32 Presumably Schaus's first name was originally Wilhelm; however, I have never seen a reference to him by it. Wilhelm was the name he gave to his only son; letter, March 26, 1986, to the author from David H. Whittier, whose stepfather was the grandson of William Schaus.
33 In Frankenstein, 158.
34 In 1854, after Schaus had left Goupil's, Knoedler published still another Mount print. The ten lithographs and two engravings published by the American Art-Union constitute the total number of prints made from Mount's paintings.
35 In Frankenstein, 163-64.
36 *Crayon* I (June 21, 1855): 412; *NYT,* March 16, 1959, 4; Jan. 2, 1860, 4.
37 *NYT,* Dec. 30, 1859, 2; Jan. 2, 1860, 4.
38 *NYT,* Dec. 9, 1858, 2.
39 *Crayon* IV (May 1857): 157; *CAJ* II (Mar.-June 1858): 45.
40 Carr, 28.
41 David C. Huntington, *The Landscapes of F. E. Church* (New York: Braziller, 1966), 1-4.
42 *NYT,* Nov. 19, 1864, 2.
43 David H. Wallace, *John Rogers: The People's Sculptor* (Middletown: Wesleyan University Press, 1967), 140, 146.
44 *CAJ* IV (Dec. 1860): 183; Rona Schneider, "The Career of James David Smillie (1833-1909)," *American Art Journal* XVI (Winter 1984): 5-6.
45 Catalogues of these exhibitions are in the collection of the Babcock Gallery, New York. I am grateful to John Driscoll of the gallery for showing them to me.
46 Jervis McEntee, "Diary," ed. Garnett McCoy, *AAAJ,* July-Oct. 1968, 27.
47 Tiffany and Company, it should be noted, also opened a free gallery, in 1860. In the following year the store exhibited the *Niagara* paintings of both Church and Gignoux. See *NYT,* Dec. 29, 1860, 2; Nov. 17, 1861, 6.

48 *NYT,* Dec. 20, 1864, 4.
49 Quoted in Martha A. S. Shannon, *Boston Days of William Morris Hunt* (Boston: Marshall Jones Co., 1923), 18–19.
50 Vedder, 273–74.
51 Vedder, 478.
52 Madeleine Fidell-Beaufort, Herbert L. Kleinfeld, and Jeanne K. Welcher, introduction to *The Diaries 1871–1882 of Samuel P. Avery, Art Dealer* (New York: Arno Press, 1979), xv–xvi; Beaufort and Jeanne K. Welcher, "Some Views of Art Buying in New York in the 1870s and 1880s," *Oxford Art Journal* V, 1 (1981): 52.
53 Fidell-Beaufort, Kleinfeld, and Welcher, xix.
54 *Appleton's Journal* IV (Dec. 3, 1870): 678.

Chapter 4

1 The following paragraphs on the fair are based on Carol Troyen, "Innocents Abroad," *American Art Journal,* autumn 1984, 3–27.
2 M. D. Conway, "The Great Show at Paris," *Harper's Magazine* XXXV (July 1867): 248–49.
3 For accounts of the American enrollment in French art academies in the nineteenth century, see H. Barbara Weinberg, *The Lure of Paris: Nineteenth-Century American Painters and Their French Teachers* (New York: Abbeville Press, 1991).
4 *NYT,* Jan. 7, 1867, 2.
5 *NYT,* Feb. 10, 1867, 4. See also Lois Marie Fink, "French Art in the United States, 1850–1870: Three Dealers and Collectors," *Gazette des Beaux-Arts* XCII (Sept. 1978): 92.
6 *Tribune,* Jan. 16, 1867, 4.
7 *NYT,* Aug. 11, 1860, 4.
8 James Jackson Jarves, *Art Studies* (New York: Derby and Jackson, 1861), 35–36, 51.
9 Madeleine Fidell-Beaufort, Herbert L. Kleinfield, and Jeanne K. Whelcher, introduction to Samuel Putnam Avery, *The Diaries 1871–1882 of Samuel P. Avery, Art Dealer* (New York: Arno Press, 1979), xxiv.
10 Quoted by Fidell-Beaufort, Kleinfield, and Welcher, xxvii.
11 Lilian M. C. Randall, introduction to George A. Lucas, *The Diary of George A. Lucas: An American Art Agent in Paris, 1857–1909* (Princeton: Princeton University Press, 1979), I: 6–10.
12 "Art Notes," *The Art Review,* n.s., I (1875): 383.
13 Calvin Tomkins, *Merchants and Masterpieces: The Story of the Metropolitan Museum of Art* (New York: E. P. Dutton, 1970), 28–29.
14 Tomkins, 238.
15 Information on Michael Knoedler's becoming an American citizen was supplied by Knoedler & Company.
16 *Catalogue of an Exhibition of Paintings and Prints of Every Description on the Occasion of Knoedler One Hundred Years* (New York: M. Knoedler, 1946), unpaginated; Leonie Knoedler Sterner, "Knoedler Century," *Art News,* April 1946, 20 (the author was the granddaughter of Michael Knoedler).
17 I am indebted to Elizabeth Broun of the National Museum of American Art for pointing out to me the importance of Cottier. My comments on his career are based on her *Albert Pinkham Ryder* (Washington: Smithsonian Institution Press,

1989).

18 Henry James, *The Painter's Eye,* ed. John L. Sweeney (Madison: University of Wisconsin Press, 1989), 43.

19 Ibid., 51.

20 "Art Notes," *The Art Journal,* n.s., III (1878): 126.

21 Lucy H. Hooper, "The Pictures at the Paris Exhibition," *The Art Journal,* n.s., III (1878): 348-49.

22 Roland Knoedler obituary, *Art Digest,* Oct. 15, 1932, 10.

23 *The Rise of the Art World in America* (New York: Knoedler & Company, 1996), 19.

24 On the Rembrandt, *NYT* , Dec. 17, 1886, 2; Dec. 28, 1886, 4; on the van Dyck, letter, George H. Story to Louis Palma di Cesnola, Jan. 15, 1900, Metropolitan Museum of Art Archives.

25 David H. Whittier to the author, March 26, 1986. Mr. Whittier's stepfather was the grandson of William Schaus.

26 *NYT,* Jan. 14, 1875, 6; Jan. 20, 1875, 8; Patricia Olivier (the sister of David H. Whittier) to the author, February 12, 1986.

27 Letter dated Sept. 21, 1887, Metropolitan Museum of Art Archives.

28 For the reference to Monti, see Robert Rosenblum and H. W. Janson, *19th-Century Art* (New York: Harry N. Abrams, 1984), 316-17.

29 Cesnola to Schaus, Sept. 21, 1887; Schaus to Cesnola, Dec. 9, 1887, Metropolitan Museum of Art Archives.

30 David H. Whittier, letter to the author.

31 *NYT,* Feb. 29, 1896, 5.

32 DeCourcy E. McIntosh, "Demand and Supply," in Gabriel P. Weisberg et al., *Collecting in the Gilded Age: Art Patronage in Pittsburgh, 1890–1910* (Pittsburgh: Frick Art and Historical Center, 1997), 120-22.

33 *NYT,* Jan. 26, 1908, 9. The *Times* was careful to point out that at an earlier date a painting by Meissonier, *Friedland,* had sold for $66,000, but had been accompanied by a portrait of the artist; the lot, in other words, had included two paintings.

34 *Macbeth Gallery Art Notes,* 42 (Feb. 1911): 665–66.

Chapter 5

1 Jack Post, "The Old Family Business," *Yankee,* Sept. 1954, 103.

2 Robert C. Vose Jr., "Boston's Vose Galleries: A Family Affair," *AAAJ* 21 (1, 1981): 8.

3 "Four Generations," *Art Digest,* March 15, 1941, 20.

4 Post, 103; Vose, 8.

5 Vose, 9; Post, 107.

6 Vose, 10.

7 Post, 107; Vose, 9.

8 Vose, 18.

9 I am indebted to Gwendolyn Owens, whose essay "Art and Commerce: William Macbeth, the Eight and the Popularization of American Art," in Elizabeth Milroy, ed., *Paintings of a New Century: The Eight and American Art* (Milwaukee: Milwaukee Art Museum, 1991), 61-84, led me to make a second, profitable examination of the Macbeth Gallery Papers, AoAA.

10 Information on Macbeth's early life in New York is taken from his diary, in the collection of AoAA.

11 Information on Keppel's early years in the trade is taken from his brief memoir, "Chiefly Personal," which serves as the introduction to his *The Golden Age of Engraving* (New York: Baker and Taylor, 1910), and from the *Dictionary of American Biography* (New York: Charles Scribner's Sons, 1933), 351-52.

12 This organization, many of whose members also were members of the NAD, was founded in 1877 out of the disgruntlement felt by young artists over the preferential treatment at NAD exhibitions given to their elders, whose paintings were hung "on the line" (at eye level), whereas those of young artists were skyed. In 1905 the two organizations amalgamated under the umbrella of the NAD. See Eliot Clark, *History of the National Academy of Design 1825–1953* (New York: Columbia University Press, 1954), 105-10.

13 See Macbeth's correspondence with Chapman, in Macbeth Papers, AoAA.

14 Keppel to Macbeth, July 23, 1906, Macbeth Gallery Papers, AoAA.

15 *Art Notes* [a Macbeth Gallery journal] 63 (April 1917): 1016.

16 Linda Skalet, "Thomas B. Clarke, American Collector," *AAAJ* 3 (1975): 2-7; H. Barbara Weinberg, "Thomas B. Clarke: Foremost Patron of American Art from 1872 to 1899," *American Art Journal,* May 1976, 65. In 1891 Clarke established a gallery of his own, Art House, for the sale of oriental art, items of Greek antiquity, and paintings by George Inness.

17 See letters from Davies and Ranger to Macbeth, in Macbeth Gallery papers, AoAA. Davies's tour of Europe was funded by Benjamin Altman, the eminent collector and department store owner.

18 According to Robert Macbeth, the dealer's son, in the gallery's *Art Notes* 75 (April-May 1922): 1282.

19 *Art Notes*, 19 (April 1902): 190-91.

20 *Art Notes*, 23 (Nov. 1903): 357.

21 Clipping marked "Providence *Bulletin* Feb. 28.05," Macbeth Gallery Papers, AoAA.

22 Van Wyck Brooks, *John Sloan: A Painter's Life* (New York: E. P. Dutton, 1953), 77.

23 Shortly before the opening on February 3, each artist put up an additional $45 to cover expenses; John Sloan, *John Sloan's New York Scene,* ed. Bruce St. John (New York: Harper and Row, 1965), 126, 186. Macbeth had originally asked for a guarantee of $500.

24 Sloan, 113.

25 Late in 1897 these three artists, along with Joseph DeCamp, Thomas W. Dewing, Willard Metcalf, Robert Reid, Edward Simmons, Edmund C. Tarbell, and J. Alden Weir had formed a mutually supportive group that came to be known as the Ten American Painters. After the death of Twachtman, in 1902, William Merritt Chase was invited to join the group. See William H. Gerdts, "The Ten: A Critical Chronology," in Gerdts et al., *Ten American Painters* (New York: Spanierman Gallery, 1990), 9-81.

26 Bennard B. Perlman, *The Immortal Eight* (Cincinnati: Northlight Publishers, 1979), 189.

27 Ibid., 178, 185.

28 William Innes Homer, *Robert Henri and His Circle* (Ithaca and London: Cornell University Press, 1969), 151, 283n.

29 R[obert] G. McIntyre, "The Macbeth Gallery: A Capsule History," in *The Role of the Macbeth Gallery* (New York: American Federation of Arts, 1962), unpaginated.

30 Homer, 152–156.

31 Conversation with Carole M. Pesner, March 27, 1999.

32 Van Wyck Brooks, *John Sloan: A Painter's Life* (New York: Dutton, 1955), 105.

33 Sloan, 186.

34 Sloan, *New York Etchings* (New York: Dover Publications, n.d.), plate 16.

35 Identified by Robert Macbeth in a letter to Jessie Walker Macbeth, June 1935, Macbeth Gallery Papers, AoAA.

36 On Evans, see William H. Truettner, "William T. Evans, Collector of American Paintings," *American Art Journal,* Fall 1971, 50–79. Truettner confines the Clausen matter to a footnote.

37 "Spurious Paintings Bring Legal Fight," *NYT*, May 15, 1908, 1. Over the years to 1915, Evans's gifts to the nation amounted to 150 paintings. See Truettner, 57.

38 *NYT,* May 15, 1908, 1; May 16, 1908, 1; May 17, 1908, 1–2; May 21, 1908, 16.

39 *American Art News,* March 5, 1910, 4, 8; April 2, 1910, 4.

40 *Art Notes*, 56 (May 1915): 884.

41 The Macbeth Gallery files in the collection of AoAA include only the letters *from* correspondents, not the gallery's letters *to* them.

42 *Art Notes* 39 (Dec. 1909): 616.

43 Francis M. Neumann, "Frederic C. Torrey and Duchamp's *Nude Descending a Staircase*," in Bonnie Clearwater, ed., *West Coast Duchamp* (Miami Beach: Grassfield Press, 1991), 21.

44 *Art Notes* 46 (Nov. 1912): 721.

45 *Art Notes* 63 (April 1917): 1027.

46 *Art Notes* 63 (April 1917): 1026–27.

47 Doreen Holger, "William Macbeth and George A. Hearn: Collecting American Art, 1905–1910," *AAAJ* 15, 2 (1975): 9–15.

48 *Art Notes* 47 (Jan. 1913): 741–42; 54 (Feb. 1915): 856.

49 David Michaelis, *N. C. Wyeth* (New York: Alfred A. Knopf, 1998), 346–47. N.C. Wyeth was Andrew Wyeth's father; he too exhibited at Macbeth's.

Chapter 6

1 Gilbert C. Fite and Jim E. Reese, *An Economic History of the United States*, 3rd ed. (Boston: Houghton Mifflin, 1973), 369–72.

2 The origin and rise to greatness of Duveen Brothers in the art world has often been described in print. The four best known accounts are by S. N. Behrman, the playwright and essayist, in his entertaining but untrustworthy *Duveen* (New York: Random House, 1952); by Edward Fowles, owner of the firm in its last years, in *Memories of Duveen Brothers* (London: Times Books, 1976); by James Henry Duveen, a member of the family and sometime member of the firm, in *The Rise of the House of Duveen* (New York: Alfred A. Knopf, 1957); and by Colin Simpson in *Artful Partners: Bernard Berenson and Joseph Duveen* (New York: Macmillan, 1986), the product of careful research in the Duveen archives at the Metropolitan Museum.

3 Simpson, 11.

4 Duveen, 14–15; Simpson, 11–12.

5 Duveen, 28–30.

6 Henri Hangjas Duveen and his wife were cousins; he had added her maiden name to his own name at the time of their marriage.

7 Simpson, 16.
8 Quoted by Simpson, 18.
9 Duveen, 64-65.
10 Henry Duveen obituary, *NYT,* Jan. 3, 1919, 13.
11 Fowles, 23.
12 Simpson, 23-24.
13 Duveen, 95-97.
14 Fowles, 8.
15 Duveen, 125-28; Simpson, 29.
16 Simpson, 30-32. Berenson dropped the "h" during the First World War so as not to be thought of German origin. He was in fact born in Lithuania.
17 Fowles, 23.
18 Simpson, 99-101.
19 Ibid., 99-101.
20 Ibid., 101-5; Fowles, 33.
21 Duveen, 293; Fowles, 39.
22 Simpson, 107-9.
23 Ibid., 107-9; Fowles, 38n.
24 Simpson, 107-9; Duveen, 213, 234.
25 Duveen, 212-17, 234; Henry Duveen obituary.
26 Simpson, 111.
27 Ibid., Fowles, 39.
28 Simpson, 112; Duveen, 289-93; Fowles, 8.
29 Fowles, 35-43.
30 Ibid., 58-59.
31 Paul Durand-Ruel, "Memoirs," in *One Hundred Years of Impressionism* (New York: Wildenstein Gallery, 1970), unpaginated; René Gimpel, *Diary of an Art Dealer,* trans. John Rosenberg (New York: Farrar, Straus and Giroux, 1966), 88. Gimpel quotes a conversation with one (unidentified) of the sons of Paul Durand-Ruel.
32 Quoted in Frances Weitzenhoffer, *The Havemeyers: Impressionism Comes to America* (New York: Harry N. Abrams, 1986), 37.
33 John Rewald, *Studies in Impressionism,* ed. Irene Gordon and Frances Weitzenhoffer (New York: Harry N. Abrams, 1985), 197.
34 Gimpel, 20, 75, 152. It is also known that Durand-Ruel was equally kind to the Barbizon artists when they were in need.
35 Weitzenhoffer, 38.
36 Published in Lionello Venturi, comp., *Les Archives de l'impressionisme: Lettres de Renoir, Monet, Pisarro, et autres. Mémoires de Paul Durand-Ruel. Documents* (Paris and New York: Durand-Ruel, 1939).
37 Denys Sutton, "One Paris in the Universe," in *Paris–New York: A Continuing Romance* (New York: Wildenstein Gallery, 1977), 22.
38 Gimpel, 88.
39 Wesley Towner, *The Elegant Auctioneers* (New York: Hill & Wang, 1970), 39-46, 117-20; Weitzenhoffer, 39-40.
40 Towner, 119-20; Weitzenhoffer, 41.
41 Sutton, 23; Weitzenhoffer, 42-43.
42 John Rewald, *Post-Impressionism: From Van Gogh to Gauguin* (New York: Museum of

Modern Art, 1956), 73.
43 Sutton, 23; Rewald, 42.
44 After 1919, when René Gimpel, Ernest Gimpel's son, abrogated the partnership, the gallery continued in New York as Wildenstein and Company.
45 Nathan Wildenstein obituary, *NYT,* April 25, 1932, 21; Ernest Gimpel obituary, *NYT,* Jan. 9, 1907, 9.
46 *Hyde's Weekly Art News,* Nov. 21, 1903. This publication, originally a weekly broadside and soon renamed *American Art News,* was the predecessor of the monthly *Art News* .
47 *American Art News,* March 18, 1905.
48 Germain Seligman, *Merchants of Art* (New York: Appleton-Century-Crofts, 1961), 45. Germain Seligman, the son of Jacques Seligmann, dropped the second "n" from his last name.
49 Ibid., 5. All information in this and the following paragraphs, apart from the dates of exhibitions, is taken from chapters 1 and 2 of Seligman's book.
50 Ibid., 24.
51 Ibid., 43. The cause of the quarrel is unknown. The third brother, Simon, had retired before its outbreak.
52 Ibid., 109-10.
53 Ibid., 121.
54 Ibid., 155-56.

Chapter 7

1 Sue Davidson Lowe, *Stieglitz: A Memoir/Biography* (New York: Farrar, Straus and Giroux, 1983), 11.
2 Dorothy Norman, *Alfred Stieglitz: An American Seer* (New York: Aperture, 1990), 9, 17, 22-23; Lowe, 57-59, 72-75.
3 Richard Whelan, *Alfred Stieglitz: A Biography* (Boston: Little, Brown 1995), 63-67.
4 Stieglitz obituary, *NYT,* July 14, 1946, 38.
5 Lowe, 74-75; Whelan, 72-73.
6 Whelan, 99-100.
7 Ibid., 103-4.
8 Lowe, 99, 106-7.
9 Agnes E. Meyer, *Out of These Roots: The Autobiography of an American Woman* (Boston: Little, Brown, 1953), 69.
10 Whelan, 134.
11 William Inness Homer, *Alfred Stieglitz and the American Avant-Garde* (Boston: New York Graphic Society, 1977), 19.
12 Whelan, 231-32.
13 Guy Pène du Bois, *Artists Say the Silliest Things* (New York: Duell, Sloan and Pierce, 1940), 258.
14 Whelan, 178.
15 *Camera Work,* April 1906, 48.
16 Francis M. Naumann, *New York Dada, 1915–23* (New York: Harry N. Abrams, 1994), 76. In 1915 Man Ray went to Stieglitz for advice on how to photograph the paintings he was to show at the Daniel Gallery.
17 Man Ray, *Self-Portrait* (Boston: Little, Brown, 1963), 19.

18 Alfred H. Barr Jr., *Matisse: His Art and His Public* (New York: Museum of Modern Art, 1951), 115.
19 Stieglitz to Daniel, June 4, 1914; Jan. 12 and June 22, 1915, Stieglitz Archive, Beinecke Library, Yale University.
20 Henry McBride, "Stieglitz and Walkowitz," *Sun* (New York), Nov. 30, 1913. Reprinted in McBride, *The Flow of Art* (New York: Atheneum, 1975), 42.
21 Man Ray, 18.
22 Van Wyck Brooks, *John Sloan: A Painter's Life* (New York: Dutton, 1959), 129–30.
23 Quoted by Norman, 59.
24 Meyer, 101.
25 Judith Zilczer, *"The Noble Buyer": John Quinn, Patron of the Avant-Garde* (Washington, D.C.: Smithsonian Institution Press, 1978), 23.
26 Zilczer, 9.
27 Aline B. Saarinen, *The Proud Possessors* (New York: Random House, 1958), 208.
28 Judith Zilczer, "Alfred Stieglitz and John Quinn: Allies in the American Avant-Garde," *American Art Quarterly* [henceforth *AAQ*] XVII (summer 1985): 18–33; B. L. Reid, *The Man from New York: John Quinn and His Friends* (New York: Oxford University Press, 1968), 263. Nor did Quinn's anti-Semitism keep him from buying the sculptures of Jacob Epstein or helping out with loans or gifts of money when Epstein was in need.
29 Lowe, 134–37.
30 Meyer, 68, 101.
31 Francis M. Naumann, introduction to Marius de Zayas, "How, When, and Why Modern Art Came to New York," *Arts Magazine,* April 1980, 96.
32 Homer, 19.
33 Milton W. Brown, *The Story of the Armory Show* (New York: Abbeville Press, 1988), 45–48.
34 Brown, 48. Another member was Jerome Meyers, whose works Macbeth also showed.
35 Brown, 227–33. The postexhibition meetings of the association's directors were marked by rancorous exchanges among the members over procedures and goals. Brown's work is the standard history of the show. All subsequent accounts, including this one, have relied on it. For interesting if cynical observations on the significance of the show, see Robert M. Crunden, *American Salons: Encounters with European Modernism* (New York: Oxford University Press, 1993), 357–70. In the years immediately following the Armory show, large exhibitions of contemporary American art were held under other auspices, including the National Arts Club, the Forum Committee, and the Society of Independent Artists. The Forum Committee consisted of six men of the art world, including Stieglitz, Robert Henri, and John Weichsel, the founder of the People's Art Guild. Their exhibition was held at the Anderson Galleries in 1916.
36 For a complete catalogue of the exhibition, see Brown, 241–328.
37 Reid, 149; Walter Pach, *Queer Thing, Painting* (New York: Harper and Brothers, 1938), 199–200.
38 Carl van Vechten, *Peter Whiffle: His Life and Works* (New York: Alfred A. Knopf, 1922), 122–23.
39 "A Layman's Views of an Art Exhibition," *The Outlook* 103 (March 29, 1913); quoted in Bennard B. Perlman, *Robert Henri: His Life* (New York: Dover Publications, 1991), 109.

40 Brown, 129.
41 Pach, 199–200.
42 Naumann, introduction to de Zayas, 104; William Schack, *Art and Argyrol: The Life and Career of Dr. Albert C. Barnes* (New York: Thomas Yoseloff, 1960), 127.
43 Francis M. Naumann, "Frederic C. Torrey and Duchamp's *Nude Descending a Staircase,*" in Bonnie Clearwater, ed., *West Coast Duchamp* (Miami Beach: Grassfield Press, 1991), 11–23.
44 "Marcel Duchamp," in *Eleven Europeans in America* (New York: Museum of Modern Art, 1944), 19–20. Duchamp does not indicate the year in which he made the gift to Torrey.
45 *Art Notes* 46 (Nov. 1912): 724.
46 *Art Notes* 48 (April 1913): 752–54.
47 Brown, 317.
48 Reid, 157–60, 198, 201. In a letter to William Butler Yeats, Reid put the cost to him at £500; the pound was then valued at $5.
49 So described in the catalogue of an exhibition held in 1941 at An American Place, the gallery of which he was then the proprietor.
50 Norman, 67.
51 Lowe, 127. Rodin's sculptures had been shown in America before 1908, but not the drawings.
52 Ibid., 432.
53 It has also been used as the title of one of the many books on O'Keeffe: Anita Pollitzer, *A Woman on Paper: Georgia O'Keeffe* (New York: Simon and Schuster, 1988), which includes the artist's correspondence with Pollitzer and a memoir of her by Pollitzer.
54 Whelan, 376.
55 *Camera Work* 47 (July 1914): 65–66. Although dated 1914, this number was not published until January 1915.
56 Homer, 194.
57 *291,* March–April, 1915, unpaginated.
58 Lowe, 206–7.
59 Stieglitz Archive.
60 Lowe, 217.
61 Judith Zilczer, "The New World's Art Center," 3. Robert Henri, W. H. deB. Nelson, and Dr. Christopher Brinton were also listed on the organizing committee, but did not actually participate.
62 Steven Watson, *Strange Bedfellows: The First American Avant-Garde* (New York: Abbeville Press, 1991), 312.
63 Watson, 317–20; Naumann, *New York Dada, 1915–23,* 183–85. *The Blind Man* was published by Duchamp, Beatrice Wood, and Henri-Pierre Roché.
64 Lowe, 433.
65 Hartley to Stieglitz, Dec. 18, 1924, Stieglitz Archive.
66 Lowe, 300–301.
67 This occurred in the 1940s at An American Place, Stieglitz's last gallery. The young collector was E. D. H. Johnson, a friend and former teacher of this writer.
68 Lowe, 65, 333.

Chapter 8

1 I am indebted to Judith Zilczer, " 'The World's New Art Center' ": Modern Art Exhibitions in New York City, 1913-1918," *AAAJ* 17 (3, 1974): 2-7, for calling my attention to these dealers and their importance.

2 For a listing of many of his purchases, see Judith Zilczer, *"The Noble Buyer": John Quinn, Patron of the Avant-Garde* (Washington, D.C.: Smithsonian Institution Press, 1978).

3 Martin Birnbaum, *The Last Romantic* (New York: Twayne Publishers, 1960), 24-29.

4 Ibid., 41.

5 Ibid., 64.

6 Zilczer, *"The Noble Buyer,"* 153; Birnbaum, 63-64.

7 In John Quinn Papers, NYPL.

8 Birnbaum, 75.

9 Ibid., 86-87.

10 Information in this and the following paragraph is taken from two sources, John Wilson Taylor and Eva Mills Taylor, *Montross: A Family History* (Staunton, Va., 1958), 325-26; and F[orbes] W[atson], "Newman Emerson Montross," *Arts Weekly*, March 18, 1932, 37-38; Van Rensselaer quoted by Watson.

11 John Sloan, *John Sloan's New York Scene,* ed. Bruce St. John (New York: Harper and Row, 1965), 197.

12 After the 1917 Montross exhibition, the Ten showed at Boston's St. Botolph Club in the same year and in 1919 at Washington's Corcoran Gallery of Art, their last exhibition.

13 Over the years of their group shows, the Ten exhibited at galleries outside New York as well as at Montross's, namely, the Kimball Gallery, Boston; M. O'Brien and Sons, Chicago; the Brerssler Gallery, Milwaukee, the J. J. Gillespie Galleries, Pittsburgh; the McClees Galleries, Philadelphia; and the Empire Galleries, Rochester, as well as at museums. See William H. Gerdts et al., *Ten American Painters* (New York: Spanierman Gallery, 1990), 177.

14 Herbert J. Seligmann, *Alfred Stieglitz Talking: Notes on Some of His Conversations, 1925–31* (New Haven: Yale University Library, 1966), 40.

15 Henry McBride, "Matisse at Montross," *Sun* (New York), Jan. 24, 1915; reprinted in Henry McBride, *The Flow of Art* (New York: Atheneum, 1975), 75.

16 Milton W. Brown, *The Story of the Armory Show* (New York: Abbeville Press, 1988), 313-14.

17 Townsend Ludington, *Marsden Hartley: The Beginning of an American Artist* (Boston: Little, Brown, 1992), 61-62.

18 *American Art News*, Jan. 22, 1910, 75.

19 *NYT,* Jan. 30, 1914, 8.

20 Quoted in Steven Watson, *Strange Bedfellows: The First American Avant-Garde* (New York: Abbeville Press, 1991), 184.

21 B. L. Reid, *The Man from New York: John Quinn and His Friends* (New York: Oxford University Press, 1968), 253. Quinn declared in a letter to Ezra Pound that he would not buy anything from Montross again, a promise to himself that he did not keep. Having failed with Montross, Quinn, along with Walt Kuhn, succeeded in securing a show for the Vorticists (their only group show in America) at the Pen-

guin Club, a private club, in 1917; see Zilczer, " 'The World's New Art Center,' " 5.

22 Joseph Solman, "The Easel Division of the WPA Federal Art Project," in Francis V. O'Connor, ed., *The New Deal Art Projects: An Anthology of Memoirs* (Washington, D.C.: Smithsonian Institution Press, 1971), 124. Other artists who showed with them at times over their four years together were John Graham, Lee Gatch, Earl Kerkam, Karl Knaths, Edgar Levy, and Ralph Rosenborg. See Isabelle Dervaux, "The Ten: An Avant-Garde Group in the 1930s," *AAAJ* 31, (2, 1991): 14–20, for an account of the group's activities.

23 The other members of the group were Ben-Zion, Louis Harris, Jack Kufeld, Louis Schanker, Joseph Solman, and Nahum Tschacbasov.

24 Unless otherwise indicated, information on Daniel and his gallery in the following paragraphs is taken from the typescript of his taped reminiscences in the collection of AoAA.

25 Julie Mellby, *Charles Daniel and the Daniel Gallery* (New York: Zabriskie Gallery, 1993), 6.

26 Man Ray, *Self-Portrait* (Boston: Little, Brown, 1963), 45.

27 Mellby, *Charles Daniel,* 6; Man Ray, 45.

28 Here and throughout his reminiscences Daniel is confused about dates and other matters. He says that he saw the watercolors just before the opening of a Marin exhibition in the fall of 1910, when in fact Stieglitz showed Marin in February of that year and not again until 1911.

29 Mellby, *Charles Daniel,* 7.

30 *Camera Work* 47 (July 1914): 33.

31 Mellby, *Charles Daniel,* 7.

32 Ibid., 7; Man Ray, 56.

33 See *American Paintings in the Ferdinand Howald Collection* (Columbus: Columbus Museum of Fine Arts, 1969). Daniel in his memoir says that Howald owned thirty-two Marins.

34 William Schack, *Art and Argyrol: The Life and Career of Albert C. Barnes* (New York: Thomas Yoseloff, 1960), 78–79.

35 E. P. Richardson, introduction to *American Paintings in the Ferdinand Howald Collection,* 4.

36 Murdock Pemberton, "A Memoir of Three Decades," *Arts,* Oct. 1955, 29–30.

37 Mellby, *Charles Daniel,* 7.

38 Julie Mellby, "Letters from Charles Daniel to Peter Blume," *AAAJ* 33 (1, 1993): 18.

39 Mellby, *Charles Daniel,* 8.

40 Daniel to Dorothy C. Walker, Daniel Papers, AoAA.

41 Stephan Bourgeois, "Art Dealers," *Creative Art* IX (Nov. 1931): 405; Richard Beer, "As They Are: The Fourth Generation," *Art News,* May 5, 1935, 11.

42 Brown, 97, 221–22, 238.

43 Quoted in Zilczer, " 'The World's New Art Center,' " 5.

44 Bourgeois to Quinn, Feb. 13, 1917; Quinn to Bourgeois, Feb. 16, 1917, John Quinn Papers, NYPL.

45 Quinn to Bourgeois, May 23, 1922, John Quinn Papers, NYPL.

46 *NYT,* Jan. 25, 1946, 25.

47 Thanks are due once again to Judith K. Zilczer for her valuable spadework in the early modern period. Her "Robert J. Coady, Forgotten Spokesman for Avant-Garde

Culture in America," *American Art Review* II (Nov.–Dec. 1975): 77–89, is the basis of the following paragraphs on Coady's career, except where otherwise noted.

48 Pierre Assouline, *An Artful Life: A Biography of D.-H. Kahnweiler, 1888-1979,* trans. Charles Ruas (New York: Grove Weidenfeld, 1990), 109–10.

49 Quoted in Zilczer, "Robert J. Coady," 86.

50 Quinn to Coady, Sept. 4, 1919, John Quinn Papers, NYPL.

51 So described by Aline B. Saarinen, *The Proud Possessors* (New York: Random House, 1958), 21.

52 Saarinen, 218.

53 In John Quinn Papers, NYPL.

54 Reid, 207.

55 Michael C. FitzGerald, *Making Modernism: Picasso and the Creation of the Market for Twentieth-Century Art* (New York: Farrar, Straus and Giroux, 1995), 112.

56 Daniel, unpublished memoir, AoAA.

57 Saarinen, 222.

58 Bryant to Quinn, Sept. 13, 1917; Quinn to Bryant, Sept. 14, 1917. In John Quinn Papers, NYPL.

59 *NYT,* Aug. 31, 1933, 19.

60 Michael Hoog, "Joseph Brummer," in Roger Shattuck et al., *Henri Rousseau* (New York: Museum of Modern Art, 1985), 228–30.

61 Brummer obituary, *NYT,* April 15, 1947, 25; Calvin Tomkins, *Merchants and Masterpieces* (New York: E. P. Dutton, 1970), 316.

62 Brummer to Quinn, Jan. 17, 1922; Quinn to Brummer, Jan. 17, 1922, in Quinn Papers, NYPL.

63 Reid, 622.

64 For accounts of the liquidation of the collection, see Reid, 653–62, and Judith Zilczer, "The Dispersal of the John Quinn Collection," *AAAJ* 19 (3, 1979): 15–20. Zilczer disagrees with Reid's conclusion that the sales of Quinn's holdings ended in a loss of $100,000 and accepts the estimate of the contemporary press and of Milton W. Brown in *American Painting from the Armory Show to the Depression* (Princeton: Princeton University Press, 1972), 95, that a substantial profit, perhaps in excess of $200,000, resulted.

65 *NYT,* Feb. 24, 1927, 23; Oct. 22, 1927, 9; Nov. 28, 1928, 26.

66 *NYT,* "Tenants Found Quickly for Remodeled Building," Dec. 14, 1941, sec. XI, 2. His tenants were the Valentine Galleries and H. Blairman and Sons.

67 Meyer to Stieglitz, Aug. 16, 1915; quoted in William Inness Homer, *Alfred Stieglitz and the American Avant-Garde* (Boston: New York Graphic Society, 1977), 195.

68 Sue Davidson Lowe, *Stieglitz: A Memoir/Biography* (New York: Farrar, Straus, and Giroux, 1983), 199–200.

69 De Zayas to Quinn, Dec. 22, 1922: Quinn to de Zayas, Dec, 30, 1922, John Quinn Papers, NYPL; Reid, 579.

70 Homer, 55; William S. Liberman, ed., *Art of the Twenties* (New York: Museum of Modern Art, 1979), 18.

71 Avis Berman, *Rebels on Eighth Street: Juliana Force and the Whitney Museum of American Art* (New York: Atheneum, 1990), 191.

72 Marius de Zayas, *How, When, and Why Modern Art Came to New York,* ed. Francis M. Naumann (Cambridge, Mass.: MIT Press, 1996), 133.

Chapter 9

1 Halpert obituary, *NYT,* Oct. 7, 1970, 50.

2 Diane Tepfer, *Edith Gregor Halpert and the Downtown Gallery Downtown: 1926-1940; A Study in American Art Patronage* (Ann Arbor: U.M.I. Press, 1989), 21–22. I am greatly indebted to this study for information of Halpert's early years. On Weichsel, see Gail Stavisky, "John Weichsel and the People's Art Guild," *AAAJ* 31 (4, 1991): 12–19, and Norman L. Kleeblatt and Susan Chevlove, *Painting a Place in America* (New York: Jewish Museum, 1991), 104–15.

3 Halpert obituary; Tepfer, 49.

4 On these artists and their public, see Nancy Boas, *The Society of Six* (San Francisco: Bedford Arts, 1988).

5 See Yunt's correspondence with the Macbeth Gallery, Macbeth Gallery Papers, AoAA.

6 Milch obituary, *NYT,* Oct. 22, 1951, 23.

7 I am grateful to Elizabeth Broun of the National Museum of American Art for pointing this out to me. On the forgeries, see her *Albert Pinkham Ryder* (Washington, D.C.: Smithsonian Institution Press, 1989), 159–63.

8 Aline B. Saarinen, *The Proud Possessors* (New York: Random House, 1958), 262.

9 This exhibition was held by Rehn simultaneously with an exhibition of paintings by ten other Americans. See Gail Levin, *Edward Hopper: An Intimate Biography* (New York: Alfred A. Knopf, 1995), 186.

10 William Zorach, *Art Is My Life* (Cleveland and New York: World Publishing Co., 1967), 88–89.

11 Tepfer, 49.

12 Avis Berman, *Rebels on Eighth Street: Juliana Force and the Whitney Museum of American Art* (New York: Atheneum, 1990), 253.

13 Susan Landauer, *The San Francisco School of Abstract Expressionism* (Berkeley and Los Angeles: University of California Press, 1996), 30.

14 Halpert interview with Harlan Phillips, Jan. 2, 1965, AoAA.

15 Belinda Rathbone, *Walker Evans* (Boston: Houghton Mifflin, 1995), 77.

16 Zorach, 89.

17 The Rockefeller folk-art collection may now be seen in Williamsburg, Virginia.

18 Several times in conversation with this writer, 1950–51, as well as in the art press.

19 Zorach, 93.

20 Edward Alden Jewell, "In the Realm of Art," *NYT,* March 4, 1934, sec. IX, 9.

21 Alan interview with Paul Cummings, Aug. 20, 1970, AoAA.

22 Others who came to her from the WPA arts project were Rainey Bennett, Raymond Breinin, O. Louis Guglielmi, and Mitchell Siporin.

23 On dining with Rockefeller, see Shahn interview with Forrest Selvig, Sept. 27, 1968, AoAA.

24 Jewell, "John Marin's Art in Two Exhibitions," *NYT,* Oct. 17, 1939, 29.

25 These figures come from the memory of this writer, who saw the works in his student days and was too impecunious to buy them. The pastel was of an apple; the painting, of a small pot with a feather in it.

26 Conversation with Halpert, c. 1961.

27 Conversation with Dorothy Schneiderman, director of the Harbor Gallery, July 1, 1993. Schneiderman was in the Downtown Gallery on that occasion.

28 Zorach, 162.
29 Conversation with Halpert, c. 1952.
30 Sanka Knox, "Halpert Art Collection Brings $3.6 Million," *NYT,* March 16, 1973, 34. The collection would undoubtedly have fetched substantially more in later years.
31 Halpert, "The Function of the Dealer," *College Art Journal* IX (autumn 1949): 55-56.
32 Janis interview with Avis Berman, Oct. 15, 1981, AoAA.
33 Alan interview, AoAA. Alan is exaggerating, of course, about both her tax liability and the narrow range of her friendships.
34 Miller interview with Paul Cummings, May 18, 1971, AoAA; Bacon interview with Cummings, May 8, 1973, AoAA.
35 Alfred Frankenstein interview with Paul J. Karlstrom, July 26, Dec. 12, 1978, Aug. 1, 1979, AoAA.
36 On the revelation that this was a Peto, see Frankenstein, *After the Hunt: William Harnett and Other American Still Life Painters, 1870–1900* (Berkeley and Los Angeles: University of California Press, 1953), 16-17.
37 Miller interview, May 25, 1971, AoAA.
38 Frankenstein interview with Paul Karlstrom, Aug. 1, 1979, AoAA.
39 For a detailed discussion of these events, see Margaret Lynne Ausfeld, *Advancing American Art: Politics and Aesthetics in the State Department Exhibition, 1946–48* (Montgomery: Montgomery Museum of Fine Art, 1984).
40 Halpert interview with Harlan Phillips, Jan. 20, 1965, AoAA; Halpert, lecture delivered at the Brooklyn Museum, Oct. 19, 1959, Halpert Papers, AoAA. On presidential disapproval of this work and Jackson Pollock's nonobjective *Cathedral* (like *Welcome Home,* retained in the exhibition), see also Jane de Hart Mathews, "Art and Politics in Cold War America," *American Historical Review* 81 (Oct. 1976): 779.
41 Frankenstein interview, Aug. 1, 1979, AOAA.

Chapter 10

1 Edward Fowles, *Memories of Duveen Brothers* (London: Times Books, 1976), 107.
2 *Art News,* Nov. 15, 1919, 1.
3 Alva Johnson, "Noble Merchandise," *New Yorker,* April 21, 1928, 29.
4 Kenneth Clark, *Another Part of the Wood* (New York: Harper and Row, 1974), 227.
5 See, for example, the before and after photographs in Colin Simpson's *Artful Partners: Bernard Berenson and Joseph Duveen* (New York: Macmillan, 1986) of Sebastiano Mainardi's *Portrait of a Lady,* which Duveen sold to Andrew Mellon.
6 Paul Mellon with John Baskett, *Reflections in a Silver Spoon* (New York: William Morrow, 1952), 298.
7 Simpson, 133-38.
8 Fowles, 66.
9 The standard biography of Berenson, on which I have drawn for this draconically reduced account, is Ernest Samuels, *Bernard Berenson: The Making of a Connoisseur* (Cambridge, Mass.: Belknap Press, 1979) and *Bernard Berenson: The Making of a Legend* (Cambridge, Mass.: Belknap Press, 1987).
10 René Gimpel, *Diary of an Art Dealer,* trans. John Rosenberg (New York: Farrar, Straus, and Giroux, 1966) 248.
11 This paragraph is a mixture of the accounts of the matter given by Samuels, *Bernard*

Berenson: The Making of a Legend, 302-3, and Fowles, 150-53. Samuels, with Berenson's letter concerning the "Botticelli" before him, corrects Fowles, who claims that Berenson described the painting as "an unusually late work of Botticelli." Nicky Mariano, in *Forty Years with Berenson* (New York: Alfred A. Knopf, 1967), 55, claims, and probably with truth on her side, that she heard Berenson refuse to give Fowles the attribution Joe hoped to get out of him.

12 Samuels, *Berenson: The Making of a Legend*, 432-37, 576-77.

13 These are mentioned by Ernest Samuels. Given Berenson's reputation as a connoisseur and the costliness of his way of life, it is reasonable to assume that he was consulted and paid by still more galleries than these.

14 Gimpel, 43-44.

15 Ibid., 38.

16 On the Frick and Bache holdings, see *The Frick Collection Handbook of Paintings* (New York: The Frick Collection, 1971) and *The Bache Collection*, 2d. ed. (New York: Jules Bache, 1939).

17 Samuels, *Bernard Berenson: The Making of a Legend*, 315-17. See also Gimpel, 239-41, 246-48.

18 Fowles, 131.

19 Andrew Decker, "The Million Dollar Belle," *Art News*, summer 1985, 94.

20 Johnson, 30; Simpson, 187-92.

21 James Thorpe, *Henry Edwards Huntington* (Berkeley and Los Angeles: University of California Press, 1994), 435.

22 Samuels, *Bernard Berenson: The Making of a Connoisseur*, 245.

23 Thorpe, 435-39.

24 Samuels, *Bernard Berenson: The Making of a Legend*, 527.

25 On the disbarments, see Levy obituary, *NYT*, Aug. 5, 1952, 19.

26 S. N. Behrman, *Duveen* (New York: Random House, 1952), 199.

27 Edward Fowles interview with John P. Morse, Aug. 21, 1959, AoAA; Behrman, *Duveen*, 239-42. The Kleinberger firm originated in Paris in 1848.

28 Fowles, 144-45; Behrman, 103-5.

29 *NYT*, July 12, 1927, 1, 3.

30 *NYT*, July 10, 1930, 1, 5.

31 Edward Fowles interview, AoAA.

32 Samuels, *Bernard Berenson: The Making of a Legend*, 389; Fowles, 194-98; John Walker, *Self-Portrait with Donors* (Boston: Little, Brown, 1974), 113.

33 Simpson, 225.

34 Behrman, 252-54; Walker, 103.

35 Walker, 129.

36 Clark, 264-66.

37 Suzanne Muchnic, *Odd Man In: Norton Simon and the Pursuit of Culture* (Berkeley and Los Angeles: University of California Press, 1998), 71.

Chapter 11

1 John Walker, *Self-Portrait with Donors* (Boston: Little, Brown, 1974), 103.

2 Apart from what is common knowledge, information in this and the following paragraph is taken from Henschel, *A Catalogue of an Exhibition of Paintings and Prints of Every Description on the Occasion of Knoedler One Hundred Years 1846–1956*, unpaginated.

3 Conversation with William Appleton, Johnston's great-grandson, c. 1990.
4 Henschel.
5 *NYT*, March 30, 1907, 9; June 24, 1907, 1; July 21, 1907, 2; Nicholas H. J. Hall, "Old Masters in a New World," in Nicholas J. Hall, ed., *Colnaghi in America* (New York: Colnaghi, 1992), 10.
6 Hall, 17–18.
7 *NYT*, May 15, 1907, 1.
8 Charles Carstairs obituary, *NYT*, July 11, 1928, 23; Henschel obituary, *NYT*, Oct. 3, 1956, 33.
9 Germain Seligman, *Merchants of Art: 1880–1950* (New York: Appleton-Century Crofts, 1961), 169–72.
10 Ibid., 172–74.
11 Edward J. Epstein, *Dossier: The Secret History of Armand Hammer* (New York: Random House, 1996), 46.
12 Ibid., 89.
13 Walker, 225–26; Robert C. Williams, *Russian Art and American Money* (Cambridge, Mass.: Harvard University Press, 1980), 157.
14 Walker, 226.
15 Ibid., 226–27; Williams, 158–61.
16 Walker, 108–10.
17 Ibid., 110–11.
18 Williams, 171–73; Walker, 119.
19 *Art News,* May 16, 1931, sec. 2, 13.
20 *NYT,* Aug. 18, 1934, 1, 8.
21 Cited by Williams, 177.
22 *Art Digest,* May 15, 1935, 15.
23 My source is the archival display of the firm's 150th-anniversary exhibition in 1996.
24 *Apollo* XXI (March 1935): 167.
25 Wesley Towner, *The Elegant Auctioneers* (New York: Hill and Wang, 1970), 457, 459.
26 Quoted in Sophy Burnham, *The Art Crowd* (New York: David McKay, 1973), 315. Burnham prints the entire transcript of Rousuck's hearing.
27 *NYT,* March 11, 1956, 58.
28 *NYT*, Aug. 26, 1956, 36.
29 *NYT*, Nov. 29, 1970, sec. II, 24.
30 Jean Clay, "The World's Foremost Art Dealers," *Réalités* (English edition), June 1959, 64.
31 Bonnie Barrett Stretch, "Buy Boldly, Sell Slowly," *Art News,* Oct. 1991, 89.
32 Clay, 66.
33 On Wildenstein's dealings with Rosenberg, see Michael C. FitzGerald, *Making Modernism* (New York: Farrar, Straus and Giroux, 1995), especially 81–84.
34 Pierre Cabanne, *The Great Collectors* (New York: Farrar, Straus, 1963), 247–48.
35 See Jonathan Napack, "The Wildenstein Family," *Spy,* Oct. 1991, 68.
36 Clay, 66.
37 Ibid., 70.
38 Ibid., 62–63; Cabanne, 244.
39 Clay, 61; Michael Lewis, "Paint by Numbers," *New Republic,* April 25, 1994, 28; Stretch, 58.

40 Correspondence between Stendahl and Wildenstein, Feb. 22, 1940 to June 14, 1943, cited in this and the following two paragraphs, Stendahl Papers, AoAA.
41 Herbert Read, introduction to René Gimpel, *Diary of an Art Dealer*, trans, John Rosenberg (New York: Farrar, Straus, and Giroux, 1966), ix–x.
42 FitzGerald, 263-65.
43 Lynn H. Nicholas, *The Rape of Europa* (New York: Alfred A. Knopf, 1994), 292. The story has been told in detail in *Le Front de l'Art* (Paris: Librairie Plon, 1961) by Rose Valland, the curator of Paris's Jeu de Paume as the war broke out and dedicated protector of national treasures as it progressed. An American film, *The Train* (1964), is loosely based on her account.
44 Hector Feliciano, *The Lost Museum* (New York: Basic Books, 1997), 136-37.
45 Nicholas, 332-33. This study is the major source of information on the Wildenstein firm's dealings with Nazi agents during the war. See also Napack, 61-68.
46 Nicholas, 90-92, 120.
47 Writing to Stendahl on May 25, Felix Wildenstein reported that Dequoy was in New York and that either Dequoy or he would travel to the West if affairs in France improved; Stendahl Papers, AoAA.
48 Nicholas, 159-60.
49 Ibid., 161-62.
50 Pierre Assouline, *An Artful Life: A Biography of D. H. Kahnweiler,* trans. Charles Ruas (New York: Grove Weidenfeld, 1988), 282-84.
51 Nicholas, 163-64.
52 Ibid., 426.
53 Stretch, 58.
54 Thomas Hoving, *Making the Mummies Dance* (New York: Simon and Schuster, 1993), 253, 270.
55 Stretch, 59.
56 Alan Riding, "Staking a Claim to Art the Nazis Looted," *NYT,* Sept. 3, 1997, 11-12.
57 Riding, 12.

Chapter 12

1 See Gilbert Seldes, *The Seven Lively Arts* (New York: Harper and Brothers, 1924), a seminal study of popular culture. His focus is on film, jazz, humorous writing, the Follies, the comics, vaudeville, and the circus.
2 Some sixty of these are listed in William S. Lieberman, ed., *Art of the Twenties* (New York: Museum of Modern Art, 1979), 11-20.
3 Francis M. Naumann, *New York Dada* (New York: Abrams. 1994), 156-57.
4 Watson, *Strange Bedfellows: The First American Avant-Garde* (New York: Abbeville Press, 1991), 355-56.
5 Ibid., 356.
6 For a full account of the exhibitions, see *The Société Anonyme and the Dreier Bequest to Yale University: A Catalogue Raisonné* (New Haven: Yale Univ. Art Gallery), 1984.
7 The most informative history of the founding and first decades of the Museum of Modern Art is Russell Lynes, *Good Old Modern: An Intimate Portrait of the Museum of Modern Art* (New York: Atheneum, 1973). Unless otherwise indicated, the following paragraphs are based on Lynes's account.
8 Calvin Tomkins, *Duchamp: A Biography* (New York: Henry Holt, 1996), 381.

9 Lynes, 3–8.
10 Ibid., 9–13.
11 On the history of the Harvard Society of Contemporary Art, see Nicholas Fox Weber, *Patron Saints* (New York: Alfred A. Knopf, 1992). Much later, with the Modern's espousal of Abstract Expressionism, Kirstein broke from it.
12 Lynes, 19-20. It was believed by some that Edith Halpert also had a say in the choice of Barr as director. See Julien Levy, *Memoir of an Art Gallery* (New York: G. P. Putnam's Sons, 1977), 99.
13 On Barr's career, see Alice Goldfarb Marquis, *Alfred H. Barr, Jr., Missionary for the Modern* (Chicago: Contemporary Books, 1989). Also see Rita Roob, "Alfred J. Barr, Jr.: A Chronicle of the Years 1902-1919" and Margaret Scolari Barr, "Our Campaigns," *The New Criterion,* special issue, summer 1987.
14 Gallatin's collection remained at New York University until 1942, when it was transferred to the Philadelphia Museum of Art.
15 Nancy Maltby, "Interpreting the New," in *Katharine Kuh* (New York: Archives of American Art, n.d.), 8. Kuh was on the curatorial staff of the Art Institute of Chicago from 1943 to 1959, after which she was art critic for the *Saturday Review.*
16 Avis Berman, *Rebels on Eighth Street: Juliana Force and the Whitney Museum of American Art* (New York: Atheneum, 1990), 64, 112, 154–59.
17 Ibid., 102–4.
18 John H. Davis, *The Guggenheims: An American Epic* (New York: William Morrow, 1978), 199, 202.
19 Quoted by Lily Harmon in her unpublished biography of J. B. Neumann.
20 Rebay obituary, *NYT,* Sept. 29, 1967, 47.
21 Wright is also represented in New York by an automobile showroom on Park Avenue.
22 Davis, 223–24.
23 Ibid., 228.
24 *NYT,* "Guggenheim Acquires 250 Works of Modern Art," May 15, 1971, 28.
25 Lynes, 271–74.
26 Harriman obituary, *NYT,* Sept. 27, 1970, 87.
27 Interview with Jeanne R. Kline, Liederman's daughter, March 16, 1982.
28 Dorothy C. Miller interview with Paul Cummings, May 18, 1971, AoAA; Lily Harmon, unpublished biography of J. B. Neumann; Willard obituary, *NYT,* Nov. 7, 1985, D57.
29 Julien Levy interview with Paul Cummings, May 30, 1975, AoAA.
30 Levy's relationship with his mother-in-law is treated in detail in Carolyn Burke, *Becoming Modern: The Life of Mina Loy* (New York: Farrar, Straus, and Giroux, 1996), 346, 370–71, 377–81, 400–401.
31 Levy, *Memoir of an Art Gallery*, 46.
32 Ibid., 71; Deborah Zlotsky, " 'Pleasant Madness' in Hartford: The First Surrealist Exhibition in America," *Arts,* Feb. 1986, 55–57.
33 Lynes, 98.
34 Quoted by Dickran Tashjian, *A Boatload of Madness: Surrealism and the American Avant-Garde, 1920–1930* (New York: Thames and Hudson, 1995), 3.
35 Julien Levy, *Surrealism* (New York: Black Sun Press, 1935), 12.
36 Levy, *Memoir,* 78; Deborah Solomon, *Utopia Parkway: The Life and Work of Joseph*

Cornell (New York: Farrar, Straus and Giroux, 1996), 60.

37 Levy, *Memoir,* 115–16.
38 Ibid., 283–85.
39 Ibid., 93.
40 John Russell, *Matisse: Father and Son* (New York: Harry N. Abrams, 1999), 37, 46–48.
41 Levy, *Memoir,* 117.
42 Russell, 389.
43 Grace Glueck, "Self-Effacing William Acquavella, Who Struck Art's Biggest Deal," *NYT,* May 10, 1990, C15, C18. The *Times* gives the figure as $143 million. Russell, 398, gives the more precise figure.
44 Matthew Spender, *From a High Place: A Life of Arshile Gorky* (New York: Alfred A. Knopf, 1999), 360–72.
45 Levy, *Memoir,* 268.
46 Virgil Thomson, *Virgil Thomson* (New York: Alfred A. Knopf, 1966), 215–17.
47 Interview with Gray Foy, December 17, 1996.
48 On his drinking, see comments by Roz Jacobs in Ingrid Schaffner and Lisa Jacobs, *Julien Levy: Portrait of an Art Gallery* (Cambridge, Mass: MIT Press, 1998), 165–66.
49 Jimmy Ernst, *A Not So Still Life* (New York: St. Martin's Press, 1984), 224.

Chapter 13

1 I am indebted to my late friend the artist Lily Harmon for permission to read her unpublished biography of J. B. Neumann and to make use of it for this book. My comments on Neumann's life are taken from her typescript.
2 When sold at auction at Sotheby's in 1985, this work fetched $9.9 million. For reasons unknown to this writer, it had been renamed *Landscape with Rising Sun.*
3 Phillips to Neumann, Jan. 4, 1926; May 5, 1930; Sept. 27, 1932; Neumann Papers, AoAA.
4 Undated letter, Neumann Papers, AAoA.
5 Neumann to Odets, March 3, 1947, Neumann Papers, AoAA; Mellon to Neumann, Nov. 15, 1947, Neumann Papers, AAoA.
6 Barbara Copeland Buenger, "Max Beckmann," in Stephanie Barron, ed., *Exiles and Emigrés* (Los Angeles: Los Angeles County Museum, 1997), 58.
7 Lynn Nicholas, *The Rape of Europa* (New York: Alfred A. Knopf, 1994), 24. The others were Bernhard Boehmer, Hildebrand Gurlitt, and Ferdinand Müller.
8 *Art News,* Sept. 1954, 7.
9 Nicholas, 4–5. See also Jimmy Ernst, *A Not So Still Life* (New York: St. Martin's Press, 1984), 173.
10 Quoted by Vivian Endicott Barnett, "Banned German Art," in Barron, ed., *Exiles and Emigrés,* 281.
11 Information from the Curt Valentin Archive, Museum of Modern Art Library.
12 Jane Wade (for Curt Valentin) to Libreria Bucholz, Madrid, Aug. 10, 1963; Federick P. Houston to Valentin, Oct. 15, 1953; in Valentin Papers, Museum of Modern Art Archives.
13 Vivian Endicott Barnett, *The Guggenheim Justin K. Thannhauser Collection* (New York: Guggenheim Museum, 1978), 12–13; Thannhauser obituary, *NYT,* Dec. 31, 1976, B8.
14 My account of events in the Goudstikkers' lives is based on conversations over

several years with my late friend Désirée Goudstikker von Saher.

15 On this effort, see Alan Riding, "Heirs Claim Art Lost to Nazis in Amsterdam," *NYT,* Jan. 12, 1998, E1, E6.

Chapter 14

1 Sources for the life of Peggy Guggenheim are her *Out of This Century* (New York: Dial Press, 1946; University Books, 1979); *Confessions of an Art Addict* (New York: Macmillan, 1960); and *Out of This Century: Confessions of an Art Addict* (New York: Universe Books, 1979), which combines the two earlier books; and Jacqueline Bograd Weld, *Peggy: The Wayward Guggenheim* (New York: E. P. Dutton, 1986). Useful for the Guggenheim background from which she emerged is John H. Davis, *The Guggenheims: An American Epic* (New York: William Morrow, 1978).

2 Davis, 73.

3 Davis, *The Guggenheims,* 73–76.

4 Davis, 238–39.

5 Weld, 308.

6 Guggenheim, *Out of This Century* (1979), 36–37.

7 Julien Levy, *Memoir of an Art Gallery,* 119.

8 Weld, 346.

9 Guggenheim, *Out of This Century* (1979), 78–85.

10 Ibid., 130–38, 163–65.

11 Ibid., 161.

12 Quoted by Guggenheim, *Out of This Century* (1979), 170–71.

13 Ibid., 196.

14 Ibid., 198.

15 Ibid., 195–96.

16 Davis, 327.

17 Weld, 210.

18 Guggenheim, *Out of This Century* (1979), 206.

19 Ibid., 209.

20 Quoted in *Peggy Guggenheim and Her Friends,* ed. Virginia M. Dortch (Milan: Berenice Art Books, 1994), 11.

21 Jimmy Ernst, *A Not So Still Life* (New York: St. Martin's Press, 1984), 213.

22 Guggenheim, *Out of This Century* (1979), 210–12.

23 Melvin P. Lader, "Howard Putzel: Proponent of Surrealism and Early Abstract Expressionism in America," *Arts Magazine,* March 1982, 85–96.

24 Ernst, 205; Guggenheim, *Out of This Century* (1979), 215.

25 Max Ernst obituary, *NYT,* April 2, 1976, 1, 37.

26 Guggenheim, *Out of This Century* (1979), 216.

27 Weld, 198.

28 Guggenheim, *Out of This Century* (1979), 224, 226.

29 Weld, 231.

30 Weld, 231.

30 Weld, 231.

31 Ibid., 245–46.

32 Levy, 254–55.

33 Melvin P. Lader, "Peggy Guggenheim's 'Art of This Century,' " in *Peggy Guggen-*

heim's Other Legacy (New York: Solomon R. Guggenheim Museum, 1988), 9.

34 Guggenheim, *Out of This Century* (1979), 252–64, 276; Weld, 260.
35 Ernst, 231.
36 Weld, 276.
37 Weld, 266–67.
38 Ernst, 206.
39 Weld, 267–68.
40 Weld, 287; Calvin Tomkins, *Duchamp: A Biography* (New York: Henry Holt, 1997), 332–33.
41 Weld, 265.
42 Ibid., 266.
43 Ernst, 235–36.
44 Quoted in *Peggy Guggenheim and her Friends,* 105.
45 Deborah Solomon, *Utopia Parkway: The Life and Work of Joseph Cornell* (New York: Farrar, Straus and Giroux, 1996), 144.
46 Lader, in *Peggy Guggenheim and Her Friends,* 10.
47 Lader, "Howard Putzel," 92.
48 Ernst, 244–45.
49 Steven Naifeh and Gregory White Smith, *Jackson Pollock: An American Saga* (New York: Clarkson N. Potter, 1989), 444.
50 Weld, 306.
51 Naifeh and Smith, 467–69.
52 Weld, 324,
53 Sidney Janis, *Abstract and Surrealist Art in America* (New York: Reynal and Hitchcock, 1944), 50, 88.
54 Janis, 87; Weld, 296.
55 Ernst, 246.
56 Guggenheim, *Out of This Century* (1979), 282.
57 Guggenheim spells his name "McPherson"; however, a letter from him in the Helen Benheim Papers, AoAA, is clearly signed "Macpherson." Macpherson is also used by *NYT* in his obituary, June 18, 1971, 42.
58 Weld, 339–40.
59 Guggenheim, *Out of This Century* (1979), 370.

Chapter 15

1 Conversation with Charles Seliger, June 24, 1997.
2 Jimmy Ernst, *A Not So Still Life* (New York: St. Martin's Press, 1984), 241.
3 Ibid., 242; Laurie Lisle, *Louise Nevelson: A Passionate Life* (New York: Summit Books, 1990), 149.
4 Melvin P. Lader, "Howard Putzel: Proponent of Surrealism and Early Abstract Expressionism in America," *Arts Magazine,* March 1982, 92.
5 Ibid., 93.
6 Coates, "Assorted Moderns," *New Yorker,* Dec. 23, 1944, 51.
7 Jacqueline Bograd Weld, *Peggy: The Wayward Guggenheim* (New York: E. P. Dutton, 1986), 336.
8 Coates, "The Art Galleries," *New Yorker,* March 30, 1946, 83. On much earlier uses of the term, in application to the painting of Kandinsky, see Bruce Altschuler, *The*

Avant-Grade Exposition (New York: Harry N. Abrams, 1994), 267, n. 39.

9 Kootz interview with Dorothy Seckler, AoAA, April 13, 1964.

10 Ibid.

11 Jewell, "The Problem of Seeing," *NYT,* Aug. 10, 1941, sec. 9, 7.

12 Macy's advertisement, *NYT,* Jan. 4, 1942, 21; Dore Ashton, *The New York School: A Cultural Reckoning* (New York: Penguin Books, 1979), 146.

13 A copy of the press release is in the Kootz Papers, AoAA.

14 Kootz obituary, *NYT,* Aug. 9, 1982, D8.

15 "57th Street," *Fortune,* Sept. 1946, 146-47. Parsons took over from Brandt in September, the month the article appeared, too late to be listed as the proprietor of the gallery. On the map, it is the gallery of Mortimer Brandt.

16 April J. Paul, "Introduction à la Peinture Moderne Americaine: Six Young American Painters of the Samuel Kootz Gallery," *Arts Magazine,* Feb. 1986, 65-71.

17 Kootz comments on this in his interview with Paul Cummings, AoAA.

18 Conversation with Irving Sandler, Sept. 29, 1997.

19 Kootz interview with Dorothy Seckler, AoAA.

20 Ibid.

21 John Bernard Myers, *Tracking the Marvelous* (New York: Random House, 1983), 114, 116.

22 Quoted in "Gambles and Gimbels" (editorial), *Art Digest,* Dec. 1, 1951, 5.

23 See "Gambles and Gimbels" and Kootz's reply to the editorial in the form of a letter he had sent to Artists Equity on the matter, *Art Digest,* Jan. 1. 1952, 4.

24 Conversation with Eleanor Ward, Feb. 12, 1982.

25 Kootz obituary, *NYT,* Aug. 9, 1982, D8.

Chapter 16

1 Betty Parsons interview with Paul Cummings, June 4, 9, AoAA; Lee Hall, *Betty Parsons: Artist, Dealer, Collector* (New York: Harry N. Abrams, 1991), 19-20.

2 Hall, *Parsons,* 22-24.

3 Calvin Tomkins, "A Keeper of the Treasure," *New Yorker,* June 9, 1975, 47.

4 Hall, *Parsons,* 25-31.

5 Tomkins, "A Keeper of the Treasure," 46; Hall, *Parsons,* 35-36.

6 Tomkins, "A Keeper of the Treasure," 48.

7 Hall, *Parsons,* 54-55.

8 Ibid., 43, 56.

9 Ibid., 61-62.

10 Tomkins, 48; Parsons interview with Paul Cummings, April 4 and 9, 1972, AoAA.

11 Tomkins, "A Keeper of the Treasure," 48-49; Hall, *Parsons,* 73.

12 Tomkins, "A Keeper of the Treasure," 51; Hall, *Parsons,* 77.

13 Tomkins, "A Keeper of the Treasure," 51.

14 Steven Naifeh and Gregory White Smith, *Jackson Pollock*: An American Saga (New York: Clarkson N. Potter, 1989), 545.

15 Calvin Tomkins, *Off the Wall: Robert Rauschenberg and the Art World of Our Time* (Garden City: Doubleday, 1980), 55-56.

16 Undated letter, Betty Parsons Papers, AoAA.

17 Ibid., 84.

18 Tomkins, "A Keeper of the Treasure," 45.

19 On their disputes and estrangements, see James E. B. Breslin, *Mark Rothko* (Chicago: University of Chicago Press, 1993), 342–48.
20 Ibid., 263.
21 Irving Sandler, "The Club," *Artforum*, Sept. 1965, 27.
22 Sandler's article "The Club" provides a full account of this loosely knit organization.
23 Interview with Esteban Vicente, Dec. 10, 1997.
24 Castelli interview with Paul Cummings, May 14–June 18, 1969, AoAA.
25 Parsons interview with Cummings, AoAA.
26 For a concise account of this matter, see B.H. Friedman, "'The Irascibles': A Split Second in Art History," *Arts*, Sept. 1978, 96–102.
27 Naifeh and Smith, 618. This was also Parsons's view. See her letter to Clyfford Still, June 20, 1950, Parsons Papers, AoAA.
28 Irving Sandler, *The New York School: The Painters and Sculptors of the Fifties* (New York: Harper and Row, 1978), 30, 33; Martica Sawin, The Hansa Gallery Revisited (New York: Zabriskie Gallery, 1997), unpaginated.
29 Castelli interview with Cummings, AoAA.
30 Bruce Altschuler, *The Avant-Garde in Exposition* (New York: Harry N. Abrams), 159–61.
31 Mimi Swartz, "Buzz and Alan," *New Yorker,* Aug. 24 and 31, 1998, 70. On Ward's background, Swartz cites her cousin, Alan Groh, who was Ward's associate at the Stable.
32 Paul Gardner, "The Stable Wasn't Just Another Gallery," *Art News,* May 1982, 111–12; interview with Eleanor Ward, Feb. 12, 1982.
33 Ashton, *The New York School,* 168.
34 Egan obituary, *NYT,* March 18, 1993, B10.
35 John Bernard Myers, *Tracking the Marvelous: A Life in the New York Art World* (New York: Random House, 1983), 198.
36 Ibid., 168.
37 Conversation with Joan Peterson, Sept. 13, 1997.
38 Lee Hall, *Elaine and Bill: Portrait of a Marriage* (New York: Farrar, Straus, and Giroux, 1993), 80–81, 154.
39 Conversation with Irving Sandler, Jan. 1, 1996.
40 Interview with Esteban Vicente.
41 Deborah Solomon, *Utopia Parkway: The Life and Work of Joseph Cornell* (New York: Farrar, Straus and Giroux, 1997), 185.
42 Miller and Cahill interview with Joan Pring, April–June 1957, Columbia Oral History Project.
43 John Brooks, "Why Fight It?," *New Yorker,* Nov. 12, 1960, 70.
44 "Chronology," in *Three Generations of Twentieth-Century Art: The Sidney and Harriet Janis Collection* (New York: Museum of Modern Art, 1972), 210.
45 Janis obituary, *NYT*, Nov. 24, 1989, sec. IV, 3.
46 Brooks, 70.
47 Janis interview with Paul Cummings, March 21–Sept. 26, 1972, AoAA.
48 Brooks, 71.
49 "Chronology," 210.
50 Brooks, 71.

51 Janis interview with Cummings, AoAA.
52 "Chronology," 211.
53 Ibid., 213.
54 Bosley Crowther, *Hollywood Rajah* (New York: Henry Holt, 1960), 305.
55 "Chronology," 213.
56 Janis interview with Cummings, AoAA. However, Guggenheim makes no mention of this recommendation in her memoirs, *Out of This Century* (New York: Dial Press, 1746; Universe Books, 1979).
57 Janis interview with Avis Berman, Oct. 15, 1981, AoAA.
58 *Decision*, Nov.-Dec. 1941, 85-95; quoted in *Three Generations of Twentieth-Century Art*, 213-14.
59 Brooks, 81.
60 Janis interview with Cummings, AoAA.
61 Gorky had not shown with Parsons, but was much admired by her; Hall, *Betty Parsons*, 94.
62 Hall, *Betty Parsons*, 101-3.
63 Thomas B. Hess, *Barnett Newman* (New York: Museum of Modern Art, 1971), 91-96.
64 Naifeh and Smith, 679-81.
65 Naifeh and Smith, 679.
66 Conversation with Grace Borgenicht, c. 1965.
67 Janis interview with Cummings, AoAA.
68 John Gruen, *The Party's Over Now: Reminiscences of the Fifties* (New York: Viking Press, 1975), 252.
69 Janis interview with Cummings, AoAA.
70 The others were Gorky, de Kooning, Pollock, Stuart Davis, Franz Kline, and Hans Hofmann.
71 Parsons Papers, AoAA.
72 Parsons interview with Paul Cummings, AoAA.
73 Still to Parsons, Dec. 11, 1953; Parsons to Still, December 16, 1953; Parsons Papers, AoAA.
74 Parsons interview with Gerald Silk, June 11, 1981, AoAA.
75 Janis interview with Avis Berman, AoAA.
76 Janis interview with Cummings, AoAA.
77 Hall, *Betty Parsons*, 127-28.
78 Janis interview with Cummings, AoAA.
79 Hall, *Betty Parsons*, 129-30.
80 Gruen, 124.
81 Roy Lichtenstein, b. 1923, was the eldest.
82 Janis, unpublished memoir, AoAA.
83 Janis interview with Cummings, AoAA.
84 Quoted in Tomkins, *Off the Wall*, 185.
85 Gruen, 203.
86 Janis interview with Cummings, AoAA.
87 Gruen, 251-52.
88 Israel Shenker, "A Pollock Sold for $2-Million, Record for American Painting," *NYT*, Sept. 22, 1973, 1, 19.

89 Hall, *Elaine and Bill,* 259-63.
90 Lee Seldes, *The Legacy of Mark Rothko* (New York: Holt, Rinehart and Winston, 1978), 128-29.
91 Ibid., 129, 138.
92 Ibid., 135.
93 Ibid., 147-49.
94 *NYT,* Nov. 23, 1977, Al, B4.
95 Reis obituary, *NYT,* Dec. 4, 1978, D4.
96 Stamos obituary, *NYT,* Feb. 4, 1997, A20.
97 *NYT,* Dec. 19, 1975, 1, 50.
98 Seldes, 323-24.
99 *NYT,* Jan. 7, 1983, 1; May 14, 1983, 27.

Chapter 17

1 In addition to works cited in the notes, my comments on the early career of Castelli are also based on my many conversations with his daughter, Nina Castelli Sundell, and his son-in-law, Michael Sundell, along with my conversations with Castelli himself and my one formal interview with him on April 8, 1993.
2 Calvin Tomkins, "A Good Eye and a Good Ear," *New Yorker,* May 26, 1980, 42.
3 Castelli interview with Laura de Coppet and Andy Warhol, in *Castelli and His Artists* (Aspen, Col.: Aspen Center for the Visual Arts, 1982), unpaginated.
4 Tomkins, "A Good Eye," 42-43.
5 Leo Castelli, in Laura de Coppet and Alan Jones, eds., *The Art Dealers* (New York: Clarkson N. Potter, 1984), 82.
6 Tomkins, "A Good Eye," 44.
7 Ibid.
8 Ibid.; interview with Leo Castelli.
9 Castelli, *New York Observer,* Nov. 22, 1993, 17.
10 Tomkins, "A Good Eye," 47.
11 De Coppet and Jones, 84.
12 Castelli interview with Cummings, May 14–June 18, 1969, AoAA.
13 Tomkins, "A Good Eye," 47.
14 Ibid., 84-85.
15 Interview with Castelli.
16 Tomkins, "A Good Eye," 51.
17 Castelli interview with Barbara Rose, July 1959, AoAA.
18 Interview with Esteban Vicente, Nov. 21, 1997.
19 Tomkins, "A Good Eye," 52; Castelli's own retelling of the story appears in his foreword to *Jasper Johns* (New York: Universe, 1997), 5–15.
20 Ibid.; Tomkins, *Off the Wall: Robert Rauschenberg and the Art World of Our Time* (Garden City: Doubleday, 1980), 141-45.
21 Tomkins, "A Good Eye," 57.
22 Unless otherwise indicated, my comments on Karp are based on countless conversations with him over the years as well as my observations of him at work.
23 De Coppet and Jones, 135.
24 Karp interview with Paul Cummings, AoAA, March 12, 1969.

25 Tomkins, "A Good Eye," 58.
26 Conversation with Karp.
27 De Coppet and Jones, 137.
28 Conversation with Ward, Feb. 12, 1982.
29 Conversation with Warhol, Castelli Gallery, 1963. Miller included two of Castelli's artists, Lee Bontecou and Edward Higgins, in the exhibition.
30 Robert Sam Anson, "The Lion in Winter," *Manhattan, Inc.*, Dec. 1984, 65.
31 Tomkins, "A Good Eye," 63; conversations with Karp.
32 David Bourdon, "What's Up in Art? Follow the Clan," *Life,* May 1, 1970, 74.
33 This observation has been quoted frequently, and in varied forms, sometimes with and sometimes without the epithet.
34 Tomkins, *Off the Wall,* 2.
35 Ibid., 3–7.
36 Ibid., 6.
37 Oldenburg published the scenarios for these pieces in his *Store Days* (New York: Something Else Press, 1967).
38 Anson, 64.
39 Tomkins, "A Good Eye," 63.
40 Fred Ferretti, "Scull's U.S. Art Brings Record $2 Million," *NYT,* Oct. 6, 1973, 6.
41 Robert Scull obituary, *NYT,* Jan. 2, 1986, B5.
42 De Coppet and Jones, 143.
43 Ibid., 144.
44 Conversation with Karp.
45 Bourdon, 71–74.
46 Edward Ball, "The Castelli Connection," *Avenue,* Feb. 1990, 85–86.
47 Interview with Margo Leavin, Jan. 15, 1984.
48 The brief life the Dilexi Gallery is chronicled in *The Dilexi Years* (Oakland: Oakland Museum, 1984).
49 De Coppet and Jones, 151–54; *The Last Time I Saw Ferus* (Newport Beach: Newport Harbor Art Museum, 1976), unpaginated.
50 "Joseph Helman," in De Coppet and Jones, 160-61.
51 De Coppet and Jones, 155–56.
52 This figure, which appeared in the press only as a rumor, was confirmed by Blum in an interview with this writer on March 19, 1998.
53 Anson, 62, 70.
54 Deborah Gimelson, "You Can Say That Again: Breaking Up Is Hard to Do," *New York Observer,* May 13, 1996, 26.
55 Interview with Blum.
56 *NYT,* Oct. 27, 1988, B6.
57 Paul Taylor, "A Lion in Winter," *NYT,* Feb. 16, 1992, II, 33.
58 Interview with Irving Blum.
59 Taylor, II, 33.
60 *NYT,* July 25, 1997, B28.

Chapter 18

1 Mueller obituary, *NYT,* May 9, 1989, D26.
2 Interview with Arnold Glimcher, April 14, 1998.

3 Comments on the Bykert Gallery are based on my interview with Klaus Kertess, Jan. 24, 1996, and several later telephone conversations.
4 Comments on Mary Boone and her gallery are based on my interview with Boone, July 10, 1996.
5 James Servin, "SoHo Stares at Hard Times," *NYT Magazine*, Jan. 20, 1991, 28.
6 "Art Dealer Arrested for Ammunition Exhibit," *NYT*, Sept. 30, 1999, B12; David Rohde, "Art Dealer Says Arrest Is an Attack on Rights," *NYT*, Oct. 1, 1999, B7; David Rohde, "Art Gallery Owner Describes Night in Jail," *NYT*, Oct. 3, 1999, 47; Barbara Stewart, "Judge Dismisses Case Involving 9-Millimeter Art, *NYT*, Dec. 7, 1999, B1.
7 Amy Virshup, "The Fun's Over," *New York Magazine*, June 22, 1987, 49-50.
8 Interview with Gracie Mansion, Oct. 27, 1996.
9 Anthony Haden-Guest, *True Colors* (New York: Atlantic Monthly Press, 1996), 141-42.
10 Virshup, 49.
11 N. R. Kleinfeld, "Bargaining at the Art Galleries: A Personal Odyssey," *NYT*, May 7, 1993, CI, C26.
12 Conversation with Grace Borgenicht, March 7, 1997.
13 Carol Vogel, "Inside Art," *NYT*, June 7, 1996, C24; Roger Bevan, "Emmerich/Sotheby's: The Way Ahead?" *The Art Newspaper*, July-August. 1996, 29.
14 Unless otherwise indicated, my observations on Larry Gagosian are based on an interview of March 9, 1998.
15 See Mark Stevens, "The Look of Power," *New York Magazine*, Jan. 22, 1996, 37-41.
16 As in "Dealers and Players," *New Yorker*, Oct. 2, 1995, 36-37.
17 Conversation with Bernice Rose, curator of drawings at the Museum of Modern Art at the time of Shafrazi's attack, February 25, 1998.

Chapter 19

1 The grandson of Hermann Wunderlich, founder of the gallery, owns the Mongerson Wunderlich Galleries in Chicago with a partner. Like the Kennedy Gallery, it deals mainly in American art of the nineteenth and early twentieth centuries.
2 McAlpin obituary, *NYT*, June 3, 1989, 11; Avis Berman, "The Katharine Kuh Gallery: An Informal Portrait," in Sue Ann Prince, ed., *The Old Guard and the Avant-Garde: Modernism in Chicago, 1910–1940* (Chicago: University of Chicago Press, 1990), 160.
3 As it did in 1999 at Sotheby's.
4 Conversation with Evelyne Z. Daitz, June 25, 1999.

INDEX

Note: Page numbers followed by letters *i* and *n* refer to illustrations and notes, respectively.